Joni Pbert, Ph.D.

W9-CPE-422

THE AUTHORITATIVE GUIDE
TO SELF-HELP BOOKS

The Authoritative Guide to Self-Help Books

JOHN W. SANTROCK

ANN M. MINNETT

BARBARA D. CAMPBELL

*Based on the highly acclaimed national survey
of more than 500 mental health professionals'
ratings of 1,000 self-help books*

THE GUILFORD PRESS
New York London

©1994 The Guilford Press
A Division of Guilford Publications, Inc.
72 Spring Street, New York, NY 10012

Printed in the United States of America

This book is printed on acid-free paper.

Last digit is print number: 9 8 7 6 5 4 3 2 1

Library of Congress Cataloging-in-Publication Data

Santrock, John W.
    The authoritative guide to self-help books : based on the
highly acclaimed national survey of more than 500 mental
health professionals' ratings of 1000 self-help books / John W.
Santrock, Ann M. Minnett, and Barbara D. Campbell.
        p.   cm.
    Includes bibliographical references and index.
    ISBN 0-89862-544-0 (hard)   ISBN 0-89862-374-X (pbk.)
    1. Self-help techniques—Bibliography.   2. Life skills—
Bibliography.   I. Minnett, Ann M.   II. Campbell, Barbara, D.
III. Title.
Z77204.S44S   1994
[BF632]
016.158—dc20   93-40425
                                                          CIP

About the Authors

John W. Santrock, Ph.D., Professor of Psychology at the University of Texas at Dallas, has authored more than 30 psychology texts, including *Psychology,* fourth edition, *Life-Span Development,* fifth edition, and *Human Adjustment.*

Ann M. Minnett, Ph.D., a developmental psychologist, is Director of Research and Evaluation at the Salesmanship Club Youth and Family Centers in Dallas, and Adjunct Assistant Professor at the University of Texas at Dallas.

Barbara D. Campbell, a research associate at the University of Texas at Dallas, has conducted research on human memory and has a long-standing interest in human adjustment and self-help books.

Acknowledgments

This large project required the help of a number of people. We especially wish to thank the more than 500 clinical and counseling psychologists who took the time from their busy schedules to complete the national survey of self-help books. We are also grateful to the many students, especially Catherine Harrelson, Craig Conners, Jamie Horton, and Patricia Green, who tracked down books, references, and reviews that were needed, and who compiled data. Bert Moore, Dean of the School of Human Development, University of Texas at Dallas, generously supported the national survey.

Thanks also go to our agent, Charlotte Cecil Raymond, for her efforts to find a home for this book, to Michael Mahoney, for his belief in the importance of the book, to Kitty Moore, Editor at The Guilford Press, for her confidence in the project, and to David Lasky, Production Editor, for his thoroughness in guiding this book through the production process.

Contents

Introduction to Self-Help
Books and
the National Survey

You have probably heard about or read one or more of the following self-help books:

Feeling Good by David Burns
What Color Is Your Parachute? by Robert Bolles
Dianetics by L. Ron Hubbard
Infants and Mothers by T. Berry Brazelton
The Courage to Heal by Ellen Bass and Laura Davis
Widowed by Joyce Brothers
The Dance of Anger by Harriet Lerner
Reclaiming the Inner Child by Jeremiah Adams
Your Perfect Right by Robert Alberti and Michael Emmons
Secrets About Men Every Woman Should Know by Barbara
    DeAngelis
Winning Through Intimidation by Robert Ringer
You Just Don't Understand by Deborah Tannen
Dr. Ruth's Guide to Good Sex by Ruth Westheimer
How to Win Friends and Influence People by Dale Carnegie
The Power of Positive Thinking by Norman Vincent Peale
How to Survive the Loss of a Love by Melba Colgrove,
    Harold Bloomfield, and Peter McWilliams
The Battered Woman by Lenore Walker
The Beverly Hills Diet by Judy Mazel and Susan Schultz
The First Three Years of Life by Burton White
Why Men Don't Get Enough Sex and Women Don't Get Enough Love
    by Jonathan Kramer and Diane Dunaway
Body Language by Julius Fast
The 7 Habits of Highly Effective People by Steven Covey

Each of these books has been at or near the top of national best-seller lists, and most have been read by at least a million people. Are they all good self-help books—do they help individuals cope effectively with problems? The consensus of mental health experts in the United States is that half of the books on this list are not good self-help books; even though these books were at or near the top of national best-seller lists, most mental health experts view them negatively. The other half of the books on this list are excellent self-help books. In this book we tell which are the good ones, which are the bad ones, and why.

HISTORY OF SELF-HELP BOOKS

Self-help books have become an important source of psychological advice for millions of Americans. Whether we want to improve our marital life, control our anger, gain self-fulfillment, raise our self-esteem, become a better parent, lose weight, solve a sexual problem, cope with stress, recover from an addiction, or tackle another problem in life, a self-help book has been written on the topic. Our preoccupation with self-improvement is nothing new; it's been around since the Bible. Although not exactly known as a self-help book author, Benjamin Franklin dispensed self-improvement advice in *Poor Richard's Almanac:* "Early to bed, early to rise, makes a man healthy, wealthy, and wise." In the 19th century, homemakers read *Married Lady's Companion* for help in managing their houses and families. And in the 1930s, Dale Carnegie's *How to Win Friends and Influence People* made him the aspiring businessman's guru.

The interest in understanding the human psyche and how to improve it heated up in the 1960s and 1970s and was accompanied by a dramatic glut of self-help books. *I'm O.K., You're O.K.* and *Your Erroneous Zones* were read by millions of Americans and made millions for their authors. They turned out to be only the tip of the iceberg.

HOW DO PEOPLE SELECT SELF-HELP BOOKS?

The self-help book market has yielded an overwhelming, bewildering array of choices. How do people select self-help books? Until this book— *The Authoritative Guide to Self-Help Books*— people simply relied on the opinions of friends, their minister, their doctor, their therapist, guest authors on talk shows, a salesperson at a bookstore, or the promotional information on the book's cover. But even personal contact with professionals—such as doctors or therapists—provides only a limited opinion about which book to purchase. Self-help books have been published at such an astonishing pace that even the well-intentioned professional has difficulty keeping up with books in a wide number of fields. The professional may be well-informed about books in one or two areas—such as depression or anxiety—but know little about books in many other areas—such as eating disorders, women's issues, motivation, relaxation/meditation, and so on.

Some self-help books have been written by professionals who have masterful insights about who we are, what we are about, and how we can improve our lives. Others, to put it mildly, leave a lot to be desired, or as one concerned therapist commented, "Many self-help books are not worth the paper they are printed on." With literally thousands of books on the market that vary greatly in quality, we wanted to know what the leading psychologists in the United States think are the best and the worst self-help books. We began searching books, research journals, and magazines to find out if anyone had conducted a survey of mental health experts to determine which books they recommend and which ones they don't, thinking we would find at least one informed guide to self-help books. We found that virtually nothing of the sort had been published.

After all, Siskel and Ebert tell us which movies to see and which ones are not worth the trip to the theater, restaurant critics inform us which restaurants are superb and which ones to avoid; automobile guides educate us about the gems and the lemons; and consumer guides dispense advice on which refrigerators, computers, televisions, and VCRs to buy. Considering the immense number of self-help books that have been written, a guide to them based on professional judgments by mental health experts is badly needed.

This Book is That Guide.

THE NATIONAL SURVEY OF CLINICAL AND COUNSELING PSYCHOLOGISTS' RATINGS OF SELF-HELP BOOKS

We recently obtained the self-help book ratings of more than 500 experts in clinical and counseling psychology from all 50 states. These mental health professionals possess the very best psychological knowledge in the United States. All are members of the clinical or counseling divisions of the American Psychological Association. To be a member of these divisions, the mental health professionals have to have obtained a doctorate from an accredited university and have been recommended for membership by their colleagues. Their ratings and comments are based on many years of experience in helping people with particular problems. We believe that their ratings and comments provide an invaluable resource for sorting through the bewildering maze of self-help books available today.

This survey of self-help books is the first one conducted on a large-scale, national basis. A number of the mental health professionals who completed our survey commented about the virtual absence of information available to the public about how to select good self-help books—which are the best ones and which are the worst ones. Their positive comments about the survey's timeliness and extensiveness bolstered our motivation for writing this book.

The self-help book industry is virtually unregulated. The people with the most influence on which self-help books sell best and worst are the wrong people—they are the publishers, the owners of large bookstore chains, and a hodgepodge of authors with a vast range of credentials, psychological knowledge, and competencies. We hope the survey and this book help to put the influence on which self-help books sell the best and the worst in the hands of informed, experienced mental health professionals whose credentials, psychological knowledge, and competencies are vastly superior to those of the merchandisers.

Self-help books are books that are written for the lay public to help individuals cope with problems and live more effective lives. Self-help books are not written for a professional audience, although increasingly psychotherapists read the books themselves and recommend them to their clients. Many therapists report that self-help books are a useful adjunct to psychotherapy.

Self-help books come in many forms. In this book we do not evaluate books that are primarily religious or autobiographical in nature. Most books that focus on health and disease—such as AIDS, cancer, and heart disease—were not included. Few self-help books that focus on ethnicity have been written and none were rated in the national survey. We do recommend two books—*Black Parenting* by James Comer and Alvin Poussaint (1992) and *The Measure of Our Success: A Letter to My Children* by Marian Wright Edelman (1992). In the next decade we are likely to see an increase in self-help books tailored to ethnic concerns. We did not include a separate category for books on gay and lesbian issues. Rather, these books were rated in the category of sexuality.

THE NATIONAL SELF-HELP SURVEY'S RATING SCALES AND CATEGORIES

We asked the mental health professionals to rate more than 350 self-help books in 33 categories. We chose these books by personally examining the shelves of major national bookstore chains, by discussing self-help books with clinical and counseling psychologists, and by reading numerous books and articles about self-help books. We left two blank spaces in each category so that the mental health experts could fill in their own choices of self-help books and rate them, if they were not on our list. More than 1,000 books were listed and rated at least once. Books that were rated by five or more mental health professionals are listed in Appendix A at the back of the book. Appendix A includes the rating of each of these books in the national survey and the number of professionals who rated them.

The following instructions were given on the survey form:

Please use this 5-point scale to evaluate the self-help books in each category (of course, if you don't know anything about the book, do not rate it):

+2	Extremely good	Outstanding; highly recommended, best or among best in category.
+1	Moderately good	Provides good advice, can be helpful; worth purchasing.
0	Average	An average self-help book.
−1	Moderately bad	Not a good self-help book; may provide misleading or inaccurate information.
−2	Extremely bad	This book exemplifies the worst of the self-help books; worst, or among worst in its category; presents inaccurate information.

The following categories of self-help books were rated by the mental health professionals:

Abuse and recovery
Addiction and recovery
Aging
Anger
Anxiety
Assertiveness
Career development
Child development and parenting
Codependency and recovery
Communication
Death, dying, and grief
Depression
Dieting and weight loss
Divorce
Eating disorders

Exercise
The family
Friendship, loneliness, and single adult life
Infant development and parenting
Love, intimacy, and marriage
Men's issues
Positive thinking and self-talk
Pregnancy
Relaxation/meditation
Self-esteem
Self-fulfillment and happiness
Self-improvement
Sexual issues and problems
Stepfamilies
Teenagers and parenting
Women's issues

After the mental health experts rated the books in specific categories, they were asked to list, regardless of category, the five best and the five worst self-help books they had come across. Space was also provided for the experts to make general comments about self-help books.

ONE TO FIVE STARS AND A DAGGER

We analyzed the responses to the national survey by computing how often the books were rated and how high or low they were rated. All books not listed at least 10 times were eliminated from the final ratings. Then, based on how often and high or low they were rated, books with positive ratings were given 1 to 5 stars; books with a negative rating were given a dagger:

★ ★ ★ ★ ★   Rated by 75 or more mental health professionals; average rating 1.15 or greater

★ ★ ★ ★   Rated by 31 or more mental health professionals; average rating 1.00 or higher

★ ★ ★   Rated 10 or more times; average rating .50 through .99

★ ★   Rated 10 or more times; average rating .25 through .49

★   Rated 10 or more times; average rating .00 through .24

†   Rated 10 or more times; average negative rating (−.01 to −1.87)

In this book, the 5-star books are Strongly Recommended, the 4-star books are Recommended, the 1-star and 2-star books are Not Recommended, and the daggered books are Strongly Not recommended. The 3-star books are interpreted as Neutral. In addition to these ratings, some self-help books were rated highly but infrequently. When books were rated +1.00 or higher but mentioned by only 10 to 30 respondents, they were assigned to the Diamonds In The Rough category (♦). These books have the potential to become 4-star or 5-star books if they become more widely known. Most categories also include books in a category called as Worth A Further Look, identified by the symbol ➋➊. These books were rated positively in the national survey but by fewer than 10 respondents. In this category also are books that were published after the survey came out that we believe deserve further examination.

HOW THE REST OF THE BOOK IS ORGANIZED

In the following chapters we present the self-help categories alphabetically—beginning with Abuse and Recovery and ending with Women's Issues. Each chapter opens with an overview of the books in the category and a description of the audiences to which the books are addressed. Then the mental health experts' ratings of the books are listed. The bulk of the chapter profiles each book in the national survey's final ratings. The profiles include a review of the book's contents and organization, why the book received high, low, or mediocre ratings, and a critique of the book by mental health experts. Books that deserve a further look are then discussed. A concluding section lists the books we recommend; it includes all 5-star and 4-star books and most "Diamonds in the Rough" and "Worth a Further Look" books. It also includes 3-star, 2-star, and 1-star books we believe deserve a more positive evaluation than they received in the national survey. In the final two chapters, the 25 best self-help books are profiled, and nine strategies for selecting a self-help book are outlined. Appendix A details the ratings of all books in the survey that were rated by five or more respondents. Appendix B is a list of notes and references.

USING THIS BOOK EFFECTIVELY

The Authoritative Guide to Self-Help Books can be used effectively by both mental health professionals and the lay public. Therapists increasingly recommend self-help books to their clients. In our national survey, 70% of the mental health professionals said that they had recommended three or more self-help books to their clients in the last year. Almost one-third had recommended six or more self-help books to their clients in the last year. Eighty-six percent of the therapists said that *good* self-help books provide a positive benefit when used in conjunction with psychotherapy.

Mental health professionals can use *The Authoritative Guide to Self-Help Books* as a professional resource for information about the quality of books that focus on a wide-ranging set of problems and circumstances. Concise book reviews that reveal each book's strengths and weaknesses can also increase therapists' knowledge of the content of a number of self-help books. *The Authoritative Guide to Self-Help Books* is the first book to present all of these reviews in one volume, so that a number of books can be quickly compared to determine their appropriateness.

Can self-help books benefit only people who are in therapy, or can they also benefit people not engaged in therapy? Debate still swirls around this issue. In our national survey, slightly more than two-thirds of the therapists said that self-help books do benefit people even if they are not involved in therapy. While no comparable information is available from a decade or two ago, in all likelihood therapists would have answered this question about the benefits of self-help books much more negatively then.

How can the lay person who is not in therapy use this book effectively? The nonprofessional has far less ability than a therapist to weave through the maze of self-help books, even in just one category, and buy the one or two books that are most beneficial. *The Authoritative Guide to Self-Help Books* can help lay people to become knowledgeable about a large number of self-help books and to learn which ones are best for them and which aren't. Chapter 35, Nine Strategies for Selecting a Self-Help Book, can help lay people to evaluate any self-help book more effectively.

CHAPTER TWO

Abuse and Recovery

Experiencing abuse transforms people into victims and changes their lives forever. Once victimized, individuals can never again feel quite as invulnerable. Determining the scope of abuse is difficult because many abused individuals never reveal their experiences. Especially disturbing in the figures that are available are the abuses perpetuated by close friends and family members. Acquaintances of the victim are implicated in almost 50% of child sexual assaults, romantic partners in 50% to 75% of sexual assaults reported by college-age and adult women. And the burden of abuse falls on women unequally: more than 75% of the reported cases of child sexual abuse involve girls and more than 90% of adult rape victims are women.

Self-help books on abuse and recovery can be categorized as books for adults who were sexually abused as children; inner child books for adults who were abused as children; books for women who have been physically and/or psychologically abused as adults by a husband or romantic partner—battered women; and books about rape, either by a stranger or by an acquaintance.

In the national survey of self-help books, only one book for adults who were sexually abused as children was rated: *The Courage to Heal* by Ellen Bass and Laura Davis.

Three other books that focus on adults who were sexually abused as children, merit a further look. They are *The Courage to Heal Workbook* by Ellen Bass and Laura Davis; *Victims No Longer* by Michael Lew, and *Allies in Healing* by Laura Davis.

Three inner child books for adults were rated: *Healing the Shame That Binds You* by John Bradshaw, *Reclaiming the Inner Child* by Jeremiah Abrams, and *Toxic Parents* by Susan Forward.

Four books for women abused as adults by their marital or romantic

---

Abuse and Recovery
BOOK RATINGS IN THE NATIONAL SURVEY

Strongly Recommended	★★★★★	*The Courage to Heal* by Ellen Bass and Laura Davis
	★★★★★	*The Battered Woman* by Lenore Walker
Neutral	★★★	*Battered Wives* by Del Martin
	★★★	*Getting Free* by Ginny NiCarthy
	★★★	*Healing the Shame That Binds You* by John Bradshaw
Not Recommended	★★	*Toxic Parents* by Susan Forward
	★★	*Abused No More* by Robert Ackerman and Susan Pickering
	★	*Reclaiming the Inner Child* by Jeremiah Abrams

---

partner made the national survey's final ratings: *The Battered Woman* by Lenore Walker; *Battered Wives* by Del Martin; *Getting Free* by Ginny NiCarthy; and *Abused No More* by Robert Ackerman and Susan Pickering.

No books that focus mainly on rape experienced in the adolescent or adult years made the final list of ratings in the national survey. However, two books about rape that deserve a further look are *I Never Called It Rape* by Robin Warshaw (on date acquaintance rape) and *Recovering from Rape* by Linda Ledra (on rape by strangers). Both of these books were given positive ratings in the national survey but were rated by fewer than 10 respondents—hence, their absence from the final ratings.

STRONGLY RECOMMENDED

★★★★★   *The Courage to Heal* (rev. ed., 1992) by Ellen Bass and Laura Davis. New York: Harper Perennial.

This is an outstanding self-help book. It has become a bible for many women who were sexually abused as children. Originally published in 1988, a revised edition appeared in 1992. Ellen Bass realized how little help was available to adult survivors of child sexual abuse through creative writing workshops she taught in the 1970s. Although not academically trained as a psychologist, she decided to offer groups for survivors and developed the I Never Told Anyone workshops, creating a safe context where women could face their own pain and anger and begin to heal. Laura Davis was sexually abused as a child and turned to Ellen Bass for help. She vividly remembers Ellen telling her over and over again, "It wasn't your fault. I believe you. Healing is possible. You're going to make it. You're going to be okay." Ellen Bass and Laura Davis both continue to hold Courage to Heal workshops for adult survivors of child sexual abuse.

The Courage to Heal begins with a brief introduction about how healing is possible. Readers answer a series of 14 questions that help them determine if they were a victim of child sexual abuse. Among other questions, they are asked whether as a child they were touched in sexual areas, shown sexual movies or forced to listen to sexual talk, and raped or otherwise penetrated. Bass and Davis then describe the nature of the many stories told by the abused women. The survivors described in the book represent a broad range of women who vary in age, economic status, race, and sexual preference. Some are in committed relationships, others are single; some are mothers, some are not. The stories are from women who were abused under different circumstances and by different perpetrators. Next, the power of writing in the healing process is underscored. A number of writing exercises are included throughout *The Courage to Heal* to help women reexperience their feelings, to grieve, to figure out how they feel, and to understand what they need.

The bulk of the book is divided into five parts: Taking Stock; The Healing Process; Changing Patterns; For Supporters of Survivors; and Courageous Women. Two sections toward the end of the book focus on counseling and healing resources. In Taking Stock, readers are led through a series of questions to which they provide answers that help them recognize the damage. Then they are encouraged to honor what they did to survive. Taking Stock covers the first stage of recovery from childhood sexual abuse for an adult: acknowledging that the sexual abuse did occur.

The second stage of recovery is spelled out in the book's next section, The Healing Process. Bass and Davis believe that before women can cope with childhood sexual abuse they have to make a commitment to heal themselves. The authors provide numerous tips about what survivors can do once they begin to remember some of the details of their abuse. These tips include where to go, who to talk to, and how to comfort themselves.

The third stage of recovery is explored in the next section, Changing Patterns, which involves getting on with your life. In this stage of recovery, readers learn about the personal power they possess, how to deal with feelings effectively, loving their body, learning to trust and develop intimate relationships, adapting to sexuality, understanding parent–child relationships, and coming to grips with their family of origin.

The fourth section of the book provides valuable advice for supporters of survivors—family members, partners, and counselors. The fifth section contains 15 stories of survivors who represent a broad range of experience. The stories are presented in hope that readers can find at least one woman with whom they can identify. The 1992 edition of *The Courage to Heal* includes a list of more than 600 resources for women survivors of child sexual abuse

This book gets extremely high marks. Any woman who knows she was sexually abused as a child or has the slightest inkling she might have been abused will benefit from this book. The writing is clear, the survivors' comments and stories are artfully woven through the book, the writing exercises are valuable therapy tools, and the authors' compassion, understanding, and insight are apparent. *The Courage to Heal* is a powerful book that can help women recognize if they were sexually abused as a child, take them step-by-step through the healing process, and help them live effective lives. Unlike some recovery books that dwell too extensively on the past, *The Courage to Heal*, after leading women to become aware of a painful past, moves on in positive ways to help them heal and recover. While *The Courage to Heal* is about a traumatic, stressful, devastating experience—child sexual abuse—every section of the book rings with hope, enthusiasm for healing, and belief in positive outcomes. Without question, *The Courage to Heal* is the best self-help book for women who were sexually abused as a child, and it was consistently recognized as such by the mental health experts in the national survey.

★★★★★   *The Battered Woman* (1979) by Lenore Walker. New York: Harper & Row.

Like *The Courage to Heal*, *The Battered Woman* is an excellent self-help book. The two books were written for different audiences—*The Courage to Heal* for adults who were abused as children, *The Battered Woman* for women who have been or continue to be abused by their husband or romantic partners. Lenore Walker, who has a private practice in Denver, Colorado, is widely recognized as one of the leading therapists who study and counsel battered women.

The Battered Woman is divided into three main parts. Part I, Psychology of the Battered Woman, includes valuable information about the myths and realities of abuse as well as psychological theories that help explain the victimization of the battered woman. Part II, Coercive Techniques in Battering Relationships, provides vivid, heart-wrenching stories told by battered women themselves. Part II, The Way Out, examines not only the dark side of legal, medical, psychological, and other services that tend to keep battered women as victims, but the services battered women themselves say would be more helpful.

Walker tells her readers that if they are female there is a 50% chance that they are battered, which shatters myth number 1: The battered woman syndrome affects only a small percentage of the population. Battered women are found in all age groups, races, ethnic and religious groups, educational levels, and socioeconomic groups. They include doctors, lawyers, corporate executives, nurses, secretaries, full-time homemakers, and others. Like rape, the battering of the American woman is a seriously underreported crime. Walker goes on to list and elaborate on 20 other myths about battered women. Then she describes common characteristics of the battered woman, such as low self-esteem; belief in the myths about battered relationships; feelings of guilt, yet denial of feelings of terror and anger; use of sex as a way to establish intimacy; and the belief that no one can help her resolve her predicament except herself.

Walker asserts that battered women undergo a process of victimization, acquiring a sense of "learned helplessness" that leaves them prey to abuse, unable to fault their abusers and unwilling to leave them. Battered women often feel that it is better to be battered than to have no man at all. Battered women also often get caught in a cycle of behavior in which tension builds and essentially inconsequential actions trigger violent outbursts, followed by a period of contrition—remorse, flowers, and the like—that serves to restore the battered woman's positive feelings for her attacker. The learned helplessness and the violence cycle that battered women experience glue together a violence-prone but often charming man and a loving woman in a guilt-ridden relationship.

The terrifying, emotionally devastating nature of battering comes across vividly in the voices of women Walker interviewed. These case studies are carefully written and inevitably disturbing. They evoke a range of emotions—from compassion to rage—and encourage analysis of our own close relationships. The case studies unabashedly present battering from a woman's perspective; indeed, Walker acknowledges from the beginning of the book that the book is written from a woman's view.

In the final part of *The Battered Woman*, Walker covers a number of options available to women who want to get out of an abusive relationship. She describes safe houses, refuges or shelters that have become the cornerstone of treatment for battered women who do not want to return home, provides valuable information about legal and medical alternatives available to battered women, and gives brief overviews of different types of psychotherapy for battered women. In the last chapter,

Designing a Better Tomorrow, a very helpful exercise is included. The reader is asked 15 questions to which answers help to identify a potential batterer.

The Battered Woman was written in 1979 and has not been revised. One of its few shortcomings is its age, which shows in the book's final section. In the decade and a half since the book was written, a number of changes in the legal, medical, and psychological aspects of battering have taken place. For example, a number of advances in feminist therapies have been made in the last decade. Many new agencies for battered women have appeared since Walker's listings were made. Walker herself has since written another book on battered women, The Battered Woman Syndrome (1984), an academic book for professionals that probably is not of major interest to most individuals wanting to read a self-help book on battering. This more scholarly treatment of the battered woman, based on in-depth interviews with 435 self-identified battered women, is much tougher reading than The Battered Woman.

All in all, The Battered Woman receives very high marks. It is the best self-help book for battered women and easily deserves its 5-star ranking. Any woman who has been in an abusive relationship with a man, who continues to be in such a relationship, or who would like to find out if her male companion is a potential abuser will benefit from this excellent self-help book.

NEUTRAL

★★★ Battered Wives (revised and updated, 1981) by Del Martin. Volcano, CA: Volcano Press.

Like The Battered Woman by Lenore Walker, Battered Wives is a book for women who have been in an abusive relationship with a man or who continue to be abused in the relationship. While the book is titled Battered Wives, Martin says that her book applies equally to unmarried women who live with violent men and that many of the examples she uses involve unmarried cohabitants. Martin is a leading authority on battered women and has been coordinator of the National Organization of Women (NOW) Task Force on Battered Women. Battered Wives was the first self-help book for battered women, initially published in 1978, then revised and updated in 1981.

In Martin's view, the underlying problem that has led to the battering of so many women is found not in the husband/wife interaction of immediate triggering events but rather in the institution of marriage itself, historically negative attitudes toward women in society, the economy, and inadequacies in legal and social services systems. Martin believes police and prosecutor functions should be constrained. She proposes specific legislation prohibiting wife abuse and argues that judges should protect the wife by not permitting probation and deemphasizing reconciliation. Other recommendations focus on gun control, equal rights, and marriage contract legislation. An especially helpful section explains how to set up a refuge or safe place for battered women.

Martin's book served the extremely important purpose of helping to bring wife battering to the attention of the American public. The book is at its best in its scathing feminist critiques of a society that badly discriminates against women. *Battered Wives* is more a sociological analysis of battered women than an in-depth psychological analysis. *Battered Wives* doesn't flow as easily as Lenore Walker's *The Battered Woman*. The textbook style of writing makes for difficult reading in many places. The riveting case studies and more personal tone in Walker's book will be more attractive to most readers. And even the 1981 revision of *Battered Wives* is dated.

★★★ *Getting Free: You Can End Abuse and Take Back Your Life* (expanded 2nd ed., 1986) by Ginny NiCarthy. Seattle, WA: The Seal Press.

Getting Free, like *The Battered Woman* and *Battered Wives*, is for women and is about battering. NiCarthy directed the Abused Women's Network in Seattle and has led groups at New Beginnings Shelter for Battered Women and the Seattle YMCA. Her book is based on her experiences in those organizations, especially what she learned from women who struggled to get free of violent partners about how they changed their lives. *Getting Free* is divided into six sections: Making the Decision to Leave or Stay; Getting Professional Help; Helping Yourself to Survival; After You Leave; The Ones Who Got Away; and New Directions. The final section—New Directions—examines topics that do not appear in the other books on battered women in the national survey and provides valuable analysis and recovery advice for abused teens and abused lesbians.

Getting Free has an extensive number of exercises for readers to fill out. With so many exercises, the book is virtually a combination of narrative and workbook. *Getting Free* has some good moments—especially when discussing support systems for recovering women—and is very easy to read, but it lacks the substance, the power, and the insightful case studies of Lenore Walker's *The Battered Woman*.

★★★ *Healing the Shame That Binds You* (1988) by John Bradshaw.
Deerfield Beach, FL: Health Communications.

Healing the Shame That Binds You has been on *The New York Times*
best-seller list and has sold more than half a million copies. Its author,
John Bradshaw, studied for the Roman Catholic priesthood and for the
past two decades has worked as a counselor, theologian, management
consultant, and public speaker. Bradshaw believes that people with a wide
array of problems, including addictions, compulsions, codependencies,
the drive to overachieve, anxieties, and character disorders developed
their problems because of toxic shame. What is toxic shame? Bradshaw
never gives a clear definition, but he does provide some hints about its
nature. He says toxic shame is present when people feel that things are
hopeless and that they are worthless. They feel defective and flawed as
a person, bad, and inadequate. Individuals with toxic shame perceive that
they lack power. Bradshaw believes that toxic shame colors a person's
entire identity. It smothers people and keeps them from living a happy
and competent life.

How do people become trapped in toxic shame? Bradshaw thinks
toxic shame has preverbal origins in negative experiences in infancy. The
negative experiences are perpetrated by shame-based parents, who have
a shame-based marriage and establish shame-based rules for their children. Such rules include heavy-handed control, the expectation of perfect behavior, and extensive blaming. Bradshaw believes that shame-based
parents shortchange their children by emotionally abandoning them.
Bradshaw says that people carry these shame-based feelings deep within
them into their adult lives.

How can people get rid of shame-based feelings? Bradshaw believes
that the healing process involves getting the shame out of hiding and
externalizing it. The externalizing involves liberating the lost inner child,
integrating disowned parts, loving the self, healing memories and improving self-image, confronting and changing inner voices, coping with
toxic shame relationships, and spiritual awakening. Bradshaw describes
a number of therapy strategies that can be used to help individuals ex-
ternalize their toxic shame.

Healing the Shame That Binds You barely received a 3-star Neutral
rating in the national survey. Some of the mental health experts rated
Bradshaw's book very positively, others rated it very negatively. The positive reviewers said that Bradshaw really "grabs" people with his description of the pain that he himself went through. He writes frankly about
his alcoholic father and his mother who was a victim of incest, as well
as his own shortcomings as a husband and a father. His emotional sensitivity comes through strongly in *Healing the Shame That Binds You*

as a direct appeal to readers. Bradshaw supporters say that he has an uncanny ability to get people to bring out their hidden problems and deal with their emotions. Enthusiasts also endorse his portrayal of the inner child in all of us, which he sees as the major source of human misery.

Critics of Bradshaw's *Healing the Shame That Binds You* give a number of reasons why they don't like the book. First, they state that toxic shame is not as widely responsible for adult problems as Bradshaw proposes. Human behavior is determined by many factors, say these experts, not by a single cause like toxic shame. Second, critics argue that adult problems are not entirely due to experiences in the early years of childhood and that Bradshaw does not adequately take into account later experiences, including those in the adult years that continue to shape people's lives. Third, some critics cite the absence of evidence for the success of Bradshaw's inner child strategies. And fourth, some mental health critics point out that the business of encouraging people to go back through their childhood and unlock mysteries and demons is heavy stuff. Some individuals uncover memories that are frightening and traumatic, and several of the critics said that self-help books and groups led by nonprofessionals are not ideal contexts for unlocking such memories.

NOT RECOMMENDED

★★ *Toxic Parents: Overcoming Their Hurtful Legacy and Reclaiming Your Life* (1989) by Susan Forward. New York: Bantam.

Author Susan Forward, Ph.D., a therapist in Southern California, tells adults that they are not to blame for what happened to them as children. Their problems as an adult in relationships, careers, and decision making, are a result of how their parents raised them. If they become depressed, its their parents' fault.

Who are the toxic parents? Forward says they are

- inadequate parents who constantly focused on their own problems.
- controlling parents who used guilt, manipulation, and overhelpfulness to dictate their children's lives.
- alcoholic parents who, immersed in their chaotic moods, had little energy or time for their children.
- verbally abusing parents who, whether overtly abusive or subtly sarcastic, demoralized their children with put-downs.
- physically abusing parents who were incapable of controlling their rage.
- sexually abusing parents who destroyed the innocence of their children.

Although number one on *The New York Times* Bestseller List, *Toxic Parents* was given a 2-star Not Recommended rating in the national survey. One of the major problems with *Toxic Parents*, said the mental health experts, is that every parent who ever lived fits at least part of Forward's description of toxic parents. It is all too easy for young adults who had very good parents to read *Toxic Parents* and then blame their parents for every problem that pops up, from minor depressions to career difficulties. To be sure, some parents do fit Forward's toxic parent category—parents who sexually and physically abused their children, verbally abused their children, or did not emotionally support their children. However, when Forward asks readers if, when they were children, their parents

- told them they were bad or worthless
- used physical pain to discipline them
- frightened them
- did anything to them that had to be kept secret

nearly every reader can respond "yes" to one or more of these "accusations." And even if parents never did any of these things, we, as human beings, like to blame others for our problems, and who is handier to blame than our parents?

Because the toxic parent category is all-encompassing, many well-meaning young people may unfortunately "trash" and verbally abuse parents who should not be disowned. The mental health experts said that college students and recent college graduates, still in the delicate stage of developing their own identity, are especially vulnerable to such overreactions. Critics of *Toxic Parents* believed that the book places too much blame on parents for young adults' problems, which can actually hinder the development of self-responsibility. According to mental health professionals, *Toxic Parents*, like *Healing the Shame That Binds You* and *Reclaiming the Inner Child*, places exclusive blame for adult problems on early experiences in life rather than on a balance of earlier and later experiences.

★★   *Abused No More: Recovery for Women from Abusive or Co-Dependent Relationships* (1989) by Robert Ackerman and Susan E. Pickering. Blue Ridge Summit, PA: T. A. B. Books.

This is a book for women abused by a marital or romantic partner who also has a substance abuse problem. In many circumstances, abusing women and abusing alcohol are related. The authors provide an in-depth look at the destructive link between spouse abuse and alcohol abuse.

They recommend a combined recovery approach for the many victims of this double jeopardy situation. Dr. Robert Ackerman is a professor of sociology at Indiana University of Pennsylvania and cofounder of the National Association for Children of Alcoholics. Susan Pickering has worked for more than 10 years as group leader in women's shelters.

Abused No More received a 2-star Not Recommended rating in the national survey of self-help books. Critics thought that the idea of a combined recovery approach for victims in the double jeopardy situation of wife abuse and alcohol abuse has merit. However, they felt that this book did not measure up to other books in the battered woman category, especially Lenore Walker's *The Battered Woman*, or to the best books in the addiction and recovery category.

★   *Reclaiming the Inner Child* (1990), edited by Jeremiah Abrams. Los Angeles, CA: Jeremy P. Tarcher.

According to the editor of this book, Jeremiah Abrams, the inner child is a vital but unconscious part of the self that we carry with us into our adult years. Abrams and other enthusiasts of the inner child concept argue that virtually every adult had an anxious and stressful childhood. Only by healing the abandoned or abused inner child and resolving old traumas can individuals adapt and cope successfully, says Abrams. *Reclaiming the Inner Child* is about a wide range of anxieties and traumas in childhood that are still unresolved in adulthood.

In the introductory chapter, Abrams paints the landscape of the inner child concept. The remainder of the book consists of thirty-seven chapters whose main contents are articles reprinted from other sources. Part I, The Promise of the Inner Child, includes a Jungian paper on archetypes; Part II, The Abandoned Child, has an article by M. Scott Peck on love and the fear of abandonment; Part III, Eternal Youth and Narcissism: The Child's Dilemma, includes a paper by Helen Luke on the little prince; Part IV, The Wounded Child Within, has a paper by Charles Whitfield on how the inner child can be healed; Part V, Recovering the Child, includes an article by John Bradshaw on liberating the lost inner child; and Part IV has a paper by Erik Erikson on the historical relevance of human childhood.

The mental health experts in the national survey gave this book a low rating, placing it in the 1-star Not Recommended category. Critics pointed to two major problems: the abstract, almost mystical nature of the inner child concept and the lack of evidence to support the concept. Critics also say that the inner child concept places too much blame on early childhood experiences and does not give enough attention to later experiences. And critics said that the inner child advocates portray life too pessimistically. The book itself is very hard to read. Other than the introductory chapter and all-too-brief openings for each part and chapter, little interpretation is offered by editor Abrams. Readers are left the almost impossible task of dissecting and understanding many very difficult articles on their own.

WORTH A FURTHER LOOK

◑◐   *I Never Called It Rape* (1988) by Robin Warshaw. New York: Harper & Row.

This book does an excellent job of revealing the facts, the tragedies, and the healing process involved in date or acquaintance rape. Robin Warshaw is a journalist who specializes in social issues. *I Never Called It Rape* is based on a *Ms.* magazine report about date or acquaintance rape. Even though any article appearing in *Ms.* magazine might be suspected of feminist bias, Warshaw's book presents an eye-opening, balanced treatment of an important national problem. The *Ms.* report benefitted considerably from the professional advice of Mary Koss, a clinical psychologist from the University of Arizona, who is a leading mental health authority on date rape.

This book is written mainly for high school, college, or young adult women, although most college and young adult men would also benefit from reading it. The *Ms.* survey revealed that 25% of women in college are the victims of rape or attempted rape and further that 84% of these victims are acquainted with their assailants. Only 5% report their rapes to the police. Warshaw, in easy-to-read fashion, combines survey results with vivid first-person accounts to explain what date rape is, how it happens, and why it was a hidden crime for so long. Warshaw herself was a victim of a violent date rape experience with an ex-boyfriend and provides graphic details of what happened. *I Never Called It Rape* also provides valuable guidelines for victims at all stages of the healing process.

I Never Called It Rape is the best self-help book available on date rape. Any female who has experienced date rape can benefit from Warshaw's portrayal of the healing process, any dating female can benefit from the book's detailed observations about how and why date rape happens, and males can benefit from the book's description of the devastating aftereffects of date rape.

◑◐   *Recovering from Rape* (1986) by Linda Ledra. New York: Henry Holt.

While *I Never Called It Rape* focuses on only one kind of rape—date rape—*Recovering from Rape* addresses all types of rape. Author Linda

Ledry, R.N., Ph.D., is director of the Minneapolis Sexual Assault Resource Service. *Recovering from Rape* is a comprehensive handbook for survivors and those close to them. Ledra offers emotional support and practical guidance on overcoming the trauma of rape. She tells victims what to expect when talking to the police, at the hospital, and if the case goes to court. Readers learn about effective ways to cope with their feelings at different points in the aftermath of rape—immediately following the assault, the next few months, and years later. Ledra gives readers hope by describing the experiences of victims who have coped and pulled through. She reassures readers that they did not deserve to be raped, guiding them from guilt or disbelief through bitterness and despair to the decision to take back control of their lives. A state-by-state list of rape crisis centers at the end of the book provides a valuable resource for anyone concerned with sexual assault.

◐◑ *The Courage to Heal Workbook* (1990) by Laura Davis. New York: Harper Perennial.

In *The Courage to Heal Workbook*, Laura Davis (coauthor of The Courage to Heal) provides an in-depth series of exercises for both women and men who were sexually abused as children. The workbook includes a combination of checklists, open-ended questions, writing exercises, art projects, and activities that take the adult survivor step-by-step through the healing process. This book is a helpful companion to *The Courage to Heal*. The workbook is organized into four main sections. Part I, Survival Skills, teaches survivors how to create a safe, supportive environment, ask for help, cope with crises, and evaluate therapy choices. Part II, Taking Stock, helps survivors examine the past, determine the effects of abuse, and develop healthier coping strategies. Part III, Aspects of Healing, focuses on specific aspects of the healing process, such as making a confrontation plan, preparing for family contact, and affirming one's progress. Part IV, Guidelines for Healing Sexually, leads the survivor to establish healthly ground rules for sexual contact.

◐◑ *Victims No Longer: Men Recovering From Incest and Other Childhood Sexual Abuse* (1990) by Michael Lew. New York: Harper Perennial.

The Courage to Heal is a book for women by women. *Victims No Longer* is a book by a man for men who were sexually abused as children. Michael Lew has a Master's degree in education and has extensively counseled male survivors of childhood sexual abuse at the Next Step Counseling and Training Center in Newton Center, Massachusetts, where he is codirector. Lew points out that our society has no room for a man as a victim. Men are simply not supposed to be abused. After all, isn't a "real man" supposed to be able to protect himself in any situation?

Victims No Longer analyzes many different kinds of sexual abuse but focuses mainly on incest. The great majority of reported cases of incestuous abuse—of both boys and girls—involve male perpetrators. The male survivors of such incest often become confused about their sexuality. Since the abuse was committed sexually, the survivor often perceives it as an act of sexual passion instead of what it really is—an aggressive, destructive violation of another human being.

Victims No Longer is similar in format to *The Courage to Heal*, with case studies woven through the book. Readers learn how to determine if they were sexually abused as children and how the healing process works, and they are given valuable information about where to turn for support. Like *The Courage to Heal*, *Victims No Longer* is not only well-written and easy to read but also warm and personal. The book fills an important void in the Abuse and Recovery self-help category and will benefit any man who was sexually abused as a child or who has a feeling that he may have been abused but is not sure.

◑◑   *Allies in Healing: When the Person You Love Was Sexually Abused as a Child* (1991) by Laura Davis. New York: Harper Perennial.

In *The Courage to Heal*, Ellen Bass and Laura Davis only briefly addressed the partners—those who need to provide important support—of adult survivors of child sexual abuse. *Allies in Healing*, was written for the partners—girlfriends, boyfriends, spouses, lovers. Davis tells couples how to deepen compassion, improve communication, and develop understanding of healing as a shared experience. Partners are taught how they can work and grow together with an adult survivor of child sexual abuse, as well as how to cope with crises that might arise. The struggles, triumphs, and courage of eight partners provide in-depth evidence of the partner's role in the healing process.

Allies in Healing received very positive ratings in the national survey on self-help books but was listed fewer than 10 times. *Allies in Healing* is a valuable companion to *The Courage to Heal* because it offers practical advice and hope for partners of survivors while helping partners tend to their own needs during the survivor's recovery.

CONCLUSIONS

In summary, we recommend:

- On women's adult recovery from child sexual abuse:

  ★★★★★ *The Courage to Heal* by Ellen Bass and Laura Davis

- On adult recovery from sexual abuse:

  ◖◗ *The Courage to Heal Workbook* by Ellen Bass and Laura Davis

- On men's adult recovery from child sexual abuse:

  ◖◗ *Victims No Longer* by Michael Lew

- For the partners of adult survivors of child sexual abuse:

  ◖◗ *Allies in Healing* by Ellen Bass

- On battered women who have been abused by their marital or romantic partner:

  ★★★★★ *The Battered Woman* by Lenore Walker

- On date or acquaintance rape:

  ◖◗ *I Never Called It Rape* by Robin Warshaw

- For adult survivors of any kind of rape and those who are close to them:

  ◖◗ *Recovering from Rape* by Linda Ledra

CHAPTER THREE

Addiction and Recovery

Most self-help book authors, as well as therapists, realize how difficult the process of recovery from an addiction is. Virtually all of the authors who write self-help books on addiction recognize that some form of therapy or ongoing self-help group is needed for recovery. Therefore, reading a self-help book on addiction is unlikely, by itself, to help a reader recover from an addiction. However, good self-help books can help determine whether an addiction is present or not, can help in the decision about what type of self-help group or therapy might be best in recovering from an addiction, and can successfully be used while participating in self-help groups or therapy.

Self-help books on addiction fall into five main categories: spiritually based books that are products of self-help groups, especially Alcoholics Anonymous (AA); books for the children and relatives of alcoholics and other substance abusers; books that focus on the addictive personality or mind; books that cover a wide range of addictions; and recently produced books that emphasize psychological, nonreligious-oriented alternatives to AA. Some mental health professionals place books that deal exclusively with love as an addiction, sex as an addiction, or eating disorders as addictions in the general category of addiction and recovery. However, in *The Authoritative Guide to Self-Help Books* these books will be discussed in the respective categories of love (Chapter 22), sex (Chapter 30), and eating disorders (Chapter 17). Many books on codependency also focus on addiction and recovery. The codependency books are also evaluated in their own chapter (Chapter 11).

In the national survey of self-help books, five books by Alcoholics Anonymous World Services or related to Alcoholics Anonymous-type programs were rated. The three books by Alcoholics Anonymous World Services are *Alcoholics Anonymous; Twelve Steps and Twelve Tradi-*

Addiction and Recovery

BOOK RATINGS IN THE NATIONAL SURVEY

Recommended	★★★★ *Alcoholics Anonymous* by Alcoholics Anonymous World Services
	★★★★ *Twelve Steps and Twelve Traditions* by Alcoholics Anonymous World Services
Diamonds in the Rough	◆ *It Will Never Happen to Me* by Claudia Black
Neutral	★★★ *One Day at a Time in Al-Anon* by Alcoholics Anonymous World Services
	★★★ *A Day at a Time* by CompCare
	★★★ *Addiction and Grace* by Gerald May
	★★★ *Adult Children of Alcoholics* by Janet Woititz
Not Recommended	★ *The Alcoholic Man* by Sylvia Carey
Strongly Not Recommended	† *Healing the Addictive Mind* by Lee Jampolsky

---

tions; and *A Day at a Time. The Alcoholic Man* by Sylvia Carey was based on interviews with individuals in AA and adopts an AA approach. *One Day at a Time in Al-Anon* is based on the self-help group approach of Al-Anon, which follows a strategy similar to AA.

Two books on children and relatives of alcoholics made the national survey's final ratings—*It Will Never Happen to Me* by Claudia Black and *Adult Children of Alcoholics* by Janet Woititz. These books are targeted to the children and relatives of alcoholics and other substance abusers who are especially vulnerable to developing certain problems themselves.

Two books that focus on the addictive personality or mind were rated in the national survey. Gerald May's *Addiction and Grace* adopts this approach, along with a strong emphasis on spiritual commitment. Lee Jampolsky's *Healing the Addictive Mind* also is based on changing an individual's addictive mind.

No books that cover a number of addictions made the final list of ratings in the national survey. However, one book in this category that was positively rated several times had only recently been published at the time of the survey—*The Truth about Addiction and Recovery* by Stanton Peele and Archie Brodsky. More will be said about this book in Worth a Further Look.

Also, no books that emphasize psychological, nonreligious alternatives to AA made the final list of ratings. Peele and Brodsky's book, *The Truth about Addiction and Recovery*, falls into the category, as does the recently published *When AA Doesn't Work for You: Rational Steps to Quitting Alcohol* by Albert Ellis and Emmett Velton, also profiled in Worth a Further Look.

RECOMMENDED

★ ★ ★ ★   *Alcoholics Anonymous* (3rd ed., 1976). New York: Alcoholics Anonymous World Services.

In the national survey, this was the highest rated of the three books published by Alcoholics Anonymous World Services. Revised twice since the first edition was published in 1939, the book is the basic text for Alcoholics Anonymous self-help groups. These groups are open and free to anyone, nonalcoholics as well as alcoholics. The average period of sobriety for AA members (who call themselves AAs) is 52 months; 29% stay sober for more than 5 years. Members range from teens to the elderly. Increasing numbers of young people have joined AA in recent years. About twice as many men as women belong. The number of AA members addicted to substances other than alcohol has increased to an estimated 38% overall. The principles of Alcoholics Anonymous have been revised and adapted by a number of self-help groups such as Narcotics Anonymous, Gamblers Anonymous, and Al-Anon (for people with a variety of addictions and their families).

Called the "Big Book" by AAs, *Alcoholics Anonymous* is divided into two basic parts. The first part describes the Alcoholics Anonymous recovery program, which relies heavily on confession, group support, and spiritual commitment to God to help individuals cope with alcoholism. Extensive personal testimonies of AA members from different walks of life make up the latter two-thirds of the book. Successive editions of the book have expanded the case histories to describe examples of alcoholics from a variety of backgrounds in hope that alcoholics who read the book can identify with at least one of them. The chapter-long stories record the experiences of pioneers of AA (such as Doctor Bob, a cofounder of AA), individuals who stopped in time (such as the housewife who drank at home, hiding her bottles in dresser drawers, but recovered through AA), and people who nearly lost all (such as a middle-aged man who began drinking heavily in college and didn't beat the addiction until he joined and stayed with AA). Brief appendices include the Twelve AA Steps and Traditions (which are outlined shortly in the review of another AA book) and several testimonials to AA by ministers and physicians. The book also explains how to join AA and attend meetings.

Alcoholics Anonymous was given a 4-star Recommended rating by the mental health experts in the national survey. AA has helped millions of individuals throughout the world to cope effectively with their addiction to alcohol. The positive and supportive atmosphere created by recovering alcoholics at AA meetings—which are held daily—make a difference in helping many people to become sober.

AA, however, is not without its critics. AA works for many but not all alcoholics. Some agnostic or atheistic alcoholics have difficulty relating to AA's strong spiritual emphasis, although AA welcomes these individuals to join its groups. Three self-help groups that have sprung up in recent years as alternatives to Alcoholics Anonymous are Rational Recovery (RR), Secular Organization for Sobriety (SOS), and Women for Sobriety (WFS). Put off by AA's religious emphasis, the new groups leave God out of their battle with the bottle and rely more on willpower than on a higher power. While AA calls drinking a disease and urges members to accept their own helplessness against it, the newer groups emphasize the importance of taking personal responsibility for recovery.

Several of the mental health professionals in the survey said that AA is too "cultish" and that an adequate research base to support the success of AA over other treatments has not been established. Another mental health expert commented that in most cases AA is not a replacement for therapy but can be useful when it precedes or is combined with therapy. Such qualifications of the AA approach by some mental health professionals in the national survey meant a 4-star Recommended rating for *Alcoholics Anonymous* rather than a 5-star, Strongly Recommended rating.

★★★★ *Twelve Steps and Twelve Traditions* (2nd ed., 1990). New York: Alcoholics Anonymous World Services.

This book is devoted to detailed discussions of the Twelve Steps and Twelve Traditions used in Alcoholics Anonymous. The Steps and Traditions represent the heart of AA's principles, providing a precise guide for members to use in their recovery. The strong spiritual nature of the Twelve Steps and Traditions is apparent.

1. We admitted we were powerless over alcohol . . . that our lives had become unmanageable.

2. We came to believe that a Power greater than ourselves could restore us to sanity.
3. We made a decision to turn our will and our lives over to the care of God *as we understood Him.*
4. We made a searching and fearless moral inventory of ourselves.
5. We admitted to God, to ourselves, and to another human being the exact nature of our wrongs.
6. We were entirely ready to have God remove all these defects of character.
7. We humbly asked Him to remove our shortcomings.
8. We made a list of all persons we had harmed, and became willing to make amends to them all.
9. We made direct amends to such people wherever possible, except when to do so would injure them or others.
10. We continued to take personal inventory and when we were wrong promptly admitted it.
11. We sought through prayer and meditation to improve our conscious contact with God *as we understood Him,* praying only for knowledge of His will for us and the power to carry that out.
12. We having had a spiritual awakening as the result of these steps, we tried to carry this message to alcoholics and to practice these principles in all our affairs.

In the 4-star *Alcoholics Anonymous,* the Twelve Steps are briefly described, much as we have done here, in an appendix, and the religious orientation of AA is not emphasized in the case studies. In *Twelve Steps and Twelve Traditions's* almost 200 pages are devoted to elaborating the basic principles of the Twelve Steps; the religious orientation of AA takes center stage.

Like its sister book, *Alcoholics Anonymous, Twelve Steps and Twelve Traditions* was given a 4-star Recommended rating in the national survey. Because the twelve steps have become so widely used, mental health experts have carefully analyzed them. Criticisms of the Twelve Steps focus mainly on their spiritual basis. Unhappy with the strong religious flavor of the Twelve Steps and AA, some mental health experts have recast the steps in nonreligious terms to appeal to a wider range of people. Before his death, the famous behaviorist B. F. Skinner put together a psychological alternative to AA's Twelve Seps in 1987:

1. We accept the fact that all our efforts to stop drinking have failed.
2. We believe that we must turn elsewhere for help.
3. We turn to our fellow men and women, particularly those who have struggled with the same problem.

4. We have made a list of the situations in which we are most likely to drink.
5. We ask our friends to help us avoid those situations.
6. We are ready to accept the help they give us.
7. We earnestly hope that they will help.
8. We have made a list of the persons we have harmed and to whom we hope to make amends.
9. We shall do all we can to make amends, in any way that will not cause further harm.
10. We will continue to make such lists and revise them as needed.
11. We appreciate what our friends have done and are doing to help us.
12. We, in turn, are ready to help others who may come to us in the same way.

A number of self-help books that reformulate the Twelve Steps in various ways have been written, but none were mentioned often enough by mental health professionals in the national survey to be included in the final listing of books.

DIAMONDS IN THE ROUGH

♦ *It Will Never Happen to Me* (1981) by Claudia Black. New York: Ballentine.

Unlike the Alcoholics Anonymous books that are directed at alcoholics themselves (although anyone can attend AA meetings), Claudia Black's book was written to help children—as youngsters, adolescents, and adults—cope with the problem of having an alcoholic parent. Black, with an impressive educational background in the field of social work, has extensively counseled many alcoholic clients who were raised in alcoholic families, as well as wives of alcoholics. She comments that virtually every one of them said, "It will never happen to me," hence the title of her book. Black believes that when people grow up in alcoholic homes, they learn to not talk, not trust, and not feel, whether they drink or not.

It Will Never Happen to Me was given the Diamonds in the Rough rating because the mental health experts did not rate it very often, but when they did they gave it a high rating. Black's book is the best self-help book for children and spouses of alcoholics. She does a good job of describing the alcoholic cycle, paints a vivid picture of the pitfalls those related to alcoholics face, and is upbeat in giving them hope for recovery and positive living. In the final chapter, Black tells readers about a number of resources relatives of alcoholics can call on in reaching out for help. Although *It Will Never Happen to Me* was written primarily for the children and spouses of alcoholics, Black's book can also benefit individuals related to people with other substance abuse addictions and eating disorders.

While *It Will Never Happen to Me* was given the highest rating of the children of alcoholics books, some mental health experts believe that all the books in the children of alcoholics category are ineffective. They are especially critical of the lack of documented success of such counseling strategies and believe that more traditional psychological approaches to therapy—such as behavioral, cognitive, or family systems—can be more effective.

NEUTRAL

★★★   *One Day at a Time in Al-Anon* (1973). New York: Al-Anon Family Group Headquarters.

Originated by a group of women married to alcoholic husbands, Al-Anon is a support group for relatives and friends of alcoholics. Like a number of self-help support groups for alcoholics and their relatives, Al-Anon members follow AA's Twelve Steps of recovery. The members of Al-Anon share experiences, strength, and hope in helping each other solve the problems created in the family of an alcoholic. Like AA, Al-Anon does not charge for its group sessions, although voluntary contributions are accepted.

One Day at a Time reflects an important principle of Al-Anon: Focus on one day at a time when living with an alcoholic. Each day is viewed as a fresh opportunity for self-realization and growth rather than for dwelling on past problems and disappointments. Like the Alcoholics Anonymous books, *One Day at a Time* has a strong spiritual emphasis. Each page is devoted to one day—from January 1 to December 31—and consists of two parts: a message and today's reminder. Religious quotations are used frequently throughout the book.

One Day at a Time is categorized as a 3-star book, placing it in the Neutral category. *One Day at a Time* has a special appeal to alcoholics and to the relatives of alcoholics who find strength in brief spiritual messages.

★★★   *A Day at a Time* (1976). Minneapolis, MN: CompCare.

This is a book of daily reflections, prayers, and catchy phrases that are intended to offer inspiration and hope to recovering alcoholics. The book is based on the spiritual aspects of Alcoholics Anonymous, especially the Twelve Steps and Twelve Traditions. Like Al-Anon's *One Day at a Time*, each page is devoted to a day—from January 1 through December 31. Each page is divided into three parts: Reflection for the Day; Today I Pray; and Today I Will Remember. The brief daily messages come from poets, philosophers, scholars, psychologists, and members of AA. A subject index guides the reader to topics highlighted on different days. Topics range from abstinence and acceptance to willingness to change and working with the program.

A Day at a Time received the lowest rating of the three Alcoholics Anonymous books that were rated in the national survey. It was given 3 stars, placing it in the Neutral category. The two AA books that were given 4 stars—*Alcoholics Anonymous* and *Twelve Steps and Twelve Traditions*—are considerably longer and more detailed about the way Alcoholics Anonymous works. Like Al-Anon's book *One Day at a Time*, *A Day at a Time* is most likely to appeal to individuals with a strong religious interest.

★★★ *Addiction and Grace* (1988) by Gerald C. May. New York: Harper-Collins

Addiction and Grace falls into the category of self-help books that combine spiritual and psychological principles to help combat any type of addiction—whether to alcohol, other drugs, sex, love, food, work, gambling, and so on. May is a psychiatrist and spiritual director who supervises the training of spiritual leaders at the Shalom Institute in Washington, DC. Reflecting his belief in the roles that relationships with others and spirituality play in addiction, his book is subtitled *Love and Spirituality in the Healing of Addictions*. May states that the deepest human need is to be in a loving relationship with God and others. However, says May, our freedom to satisfy this need is restricted by many different addictions (including fame as well as drugs) that use up our desire. May describes how to resist the entrapments of life's many addictions, especially through a better understanding and adoption of religious principles, including grace.

Addiction and Grace may appeal to individuals with a strong spiritual orientation. The 3-star rating by the mental health experts in the national survey places the book in the Neutral category. *Addiction and Grace* is not a well-written book. Most people searching for a self-help book on addiction will find its writing style too abstract and technical to benefit them. The book also uses the term addiction too broadly: About everything a person does is subject to becoming an addiction that interferes with positive living. For example, most mental health experts don't include self-improvement and anchovies on their list of addictions, but May does!

★★★   *Adult Children of Alcoholics* (expanded edition, 1990) by Janet Woititz. Deerfield Beach, FL: Health Communications.

Janet Woititz is the "mother" of the ACoA (Adult Children of Alcoholics) movement. *Adult Children of Alcoholics* was originally written only for children of alcoholics and was first published in 1983. Woititz believes that the current edition of the book can help individuals in other types of problem families as well, such as those with a member addicted to gambling, drug abuse, or overeating. Woititz, who has a doctorate in education, is the founder and president of the Institute for Counseling and Training in West Caldwell, New Jersey, which specializes in working with dysfunctional families.

Woititz believes that no one has an ideal childhood, so we are all recovering in some way or another. She argues that because there are so many alcoholic families and because they have been so widely studied by ACoA counselors, some basic problems and vulnerabilities of adult children of alcoholics can be described. Woititz says that reading her book, *Adult Children of Alcoholics,* is the first step to recovery. She also endorses Al-Anon and its Twelve-Step program to recovery.

According to Woititz, the key to recovery is learning the principle of detachment, whether you are recovering from an addiction or are living with an addict. In her view, because adult children of alcoholics *all* received inconsistent nurturing as children, as adults they hunger for nurture and are too emotionally dependent on their parents. They have to separate themselves from their parents in the least stressful way possible, she says. Woititz thinks the detachment process takes about six months to a year. Then they are ready to join an ACoA support group. By detachment from parents and joining an ACoA group, emotions held back for years will surface and the road to recovery will open up.

The ACoA movement has been very popular among adult children of alcoholics, and *Adult Children of Alcoholics* continues to be a widely read self-help book; it was on *The New York Times* best-seller list for more than 45 weeks and has sold more than 2 million copies. However, the opinions of the mental health experts in our national survey were mixed, giving *Adult Children of Alcoholics* a 3-star Neutral rating.

One of the main criticisms of the book is its emphasis that the adult children of alcoholics can never be completely cured; they always will be in some phase of recovery because of the traumatic childhood they experienced. Critics say that ACoA books and groups cause people to get locked into their traumatic past and ruminate too much about early experiences in their life. Some mental health experts believe that the successful strategy for recovery should focus more on an individual's current coping strategies and experiences than on a sea of early problems. When ACoA advocates tell their clients that they cannot be cured, the clients may think that means that they can never change, which many mental health experts believe is unfortunate. Some mental health experts also do not agree with Woititz's belief that everyone living in a family with an alcoholic has the same vulnerabilities and develops the same problems. Rather, they advocate taking into account differences in family members' reactions to having an alcoholic in the family. Not everyone growing up in a family with an alcoholic develops serious problems; even those who do aren't necessarily in recovery for the rest of their lives, say the detractors.

NOT RECOMMENDED

★ *The Alcoholic Man* (1990) by Sylvia Carey. Los Angeles, CA: Lowell House.

In *The Alcoholic Man*, Sylvia Carey, who has a Master's degree in family counseling, describes her extensive interviews with 18 men who remained sober from 30 days to 43 years. Carey is a Los Angeles-based counselor who herself was addicted to alcohol for 8 years and is now 21-years sober. The alcoholic men share their triumphs and problems, providing insights about the journey to recovery. *The Alcoholic Man* provides information for not only alcoholics but their families and friends as well, helping them understand the nature of alcoholism and recovery from it. All of the men interviewed by Carey were members of Alcoholics Anonymous, although the book is not about AA per se but rather about the recoveries of the 18 men.

This book was given a 1-star Not Recommended rating by the national panel of mental health experts. Critics pointed out that the book is a hodgepodge of 18 disconnected stories, with no consistent theme or "hook"—like the twelve steps and traditions of the Alcoholics Anonymous books—that readers can hang on to. In the final few pages, a brief overview of AA is given, about the only consistent theme in the book. The AA books themselves provide better depth and definable steps to recovery than *The Alcoholic Man*.

STRONGLY NOT RECOMMENDED

† *Healing the Addictive Mind* (1991) by Lee Jampolsky. Berkeley, CA: Celestial Arts.

In this New Age book, Lee Jampolsky, Ph.D., a psychologist in private practice in Carmel, California, suggests coping with an addiction by achieving inner peace. He believes inner peace can be accomplished by releasing fear and letting love in. Doing this, he says, frees a person from the need for—and dependency on—outside forces and situations. The book is divided into two parts, the first offering an understanding of addiction in general and how it affects people's lives, the second providing daily lessons designed to help individuals choose peace more consistently.

Healing the Addictive Mind received a very unfavorable review by the mental health experts in the national survey. With a negative overall rating, the book was placed in the Strongly Not Recommended category. Critics of the book point out that Jampolsky's inner peace system is not widely accepted or tested. They believe it is unlikely that this book will help a reader cope with addiction.

WORTH A FURTHER LOOK

◑◑ *The Truth about Addiction and Recovery* (1991) by Stanton Peele and Archie Brodsky. New York: Simon & Schuster.

Drawing on recent research and detailed case studies, the authors conclude that addictions—whether to food, cigarettes, sex, alcohol, or drugs—are not diseases, and they are not necessarily lifelong problems. Stanton Peele, a psychologist and health-care researcher, is a leading authority in the addiction field. Archie Brodsky is a researcher in the Program in Psychiatry and Law at Harvard Medical School.

Instead of medical treatment or a Twelve-Step program like AA, Peele and Brodsky recommend their "life process program" that emphasizes coping with stress and achieving one's goals. *The Truth about Addiction and Recovery* is divided into three parts. In Part I, From Alcoholism to Shopping Addiction: Addiction Is Not a Disease, separate chapters are included on alcoholism, different drugs, smoking, obesity, gambling, and love and sex. In Part II, The Life Processes Program: Skills for Taking Control of Your Life, separate chapters address such topics as how to assess your values and what is really important to you, how to carry out plans of change, and how to develop life skills. In Part III, Changing Communities, Changing Lives, separate chapters examine how to prevent addiction in children, how to establish communal ties, and where you have been and need to go.

Distinguished psychotherapist Albert Ellis believes that the book should be required reading for addicts, their associates, and those who try to treat them. Carol Tavris, author of the well-received self-help book *Anger: The Misunderstood Emotion*, says that *The Truth about Addiction and Recovery* is a calm, reasoned, and highly effective alternative to the disease model of addiction and other bad habits that can be very helpful to people with an addiction and to their relatives. While *The Truth about Addiction and Recovery* does include a number of case studies, the book is more like a textbook than the other books in this category. For example, a number of research studies and academic sources are cited to support the author's interpretations and recommendations. The book is a trade off, well-documented but somewhat difficult to digest.

◐◐   *When AA Doesn't Work for You: Rational Steps to Quitting Alcohol* (1992) by Albert Ellis and Emmett Velton. Fort Lee, NJ: Barricade Books.

A second book worth a further look is Albert Ellis and Emmett Velton's *When AA Doesn't Work for You: Rational Steps to Quitting Alcohol.* The authors acknowledge that AA works for many people but not for everybody. Ellis is a well-known cognitive therapist who has written several books that are rated in later chapters in *The Authoritative Guide to Self-Help Books*. Ellis's approach is called rational emotive therapy, which attempts to turn irrational thought patterns into rational ones. Emmett Velton is a therapist who has used rational emotive therapy for more than 20 years to help recovering alcoholics.

When AA Doesn't Work for You begins with several chapters that help readers determine whether they have a drinking problem or not and introduces rational emotive therapy as the best strategy for recovery. A number of helpful step-by-step methods, including the use of a daily journal and homework assignments, are provided in later chapters. Maladaptive thought patterns and conversations, followed by specific ways to replace them with more adaptive ones, are woven throughout the book. Unlike many of the books in the addiction and recovery category, Ellis and Velton's book does not include spiritual commitment in the recovery process. Ellis and Velton believe AA's notion of the alcoholic's powerlessness is an irrational idea. Self-control and personal responsibility rather than control by a higher power are stressed.

Rational Recovery (RR), one of the increasing number of nonreligious self-help groups for recovering alcoholics and their relatives that have been formed in recent years, traces its roots directly to the ideas of

Albert Ellis and his rational emotive therapy. RR teaches that what leads to persistent drinking is a person's belief that he or she is powerless and incompetent. Using Ellis's approach, a moderator (usually a recovered RR member) helps guide group discussion and get members to think more rationally and act more responsibly. While AA stresses that alcoholics can never fully recover but instead are always in some phase of recovery, RR tells members that recovery is not only possible but that it can happen in a year or so.

CONCLUSIONS

In summary we recommend:

- On Alcoholics Anonymous and related strategies of recovery:

  ★★★★ *Alcoholics Anonymous* by Alcoholics Anonymous World Services

  ★★★★ *Twelve Steps and Twelve Traditions* by Alcoholics Anonymous World Services

- For children and relatives of alcoholics or other types of substance abusers:

  ◆ *It Will Never Happen to Me* by Claudia Black

- On an alternative to AA:

  ◑◑ *The Truth about Addiction and Recovery* by Stanton Peele and Archie Brodsky

  ◑◑ *When AA Doesn't Work for You: Rational Steps to Quitting Alcohol* by Albert Ellis and Emmett Velton

- On a wide range of addictions:

  ◑◑ *The Truth about Addiction and Recovery* by Stanton Peele and Archie Brodsky

CHAPTER FOUR

Adult Development

For too long, psychologists believed that development was something that happens only to children. To be sure, growth and development are dramatic in the first two decades of life, but a great deal of development goes on in the adult years of life, too. In this chapter we consider only self-help books for people in the early and middle adulthood years, from the early 20s through the late 50s or early 60s. In Chapter 5, Aging, we explore self-help books for and about older adults.

The adult years are important not only to the adults who are passing through them but to their children, who as they become adults often want to better understand their parents and improve their relationship with them. The changes in body, personality, and ability through the adult years can be considerable. Adults want to know how to adjust to these changes and how to make transitions in their adult life more smoothly. They also want to know how to cope with the important adult themes of love and work.

Self-help books on adult development can be divided into five categories: books that focus on stages of adult development as crises, especially the midlife crisis; books that emphasize life events and themes of adult development such as love and work; books that deal with a specific life event or transition in adult development, such as menopause; books that explore adults' relationships with their parents; and books that examine loss and growth in adulthood.

In the national survey of self-help books, two books that focus on stages of adult development as crises, especially the midlife crisis, made the final ratings: *Seasons of a Man's Life* by Daniel Levinson and *Passages* by Gail Sheehy.

Only one book that emphasizes life events and themes of adult development, such as love and work, was rated: *Lifelines* by Sharan Merriam and M. Carolyn Clark.

Adult Development
BOOK RATINGS IN THE NATIONAL SURVEY

Recommended	★★★★ *Necessary Losses* by Judith Viorst
	★★★★ *Seasons of a Man's Life* by Daniel Levinson
Neutral	★★★ *Making Peace with Your Parents* by Harold Bloomfield
	★★★ *Passages* by Gail Sheehy
	★★★ *Lifelines* by Sharan Merriam and M. Carolyn Clark
	★★★ *When You and Your Mother Can't Be Friends* by Victoria Secunda
	★★★ *How to Deal with Your Parents* by Lynn Osterkamp

No books that deal with a specific life event or transition made the final list, although Gail Sheehy's *Silent Passages,* a book about menopause that was published too late to be included in the national survey, deserves a further look.

Three books that explore adults' relationships with their parents were rated: *Making Peace with Your Parents* by Harold Bloomfield, *When You and Your Mother Can't Be Friends* by Victoria Secunda, and *How to Deal with Your Parents* by Lynn Osterkamp.

One book that examines loss and growth in adulthood was rated: *Necessary Losses* by Judith Viorst.

RECOMMENDED

★★★★ *Necessary Losses* (1986) by Judith Viorst. New York: Simon & Schuster.

Necessary Losses describes how we can grow and change through the losses that are an inevitable part of our lives. The book was on *The New York Times* best-seller list for over a year. Author Judith Viorst has been a contributing editor to *Redbook* magazine. After almost two decades of work as a professional writer, Viorst wanted to learn more about psychology, so she studied at the Washington Psychoanalytic Institute for six years. Through her therapy experiences, she concluded that many people struggle with many different types of loss.

When we think of loss, we often think of the loss, through death, of the people we love. But Viorst talks about loss as a far more encompassing theme of life. She says we lose not only through death but also by leaving and being left, by changing and letting go and moving on. Viorst also describes the losses we experience through our impossible expectations, illusions of freedom and power, and illusions of safety, and the loss of our own younger self, the self we always thought would be unwrinkled, invulnerable, and immortal.

Necessary Losses is divided into four sections. The first section, The Separate Self, deals with such topics as the high cost of separation, standing alone, and lessons in love. The second section, The Forbidden and the Impossible is concerned with the losses involved in facing the limitations of our power and deferring what is forbidden and impossible. The third section, Imperfect Connections, describes the losses we experience when we relinquish our dreams of ideal relationships and come to terms with the human realities of imperfect connections. The last section, Loving, Losing, Leaving, Letting Go, fittingly faces the losses—often multiple—of the second half of life, our final losing, leaving, and letting go.

Although loss is often a depressing circumstance that most of us try to avoid, Viorst gives a positive tone to the emotional struggles we go through in loss. She believes that through the loss of our mother's protection, the loss of impossible expectations we bring to relationships, the loss of our younger selves, and the loss of loved ones through separation and death, we gain a deeper perspective, true maturity, and fuller wisdom about life.

Necessary Losses is a good self-help book. It received a 4-star Recommended rating in the national survey and was the highest-rated book in the adult development category. Viorst writes extraordinarily well and her sensitive voice comes through clearly in *Necessary Losses*. The extensive psychoanalytic training she underwent prior to writing this book also served her well in explaining the nature of loss. Most adults can benefit from reading this book and will find themselves time after time relating to the examples of loss she provides. Benjamin Spock, famous author of parenting self-help books, said that this perceptive book should absorb anyone who admits to being human.

★★★★ *Seasons of a Man's Life* (1978) by Daniel J. Levinson. New York: Ballantine.

Seasons of a Man's Life, a national bestseller, falls into the category of adult development books that outline a number of stages adults pass through with a special emphasis on the midlife crisis. Author Levinson is a well-respected clinical psychologist and professor at Yale University. The book's title accurately reveals that *Seasons of a Man's Life* is more appropriate reading for men than for women.

In this book, Levinson and his colleagues reported the results of their extensive interviews with 40 middle-aged men. The interviews were conducted with hourly workers, business executives, academic biologists, and novelists. Conclusions are bolstered with biographies of famous men and memorable characters in literature. Although Levinson's main interest focuses on midlife change, he describes a number of stages and transitions in the life cycle, ranging from 17 to 65 years of age.

Levinson believes that successful adjustment requires mastering developmental tasks at each stage. He sees the twenties as a novice phase of adult development. At the end of the teenage years, people need to make a transition from dependence to independence, a transition marked by the formation of a dream—an image of the kind of life desired, especially in terms of a career and marriage. From about 28 to 33, people go through a transition period in which they must face the more serious question of determining their development. In the thirties, individuals enter a phase of "Becoming one's own man" (or *Boom*). By age 40, people have reached a stable location in their careers, have outgrown their tenuous attempts at learning to become an adult, and now must look forward to the kind of life they will lead as middle-aged adults.

In Levinson's view, the change to midlife takes about five years and requires men to come to grips with four major conflicts that have existed since adolescence: (1) being young versus being old, (2) being destructive versus being constructive, (3) being masculine versus being feminine, and (4) being attached to others versus being separated from them. Levinson reports that 70 to 80% of the men he interviewed found the midlife transition (ages 40 to 45) tumultuous and psychologically painful. Levinson says that adults can effectively cope with the midlife transition by reducing the polarities of the four major conflicts and accepting each as an integral part of their being.

Seasons of a Man's Life received a 4-star Recommended rating in the national survey of self-help books. Levinson's book is one of several that helped to form the American public's image of a midlife crisis. Some critics lavished praise on the work. Distinguished psychologist Robert R. Sears of Stanford University commented that Levinson's view is a companion to Freud's stage view of sexuality and Erikson's life cycle view. He also remarked that the biographies are of outstanding quality. Professor Peter Newton of the University of California at Berkeley said that *Seasons of a Man's Life* is a work of great value that will help adults live more intelligently and have greater insights into their adult years.

Seasons of Man's Life is almost two decades old now, and it is not without its critics. Some experts on adult development believe that the book overdramatizes the midlife crisis. While Levinson found that 70 to 80% of the men in his study experienced a midlife crisis, others have found that the percentage in the general population is not nearly as high. Critics also point out that Levinson does not adequately take into account individual variations in how people go through midlife. Also, Levinson's central focus is career choice and work achievement. He does not adequately address women's concerns about relationships, interdependence, and caring.

NEUTRAL

★ ★ ★   *Making Peace with Your Parents* (1983) by Harold Bloomfield. New York: Random House.

This book falls into the category of adults' relationships with their parents. Author Harold Bloomfield, M.D., is a practicing psychiatrist and director of psychiatry at the North County Holistic Health Center in Del Mar, California. His psychiatric training was at Yale University Medical School. He is also a coauthor of the strongly recommended *How to Survive the Loss of a Love* that focuses on coping with the death of a loved one (Chapter 11).

According to Bloomfield, whatever your age, if you are to become a fulfilled and competent person, you need to resolve the issues in your life that involve your relationship with your parents. Drawing on insights from his clinical practice, research in the area of adult children–parent relationships, and personal experiences in his own family, Bloomfield describes the problems many adults encounter in expressing love and anger toward their parents. He believes that underneath adults' anger and resentment is a deep desire to love and be loved by their parents.

Making Peace with Your Parents contains exercises and case studies that help adults improve their communication with their parents, cope effectively with difficult parents, unravel parental messages about love, sex, and marriage, and deal with parents' aging, dying, and death. Bloomfield especially believes that adults have to "become their own best parent" by nurturing themselves and engaging in self-responsibility instead of relying on their parents to satisfy such important needs.

Making Peace with Your Parents received a 3-star Neutral rating in the national survey. This book just missed making the 4-star Recommended category. Several of the mental health experts said that *Making Peace with Your Parents* is an excellent book for adults who have a great deal of anger toward their parents. Its message of self-responsibility is an important one, and the clear examples can help adults become aware of how their relationships with their parents have continued to shape their lives as adults.

★ ★ ★   *Passages: Predictable Crises of Adult Life* (1976) by Gail Sheehy. New York: E. P. Dutton.

Like *Seasons of a Man's Life, Passages* is about stages of adult development that all adults supposedly pass through. In the mid-1970s Sheehy's book was so popular that it topped *The New York Times* best-seller list for 27 weeks. Author Gail Sheehy is a journalist.

Sheehy argues that we all go through developmental stages roughly bound by chronological age. Each stage brings problems people must solve before they can progress to the next stage. The periods between the stages are called passages. Sheehy uses catchy phrases to describe each stage: "the trying 20s," "catch 30," "the deadline decade (35 to 45 years of age)," and "the age 40 crucible." Sheehy's advice never waivers: Adults in transition may feel miserable, but those who face up to agonizing self-evaluation, who appraise their weaknesses as well as their strengths, who set goals for the future, and who try to be as independent as possible will more often find happiness than those who do not fully experience these trials. Sheehy believes that these passages earn people an authentic identity, one that is not based on the authority of one's parents or on cultural prescriptions. Adults construct an authentic identity by fully experiencing life's crises and transitions and by psychologically analyzing their lives.

Passages received a 3-star Neutral rating in the national survey of self-help books. Not surprisingly, given its popularity among the public, *Passages* was one of the most frequently rated books. However, the reviews by the mental health experts were mixed. On the positive side, some mental health experts feel that *Passages* has given people in their thirties, forties, and fifties new insights about developmental stages and transitions in adult development. In a 1991 Library of Congress and Book-of-the-Month Club survey of the books that have most influenced people's lives, *Passages* was in the top ten. On the negative side, some experts on adult development believe that Sheehy's book, like Levinson's *Season of a Man's Life*, describes midlife as too much of a crisis and does not adequately consider the many individual ways people go through midlife. Sheehy's *Passages* may be biased toward individuals who are under a great deal of stress because a disproportionate number of the people she interviewed for her book were divorced.

Adult development expert Bernice Neugarten, professor of human development at the University of Chicago, said that choices and dilemmas in adult development do not spring forth at 10-year intervals as Sheehy implies. Decisions are not made and left behind as if they were merely beads on a chain. Neugarten argues that most adulthood themes appear and reappear throughout adulthood. Issues of intimacy and freedom can haunt couples throughout their relationship. Feeling the pressure of time, reformulating life's goals, and coping with success and failure are not the exclusive property of adults of a particular age.

An increasing number of psychologists have studied adult development in the more than two decades since Sheehy wrote *Passages*. The growing consensus of the adult development experts is that self-help books like *Passages* and *Seasons of a Man's Life* present a misconception of midlife. It is not just self-help books, though, that have promoted the concept of midlife as a crisis and turbulent time. So have other media sources, such as television and magazines. The reality is that few middle-aged males drive off into the sunset in a Porsche 911 with a 25-year-old striptease dancer. As with adolescent turmoil, midlife crises are much rarer than the popular press's stories would have us believe.

★★★　*When You and Your Mother Can't Be Friends* (1990) by Victoria Secunda. New York: Delacourte Press.

When You and Your Mother Can't Be Friends is in the category of adult development books that focus on adult children's relationships with their parents. Author Victoria Secunda is a journalist whose work has appeared in magazines such as *New Woman*.

As the title of this book suggests, Secunda writes about the problems that can unfold in mother–daughter relationships when daughters have become adults — daughters who have not resolved unhappy childhood attachments to their mothers and who continue to have unhappy relationships with their mothers. Secunda believes that many adult women won't admit or explore their emotional confusion about their mothers. Yet honesty is exactly what is needed to go beyond mother–daughter bitterness, she says. One problem is that many adult daughters may not recognize how their relationship with their mothers has skewed their adulthood. Such women may play out their unresolved disaffection with husbands and lovers, coworkers and friends, and especially with their own children.

Secunda's book has an optimistic tone. Adult daughters can resolve an unhappy relationship with their mothers and develop an affectionate truce. Friendship with their mothers can even develop. *When You and Your Mother Can't Be Friends* includes excerpts from interviews Secunda conducted with more than 100 adult daughters. The excerpts are interspersed throughout the book to help adult daughters come to know, understand, and accept their mothers. Secunda also interviewed a number of experts on adults' relationships with their parents and includes their insights in the book.

When You and Your Mother Can't Be Friends received a 3-star Neutral rating in the national survey. Some of the mental health experts said that this is an excellent book for adult daughters who have problematic relationships with their mothers. They said that this is an easy-to-read book with many examples that adult daughters will be able to relate to. And they liked Secunda's optimistic tone and the hope she presents for resolving many of the conflicts. Several other mental health professionals marked down the book, citing it as stereotyping adult daughter–mother relationships and giving too little attention to individual variations in adult daughter–mother relationships.

★★★   *Lifelines: Patterns of Work, Love, and Learning in Adulthood* (1981) by Sharan Merriam and M. Carolyn Clark. San Francisco: Jossey-Bass.

Lifelines is about the importance of three adult developmental themes: work, love, and learning. Author Sharan Merriam is a professor of adult education at the University of Georgia and a nationally recognized expert on adult development. M. Carolyn Clark is a professor of adult education at Texas A&M University.

Lifelines takes a very different approach to adult development than the stage approaches of Levinson in *Seasons of a Man's Life* and Sheehy in *Passages*. Merriam and Clark believe that the three most important dimensions of adult development are work, love, and learning. They argue that by understanding patterns of work, love, and learning, adults can find new meaning in day-to-day existence, work creatively through problems, and uncover opportunities for growth. The authors draw on their research study of more than 400 adults to illustrate their beliefs in the importance of work, love, and learning in adulthood. They show how basic concerns and common experiences such as first jobs, parenthood, family illnesses, and divorce shape our identities as adults. Thus, instead of an emphasis on stages and a midlife crisis, *Lifelines* places importance on the life events we experience and how we cope with them as the keys to understanding adult development.

Lifelines received a 3-star Neutral rating in the national survey of self-help books. The mental health professionals felt that this book conveys some important ideas about adult development, especially the emphasis on coping with life events and key themes in adult development rather than stages and a midlife crisis. However, they commented that the book is too high level for most self-help book readers, who will be turned off by the textbooklike quality of the writing and the inclusion of many graphs. The authors do include personal stories and conversations but in most sections the anecdotes are overshadowed by the academic writing.

The ideas in *Lifelines* portray an important alternative to the stage–crisis approach of Levinson and Sheehy. Unfortunately, an easy-to-read self-help book that presents the life events approach to adulthood themes has yet to be written.

★ ★ ★   *How to Deal with Your Parents* (1992) by Lynn Osterkamp. New York: Berkley Books.

This book was written for adult children who want to understand and improve their relationships with their parents. Author Lynn Osterkamp, Ph.D., is a nationally recognized expert on family conflict and communication who works at the University of Kansas in Lawrence, Kansas. She helps the reader answer several important questions:

- Why are so many grown-up people still worrying about what their parents think?
- Why can't I talk to my parents the way I talk to other people?
- Why do we keep having the same arguments?
- How can I stop feeling guilty?
- How can I change family gatherings and holidays?
- How can I stay out of their relationship and keep them out of mine?
- What role would I like for my parents to play in my life today?
- How can I make lasting changes?

Osterkamp's analysis of adult children–parent relationships can especially benefit adults in their twenties and thirties who want to get along better with their parents. The book is filled with personal accounts and identifies problems readers may be having with their parents. Osterkamp gives specific ways to communicate more effectively with parents. And she motivates the reader to develop a step-by-step action plan to accomplish relationship goals.

How to Deal with Your Parents, subtitled *When They Still Treat You Like a Child*, received a 3-star Neutral rating in the national study of self-help books. Few psychologists rated the book, not surprising because the book was published only shortly before the survey was sent out. We believe that *How to Deal with Your Parents* is a good self-help book that will benefit many young adults seeking to better understand and improve their relationships with their parents. We think the book will receive increasingly favorable reviews by mental health professionals as they become more familiar with it. *How to Deal with Your Parents* is well written and well researched, and it is full of helpful examples and wise advice.

WORTH A FURTHER LOOK

❶ ❶   *The Silent Passage* (1992) by Gail Sheehy. New York: Random House.

The Silent Passage is about menopause, the time in middle age — usually in the late forties or early fifties — when a woman's menstrual periods and childbearing capability cease. Production of the hormone estrogen drops considerably. Journalist Gail Sheehy is also the author of the widely read adult development book *Passages*. To better understand menopause, Sheehy interviewed many middle-aged women and talked with experts in a number of fields.

Sheehy argues that the passage through menopause is seldom easy for women because of distracting symptoms, confusing medical advice, unsympathetic reactions from loved ones, and the scornful attitudes of society. For these reasons, menopause has been a lonely and emotionally draining experience for many women. Sheehy's goal is to erase the stigma of menopause and help women understand that it is a normal physical process. She describes her own difficult experiences and reports the frustrations of many women she interviewed. Sheehy's optimism comes through in her hope that menopause will come to be known as "the gateway to a second adulthood" for women.

The Silent Passage was published after the national survey of self-help books was conducted. In a few short months, the book joined bestseller lists around the country. When we went to check out *The Silent Passage* from a public library, 86 people were on the waiting list for the library's 8 copies! Sheehy is a masterful writer and the book is quick and easy reading (it's a small-format book only about 150 pages). Few self-help writers' books ring with the clear-toned prose that Sheehy's do.

However, while Sheehy has not overstated the stigma attached to menopause or the inadequate attention it has been given by the medical community (which is male-dominated), many medical and psychological experts simply don't believe that menopause is the widespread problem Sheehy thinks it is. In a large random sample of 8,000 women, Harvard sociologist John McKinlay and epidemiologist Sonja McKinlay did not find the lonely feelings and emotionally draining experiences associated with menopause nearly as often as Sheehy reports. Critics say that just as Sheehy overdramatized midlife as a crisis, so she as done with menopause. They fault Sheehy for being far too alarmist and morbid about menopause, arguing that menopause is not nearly as tumultuous and traumatic as Sheehy portrays it.

CONCLUSIONS

In summary we recommend:

- For adult daughters seeking to understand and improve their relationship with their mothers:

    ★★★★ *Necessary Losses* by Judith Viorst

- For young adults looking to better understand and improve their relationships with their parents:

    ★★★ *How to Deal with Your Parents When They Still Treat You Like a Child* by Lynn Osterkamp

- For men wanting to learn about stages of adult development and the midlife crisis:

    ★★★★ *Seasons of a Man's Life* by Daniel J. Levinson

CHAPTER FIVE

Aging

More than a century ago Oliver Wendell Holmes said, "To be seventy years young is sometimes far more cheerful and hopeful than to be forty years old." In Holmes' day, being 70 years young was unusual. The average life expectance was less than 45 years then. In the ensuing century we have gained an average of more than thirty years of life, mainly because of improvements in sanitation, nutrition, and medical knowledge.

For too long the aging process was thought of as an inevitable, irreversible decline. Aging involves both decline and growth, loss and gain. The old view of aging argued that we should passively live out our final years. The new view stresses that while we are in the evening of our lives when we become older, we are not meant to live out our remaining years passively. Everything we know about older adults suggests that the more active they are, the happier and healthier they are.

Self-help books on aging cover four different areas: aging in general, with a primary emphasis on the medical and physical dimensions; aging in general, with a main emphasis on the social, psychological, and life style aspects; how to live longer; and Alzheimer's disease.

In the national survey, three books on aging in general with an emphasis on the medical and physical dimensions were rated: *Complete Guide to Health and Well-Being After 50* by Robert Weiss and Genell Subak-Sharpe; *Aging Well* by James Fries; and *The 50+ Wellness Program* by Harris McIlwain and others.

One book on aging in general with an emphasis on the social, psychological, life-styles aspects was rated: *It's Better to Be Over the Hill than Under It* by Eda LeShan. A second book—*Your Renaissance Years* by Robert Veninga—made the Worth a Further Look category.

One book on how to live longer was rated: *How to Live Longer and Feel Better* by Linus Pauling.

Aging

BOOK RATINGS IN THE NATIONAL SURVEY

Diamonds in the Rough	◆ *The 36-Hour day* by Nancy Mace and Peter Rabins
	◆ *It's Better to Be Over the Hill than Under It* by Eda LeShan
Neutral	★★★ *The Diminished Mind* by Jean Tyler and Harry Anifantakis
	★★★ *Complete Guide to Health and Well-Being after 50* by Robert Weiss and Genell Subak-Sharpe
	★★★ *Aging Well* by James Fries
	★★★ *How to Live Longer and Feel Better* by Linus Pauling
Not Recommended	★ *The 50+ Wellness Program* by Harris McIlwain and Lori Steinmeyer, Debra Fulgham, R. E. Fulgham, and Robert Bruce

---

Two books on Alzheimer's disease were rated: *The 36-Hour Day* by Nancy Mace and Peter Rabins and *The Diminished Mind* by Jean Tyler and Harry Anifantakis.

DIAMONDS IN THE ROUGH

◆ *The 36-Hour Day: A Family Guide to Caring For Persons with Alzheimer's Disease, Related Dementing Illness and Memory Loss in Later Life* (1981) by Nancy Mace and Peter Rabins. Baltimore, MD: The Johns Hopkins University Press.

The 36-Hour Day is a family guide to caring for persons with Alzheimer's disease and related diseases in older adults. Author Nancy Mace is coordinator of teaching services in the Department of Psychiatry at the Johns Hopkins University Medical School. Coauthor Peter Rabins, M.D., is a professor in the Department of Psychiatry at the same medical school.

Alzheimer's disease is a progressive, irreversible brain disorder characterized by gradual deterioration of memory, reasoning, language, and eventually physical functioning. Alzheimer's disease was discovered in 1906 and researchers have still not found a cure for it. Approximately 2.5 million people over the age of 65 in the United States have Alzheimer's disease. As more people live to older ages, predictions suggest that Alzheimer's disease could triple in the next 50 years.

The authors say that for those who care for a person with Alzheimer's or related diseases, every day seems as if it is 36 hours long. *The 36-Hour Day* is a guide for the home care of older adults in the early and middle stages of these diseases. *The 36-Hour Day* prepares the family for many different aspects of home care, from dealing with baffling and unpredictable behaviors to helping the afflicted relative live a life as full and satisfying as possible. The family is also helped to recognize the point beyond which home care is no longer enough, and guidance in choosing a nursing home or other care facility is provided. Various support groups that have been formed to help families with an Alzheimer's member are also described.

The 36-Hour Day made the Diamonds in the Rough category in the national survey. This is a good self-help book for families who have an Alzheimer's relative. It provides practical advice with specific examples that help readers learn how to care for an impaired relative on a day-to-day basis. *The 36-Hour Day* is easy to read and insightful and can help families provide a better life for a relative with Alzheimer's disease.

♦   *It's Better to Be Over the Hill than Under It: Thoughts on Life over Sixty* (1990) by Eda LeShan. New York: Newmarket Press.

It's Better to Be Over the Hill than Under It covers a wide range of aging topics related mainly to the social, psychological, and life style aspects of aging. Author Eda Leshan is a family life educator who has written more than 20 books as well as a weekly column on life over 60 for *Newsday.* She lives in New York City.

This book consists of what LeShan believes are her best columns from the *Newsday* series. The articles are divided into three sections: Loving and Living; Memories; and Growing and Changing. The 75 essays range from "An Open Letter to the Tooth Fairy" to "Nothing Is Simple Anymore" to "Divorce after Sixty." Many life issues that have to be dealt with in old age are covered: money, love, sex, anger, facing mortality, work, marriage, friendship, retirement, holidays, grandparenting, children, and so on. Woven through the essays is hope for older adults, hope that will allow them to love and grow and to keep their minds and bodies active and alive.

LeShan says that the most important thing she learned from writing these essays is that the critical emotional adjustment in the final stage of life is acceptance. The real test for older adults, she says, is not looking back but rather dealing with the present, no matter what the inevitable aspects of aging are, and anticipating each day ahead.

It's Better to Be Over the Hill than Under It received the Diamonds in the Rough rating in the national survey. This Erma Bombeck-like viewpoint on old age is extremely enjoyable reading. LeShan is a masterful writer who mixes wit with sage advice. The book is especially good for older adults who feel caught in a rut and need their spirits lifted. And it is good reading for the middle-aged and young adult children of older parents, helping them to become knowledgeable about the changes that are taking place in their aging parents.

NEUTRAL

★ ★ ★   *The Diminished Mind: One Family's Extraordinary Battle with Alzheimer's* (1991) by Jean Tyler and Harry Anifantakis. Blue Ridge Summit, PA: TAB Books.

Like *The 36-Hour Day, The Diminished Mind* is about one of older adults' most horrifying diseases—Alzheimer's. Author Jean Tyler tells the true story of her husband Manley's devastating battle with Alzheimer's. Harry Anifantakis is a professional writer.

Manley Tyler was a loving husband and respected elementary school principal before the onset of Alzheimer's disease. Jean Tyler sensitively describes the pain and grief of her husband's slow, 15-year decline and his eventual death. Alzheimer's hits most older adults much later than it did Manley Tyler. He was only 42-years-old when he first showed the disease's symptoms. His case is also special because he fought the disease longer than most do. Jean Tyler relates the progressive deterioration of memory and judgment that made it impossible for him to complete even the simplest of tasks and made him increasingly prone to hostile behavior and paranoia.

The Diminished Mind made the 3-star Neutral category in the national survey. While this book speaks volumes about the emotionally draining experiences and losses involved in Alzheimer's, it also carries some important messages for the survivor's of an Alzheimer's victim. They can emerge from the experience with fond memories of their loved one and a stronger understanding of what it means to be human.

★ ★ ★   *Complete Guide to Health and Well-Being after 50* (1988) by Robert Weiss and Genell Subak-Sharpe. New York: Times Books.

Complete Guide to Health and Well-Being after 50 profiles a wide array of physical and mental health issues. Author Robert Weiss, M.D., serves as dean and professor in the Columbia University School of Public Health for almost two decades. Coauthor Genell Subak-Sharpe has written, edited, or coedited more than 20 health and medical books.

The full title of this book is actually *The Columbia University School of Public Health Complete Guide to Health and Well-Being after 50*. The book was produced under the auspices of the Columbia University School of Public Health. The word "complete" in the title is appropriate. This book provides information about an encyclopedic number of physical and mental health issues that older adults face. The topics range from medical and physical concerns such as heart disease, arthritis, and cosmetic surgery to psychological and life style concerns such as coping with stress and retirement.

The *Complete Guide to Health and Well-Being after 50* is divided into five main parts. Part I, Health and Fitness, includes discussion of nutrition, exercise, breaking bad habits, and looking your best in the later years. Part II, Emotional Well-Being and Relationships, covers the mid-life crisis, changing relationships. lifelong learning, and retirement. Part III, A Preventive Approach to Diseases of Aging, explores heart disease, cancer, arthritis, and mental functioning in aging, and Part IV, Health Resources for Older People, tells older adults how to use the health care system effectively. Part V, Death, evaluates the importance of coming to terms with mortality.

Most self-help books don't have elaborate charts and tables. This one is filled with them, along with many illustrations, exercises, diets, and self-tests.

The *Compete Guide to Health and Well-Being after 50* made the 3-star Neutral category in the mental health professionals' ratings in the national survey. Several of the mental health experts said that this book is an excellent guide that provides solid descriptions of the health problems of the elderly and the best ways to deal with them. One of the respondents commented that the chapter on using the health care system wisely is exceptionally good. As would be expected in a book written by public health experts, *Complete Guide to Health and Well-Being after 50* is strongly tilted toward a presentation and exploration of physical health issues. Coverage of the psychological and social dimensions of aging is not as thorough and not as insightful as the physical health discussions.

★★★   *Aging Well* (1989) by James Fries. Reading, MA: Addison-Wesley.

Aging Well, like *Complete Guide to Health and Well-Being after 50*, explores a wide range of topics on aging with a stronger emphasis on the medical and physical dimensions of aging than on the life style dimensions. Arthur James Fries, M.D., is a professor of medicine at Stanford University and a world-renowned expert on aging.

Fries believes that we have the capability to age well—with grace and wisdom, energy and vitality. Aging well is not an easy task, he says. It requires a basic understanding of the aging process, a good plan, work, and persistence.

Aging Well is divided into three main parts. Part I, Vitality and Aging, communicates the value of pride and enthusiasm in preventing disease and maintaining vitality, as well as providing a wealth of understanding about specific diseases such as arthritis and osteoporosis. Part II, General Concerns, describes the five keys to a healthy senior life style: selecting and dealing with doctors, sexual issues, retirement, chronic illness, and completing a plan that will ensure that your wishes are carried out after you die. Part III, Solutions, is a step-by-step guide to managing a full range of medical problems, including pain, urinary tract problems, and heart problems.

Fries provides a positive outlook on aging. He believes that while the aging process may slow us down, our older years can still yield the richest moments of our lives.

Aging Well received a 3-star Neutral rating in the national survey. Several mental health professionals gave Fries's book very high marks, stating that *Aging Well* is the best overall guide to the aging process available in the self-help market. The book is well-written and thorough. Fries's expertise on aging clearly comes through in his evaluation of many aging topics. The book is especially helpful as a guide to consult when physical and medical problems arise.

★ ★ ★   *How to Live Longer and Feel Better* (1986) by Linus Pauling. New York: W. H. Freeman.

This book provides a regimen that the author believes will add years to your life and make you feel better. Linus Pauling, Ph.D., is a two-time Nobel Prize Winner, first in chemistry in 1952 and then in peace in 1962.

How to Live Longer and Feel Better shows how vitamins work and how to make them work for you. Pauling especially believes that vitamin C is responsible for producing and maintaining the body's supply of collagen, which he calls the "glue" that holds the body together. He argues that megadoses of vitamin C and other critical vitamins can slow down the aging process, makes us look younger, and help us feel better. How much vitamin C? Pauling urges readers to take up to 18 grams of vitamin C every day. He also says to consume 25,000 International Units of vitamin A and 1,600 IU of vitamin E every day, plus other micronutrients almost 100 times in excess of recommended daily allowances established by the Food and Nutrition Board of the National Academy of Sciences.

How to Live Longer and Feel Better was placed in the 3-star Neutral category in the ratings in the national survey. In the past, Pauling's ideas clashed with those of the medical establishment, but very recently researchers are finding that vitamin supplements of C, E, and betacarotene may help slow the aging process and improve the health of older adults. Pauling portrays himself as a misunderstood, maligned maverick whose ideas will eventually be accepted by the medical community. He has taken his case to the public in books such as *How to Live Longer and Feel Better* and an earlier book, *Vitamin C, the Common Cold, and the Flu.* The recent research on vitamins does not recommend taking as much vitamin C as Pauling does and there still are a lot of blanks and uncertainies in the vitamin and aging controversy. In most cases large doses of vitamin C are harmless; the excess is simply excreted.

NOT RECOMMENDED

★ *The 50+ Wellness Program* (1990) by Harris McIlwain, Debra Fulgham, R. E. Fulgham, and Robert Bruce. New York: John Wiley & Sons.

The 50+ Wellness Program describes a multifaceted program for maintaining nutritional, financial, and emotional well-being for adults who are 50 years of age and older. Senior author Harris McIlwain, M.D., is a gerontologist and rheumatologist.

This book is divided into three main parts. Part I, Eliminating Risk Factors, includes discussion of the signs and symptoms of aging, prevention and early detection of disease, and medical examinations. Part II, Formulating a Plan for Healthy Living, describes nutrition, exercise, wellness, and disease. Part III, Responding to Life Changes, covers specific health problems, life style and coping issues, and planning for financial changes.

The 50+ Wellness Program was placed in the 1-star Not Recommended category in the ratings in the national survey. It was the lowest-rated book in the aging category. The mental health experts felt that the comprehensive guides written by Robert Weiss and Genell Subak-Sharpe (*Complete Guide to Health and Well-Being after 50*) and James Fries (*Aging Well*) are much easier to read, provide more insightful analysis of aging issues, and are more helpful in coping effectively with the aging process.

WORTH A FURTHER LOOK

◑ ◑ *Biomarkers* (1991) by William Evans and Irwin Rosenberg. New York: Simon & Schuster.

This book is based on research data from the USDA Human Nutrition and Research Center at Tufts University. Author Evans is the chief of the Human Physiology Laboratory at the Human Nutrition and Research Center and a fellow in the American College of Nutrition. Coauthor Rosenberg is director of nutrition research in aging at Tufts and is former President of the American Society of Clinical Nutrition.

The authors document how 50 minutes of aerobic exercise and strength training a day can slow the aging process. They identify 10 biomarkers—key physiological factors—that are associated with youth and vitality:

- Lean body mass
- Strength
- Basal metabolism rate
- Body fat percentage
- Aerobic capacity
- Blood pressure
- Insulin sensitivity
- Cholesterol/HDL ratio
- Bone density
- Body temperature regulation

The authors provide dietary guidelines, self-tests for evaluating physical fitness, and exercise programs for every fitness level.

This is a good self-help book for middle-aged and older adults. The authors do an excellent job of showing how we can age successfully and literally slow the aging process through regular exercise and sensible nutrition, although the writing is too technical in places.

◑ ◑ *Your Renaissance Years* (1991) by Robert Veninga. Boston: Little, Brown.

Your Renaissance Years focuses on the life style dimensions of aging, especially how to cope effectively with retirement. Author Robert Veninga, Ph.D., is a professor in the School of Public Health at the University of Minnesota.

Your Renaissance Years is subtitled *Making Retirement the Best*

Years of Your Life. Veninga begins by describing the secrets of successful retirement and getting the reader to consider early retirement. Subsequent parts of the book focus on the following retirement concerns and issues: money, housing, health, leisure, relationships, and spirituality. Case histories of 135 retirees are interspersed through *Your Renaissance Years.*

Your Renaissance Years was positively rated in the national survey but by only eight respondents. This book was published just prior to the national survey, so few of the mental health professionals were familiar with it. Several of the respondents who did rate it felt that it is the best available self-help book on the retirement issues. *Your Renaissance Years* does provide an in-depth look at how you can cope effectively with many different retirement issues, and it is well-written.

CONCLUSIONS

In summary, we recommend:

- On aging in general with emphasis on the medical and physical dimensions of aging:

    ★★★ *Complete Guide to Health and Well-Being after 50* by Robert Weiss and Genell Subak-Sharpe

    ★★★ *Aging Well* by James Fries

    ◑◑ *Biomarkers* by William Evans and Irwin Rosenberg

- On aging in general with emphasis on the life style dimensions of aging:

    ◆ *It's Better to Be Over the Hill than Under It* by Eda LeShan

- On Alzheimer's disease:

    ◆ *The 36-Hour Day* by Nancy Mace and Peter Rabins

- On retirement:

    ◑◑ *Your Renaissance Years* by Robert Veninga

CHAPTER SIX

Anger

Anger is a powerful emotion. People who have fiery tempers—who become furious when they are criticized, get angry when they are slowed down by others' mistakes, fly off the handle, say nasty things when they get mad, feel like hitting someone when they are frustrated, and whose blood boils when they are under pressure—hurt not only others but themselves as well. Everybody gets angry sometimes, but for most of us, it's only mild anger a couple of times a week. The mild anger often emerges in response to a loved one or a friend performing what we perceive to be a misdeed—being late, promising one thing and doing another, or neglecting a duty, for example. Other people's bouts of anger are enraged, agitated, out-of-control, and frequent. A number of self-help books have been written for individuals who harm others and themselves because they cannot control their anger.

Self-help books on anger can be divided into four categories: books that cover a wide range of anger problems; books designed to help women understand and cope with anger in their lives; books that stress a cognitive (how to change your thoughts) or behavioral (how to replace maladaptive behaviors with adaptive ones) approach to getting a handle on anger; and books that advocate a "let it all out" catharsis approach to anger.

In the national survey of self-help books, one book that addresses a wide range of anger problems was included in the final ratings: *Anger: The Misunderstood Emotion* by Carol Tavris.

One book on anger that is written for women was rated: *The Dance of Anger* by Harriet Lerner.

Two cognitive or behavioral books on anger were rated: *When Anger Hurts* by Matthew McKay, Peter Rogers, and Judith McKay and *Anger: How to Live With and Without It* by Albert Ellis. A third book, *Dr.*

Anger
BOOK RATINGS IN THE NATIONAL SURVEY

Strongly Recommended	★★★★★	*The Dance of Anger* by Harriet Lerner
	★★★★★	*Anger: The Misunderstood Emotion* by Carol Tavris
Neutral	★★★	*When Anger Hurts* by Matthew McKay, Peter Rogers, and Judith McKay
	★★★	*Anger: How to Live with and without It* Albert Ellis
	★★★	*The Angry Book* Theodore Rubin
Not Recommended	★★	*Anger: Deal with It, Heal with It, Stop It from Killing You* by Bill Defoore

---

Weisinger's Anger Work Out Book by Hendrie Weisinger made the Worth a Further Look category: It was positively rated but by fewer than 10 psychologists.

Two books that emphasize the "let it all out" catharsis approach made the final ratings: *Angry Book* by Theodore Rubin and *Anger: Deal with It, Heal with It, Stop It from Killing You* by Bill Defoore.

STRONGLY RECOMMENDED

★ ★ ★ ★ ★   *The Dance of Anger: A Woman's Guide to Changing the Patterns of Intimate Relationships* (1985) by Harriet Lerner. New York: Harper Perennial.

The Dance of Anger is a book written mainly for women about the anger in their lives, both theirs and that of the people they live with, especially men. *The Dance of Anger* is an excellent self-help book. It has sold more than a million copies and deservedly has been on *The New York Times* best-seller list. Harriet Lerner is a widely respected psychotherapist at the famous Menninger Clinic in Topeka, Kansas.

Lerner believes that women have more difficulty coping with anger than men do. She says that expressions of anger are not only encouraged more in boys and men but may be glorified to maladaptive extremes. In contrast, girls and women have been denied even a healthy and realistic expression of anger. Lerner argues that to express anger—especially openly, directly, or loudly—traditionally makes a woman unladylike, unfeminine, unmaternal, and sexually unattractive. Society has taught women to be passive and quiet, not angry. Many women fear that if they express anger they will rock the relationship boat. Lerner explains the difficulties women have in getting angry and describes how they can use their anger to gain a stronger, more independent sense of self. Numerous patterns of anger in intimate relationships are woven throughout *The Dance of Anger*. Most women—and men—will be able to recall instances in which one or more of these patterns caused problems in their lives.

Rooted in both family systems and psychoanalytic theory, *The Dance of Anger* has nine chapters and an epilogue. In the early chapters, Lerner addresses styles of managing anger that don't work for women in the long run—silent submission, ineffective fighting and blaming, and emotional distancing. She also paints the cultural context of an American society that has created these ineffective styles in women. And she motivates women to develop the courage to change these old, protective ways.

In Chapter 3, Lerner describes the circular dances of couples. She says that when we have a problem, we often look for someone to blame. Consider the all-too-familiar situation of the nagging wife and the withdrawing husband. The more she nags, the more he withdraws, and the more he withdraws, the more she nags. Some people look at this situation and say that because she nagged first, she is to blame. Someone else might look at the situation and say that because he became unavailable and remote, she had no option but to go after him. From Lerner's family systems perspective, it doesn't mater who started it. What matters is that each person is provoking the other. The problem is not in her alone or in him alone but rather in their interconnectedness. Lerner goes on in later chapters to provide valuable advice about how to deal with anger when interacting with "impossible" mothers, with children, and in family triangles. In a later chapter, Lerner outlines a number of strategies that will help women break out of circular dances and handle anger more constructively. In the Epilogue, she gives wise guidelines for going beyond self-help, believing that trying to deal with anger should not be an isolated task.

The mental health experts in the national survey rated *The Dance of Anger* very positively. It was the highest-rated book on anger and made the 5-star Strongly Recommended category. It is a careful, compassionate exploration of women's anger and an insightful guide for turning anger into a constructive force that can reshape women's lives. Distinguished self-help author Carol Tavris says that *The Dance of Anger* gives readers information they can use to manage their anger wisely and well. Thomas Gordon, founder of Parent Effectiveness Training, recommends

Lerner's book, believing that it helps women to accept their anger and gives them the strength to do something constructive with it. Regardless of their ages, backgrounds, or life experiences, virtually all women— and many men—can gain considerable knowledge about how to make close relationships more adaptive and less harmful by reading *The Dance of Anger*.

★ ★ ★ ★ ★   *Anger: The Misunderstood Emotion* (revised and updated, 1989) by Carol Tavris. New York: Touchstone Books.

This also is an excellent self-help book. While Lerner's *The Dance of Anger* was written primarily for women, Tavris's *Anger: The Misunderstood Emotion* covers wider terrain. Indeed, it is hard to come up with any facet of anger—from wrecked friendships to wars—that Tavris does not address. The first edition of *Anger: The Misunderstood Emotion* appeared in 1982. The revised and updated edition includes new and expanded coverage of highway anger, violence in sports, young women's anger, and family anger, and it suggests strategies for getting through specific anger problems. Carol Tavris, Ph.D. is a social psychologist, writer, and lecturer who lives in Los Angeles.

Anger: The Misunderstood Emotion consists of 10 extraordinarily well-written, entertaining chapters. In the first several chapters, Tavris debunks a number of myths about anger and highlights anger's cultural rules. She persuasively argues that the "letting it all out" catharsis approach is not the best solution for defusing anger and coping effectively with stress. Tavris says that one of the main results of venting anger is to raise the noise level of our society. She dislikes pop-psych approaches that tell people anger is buried within them and argues that such notions are dangerous to the mental health of the participants and to the social health of the community. While such views get people agitating, shouting, ventilating, and boiling over, they rarely recognize or fix the circumstances that make people angry in the first place. Tavris believes that no amount of shouting or pillow pounding will extricate us from life's problems. She also sharply criticizes psychotherapy approaches that are based on the belief that inside every tranquil soul there is a furious one screaming to get out.

In Chapters 3 and 4, the toll of anger on the body is explored and a number of myths about anger's involvement in stress and illness are exploded. The precision of Tavris's work is exemplified in her discussion of the kind of behavior associated with heart disease. She carefully documents how the behavior involves not just any type of anger but rather anger that is overexpressed. Later chapters present very helpful ideas about anger in marital relationships and situations involving justice.

In the final two chapters, Tavris tells readers how to rethink anger and make more adaptive choices. Following are some of her wise suggestions:

- When your anger starts to boil and your body is getting aroused, work on lowering arousal by waiting. You will usually simmer down if you wait long enough.
- Cope with the anger by neither being chronically angry over every little bothersome annoyance nor passively sulking.
- Form a self-help group with others who have been through similar experiences with anger. The other people are likely to know how you are feeling, and together you might come up with some good solutions to anger problems.
- Take action to help others; it can out your own miseries in perspective. Women who organized Mothers Against Drunk Drivers did this.
- Seek ways of breaking out of your usual perspective. Some people have been rehearsing their "story" for years, repeating over and over the reasons for their anger. Retelling the story from other participants' points of view often helps people find routes to empathy.

Carol Tavris is an insightful psychologist and masterful writer. The 1989 edition of *Anger: The Misunderstood Emotion* is current and well-researched. Tavris's delivery is witty and eloquent. *Anger: The Misunderstood* was given a 5-star Strongly Recommended rating by the mental health professionals in the national survey. Distinguished anthropologist Ashley Montagu, author of *The Nature of Human Aggression*, said that *Anger: The Misunderstood Emotion* is the best book of its kind ever written. Anyone wanting to cope more effectively with the anger in their lives will find this book a welcome tonic.

NEUTRAL

★ ★ ★   *When Anger Hurts* (1989) by Matthew McKay, Peter Rogers, and Judith McKay. Oakland, CA: New Harbinger.

When Anger Hurts presents a cognitive-behavioral approach to coping with anger. Matthew McKay, Ph.D., and Peter Rogers, Ph.D., are codirectors of Families in Transition and Haight-Ashbury Psychological Services in San Francisco. Judith McKay has a background in nursing and currently works at Alto Bates Hospital in Berkeley, California.

When Anger Hurts, subtitled *Quieting the Storm Within*, is divided into three main sections that focus on understanding anger, building skills to cope with anger, and dealing with anger at home. The middle section on building skills to cope with anger contains a number of helpful strategies, including how to control stress step by step, how to keep anger from escalating, how to use healthy self-talk to deal with angry feelings, and how to engage in problem-solving communication when anger is harming relationships. The authors instruct readers in the specifics of keeping an anger journal. They believe that the observations and recordings made in the journal help individuals to actively cope with their anger. Journal exercises for dealing effectively with anger are provided throughout the book.

Based on the ratings in the national survey of mental health professionals, *When Anger Hurts* was given 3 stars placing it in the Neutral category. This was the highest-rated of the 3-star books in the anger category and has received positive recommendations by cognitive and behavioral psychologists. Cognitive therapist Albert Ellis commented that *When Anger Hurts* is a good book with practical and down-to-earth advice. Leading family behaviorist Gerald Patterson said that McKay and his colleagues have described sensible ways to control anger.

★ ★ ★   *Anger: How to Live with and without It* (1977) by Albert Ellis. Secaucus, NJ: Citadel Press.

Anger: How to Live with and without It is one of well-known cognitive therapist Albert Ellis's many books on how to cope more effectively. In this book, Ellis applies his rational emotive therapy to helping people deal with anger. He provides step-by-step instructions for how to cognitively and behaviorally rearrange anger. Readers are given a number of homework assignments to help them rethink how they deal with anger.

Anger: How to Live with and without It received a 3-star rating in the national survey, placing it in the Neutral category. It is not nearly as well written as Lerner's and Tavris's books, and it is more narrow and dated than the behavioral and cognitive approach presented by Matthew Mckay and his colleagues in *When Anger Hurts*. Some of Ellis's more recent books are less academically written and easier to read.

★ ★ ★   *The Angry Book* (1969) by Theodore Rubin. New York: McMillan.

The Angry Book is a psychoanalytically oriented book that advocates the "let it all out" catharsis approach to anger. Author Theodore Issac Rubin, M.D., was trained at the American Institute for Psychoanalysis.

Rubin warns readers of the dangers that await them if they bottle up their anger and "twist" or "pervert" it. He says a "slush fund" of accumulated, unexpressed anger builds up in your body, just waiting for the opportunity to produce high blood pressure, depression, alcoholism, sexual problems, and other diseases. At the end of *The Angry Book*, Rubin asks readers 103 questions that are intended to give them therapeutic guidance. One of these questions asks readers whether they have ever experienced the good, clean feeling that comes after expressing anger, as well as the increased self-esteem and feeling of peace with oneself and others such expression brings. Another question asks if readers are aware that people can feel loving and make love after a "fight" because an emotional traffic jam has been cleared.

The "let it all out" ventilationist approach advocated by Rubin has been widely accepted by many clinical psychologists, psychiatrists, and lay people. They believe that holding anger inside us causes many problems and harms our coping ability. Rubin's "let it all out" approach directly contradicts the approach advocated by Carol Tavris in *Anger: The Misunderstood Emotion* and the approaches recommended by Matthew McKay and his colleagues in *When Anger Hurts* and Albert Ellis in *Anger: How to Live With or Without It*.

The Angry Book barely made the 3-star Neutral category. The mental health professionals in the national survey felt that the psychoanalytically based approach of Harriet Lerner in *The Dance of Anger* is much more in line with contemporary thinking on the healthy expression of anger. Carol Tavris provides a well-thought-through, well-documented critique of the "let it all out" approach and a thorough critique of Rubin's book in *Anger: The Misunderstood Emotion.* In response to Rubin's question "Are you aware that your anger will not kill anyone and that no one's anger will kill you?" Tavris responds, "Yes, but only because I am a woman who has never been beaten by her husband or father. I imagine that thousands of battered wives in this country would have a far different response." And in response to Rubin's question "Are you aware that people can feel loving and make love after a 'fight' because an emotional traffic jam has been cleared?" Tavris responds, "Those are other people, then, because most people report that they need time to cool down after a quarrel before they 'feel loving' again. Besides, the trendy notion that fighting is sexy produces an association between sex and aggression that I, for one, find abhorrent."

★ ★ *Anger: Deal with It, Heal with It, Stop It from Killing You* (1981) by Bill Defoore. Deerfield Beach, FL: Health Communications.

This book also takes a "let it all out" catharsis approach to handling anger and emphasizes the role of the inner child in causing anger problems.

Author Bill Defoore, Ph.D., is associated with the Institute for Personal and Professional Development in Irving, Texas. Defoore especially advocates participation in anger work as a tonic for anger problems. Anger work involves engaging in exercises that release the physical tension associated with anger. According to DeFoore, these exercises will help you become more relaxed and better able to think and communicate effectively. DeFoore recommends screaming alone in your car, hitting a punching bag, smashing a mat as hard as possible, and other anger releases. He believes that venting pent-up tension in this manner will drain off angry feelings and keep people from exploding with rage at their spouses, their children, their work associates, and other friends.

DeFoore's book was given a 2-star Unrecommended rating in the national survey of mental health professionals. The criticism of Rubin's *The Angry Book* can also be leveled at DeFoore's *Anger: Deal with It, Heal with It, Stop It from Killing You*. The consensus of the mental health experts in the national survey was that the "let it all out" ventilation approach may temporarily make people feel better, but it rarely deals with the circumstances that lead to the anger in the first place. Unlike Lerner's and Tavris's excellent books on anger, DeFoore's book ignores the large research base of information about anger.

WORTH A FURTHER LOOK

◗ ◗   *Dr. Weisinger's Anger Work Out Book* (1985) by Hendrie Weisinger. New York: Quill.

This is a cognitively and behaviorally oriented workbook of 22 detailed exercises for working through anger problems. Hendrie Weisinger, Ph. D., is a psychotherapist who practices in the Los Angeles area. He has worked extensively with clients to help them manage their anger and gives workshops on how to take criticism and control anger. Among the exercises in Weisinger's book are Looking Good (on monitoring thoughts and behavior); The Good, the Bad, and the Ugly (on assessing anger); Getting Physical (on training to hear the body talk before it yells); Time Bomb (on detecting what ticks us off and how to defuse anger); Lover and Others (on how to help a lover work out anger), Family Feud (on how to work out anger in the family); and Anger and Good Company (on ways to cope more effectively with anger that will improve job performance).

The exercises in *Dr. Weisinger's Anger Work Out Book* include many specific strategies that have been documented to reduce anger, including exercise, relaxation, getting support from others, self-monitoring, taking the perspective of others, self-disclosure, problem solving, laughing and playing, and talking peacefully with others. While its catchy chapter titles might imply a pop-psych book, Weisinger's how-to exercises are solidly rooted in sound psychological principles. The book is well-written; readers should have no difficulty following the instructions on how to do the exercises. The workbook comes highly recommended by both Thomas Gordon, founder of Parent Effectiveness Training, and Ronald Podell, professor of psychiatry and director of the Center for Mood Disorders at UCLA.

CONCLUSIONS

In summary, we recommend:

- On coping with anger in many different facets of life:

  ★★★★★ *Anger: The Misunderstood Emotion* by Carol Tavris

- For women who want to understand and deal with anger, especially in marital and family relationships:

  ★★★★★ *The Dance of Anger* by Harriet Lerner

- A workbook with practical exercises for learning to cope effectively with their anger.

  ◖◗ *Dr. Weisinger's Anger Work Out Book* by Hendrie Weisinger

---

CHAPTER SEVEN

Anxiety

Anxiety is a highly unpleasant feeling that comes in different forms. Sometimes anxiety is a diffuse, vague feeling, at others a fear of something specific. People who have an anxiety disorder often feel motor tension (they are jumpy, trembling, or can't relax), are hyperactive (they feel dizzy, their heart races, or they perspire), and are apprehensive.

A current controversy swirls around the reasons people become anxious. Some mental health experts, especially in the medical field, believe that anxiety is biologically determined and should be treated with drugs. Other mental health experts, including many psychologists, argue that anxiety is primarily caused by what we experience and how we think. They stress that helping people reduce their anxiety involves rearranging their environment and how they cognitively interpret their world.

Topics of self-help books on anxiety fall into five main categories: the biological basis of anxiety and its treatment through drug therapy; the cognitive and experiential basis of anxiety and its treatment through psychotherapy; panic attacks; obsessive-compulsive disorders; and phobias.

Two books that describe the biological nature of anxiety and its treatment through drugs were rated in the national survey: *The Anxiety Disease* by David Sheehan and *The Good News About Panic, Anxiety, and Phobias* by Mark Gold.

One book that stresses the cognitive and experiential basis of anxiety and its treatment through psychotherapy rather than drug therapy was rated: *Anxiety Disorders and Phobias: A Cognitive Perspective* by Aaron Beck and Gary Emery.

Three books that mainly explore panic attacks were rated: *Don't Panic* by Reid Wilson; *Anxiety and Panic Attacks* by Robert Handly; and *The Panic Attack Recovery Book* by Shirley Swede and Seymour Jaffe.

Anxiety

BOOK RATINGS IN THE NATIONAL SURVEY

Strongly Recommended	★★★★★	*Anxiety Disorders and Phobias* by Aaron Beck and Gary Emery
Recommended	★★★★	*Don't Panic* by Reid Wilson
	★★★★	*Obsessive-Compulsive Disorders* by Steven Levenkron
Neutral	★★★	*Peace from Nervous Suffering* by Claire Weekes
	★★★	*Anxiety and Panic Attacks* by Robert Handly
	★★★	*The Panic Attack Recovery Book* by Shirley Swede and Seymour Jaffe
	★★★	*The Anxiety Disease* by David Sheehan
	★★★	*The Good News about Panic, Anxiety, and Phobias* by Mark Gold

---

One book on obsessive-compulsive disorders was rated in the national survey: *Obsessive-Compulsive Disorders* by Steven Levenkron.

One book on a specific phobia—agoraphobia—was rated: *Peace from Nervous Suffering* by Claire Weekes.

STRONGLY RECOMMENDED

★★★★★ *Anxiety Disorders and Phobias: A Cognitive Perspective* (1985) by Aaron Beck and Gary Emery. New York: Basic Books.

Anxiety Disorders and Phobias provides information about different types of anxiety and how sufferers of anxiety can rearrange their thoughts to overcome the anxiety that is overwhelming their lives. Author Aaron Beck, M.D., is an internationally acclaimed expert on anxiety disorders and depression. Beck is a psychiatrist at the University of Pennsylvania Medical School and director of the Center for Cognitive Therapy in Philadelphia. Coauthor Gary Emery, Ph.D., is director of the Los Angeles Center for Cognitive Therapy and is a professor in the psychology department at UCLA.

Anxiety Disorders and Phobias is divided into two parts. In Part I,

Beck describes the nature of anxiety and how it is distinguished from fear, phobia, and panic. He believes that the core problem for anxiety sufferers is their sense of vulnerability and their ineffective cognitive strategies for coping with anxiety. Beck pinpoints a number of patterns in life that lead to different types of anxiety and phobias and how they can be reduced or eliminated by altering the way we think and interpret our world.

In Part II of *Anxiety Disorders and Phobias*, Emery outlines a treatment program based on cognitive therapy that can help individuals cope effectively with anxiety and phobias. Separate chapters tell readers how to change the way they develop images of themselves and their world, how to change your feelings, and how to modify your behavior.

Anxiety Disorders and Phobias was the highest-rated anxiety book and made the 5-star Strongly Recommended category in the national survey. A number of the mental health experts in the national survey commented about the effectiveness of Beck's cognitive approach in helping individuals overcome their anxieties. Distinguished psychotherapist Hans Strupp, professor of psychology at Vanderbilt University, said that *Anxiety Disorders and Phobias* tackles difficult anxiety problems with considerable success. Gerald Klerman, professor of psychiatry at Harvard Medical School, commented that Beck and Emery's book provides a solid groundwork for understanding the cognitive approach to reducing anxieties and phobias.

Although *Anxiety Disorders and Phobias* received rave reviews in the academic community, it is not a self-help book. It is written at a very high level that is appropriate for psychotherapists or for graduate students in psychology. Only lay readers who are already fairly sophisticated about the nature of psychological problems and how they can be treated or who seek an intellectual challenge will want to tackle *Anxiety Disorders and Phobias*. Clinicians will find it an excellent resource for furthering their knowledge of the cognitive therapy approach to anxiety and phobias.

RECOMMENDED

★ ★ ★ ★	*Don't Panic: Taking Control of Anxiety Attacks* (1986) by Reid Wilson. New York: Harper & Row.

Don't Panic was the highest-rated book on panic disorder in the national survey. Author Reid Wilson, Ph.D., specializes in the treatment of panic and anxiety disorders. He is director of the Clinical Hypnosis Training Program at the Southeast Institute in Chapel Hill, North Carolina.

Panic disorder is an anxiety disorder in which the main feature is recurrent panic attacks marked by the sudden onset of intense apprehension or terror. People who suffer from panic disorder may have feelings of impending doom but aren't necessarily anxious all the time. The unanticipated anxiety attacks include such symptoms as severe palpitations, extreme shortness of breath, chest pains, trembling, sweating, dizziness, and a feeling of helplessness. Victims fear they will die, go crazy, or do something they cannot control.

Wilson describes a self-help program for coping with panic attacks. *Don't Panic* is divided into two parts. In Part I, readers learn what panic attacks are like, how it feels to undergo one, and what type of people are prone to panic attacks. Advice is given on how to sort through the physical and psychological aspects of panic attacks. In Part II, readers learn how to conquer panic attacks, especially through self-monitoring.

Don't Panic made the 4-star Recommended category in the national survey. Several of the mental health experts were especially impressed with the many examples of individuals who experienced panic attacks and successfully coped with them. Other experts thought the concrete suggestions for specific actions to take at the onset of a panic attack and during the attack were beneficial. These actions include breathing exercises, focused thinking, mental imagery, and deep muscle relaxation. Aaron Beck, whose book (with Gary Emery) was at the top of the anxiety self-help book ratings, said that *Don't Panic* is an insightful portrayal of panic attacks and provides hope and guidance for those who suffer from panic attacks. Wilson's book is much easier reading than Beck and Emery's *Anxiety Disorders and Phobias*, but it covers a more limited domain, confining its discussion to panic attacks alone.

★ ★ ★ ★   *Obsessive-Compulsive Disorders* (1991) by Steven Levenkron. New York: Warner Books.

Obsessive-Compulsive Disorders is, as the title implies, about one category of anxiety — obsessive-compulsive disorders. This is the only book on obsessive-compulsive disorders that made the final ratings in the national survey. Author Steven Levenkron maintains a private practice in New York City and in White Plains, New York.

Obsessive-compulsive disorders are anxiety disorders in which an individual has anxiety-provoking thoughts that will not go away (obsession) and/or feels the urge to perform repetitive, ritualistic behaviors usually designed to prevent or produce a future situation (compulsion). Obsessions and compulsions are different problems, but often both are displayed by the same person. Some common compulsions are excessive checking, cleansing, and counting.

Levenkron believes obsessive-compulsive disorder (OCD) is the personality's attempt to reduce anxiety, which may stem from a painful childhood or a genetic tendency toward anxiousness. Levenkron developed therapy techniques to help people who suffer from OCD that include the help and support of parents, teachers, physicians, and friends. His book includes a large number of case histories to illustrate the problems people who have OCD encounter and how they can overcome their problem. Levenkron argues that people can reduce or eliminate their obsessions and compulsions if they follow four basic steps: (1) rely on a family member or a therapist for support and comfort; (2) unmask their rituals; (3) talk in depth to trusted family members or a therapist; and (4) control their anxiety.

Obsessive-Compulsive Disorders attained the 4-star Recommended category in the national survey. Several of the mental health experts lauded Levenkron's excellent choice of case studies that let readers who have obsessions and/or compulsions see how others have successfully coped with their problems. Michael Kenin, a psychiatrist on the staff of Lenox Hill Hospital in New York City, said that this book reveals a compassionate understanding of obsessive-compulsive disorders. Raymond Vath, a psychiatrist at the University of Washington, commented that *Obsessive-Compulsive Disorders* is an outstanding book that has made an important contribution to how OCD should be treated.

NEUTRAL

★ ★ ★   *Peace from Nervous Suffering* (1972) by Claire Weekes. New York: Hawthorn Books.

Peace from Nervous Suffering is about one type of phobia—agoraphobia, the fear of entering unfamiliar situations, especially open or public spaces. It is the most common type of phobic disorder. Claire Weekes, M.D., Ph.D., is a mental health consultant to the Rachel Forster Hospital in Sydney, Australia.

People with a generalized anxiety disorder can't pinpoint the cause of their nervous feelings, but those with phobias—anxiety disorders involving overwhelming, persistent fear of particular objects or situations—can. In agoraphobia, the fear is of leaving the safety of home. Weekes believes that the cure for agoraphobia involves four rather simple rules: (1) face the phobia, don't run away from it; (2) accept it, don't fight it; (3) float past it, do not stop and listen in; and (4) let time pass and don't be impatient. Weekes includes an extensive number of case studies from around the world in which agoraphobics have successfully overcome their fear of leaving the safety of their home.

Peace from Nervous Suffering was given 3 stars and placed in the Neutral category in the national survey ratings. On the positive side, Weekes's book was one of the first ever to deal with agoraphobia, and it helped many people recognize their problem and overcome it. On the negative side, several of the mental health experts said *Peace from Nervous Suffering* is somewhat dated. It is more than two decades old, and many advances, especially cognitive and medical treatments, in treating phobias have been made since the book was written.

★ ★ ★   *Anxiety and Panic Attacks: Their Cause and Cure* (1985) by Robert Handly. New York: Fawcett Crest.

Anxiety and Panic Attacks is mainly about panic attacks and agoraphobia. Author Robert Handly is president of Robert Handly Associates, a human resources consulting firm in Dallas, Texas. He conducts workshops on motivation, stress management, and goal achievement.

Handly describes his own struggle with agoraphobia and the successful strategies he used to overcome it. He believes that five basic principles are involved in coping with anxiety and panic attacks:

- Use the creative powers of your unconscious mind to help yourself.
- Use visualizations and affirmations to improve your self-image. This will help you turn fear into self-confidence.
- Use rational and positive thinking to see yourself and events as they really are and also to visualize how you want them to be.
- Act as if you are already who you want to be.
- Set goals to be the person you want to be.

Handly also stresses the importance of physical health, fitness, and good nutrition in overcoming anxiety.

Anxiety and Panic Attacks received a 3-star Neutral rating in the national survey. Among the positive points of this book are its easy-to-read writing style and in-depth analysis of one person's experience (the author's) with panic attacks and agoraphobia. However, several of the mental health experts in the survey marked the book down for its inattention to some of the current developments in treating panic disorder and agoraphobia and for its rather loose inclusion of many different ideas that have not been well tested.

★ ★ ★   *The Panic Attack Recovery Book* (1987) by Shirley Swede and Seymour Jaffe. New York: New American Library.

As the title suggests, this book addresses a particular type of anxiety— panic attacks. Shirley Swede, a former sufferer of agoraphobia, is the founder of PASS—the Panic Attack Sufferers' Support Group. Seymour Jaffe, M.D., is PASS's chief consultant.

The PASS program is based on seven steps to recovery from panic attacks:

1. *Diet.* Eat a healthy balanced diet. Suggestions for foods to avoid and foods/supplements to include are detailed.
2. *Relaxation.* Relaxation exercises are given and the importance of relaxation is emphasized.
3. *Exercise.* The importance of aerobic exercise is discussed and several types of exercises are listed.
4. *Attitude.* Positive thinking is stressed.
5. *Imagination.* Pretending you feel confident can often help you through difficult times and make further experiences more pleasant.
6. *Social Support.* PASS believes that the individual should seek support and "strokes" from any social network but that a support group of panic attack sufferers is likely to be the most beneficial. How to set up such a neighborhood group is included.
7. *Spiritual Values.* Faith, hope, and forgiveness are essential for recovery.

The Panic Attack Recovery Book is divided into four parts. Part I discusses the biological bases of panic disorders and prepares the reader for the program regime; Part II details the seven-step PASS program; Part III helps the sufferer plan and actually take a trip using the skills taught in the program; and Part IV offers twenty personal stories of individuals who have overcome their panic attacks.

This book was given a 3-star Neutral rating in the national survey. It is an informative blend of personal experience (Ms. Swede) and medical knowledge (Dr. Jaffe) that panic attack sufferers may find enlightening and helpful. The advice on how to establish a neighborhood support group is especially good, and the personal accounts of recovery from panic attacks (presumably from PASS members) provide encouragement to people to help them deal more effectively with anxiety.

★ ★ ★   *The Anxiety Disease* (1983) by David Sheehan. New York: Charles Scribner & Sons.

The Anxiety Disease is about the biological factors involved in anxiety and how anxiety can be conquered through the use of appropriate drugs and behavior therapy. David Sheehan, M.D., is the director of the anxiety research program in the Department of Psychiatry at the Massachusetts General Hospital and also a professor of psychiatry at Harvard University Medical School.

Sheehan describes a number of case studies from his psychiatry practice to illustrate how to recognize anxiety problems and successfully treat them. He believes that anxiety disorders progress through seven stages— spells, panic, hypochondriacal symptoms, limited phobias, social phobias, agoraphobia/extensive public avoidance, and finally depression— and that recovery from an anxiety disorder occurs in four phases—doubt, mastery, independence, and readjustment. Individuals go through the phases as their medications eliminate chemically induced panic attacks and therapy overcomes their avoidance tendencies.

The Anxiety Disease received a 3-star Neutral rating in the national survey. Some of the mental health experts said that Sheehan's biological approach is a very effective way to treat anxiety disorders, especially panic attacks. Others did not like Sheehan's biological, drug-based approach to reducing anxiety.

★ ★ ★ *The Good News about Panic, Anxiety, and Phobias* (1988) by Mark Gold. New York: Villard Books.

The Good News about Panic, Anxiety, and Phobias, like *The Anxiety Disease,* stresses the biological basis of anxiety disorders and their treatment through the use of drugs. Mark Gold, M.D., is the research director at Fair Oaks Hospital in New Jersey and Florida. He is a recognized authority on the biological mechanisms involved in anxiety disorders.

Gold asserts that if a person has an anxiety disorder it is not the person's fault. Instead, the disorder is the fault of inherited dysfunctions in the biochemistry of the person's body. Gold recommends variations in drug therapy for different types of anxiety disorders. At the end of the book, he provides a state-by-state listing of resources and medical experts on anxiety disorders.

The Good News about Panic, Anxiety, and Phobias received a 3-star Neutral rating in the national survey. It was the lowest-rated 3-star book. Undoubtedly, had the national survey included a large number of psychiatrists, books such as Gold's and Sheehan's would have been rated higher. Gold's book is more up to date than Sheehan's.

CONCLUSIONS

In summary, we recommend:

- For clinicians and others with a fairly sophisticated knowledge of psychological problems:

  ★★★★★ *Anxiety Disorders and Phobias* by Aaron Beck and Gary Emery

- On reducing or eliminating panic attacks:

  ★★★★ *Don't Panic* by Reid Wilson

- On coping more effectively with an obsessive-compulsive disorder:

  ★★★★ *Obsessive-Compulsive Disorders* by Steven Levenkron

- On the biological basis of anxiety and its treatment through drug therapy:

  ★★★ *The Good News about Panic, Anxiety, and Phobias* by Mark Gold

CHAPTER EIGHT

Assertiveness

Famous behavior therapist Joseph Wolpe says that there are essentially three ways to relate to others. The first is to be aggressive, considering only ourselves and riding roughshod over others. The second is to be nonassertive, always putting others before ourselves and letting others run roughshod over us. The third approach is the golden mean—to be assertive, placing ourselves first, but taking others into account.

In most cultures, women have traditionally been socialized to be nonassertive and men to be aggressive. In today's world, an increasing number of women have stepped up their efforts to reduce their passivity and be more assertive, and more men are choosing to be less aggressive. Many mental health professionals believe that our society would benefit from increased assertiveness by women and decreased aggression by men. Breaking out of traditional patterns, though, can be difficult and stressful. But in the case of working hard to become more assertive, it's clearly worth the effort.

While all books on assertiveness tell how to act in our own best interests, stand up for our legitimate rights, and express our views openly and directly, there are five variations on this basic theme: assertiveness training, with an emphasis on behavior modification and communication skills; assertiveness training for women; becoming more aggressive; taking charge; and learning the emotional and spiritual aspects of becoming more assertive.

Five books in the national survey approach assertiveness from the perspective of assertiveness training, including an emphasis on behavior modification and communication skills: *Your Perfect Right* by Robert Alberti and Michael Emmons; *Stand Up, Speak Out, Talk Back* by Robert Alberti and Michael Emmons; *When I Say No, I Feel Guilty* by Manuel Smith; *Don't Say Yes When You Want to Say No* by Herbert Fensterheim and Jean Baer; and *The Gentle Art of Verbal Self-Defense* by Suzette Elgin.

One book in the national survey focuses exclusively on assertiveness training for women: *The Assertive Woman* by Stanlee Phelps and Nancy Austin.

Three books in the survey advocate the importance of becoming more aggressive: *Creative Aggression* by George Bach and Herb Goldberg; *Looking Out for Number One* by Robert Ringer; and *Winning Through Intimidation* by Robert Ringer.

Three books in the survey advocate the importance of taking charge to become more assertive: *How to Take Charge of Your Life* by Mildred

---

Assertiveness
BOOK RATINGS IN THE NATIONAL SURVEY

Strongly Recommended	★★★★★	*Your Perfect Right* by Robert Alberti and Michael Emmons
Recommended	★★★★	*Stand Up, Speak Out, Talk Back* by Robert Alberti and Michael Emmons
	★★★★	*When I Say No, I Feel Guilty* by Manuel Smith
Diamonds in the Rough	♦	*The Assertive Woman* by Stanlee Phelps and Nancy Austin
Neutral	★★★	*Don't Say Yes When You Want to Say No* by Herbert Fensterheim and Jean Baer
	★★★	*Good-Bye to Guilt* by Gerald Jampolsky
	★★★	*How to Take Charge of Your Life* by Mildred Newman and Bernard Berkowitz
	★★★	*The Gentle Art of Verbal Self-Defense* by Suzette Elgin
Not Recommended	★★	*Creative Aggression* by George Bach and Herb Goldberg
	★	*Pulling Your Own Strings* by Wayne Dyer
	★	*Control Freaks* by Gerald Piaget
Strongly Not Recommended	†	*Looking Out for Number One* by Robert Ringer
	†	*Winning Through Intimidation* by Robert Ringer

Newman and Bernard Berkowitz; *Pulling Your Own Strings* by Wayne Dyer; and *Control Freaks* by Gerald Piaget.

One book in the survey emphasizes the role of emotional and spiritual factors in becoming more assertive: *Good-bye to Guilt* by Gerald Jampolsky.

STRONGLY RECOMMENDED

★ ★ ★ ★ ★   *Your Perfect Right: A Guide to Assertive Living* (6th ed., 1990) by Robert Alberti and Michael Emmons. San Luis Obispo, CA: Impact.

Your Perfect Right, a national best seller, emphasizes the importance of developing better communication skills in becoming more assertive. Initially published in 1970, the most recent edition of the book came out in 1990. Author Robert Alberti, Ph.D., and Michael Emmons, Ph.D., are counseling psychologists and former professors at California Polytechnic State University at San Luis Obispo.

Your Perfect Right is divided into two main parts: Part I speaks to the self-help reader who wants to learn how to become more assertive; Part II is a guide for assertiveness training leaders that teaches them techniques to help others become more assertive.

In Part I, the reader learns how to distinguish assertive, nonassertive, and aggressive behavior and why assertive behavior is the best choice. Among the key components of assertive behavior are self-expression, honesty, directness, self-enhancement, not harming others, being socially responsible, and learned skills. Readers fill out a questionnaire to evaluate their own level of assertiveness, and then they learn about the obstacles they will face in trying to be more assertive. Step-by-step procedures are presented for getting started and for gaining the confidence to stand up for their own rights. An excellent chapter on "soft assertions" gives information about how to be more assertive with friends and family members. Being assertive with friends and family members makes relationships with these important people more open and honest and less harmful. Interactions in school, work, and community are also covered, with tips on how to be assertive in those contexts. Readers also learn how anger needs to be expressed in assertive, nonaggressive ways. Throughout the first part of the book numerous real-life situations that call for assertive behavior are presented, with practical advice on how to handle them.

Part II, written mainly for mental health practitioners, is brief. Although primarily for the professional, the self-help reader can acquire some valuable information about assertiveness from this section. A special benefit is the thorough discussion of how assertiveness training groups work.

An extensive list of further readings about assertiveness, along with brief descriptions of the books, is provided toward the end of the book. *Your Perfect Right* also includes two appendices. The first is titled "The Universal Declaration of Human Rights" and describes thirty articles that address the assertiveness rights of human beings. The second appendix discusses principles for the ethical practice of assertiveness training.

Your Perfect Right received the 5-star Highly Recommended rating in the national survey and was widely known — almost 300 respondents rated it. Some mental health professionals call *Your Perfect Right* "the assertiveness bible," they think so highly of it. For more than two decades, this book has helped many nonassertive people become more assertive and many aggressive people realize that they should respect the rights of others and tone down their hostile tendencies. In summary, this is an excellent self-help book.

RECOMMENDED

★ ★ ★ ★   *Stand Up, Speak Out, Talk Back* (1975) by Robert Alberti and Michael Emmons. New York: Pocket Books.

Stand Up, Speak Out, Talk Back tackles the same problem as its sister book, *Your Perfect Right:* how to become more assertive by improving communication skills. The authors discuss developing the self-confidence and specific strategies that will help you become more assertive.

Stand Up, Speak Out, Talk Back is divided into three main parts. Part I asks readers the extent to which they feel they are in charge of their lives. To help readers accurately answer this important question, the authors put readers in various situations and ask how they would respond. They learn how people respond nonassertively, assertively, and aggressively in these contexts. Alberti and Emmons give artful advise on how to become assertive without stepping on others.

Part II introduces the Assertiveness Training Program, developed by Alberti and Emmons, which is based on the idea that it is easier to change people's behavior than to change their attitudes. The authors propose a thirteen-step training program for becoming more assertive. The steps are clearly described and easy to understand. Even so, many nonassertive people don't have the confidence to try out the steps. Alberti and

Emmons do a good job of building up the reader's confidence to try out this program. Readers also learn some fascinating strategies for using nonverbal behavior—eye contact, body posture, gestures, facial expressions, voice, and timing—in their effort to present themselves more assertively.

Part III tells readers how to help others learn to be more assertive, how to form an assertiveness group, and how in some situations it is necessary to go beyond assertiveness. At this point, readers are told how to handle potential adverse reactions to their assertiveness, and situations are presented in which one might not want to assert oneself (such as when interacting with overly sensitive people). As in *Your Perfect Right*, Alberti and Emmons include an appendix that presents the thirty articles in their "Universal Declaration of Human Rights."

Stand Up, Speak Out, Talk Back received the 4-star Recommended rating in the national survey. This rating places it lower than its sister book, the 5-star Highly Recommended *Your Perfect Right*. Also, *Stand Up, Speak Out, Talk Back* is not as widely known as *Your Perfect Right*—fewer than 100 respondents rated it. Nonetheless, the mental health experts in the national survey still perceived *Stand Up, Speak Out, Talk Back* to be the second best self-help book in the assertiveness category. Either of the Alberti/Emmons books can help in learning to become more assertive. Both are easy-to-read and include vivid presentations of situations the reader can relate to in seeking to become more assertive.

★ ★ ★ ★   *When I Say No, I Feel Guilty* (1975) by Manuel Smith. New York: Bantam Books.

When I Say No, I Feel Guilty was especially written for people who feel that they are always being talked into doing something they don't want to do. It falls into the category of assertivenss books that emphasize the importance of learning better communication skills to become more assertive. Author Manuel Smith, Ph. D., is a clinical psychologist in Los Angeles, California.

When I Say No, I Feel Guilty contains 11 chapters that cover such important assertiveness topics as how other people violate our rights, 10 articles that make up an assertiveness bill of rights, the importance of persistence in becoming assertive, how to assertively cope with supervisors and experts, how to work out compromises and say "no," and how to be assertive in sexual encounters. Interspersed through the book are 34 annotated dialogues that illustrate basic assertive skills, such as calm persistence in getting what we want; disclosing our worries to others; agreeing with critical truths and still doing what we want; asserting our negative points; prompting criticism; and keeping our self-respect. The dialogues help to detect hidden meanings in communication and how to counter others' remarks.

When I Say No, I Feel Guilty received a 4-star Recommended rating in the national survey and was rated by a large number of respondents—more than 200. Some of the mental health professionals praised the book, commenting about the down-to-earth advice on how to become more assertive. They especially liked the many examples of timid people who gained the skills and confidence to stand up to such aggressive people as deceitful auto mechanics and obnoxious relatives. Some critics, however, said that the book oversimplifies some of the issues in becoming more assertive. For example, at one point Smith states that in a hit-and-run accident, a riot, a robbery, or a mugging, assertiveness is of little value to the victim.

DIAMONDS IN THE ROUGH

◆   *The Assertive Woman: The New Look* (2nd ed., 1987) by Stanlee Phelps and Nancy Austin. San Luis Opismo, CA: Impact.

The Assertive Woman, as the title implies, is about how women can become more assertive. It is written by two women, Stanlee Phelps, who has a Master's degree in social work and is a human relations consultant, and Nancy Austin, who has an M.B.A. and is a motivational speaker and business management consultant. Austin is also the coauthor (with Tom Peters) of the best-selling book *A Passion for Excellence.*

The Assertive Woman was initially published in 1975, then revised in 1987. It deals with the special obstacles women encounter in trying to assert themselves in a society that stereotypes women as passive and dependent. According to Phelps and Austin, assertive women demonstrate that they are capable of choosing their own life, free of the dictates of tradition, husband, children, and bosses. They may *choose* to become a homemaker, *elect* to enter a male-dominated profession, or *opt* to have only one child. In their sexual relationships, they feel comfortable in taking the initiative or in firmly saying "no" to sexual overtures.

Twenty-four straight-to-the-point chapters take the reader through the gamut of issues facing today's woman in her quest to become more assertive. Phelps and Austin say that they themselves had a lot to learn about becoming assertive women in a male-dominated society. They ask women to begin by measuring their "Assertiveness Quotient," and then they present examples of assertive and nonassertive behavior displayed by women.

Women are asked to partake in a lot of soul searching so that they can get in touch with their true feelings and attitudes, their bodies, and their relationships. The authors also warn women about falling into some common traps, such as trying to meet everyone's needs and being "superwoman." With gentle encouragement and support, Phelps and Austin tell women about the importance of a positive body image, handling compliments as well as criticism, saying "no," acknowledging anger, and revealing sensitive feelings in becoming assertive. How women can become more assertive in their family and at work is addressed at length. The book closes with answers to questions most often asked by women who attend the assertiveness seminars offered by the authors.

The mental health professionals' rating in the national survey place *The Assertive Woman: The New Look* in the Diamonds in the Rough category. The book received a very positive rating but was evaluated by too few respondents to earn a 4-star or 5-star rating. *The Assertive Woman* is a very good self-help book for women who want to learn how to turn their passive, dependent, nonassertive behavior patterns into more assertive ones. It is easy reading, and the 1987 edition includes a number of contemporary ideas on assertiveness training for women that were not included in the first edition.

NEUTRAL

★ ★ ★   *Don't Say Yes When You Want to Say No* (1975) by Herbert Fensterheim and Jean Baer. New York: Dell Books.

Don't Say Yes When You Want to Say No is a behaviorally oriented approach to becoming more assertive. Herbert Fensterheim, Ph.D., practiced psychoanalytically based therapy for 20 years and then turned to behavior therapy to help people with their problems. Jean Baer, his wife, is a professional writer.

Don't Say Yes When You Want to Say No contains 13 chapters, seven of which are devoted to the behavioral approach to assertiveness training. In the early chapters, the reader learns how to target assertiveness difficulties, use behavioral rehearsal and other strategies to learn to say "no," call on assertiveness training techniques to develop a social network of friends and acquaintances, develop self-control, and learn assertiveness skills that help at work. An assertiveness guide for individuals of different sexual orientations is also provided. Other chapters explore a wide range of topics, some of which are not found in other assertiveness self-help books. Using assertiveness to help cope with depression and eating disorders is an example. Behavioral plans for making a marriage work and improving the quality of sexual relationships are discussed.

Don't Say Yes When You Want to Say No received a 3-star Neutral rating in the national survey. Soon after it was published in 1975 it was given an honorable mention in the media awards established by the American Psychological Association. However, because the book was published almost two decades ago, it has become dated in some ways; for example, in discussing mental disorders the outmoded category of neurosis is used. Some critics feel that the book includes too many topics under the umbrella of assertiveness training and skills, in the process telling the reader too little about any of them. In general, the mental health professionals strongly preferred the assertiveness books by Robert Alberti and Michael Emmons to Fensterheim and Baer's book.

★ ★ ★   *Good-Bye to Guilt* (1985) by Gerald Jampolsky. New York: Bantam Books.

Good-Bye to Guilt presents an emotionally and spiritually based approach to becoming more assertive. Author Gerald Jampolsky, M.D., practiced psychiatry for a number of years, then gave it up to establish the Center for Attitudinal Healing in California. Attitudinal healing is Jampolsky's term for the process of letting go of past negative thoughts about guilt, fear, and condemning judgments.

Good-Bye to Guilt is divided into two main parts. In Part I, the reader learns about the spiritual transformations involved in moving from fearfulness (of love, death, having fun, and much more) to forgiveness (letting go) to unconditional love (for/from God, for self, and for others). Jampolsky believes that God is a nonphysical, spiritual love force rather than a Judeo–Christian deity.

Part II is the majority of the book—fourteen lessons that apply the knowledge learned in Part I to real-life situations. Among the chapters in Part II are Only My Condemnation Injures Me and In My Defenselessness My Safety Lies. Exercises such as Becoming One with a Flower introduce vivid images of the spiritual healing process.

Good-Bye to Guilt received a 3-star Neutral rating in the national survey. Some of the mental health professionals liked Japolsky's spiritual, emotional approach to becoming more assertive. Others criticized the approach. One mental health expert commented that *Good-Bye to Guilt* is a Christianized version of EST. Another critic said it is a blend of pop psychology and ecstatic religion. Yet another critic said that Jampolsky has good intentions but questioned his assertion that self-revelation and unconditional love are the keys to getting rid of guilt and becoming more assertive.

★ ★ ★   *How to Take Charge of Your Life* (1977) by Mildred Newman and Bernard Berkowitz. Fort Worth, TX: Harcourt Brace.

How to Take Charge of Your Life presents an approach that is very different from the assertiveness training/communication skills approach of such books as *Your Perfect Right, The Assertive Woman,* and *When I Say No, I Feel Guilty.* To take charge of life, Newman and Berkowitz tell readers that they need to increase their self-awareness, accept responsibility for themselves, and increase their self-esteem. Mildred Newman has a Master's degree and is married to Bernard Berkowitz, Ph.D. They live in New York City and are therapists there. Their approach is psychoanalytically based.

This is a very brief book—small in size and only about 100 pages long—that uses fables and catchy phrases. The authors tell the reader to "be the rider, not the horse" and that "the only way to break old habits is to start a new one." They also warn readers that their behavior is often controlled and manipulated by others without consent—and that they should do something about it.

How to Take Charge of Your Life received a 3-star Neutral rating in the national survey. Critics of the book said that the authors offer very few effective strategies for taking charge of life and becoming more assertive. A motivational pitch to "be the rider, not the horse" doesn't provide detailed strategies to help people become more assertive.

★ ★ ★   *The Gentle Art of Verbal Self-Defense* (1980) by Suzette Elgin. Englewood Cliffs, NJ: Prentice-Hall.

The Gentle Art of Verbal Self-Defense presents a communication skills approach to becoming more assertive. Author Suzette Elgin is a retired linguistics professor and founder of the Ozark Center for Language Studies.

This book contains 18 chapters that train readers in "verbal judo," which involves using an opponent's strength and momentum as tools for self-defense. Elgin describes four basic principles of verbal self-defense that are important to master:

1. Know that you are under attack.
2. Know what kind of attack you are facing.
3. Know how to make your defense fit the attack.
4. Know how to follow through.

A number of examples and exercises help readers learn to use these principles. Effective and appropriate use of voice, posture, mannerisms, and charisma are explained. Specific strategies for college students to use with college instructors are also given. And tips for verbal self-defense with men and women are provided.

The Gentle Art of Verbal Self-Defense received a 3-star Neutral rating in the national survey. This was the lowest rated 3-star book. On the positive side, the book includes effective verbal strategies for seizing control of a situation, and the extensive exercises are good learning devices. However, the consensus of the mental health experts in the national survey was that books such as *Your Perfect Right* and *Stand Up, Speak Out, Talk Back* do a better job of teaching the communication skills necessary to become more assertive.

NOT RECOMMENDED

★ ★   *Creative Aggression: The Art of Assertive Living* (1974) by George Bach and Herb Goldberg. Garden City, NY: Doubleday.

Creative Aggression states that we need to accept the aggressive nature of human beings, and it shows how to use aggression constructively. Author George Bach, Ph.D., has been the director of the Institute of Group Psychotherapy in Los Angeles, California. He is one of the pioneers in group psychotherapy. Coauthor Herb Goldberg, Ph.D., is a practicing psychotherapist and professor of psychology at California State University at Los Angeles. Goldberg also has been a lèader in the men's movement, and two of his books on men's issues are evaluated in Chapter 23.

Bach and Goldberg present a number of case studies to make the point that dangerous hostility often lies beneath the surface of "nice" mothers, fathers, teachers, bosses, and just about everyone. The authors say that all of this niceness can drive one batty and that the only way to effectively combat it is to rely on natural aggressive tendencies. The rather bizarre chapter titles include Combatting the Mind Raper, The Myth of the Nice Guy/Mother/Father, and Fusion: Aggression in the Service of Eros.

Creative Aggression received a 2-star Not Recommended rating in the national survey. Many mental health professionals do not advocate the "aggression is natural" approach to becoming more assertive. Such an approach, said the critics, all too often leads an individual to run roughshod over someone else, causing so much anger and hostility on the part of the other person that the doors of communication close.

★ *Pulling Your Own Strings* (1977) by Wayne Dyer. New York: Thomas Y. Crowell.

Pulling Your Own Strings has been a huge success in the self-help market, with more than three million copies of the book sold since its publication in 1977. The book falls into the category of assertiveness books that advocate taking charge of life. Author Wayne Dyer, Ph.D., is a well-known self-help book author. One of his other very popular self-help books — *Your Erroneous Zones* — is profiled and evaluated in Chapter 28.

Dyer believes that every person has a responsibility to not act the part of the victim. He urges readers to be courageous, to realize what they can and cannot change about their lives, and to value themselves. Readers learn how to operate from a position of strength rather than weakness and how to teach others about how they expect to be treated. The book closes with a 100-item checklist for making a "take charge" profile.

Dyer presents many anecdotes from patients, literary figures, and people from all walks of life throughout the book as examples. A number of self-tests help readers monitor progress in learning how to take control of their lives. Dyer is an entertaining writer and knows how to grab a reader's attention. Each chapter opens with a one-liner, such as "There is no such thing as a well-adjusted slave."

Although *Pulling Your Own Strings* was a runaway best seller when it first came out in the late 1970s, the mental health professionals in the national survey were not kind to the book. Their ratings placed it in the 1-star, Not Recommended category. *Pulling Your Own Strings* was published at a time when the American public was becoming attuned to the importance of looking out for one's own needs instead of worrying exclusively about others' needs. A number of the mental health experts in the national survey criticized Dyer's approach as too "me" oriented, which promotes selfishness and egocentrism while not adequately taking into account the needs and feelings of others. Most mental health experts today recommend a more balanced approach that recognizes the importance of both self-attention and consideration of others. Some of the mental health professionals in the national survey also felt that *Pulling Your Own Strings* is biased against women.

★ *Control Freaks: Who Are They and How To Stop Them From Running Your Life* (1991) by Gerald Piaget. New York: Doubleday.

Control Freaks, like *Pulling Your Own Strings*, falls into the category of assertiveness books that focus on the importance of taking charge of life. Author Gerald Piaget, Ph.D., a professor of psychology at Stanford University Medical School, is a self-confessed control freak.

Piaget's book is especially directed at the victims of control freaks, advising them on how to remain independent of another person's control. The book describes the types of tactics control freaks use and how they manipulate others. Readers also learn step-by-step techniques to arm themselves against others' efforts at dictating life. Piaget's strategies are based on the akido martial arts system of defense. In this system, yielding to and pressing your opponent, rather than confrontation, are advocated. Frequent anecdotes and end-of-chapter exercises are included.

Control Freaks received a 1-star Not Recommended rating in the national study. The book came out just before the national survey was conducted and only 11 mental health professionals rated it. Piaget does present some strategies that are worth further consideration, so this book may be evaluated more positively as more mental health experts become familiar with it.

STRONGLY NOT RECOMMENDED

† *Looking Out for Number One* (1977) by Robert Ringer. Beverly Hills, CA: Los Angeles Book Company.

Looking Out for Number One urges readers to become more aggressive and, as the title implies, to look out for themselves in order to get what they want and deserve in life. When it first was published in the late 1970s, *Looking Out for Number One* was on *The New York Times* bestseller list for over a year. Author Robert Ringer is a businessman.

Ringer tells readers to go beyond being assertive, to aggressively go after the prizes of the world and not worry about others who get in the way; if you don't get the prizes, they will. Moreover, Ringer says that everybody else is trying to interfere with our quest for winning and succeeding. To find success and happiness, Ringer says readers must cross seven hurdles:

- *Perspective Hurdle.* To overcome this hurdle you have to focus on your own problems but avoid overmagnifying the importance of each problem.
- *Reality Hurdle.* You should base your life on facts instead of imaginary, impractical, or utopian wants and desires.
- *People Hurdle.* You have to be firm and not allow others' harmful traits to hurt you.
- *Crusade Hurdle.* You need to avoid crusades—they only complicate your life.

- *Financial Hurdle.* Looking out for number one—yourself—means taking risks and trying to make a lot of money.
- *Friendship Hurdle.* You should try to enjoy both the social and the solitary aspects of life.
- *Love Hurdle.* Even if you have a lover, you should maintain your own identity and show a very strong interest in yourself.

Although it was a national best seller in the late 1970s, *Looking Out for Number One* was given a negative rating by the mental health experts, which placed it in the Strongly Not Recommended category. More even than Dyer's *Pulling Your Own Strings, Looking Out for Number One* encourages people to have little consideration for others, to be egocentric, and to be hedonistic. Ringer's book also comes across as male-centered and male-dominant. This type of self-help book played well in the 1970s and early 1980s, especially with businessmen, but such books have not been as popular in the last decade. The negative rating of the book by the mental health experts in the national survey probably indicates that this book has not served people well in their desire to be more assertive and happier.

† *Winning Through Intimidation* (1973) by Robert Ringer. Beverly Hills, CA: Los Angeles Book Company.

Winning Through Intimidation, like its sister book by Ringer, *Looking Out for Number One,* approaches the problem of becoming more assertive by telling readers to be more aggressive. Ringer explains how his education at Screw University gave him the background to develop four theories that have helped him to earn millions of dollars in real estate:

- *Theory of Relativity.* Honesty is subjective; everybody interprets honesty individually.
- *Theory of Relevance.* Regardless of interest or appeal, the primary factor to consider is whether or not something is relevant to what you are trying to achieve.
- *Thirty-Year Theory.* Recognize that you are going to die; you have about thirty years to win.
- *Ice Ball Theory.* There is little to be gained by taking yourself seriously.

Winning Through Intimidation was the lowest-rated book in the assertiveness category in the national survey. Its negative rating placed it in the Strongly Not Recommended category. According to the mental health experts, *Winning Through Intimidation* has many of the same faults and flaws as *Looking Out for Number One*. Several of the experts described Ringer's approach as pretentious, arrogant, and condescending. In fairness to Ringer, his book was mainly written for businessmen with the objective of winning at business and making more money. But even for that objective, the consensus of the mental health community was that *Winning Through Intimidation* should be avoided.

CONCLUSIONS

In summary, we recommend:

- On becoming more assertive by improving communication skills:
    - ★★★★★ *Your Perfect Right* by Robert Alberti and Michael Emmons
    - ★★★★★ *Stand Up, Speak Out, and Talk Back* by Robert Alberti and Michael Emmons
    - ★★★★ *When I Say No, I Feel Guilty* by Manuel Smith

- For women who want to become more assertive:
    - ◆ *The Assertive Woman: A New Look* by Stanlee Phelps and Nancy Austin

---

CHAPTER NINE

Career Development

Most of us, regardless of age, are still in the process of exploring, planning, or making decisions about our career path. Too often we perceive developing a good career plan as a one-time event, the steps toward making a single, major job commitment. But each of us probably experiences changes in our lives that require modifications in our careers, adjustments in our career goals, and sometimes a change of careers. In fact, the average worker now makes five to six job transitions in a lifetime.

The importance of better understanding career development has never been more apparent than it is today. Tough economic times and stringent measures by businesses have translated into loss of jobs by many college-educated individuals. Other changes include a work force that is rapidly becoming increasingly diverse, service-oriented, and internationally linked. Many jobs are becoming more complex and cognitively demanding. Workers are increasingly perceiving the workplace as a setting for promoting the individual's health and well-being. And now, more than ever, people are concerned about the role of work in their lives, wanting to strike the best balance between work and other life tasks for them.

The topics of the self-help books on career development in the national survey can be grouped in five different categories: career choice, job hunting, and interviewing; work and its meaning in life; education and work; career change; and effective communication in the workplace. A large number of self-help books on specific aspects of careers and work have been written—how to become a better salesperson, how to be an effective manager, how to improve the corporate workplace, and so on. Such books were not included in this survey.

Three books on career choice, job hunting, and interviewing were rated: *What Color Is Your Parachute?* by Richard Bolles; *Knock 'em Dead* by Martin Yate; and *The 100 Best Companies to Work for in America* by Robert Levering, Milton Moskowitz, and Michael Katz.

Career Development
BOOK RATINGS IN THE NATIONAL SURVEY

Strongly Recommended	★★★★★	*What Color Is Your Parachute?* by Richard Bolles
Recommended	★★★★	*Staying the Course* by Robert Weiss
	★★★★	*Win–Win Negotiating* by Fred Jandt
Neutral	★★★	*Shifting Gears* by Carole Hyatt
	★★★	*Knock 'em Dead* by Martin Yate
	★★★	*Do What You Love, the Money Will Follow* by Marsha Sinetar
Not Recommended	★★	*The Portable MBA* by Eliza Collins and Mary Devanna
	★★	*The 100 Best Companies to Work for in America* by Robert Levering, Milton Moskowitz, and Michael Katz

---

Two books on work and its meaning in life made the final ratings: *Staying the Course* by Robert Weiss and *Do What You Love, the Money Will Follow* by Marsha Sinetar. One book in this category is profiled in the Worth a Further Look section: *Lives Without Balance* by Steven Carter and Julia Sokol.

One book on education and work made the final ratings: *The Portable MBA* by Eliza Collins and Mary Devanna. A second book—*The Three Boxes of Life* by Richard Bolles—is evaluated in the Worth a Further Look section.

One book on career change made the final ratings: *Shifting Gears* by Carole Hyatt.

One book on effective communication in the workplace was rated: *Win–Win Negotiating* by Fred Jandt.

STRONGLY RECOMMENDED

★ ★ ★ ★ ★   *What Color Is Your Parachute?* (1992) by Richard Bolles. Berkeley, CA: Ten-Speed Press.

What Color Is Your Parachute? is an extremely popular book about job hunting. Author Richard Bolles is an Episcopal priest who changed from pastoral counseling to career counseling. He currently spends his time as a professional writer, updating *Parachute* every year.

What Color Is Your Parachute? was first published in 1970. Since 1975, an annual edition of the book with updates on job hunting has appeared. This is an enormously successful self-help book that has become the career seeker's bible. Bolles tries to answer concerns about the job-hunting process and gives many sources that can provide further valuable information. Unlike many books on job hunting, *What Color Is Your Parachute?* does not assume that readers are recent college graduates seeking their first jobs. Bolles spends considerable time discussing job hunting for people seeking to change careers. Bolles describes a number of myths about job hunting and successfuly debunks them. He also provides invaluable advice about where jobs are, what to do to get hired, and how to cut through the red tape and confusing hierarchies of the business world to meet the key people who are most likely to make the hiring decision. The book has remained appreciably the same over the years with updates as appropriate. Recent editions have added material on job hunting for handicapped workers, how to effectively use career counselors, and how to find a mission in life.

What Color Is Your Parachute? is divided into two main parts. In Part I, Bolles tells about the nuts-and-bolts of the job hunt and presents a systematic approach for tackling even the toughest aspects of job hunting and career change. Readers pinpoint what skills they most enjoy using, where they want to use their skills, and how to find the person who has the power to hire them. In Part II, several appendices provide unusually detailed advice on other resources that will help in the job-hunting quest: workbooks, books on many topics related to job hunting and careers, career counselors, and workshops. In the most recent editions, Bolles's discussion of finding a mission in life has been moved from the appendices section to an epilogue. Here Bolles talks about job hunting from a religious point of view.

What Color Is Your Parachute? received a 5-star Strongly Recommended rating in the national survey. Not surprisingly, given its popularity over the last two and a half decades, it was one of the most frequently rated books—more than 300 mental health professionals evaluated it. *What Color Is Your Parachute?* is an excellent self-help book about job hunting and career change. Bolles writes in a warm, engaging, personal tone. His chatty comments are often witty and entertaining, and the book is attractively packaged with cartoons, drawings, and many self-administered exercises.

The mental health professionals in the national survey were uniform in their recommendation of *What Color Is Your Parachute?* as the best self-help book in the career development category. Several of the mental health experts said that one of Bolles's gifts is the ability to convince readers that job hunting does not need to be a dull, arduous, overwhelming task. Others commented that the book is the best contribution there has ever been to the career planning/job hunting field.

RECOMMENDED

★ ★ ★ ★   *Staying the Course: The Emotional and Social Lives of Men Who Do Well at Work* (1990) by Robert Weiss. New York: Free Press.

Staying the Course is about the emotional and social lives of men who do well at work. Author Robert Weiss, Ph.D., is a well-known and highly respected sociologist. He is a professor of psychology at the University of Massachusetts—Boston and a lecturer at Harvard University. He is the author of several other books, including *Marital Separation* and *Going It Alone.*

Staying the Course is based on Weiss's interviews with eighty men, aged 35 to 55, in upper-middle-class occupations. Weiss explores the nature of the men's work and nonwork lives—their activities, relationships, goals, and stresses. He also delves into their psychological lives to discover what has motivated them to meet their obligations year after year after year. Even in the face of setbacks in life, Weiss found that men who "stayed the course" had established social status and self-worth at work, had experienced emotional and social support from their marriage and family, and had benefitted from the loyalty of friendships. Weiss says that all too often in our society successful men are portrayed as exploiters of society. He found this not to be the case in his study. The successful men had made compromises with their youthful dreams and developed respected and caring relationships both in and out of the workplace. Their lives revolved around steady career advancement instead of ruthless ambition and they cared more about family stability than sexual conquest.

These men sound curiously like Jim Anderson in *Father Knows Best* and Ozzie Nelson in *The Nelsons.* These are very responsible men, according to Weiss, who have met their obligations at work, at home, and in the social arena. They have a strong motivation to be good men and be perceived by others as good men.

Staying the Course received a 4-star Recommended rating in the national survey. Several of the mental health professionals commented about the high quality of Weiss's research, his careful interpretation, and the insights that middle-class men can gain from the interviews. However, several critics said that there is something of an old-fashioned cast to Weiss's men and his interpretation of their lives. Feminists especially do not appreciate some of the conclusions that can be drawn from Weiss's work, among them, this one: If wives work, their jobs are secondary in terms of economics and status.

★ ★ ★ ★ *Win–Win Negotiating: Turning Conflict into Agreement* (1985) by Fred Jandt. New York: John Wiley & Sons.

Win–Win Negotiating is about how to turn conflict into agreement in the business world. Fred Jandt, Ph.D., has conducted seminars on conflict management for Baylor University, for many large firms such as Blue Cross and Xerox, and for the United States government.

The main themes of *Win–Win Negotiating* are that conflict is inevitable but is not always bad and that if everyone involved makes an honest effort, the conflict can be resolved. In the first four chapters, Jandt describes the basic nature of conflict and includes a self-assesment so that readers can determine how they deal with conflict, then identify the sources of conflict. Jandt says there never is only one source of conflict and that people have to learn how to communicate in ways that will help to resolve differences. He shows the reader how to keep minor disagreements from turning into major bouts.

Jandt makes the important point that when one party is the "winner" in a conflict, in the long run both parties often lose. The eventual losses result from the losing party either avoiding future contact or trying to get even. Ultimately, the relationship usually dies. Thus, the goal is to develop a solution that will satisfy both parties and let the relationship continue in much the way it has existed in the past. Jandt suggests beginning with a list all of the possible ways that a particular conflict can be resolved, including those that might at first glance seem ridiculous. Often a solution can be put together from this long list. Other strategies Jandt recommends include both parties first assaying and then displaying their strengths, learning this professional negotiators operate, using the "Mini-Max Strategy (which outlines who should give what and who should take what), unpacking (finding multiple ways to help opponents get a good deal), and dealing with "hardball" negotiators.

Win–Win Negotating received a 4-star Recommended rating in the national survey. Several of the mental health professionals commented that the book provides a good introduction for learning how opponents or adversaries think and how they negotiate their positions. Others liked Jandt's underlying message that the relationship is more important than the conflict. Anyone who wants to learn about negotiating techiques and resolving conflict in the workplace can benefit from reading *Win–Win Negotiating*.

Another good self-help book on negotiation is *Getting to Yes* by Roger Fisher and Robert Ury. It is reviewed in chapter 12, Communication, because it covers negotiation in a number of different contexts—with friends, neighbors, marital partners, and so on, as well as with business associates—whereas *Win–Win Negotiating* is primarily about negotiation in the workplace.

NEUTRAL

★ ★ ★   *Shifting Gears* (1990) by Carole Hyatt. New York: Simon & Schuster.

Shifting Gears provides advice for individuals who voluntarily or involuntarily change careers. Author Carole Hyatt has conducted market research and research on social behavior. She has been president of Hysatt-Esserman Research Associates, which has served as a consultant to many Fortune 500 companies. She lives in New York City.

Hyatt calls attention to data that suggest that most people go through several career changes. Hyatt uses the results of interviews with 300 individuals who succeeded in career transitions to develop a framework for self-guidance in making career transitions. She advises how to

- Adapt to today's marketplace.
- Determine your work style.
- Identify trigger points that require change.
- Understand the most common reasons for getting stuck in transition.
- Explore the psychological barriers to change and overcome them.
- Learn strategies to define an appropriate career path and repackage yourself.

Shifting Gears received a 3-star Neutral rating in the national survey. The book is a recent addition to the self-help literature and was not well known among the mental health professionals—only 20 rated it. Thomas Horton of the American Management Association commented that Hyatt's book provides hope and valuable guidance for people who either are contemplating career change or are out of work.

★ ★ ★ *Knock 'em Dead* (1992) by Martin Yate. Holbrook, MA: Bob Adams Publishers.

Knock 'em Dead is an annually updated guide to job interviewing. Author Martin Yate is an employment consultant to a number of corporations and recruitment firms.

Knock 'em Dead is subtitled *With Great Answers to Tough Interview Questions.* Yate gives the best answers to a number of key questions likely to be asked in a job interview, such as

- Why do you want to work here?
- How much money do you want?
- What can you do that someone else can't?
- What decisions are the most difficult for you?
- What is your greatest weakness?
- Why were you fired (if you lost your last job)?

According to Yate, the best jobs go to the best-prepared rather than the best-qualified candidates. Yate prepares the potential interviewee with the inside scoop on stress interviews, salary negotiations, executive search firms, and drug testing. He also provides advice about how to respond to illegal questions and other "hardball" tactics. And in the most recent editions Yate has added sections on dress and body language.

Knock 'em Dead received a 3-star Neutral rating in the national survey. The book was not well known among the mental health professionals; it was rated by only 15 respondents. The experts who did rate it thought that *Knock 'em Dead* gives sound advice for job interviewing. They said that Yate is direct and to the point in communicating how to handle tough interviews. Yate's book provides much greater details about the interview process itself than Bolles's *What Color Is Your Parachute?* which gives a much broader overview of job search skills.

★ ★ ★ *Do What You Love, the Money Will Follow* (1987) by Marsha Sinetar. New York: Dell.

Do What You Love, the Money Will Follow provides a general overview of career choice and development. Author Marsha Sinetar, Ph.D., is an organizational psychologist, mediator, and writer.

This book is subtitled *Discovering Your Right Livelihood,* and that is what Sinetar tries to encourage readers to do. Sinetar strongly believes that people should try to find jobs that fulfill their needs, talents, and passions. She provides a step-by-step guide to doing this and includes dozens of real-life examples of how people have overcome their fears, taken risks, and found work that allows them to express themselves and grow. In *Do What You Love, the Money Will Follow*, readers learn how to get in touch with their inner selves and true talents, evaluate and build their self-esteem, get rid of their "shoulds," overcome resistance, and get out of an unfulfillling job and into a fulfilling one.

Do What You Love, the Money Will Follow barely received a 3-star Neural rating in the national survey. The book was given mixed reviews. Some of the mental health professionals felt that Sinetar does a good job of helping people stuck in a job they don't like to break free and find a job they truly enjoy doing. Others said that Sinetar's approach borders on naiveté and might encourage people to leave jobs they probably shouldn't in search of the ultimate, perfect job. Sinetar's book is the diametric opposite of books that explain how to become a millionaire by age 35. In that sense, it has redeeming qualities. But critics felt that at times it goes too far in playing down the material aspects of job satisfaction.

NOT RECOMMENDED

★ ★   *The Portable MBA* (1990) by Eliza Collins and Mary Devanna. New York: John Wiley & Sons.

The Portable MBA presents the basic information that is taught in America's MBA programs in a single book of less than 400 pages. Author Eliza Collins is associated with the Center for Executive Development in Cambridge, Massachusetts. For thirteen years she was editor of *The Harvard Business Review*. Coauthor Mary Devanna is associate dean of the Graduate School of Business at Columbia University.

The Portable MBA presents the top wisdom from America's best university programs. It covers an extensive range of topics, from how to effectively manage people to quantitative methods to developing business strategies. Collins and Devanna persuaded professors from some of America's leading business schools—Harvard, Columbia, Wharton, Stanford, and MIT—to write chapters on their specialties. The book is especially designed for business managers who want to sharpen their decision-making skills, for technical supervisors who want to move into management, for students entering the work force, and for MBAs who feel they need a refresher. The authors are careful to point out that while their book provides knowledge equivalent to the first year in America's leading MBA programs, there is no substitute for actually going through an MBA program.

The Portable MBA received a 2-star Not Recommended rating in the national survey because it was not well known: it was evaluated by only 15 respondents. Noel Tichy, professor in the Graduate School of Business Education at the University of Michigan said that *The Portable MBA* is must reading for all business leaders and that many MBA curricula around the country could be improved by including some of the information in this book, especially the material on the fundamentals of competition.

★ ★   *The 100 Best Companies to Work for in America* (1984) by Robert Levering, Milton Moskowitz, and Michael Katz. New York: Signet.

This book, as its title states, profiles the best companies to work for in America. To determine the top American companies to work for, three businessmen and writers first solicited recommendations, then visited and read extensively about the companies. *The 100 Best Companies to Work for in America* gives companies a rating of 1 to 5 blocks for everything from pay to ambience. The authors also choose a positive and a negative trait to highlight with a cute one-liner at the beginning of each company's evaluation.

The authors' conclusions about what makes a company a good one to work for are hardly surprising: The company sells high-quality goods or services, provides liberal benefits and perks such as country club memberships and stock options, has a nonadversary posture toward employees, favors promotion from within, has pleasant surroundings, has top management that is caring, and has a positive corporate identity.

The 100 Best Corporations to Work for in America received a 2-star Not Recommended rating in the national survey. Several of the respondents felt that the authors have done a good job of thoroughly researching the quality of life at a large number of American comapnies and provide helpful insights about the best comapanies to work for. One fault of the book is its neglect of many women's concerns — maternity leave, day-care opportunities, and records of hiring and firing women. Also, the book is now almost a decade old, and some of the companies' ratings would no doubt be different if the authors reevaluated them today. In fact, a revised edition of *The 100 Best Corporations to Work for in America* was published in 1993.

WORTH A FURTHER LOOK

◑ ◑   *The Three Boxes of Life* (1981) by Richard Bolles. Berkeley, CA: Ten-Speed Press.

The Three Boxes of Life is Bolles's second book on career issues, written after *What Color Is Your Parachute?* For Bolles, the three boxes of life are: learning, working, and playing. *The Three Boxes of Life* comes with two subtitles: *And How to Get Out of Them* and *An Introduction to Life/Work Planning.*

Bolles's main argument is that while one of the boxes—learning (schooling/education), working (developing a career) or playing (retirement)—predominates at different pointsin a person's life, the three boxes can and should be brought into better balance throughout life through careful planning. The author asks readers to evaluate their own interests and skills, to explore what's available in each of the three boxes, and then to make decisions about how to achieve a satisfying and rewarding life. An important argument in *The Three Boxes of Life* is that none of the three boxes alone adequately prepares us for the next stage in life, so we must learn at each stage how to cope with a number of life options. The essential strategy is to infuse every stage of life with learning, working, and playing rather than exclusively focusing on learning early in life, followed by working and finally playing.

As in *What Color Is Your Parachute?* Bolles writes in a warm, personal, and engaging manner. *The Three Boxes of Life* is full of exercises, self-assesments, drawings, and entertaining asides. The book also includes several appendices on life/work planning and suggestions for further reading.

The Three Boxes of Life was positively rated but by only a few respondents, hence its relegation to the Worth a Further Look category. The mental health professionals who did rate *The Three Boxes of Life* said that it is helpful adjunct to *What Color Is Your Parachute?* Its in-depth coverage of life planning augments *Parachute's* sharp focus on career development and job hunting. They also commented that Bolles's message of balancing three of life's most important agendas—learning, working, and playing—throughout life's journey is a wise one.

◑ ◑   *Lives without Balance* (1992) by Steven Carter and Julia Sokol. New York: Villard Books.

Lives without Balance is about work and its meaning in life. Authors Steven Carter and Julia Sokol are professional writers.

In *Lives without Balance,* the authors describe the problem of having an unbalanced life because of outdated values and false premises. Among the modern, destructive myths highlighted by the authors are the limitless credit card; you are the master of your own fate; think and grow rich; you can have it all; and you can do it all. Using catchy phrases themselves, the authors evaluate four types of unbalanced lives: the downward slide, the never-ending treadmill, the uncontrollable escalator, and the roller coaster. Carter and Vokol also analyze image fixes-power fixes, glamor fixes, buying and selling fixes, job perks fixes, and status fixes—along with the problems entangled in the fixes.

Lives without Balance was published after the national survey was conducted. The book raises some important issues, and the authors stimulate thought about various dimensions of work, careers, and meaning in life.

CONCLUSIONS

In summary, we recommend:

- On career choice, job hunting, and interviewing:

  ★★★★★ *What Color Is Your Parachute?* by Richard Bolles

  ★★★ *Knock 'em Dead* by Martin Yate

- On work and its meaning for traditional males and traditional females:

  ★★★★ *Staying the Course* by Robert Weiss

- On work and its meaning in life:

  ◐◐ *The Three Boxes of Life* by Richard Bolles

  ◐◐ *Lives without Balance* by Steven Carter and Julia Sokol

CHAPTER TEN

Child Development
and Parenting

Playwright George Bernard Shaw once commented that while parenting is a very important occupation, no test of fitness for it is ever imposed. If a test were imposed, some parents would turn out to be more fit than others. Most parents do want their children to grow into socially mature individuals, but they often are not sure about what to do to help their children reach this goal. One reason for the frustration of parents is that they often get conflicting messsages about how to deal with their children. One "expert" may urge them to be more permissive with their children, another may tell them to place stricter controls on them or they will grow up to be spoiled brats.

Child development and parenting is one of the largest categories of self-help books. If parents are not confused about what to do before they go to a bookstore to buy a self-help book on parenting, they may become confused when they see the bewildering array of book choices, all promising to help them turn out a happier, more competent child. The ratings of the mental health experts in the national survey provide valuable advice about how to thread through the maze of parenting self-help books.

Because the child development and parenting category contains so many books, we had to make some decisions about which books to include and which to exclude. We primarily included books that deal with parenting in general rather than parenting strategies for specific problems. For example, we evaluate parenting books on communication and discipline but for the most part do not rate books that exclusively cover such topics as learning disabilities or mental retardation. Of course, some of the general parenting books include such specific topics in their overview of parenting and child development. Also you might want to look at the books in four other categories that are related to child development and parenting: Chapter 19, The Family; Chapter 21, Infant Development and

Parenting; Chapter 25, Pregnancy; and Chapter 33, Teenagers and Parenting.

The topics of the self-help books on parenting and child development that were rated in the national survey fall into the following nine categories: normal child development and suggestions about how to cope with typical problems at each period of development; toddlers and parenting; preschool children and parenting; parent education and improving communication between parent and child; discipline techniques; the state of childhood in America; fathers; psychological effects of parents who are naricissistic and emotionally unavailable; and sleep problems.

Two books that describe normal child development and provide suggestions for parents about how to cope with typical problems at each period of development were rated: *To Listen to a Child* by T. Berry Brazelton and *Your Baby and Child* by Penelope Leach. Two other books in this category are reviewed in the Worth a Further Look section—*Good Behavior* by Stephen Garber, Marianne Garber, and Robyn Spizman, and *Dr. Mom* by Marianne Neifert.

One book in the survey focuses on understanding and parenting toddlers: *Toddlers and Parents* by T. Berry Brazelton.

One book provides advice for parents about children's development in the preschool years: *The Preschool Years* by Ellen Galinsky and Judy David.

Three books focus on parent education and improving communication between parent and child: *Between Parent and Child* by Haim Ginott; *Parent Effectiveness Training* by Thomas Gordon; and *How to Talk so Kids Will Listen and How to Listen so Kids Will Talk* by Adele Faber and Elaine Mazlish. A fourth book—*Systematic Training for Effective Parenting* by Don Dinkmeyer and Gary McKay—is profiled in Worth a Further Look.

Four books give parents information about how to discipline their children more effectively: *Children: The Challenge* by Rudolph Dreikurs, *Living with Children* by Gerald Patterson, *Positive Discipline* by Jane Nelson, and *How to Discipline Your Six- to Twelve-Year-Old without Losing Your Mind* by Jerry Wyckoff and Barbara Unell.

One book examines the state of childhood in America: *The Hurried Child* by David Elkind.

One book evaluates the father's role in the child's development: *The Father's Almanac* by S. Adams Sullivan.

No books on narcissistic, emotionally unavailable parents made the final ratings, but one book on this topic—*The Drama of the Gifted Child* by Alice Miller—is profiled in the Worth a Further Look section.

No books on children's sleep problems made the final rating, but

---

Child Development and Parenting
BOOK RATINGS IN THE NATIONAL SURVEY

Strongly Recommended	★★★★★	*To Listen to a Child* by T. Berry Brazelton
	★★★★★	*Toddlers and Parents (2nd ed.)* by T. Berry Brazelton
	★★★★★	*Between Parent and Child* by Haim Ginott
	★★★★★	*Children: The Challenge* by Rudolph Dreikurs
	★★★★★	*The Hurried Child* by David Elkind
Recommended	★★★★	*Your Baby and Child* by Penelope Leach
	★★★★	*Parent Effectiveness Training* by Thomas Gordon
Diamonds in the Rough	◆	*How to Talk so Kids Will Listen and How to Listen so Kids Will Talk* by Adele Faber and Elaine Mazlish
	◆	*Living with Children* by Gerald Patterson
	◆	*Positive Discipline* by Jane Nelson
	◆	*The Preschool Years* by Ellen Gallinsky and Judy David
Neutral	★★★	*The Father's Almanac* by S. Adams Sullivan
	★★★	*How to Discipline Your Six- to Twelve-Year-Old without Losing Your Mind* by Jerry Wyckoff and Barbara Unell

---

Solve Your Child's Sleep Problems by Richard Ferber is evaluated in the Worth a Further Look section.

STRONGLY RECOMMENDED

★ ★ ★ ★ ★   *To Listen to a Child* (1984) by T. Berry Brazelton. Reading, MA: Addison-Wesley.

To Listen to a Child addresses development throughout the childhood years. Author T. Berry Brazelton, M.D., has recently been referred to as "America's baby doctor," a title once reserved for Benjamin Spock. The title came about through Brazelton's widespread television appearances and the numerous popular books he has written in the last several decades on infant and child development. Brazelton is a professor at Harvard University Medical School and chief of the Child Development Unit of the Children's Hospital Medical Center in Boston.

The focus in *To Listen to a Child* is primarily on problematic events that arise in the lives of children. Fears, feeding and sleep problems, stomachaches, and asthma are among the normal problems of growing up that Brazelton evaluates. He assures parents that it is only when they let their own anxieties interfere that these problems (such as bedwetting) become chronic and guilt-laden. Each chapter closes with practical guidelines for parents.

To Listen to a Child is divided into three main parts. Part I focuses on love and fears experienced by small children. Brazelton describes the "dance of love" between infants and their parents and outlines common fears young childen often have. He also discusses sadness and thumbsucking. One chapter addresses the spacing of children and the effects a new baby has on older children.

Part II deals with common issues parents with young children encounter, which include discipline and the young child's search for limits, as well as feeding and sleeping problems. Especially helpful is Brazelton's commentary about the parents' bed and his belief that both the parents' welfare and the child's welfare should be taken into account when making decisions about where the child sleeps.

Part III is about children's psychosomatic problems, such as stomachaches, headaches, croup, seizures, asthma, and bedwetting. The final chapter focuses on the hospitalized child, including how to prepare the child for the hospital stay and how to interact with the child at the hosital.

To Listen to a Child received a 5-star Strongly Recommended rating in the national survey. The book is easy to read, includes extremely well-chosen and clearly explained examples, and is warm, personal, and entertaining. The book's descriptions are not as detailed as those in some other books that focus on a specific period of development—for example, Brazelton's *Toddlers and Parents*—but it is a very good resource for parents to refer to throughout the childhood years when normal problems emerge.

★ ★ ★ ★ ★   *Toddlers and Parents* (2nd ed., 1989) by T. Berry Brazelton. New York: Delacorte Press.

Toddlers and Parents is about normal child development and advises parents how to handle typical problems and issues that arise during the toddler years. First written in 1974, Brazelton's 1989 revision of the book more fully addresses the concerns of changing family life styles, fathers, single-parent families, and dual-career families. *Toddlers and Parents* carefully explores the development of the toddler through the "terrible twos"—at 1 year, 15 months, 18 months, 2 years, and 30 months.

Each of the eleven chapters interweaves the narrative of an individual child's experiences (i.e., the birth of a sibling or a typical day at a day-care center) with Brazelton's moment-by-moment descriptions of what the child may be feeling, explanations of the child's behavior, and supportive suggestions for parents that help them cope with their own feelings as well as their child's behavior. Among the topics addressed by Brazelton:

- The toddler's declaration of independence from parents at about 1 year of age, a time when the toddler becomes alternately demanding and dismissing
- The nature of working parents' family life and their toddler's development at 18 and 30 months
- Life with a toddler of different ages in nontraditional families— divorced, stepfamily
- Special considerations for withdrawn, demanding, and unusually active toddlers
- Sibling rivalry
- Coping with the 18-month old's frequent "No's"
- Day-care centers
- The 30-month-old's developing self-conrol and self-awareness

Toddlers and Parents received a 5-star Strongly Recommended rating in the national survey. It is an excellent self-help book for the parents of toddlers. The writing is clear, the examples are extraordinarily well-chosen, and the tone is warm and personal. Brazelton not only provides parents with a guide to survival with a toddler but helps them develop a sense of delight in the struggles and triumphs their toddler is going through.

★ ★ ★ ★ ★   *Between Parent and Child* (1965) by Haim Ginott. New York: Avon Books.

Between Parent and Child provides parents with a guide to improving communication with their children and understanding their children's feelings. Author Haim Ginott, Ph.D., was a clinical psychologist at Columbia University and conducted workshops in child psychotherapy and parental guidance. Ginott died in 1973.

Ginott wrote *Between Parent and Child* to help parents understand the importance of listening to the feelings behind their child's communication. Ginott says that children who feel understood by their parents do not feel lonely and develop a deep love for their parents. Ginott describes a communication technique he calls "childrenese," which is based on parents' respect for the child and self-respect and statements of understanding preceding statements of advice or instruction.

Between Parent and Child contains twelve chapters. In early chapters, Ginott lays out his ideas on how to improve communication with children, including advice on praise and criticism, avoidance of self-defeating patterns, and how to handle responsiblity and independence on the part of the child. Ginott also gives advice on discipline, including permissiveness and setting limits, jealousy, sources of anxiety in children's lives, sex education, and sex roles. In two final chapters, he helps parents understand when their child needs professional help and when they the parents need professional help. The book concludes with suggestions for further reading and information about where to go for help.

Between Parent and Child received a 5-star Strongly Recommended rating in the national survey. Since its publication in 1965, millions of copies of the book have been sold. It was never revised. *Between Parent and Child* has been praised for being simple and clear. Many mental health professionals believe that the book provides important advice for parents in helping them understand children's feelings and how to communicate more effectively with their children. Although almost three decades old, *Between Parent and Child* continues to be one of the books that many mental health professionals recommend for parents.

Critics of the book cite its age as a problem. For example, the material on sex education and sex roles is severely outdated, as are the appendices on further reading and where to get help; mothers are always at home and fathers are off at work. Some mental health professionals also believe *Between Parent and Child* is too simplistic.

★ ★ ★ ★ ★ 　*Children: The Challenge* (1964) by Rudolph Dreikurs. New York: Hawthorn Books.

Children: The Challenge tells parents how to discipline their children effectively. Author Rudolf Dreikurs, M.D., was a Viennese psychiatrist who collaborated with famous psychoanalyst Alfred Adler in conducting child guidance clinics. Dreikurs came to Chicago in 1937 where he maintained a private practice, was a professor of psychiatry at the University of Chicago School of Medicine, and was director of the Alfred Adler Institute.

Dreikurs believes that parents have to learn how to become a match for their children by becoming wise to their children's ways and capable of guiding them without letting them run wild or stifling them. Unfortunately, says Dreikurs, most parents don't know what to do with their children.

Dreikurs teaches parents how to understand their children and meet their needs. He stresses that the main reason for children's misbehavior is discouragement. Discouraged children often demand undue attention. Parents usually respond to this negative attention-getting behavior by trying to impose their will on the children, who in turn keep misbehaving. Dreikurs says that parents who get caught up in this cycle are actually rewarding their children's misbehavior. He tells parents instead to remain calm and pleasant when disciplining the child.

Children: The Challenge consists of thirty-nine brief chapters, each involving a different type of discipline problem in which children misbehave and parents respond inappropriately. Dreikurs clearly spells out effective ways to handle each of these situations. He teaches parents to be firm without being dominating, to induce respect for order and the rights of others, to stay out of power struggles and conflict, to refrain from being overprotective, and to have the courage to say "no."

Dreikurs says that a "family council" is essential for solving family problems. Parents should set aside a precise hour on a specified day of the week at which time all family members meet and have an equal vote to determine rules and courses of action. The majority rules in Dreikurs's family council and decisions must be followed and not rescinded until the next weekly meeting.

Children: The Challenge received a 5-star Strongly Recommended rating in the national survey. It is an excellent guide for parents to use in learning how to discipline their children more effectively. The book is easy to read, the examples are clear and plentiful, the strategies for discipline are good ones, and a wide range of situations in which discipline is called for is presented. Although written almost three decades ago, *Children: The Challenge* still is the most widely recommended book on parental discipline of children by mental health professionals in the 1990s.

★ ★ ★ ★ ★   *The Hurried Child: Growing Up too Fast too Soon* (rev. ed., 1988) by David Elkind. Reading, MA: Addison-Wesley.

The Hurried Child describes a pervasive and harmful circumstance that all too many American children experience—that of growing up too fast and too soon. Author David Elkind, Ph.D., is a widely recognized expert on children's and adolescents' lives. He has written extensively about children in professional journals, books, and magazines. He has been president of the National Association of Young Children and is currently a professor of psychology at Tufts University in Medford, Massachusetts.

Elkind believes that many parents in today's achievement-oriented America place too much pressure on children to grow up too soon. Elkind says parents too often push children to be a "superkid," competent to deal with all of life's ups and downs. He believes that parents have invented the "superkid" to alleviate their own anxiety and guilt. But he doesn't just point the blame at parents alone; he also faults schools and the media.

Single-parent families and families in which both parents work outside the home are especially vulnerable, says Elkind. In such families, parents sometimes place heavy domestic burdens on children too early, unwittingly use their children as confidants, or give their children too much freedom, only to withdraw it when the children reach adolescence.

Elkind also argues that too many parents expect their children to excel intellectually and place too many achievement demands on them early in their lives. The excessive expectations can be found not only in children's academic journeys but also on the athletic field, where parental pressures let children know that to be fully loved they have win.

What does Elkind think parents should do in our contemporary world? He recommends respecting children's own developmental timetables and needs, encouraging children to play and fantasize, making sure that expectations and support are in reasonable balance, and being polite.

The Hurried Child received a 5-star Strongly Recommended rating in the national survey. The majority of mental health professionals who rated the book felt that Elkind's theme of children being hurried to grow up too soon is an important one to highlight. They also lauded his insightful analysis that too often parents want children to be stars but don't give them the time and support necessary to develop their potential. One criticism of the book faults its failure to give parents day-to-day prescriptions for remedying hurried children's lives.

RECOMMENDED

★ ★ ★ ★ *Your Baby and Child: From Birth to Age Five* (2nd ed., 1991) by Penelope Leach. New York: Knopf.

Your Baby and Child describes normal child development from birth to five years of age and provides suggestions for parents about how to cope with typical problems at different ages in infancy and the early childhood years. Author Penelope Leach, Ph.D., is English. She has taught child psychology at the London School of Economics and conducted research on children's development. She also is the author of several other books on development, including *Babyhood*, which is reviewed in Chapter 21, Infant Development and Parenting.

In *Your Baby and Child,* Leach describes the basics of what parents need to know about feeding, sleeping, eliminating, teething, bathing, and dressing at each period of early development—during the first six months, six to twelve months, one to two-and-a-half years, and two-and-a-half to five years. Nontechnical graphs of growth rates are easy to interpret. Leach also explores the young child's emotional world, telling parents what children are feeling and experiencing in different periods of development. Despite describing what is normal development in different periods, Leach carefully points out individual variations in growth and development. She concludes that when parents have a decision to make about their child, their best choice is usually to go "by the baby"—their sensitive reading of what the child's needs are—rather than "by the book" and what is generally prescribed for the average child.

The index in *Your Baby and Child* cleverly doubles as a glossary of terms. The final pages in the book are a handy illustrated guide to first aid, accidents, safety, infectious diseases, and nursing. Leach also suggests developmentally appropriate games and toys.

Your Baby and Child received a 4-star Recommended rating in the national survey and came close to making the 5-star category (its average rating was high enough but it was rated by only 32 respondents). Leach's extensive experience with children comes through in her sensitive, insightful suggestions for how to handle children at different developmental levels in the first five years of life. The material is extensive, well-organized, and packed with more than 650 well-executed charts, drawings, and photographs. This is a good self-help book for parents to use as a resource guide as their child ages from birth to five years of age.

★ ★ ★ ★   *Parent Effectiveness Training: The Tested New Way to Raise Responsible Children* (1975) by Thomas Gordon. New York: Peter Wyden.

Parent Effectiveness Training was first published in 1970, then revised in 1975. It is a book designed to educate parents about the nature of children's development and to help them communicate more effectively with their children. Author Thomas Gordon, Ph.D., is a clinical psychologist who has been a professor of psychology at the University of Chicago.

The book opens with a discussion of how parents are blamed but not trained (which underscores the rationale for Gordon's Parent Effectiveness Training program). Gordon tells parents what they should and can be. He advocates an authoritative parenting strategy that involves being neither permissive nor punitive but that rather emphasized nurturing and setting clear limitations. Gordon provides especially good advice about how to communicate more effectively with children. Included in his recommendations are how to engage in active listening, how to make frank statements of feeling without placing blame, and how to deal with children's problems. Gordon's approach enables parents to show children how to solve their own problems rather than inappropriately accusing or blaming children or laying guilt trips on them.

The sixteen chapters of *Parent Effectiveness Training* contain very detailed examples of such important aspects of parent–child communication as how to talk so children will listen, how to put "I" messages to work, and how to listen so that children will talk. Strategies for modifying a child's behavior and setting limits are discussed under the topics of how to change unacceptable behavior by changing the environment and the nature of parental power.

Parent Effectiveness Training received a 4-star Recommended Rating in the national survey, barely missing the 5-star category. Its widespread popularity was reflected in the large number of respondents who rated the book—more than 250. *Parent Effectiveness Training* the book and Parent Effectiveness Training the course, taught through numerous parenting groups and classes across the country, have helped millions of parents gain a better understanding of their children and how to communicate more efffectively with them. Despite its almost quarter of a century age, *Parent Effectiveness Training* remains one of the best books available for improving parent–child communication.

DIAMONDS IN THE ROUGH

◆ *How to Talk So Kids Will Listen and How to Listen So Kids Will Talk* (1980) by Adele Faber and Elaine Mazlish. New York: Avon.

How to Talk So Kids Will Listen and How to Listen So Kids Will Talk, like *Parent Effectiveness Training*, focuses on helping parents communicate more effectively with their children. Authors Adele Faber and Elaine Mazlish worked with famous self-help book author Haim Ginott in developing parenting communication workshops. They have taught at the New School for Social Research in New York.

This very easy-to-read book is divided into seven chapters that are liberally sprinkled with cartoons and exercises. The chapters focus on helping children deal with their feelings, helping parents deal with their own negative feelings, and creating a spirit of cooperation between parents and children; alternatives to punishment; encouraging children's autonomy; praising children; freeing children from playing roles; and putting all of the pieces together for rearing a happy and competent child.

How to Talk So Kids Will Listen and How to Listen So Kids Will

Talk received a Diamonds in the Rough rating in the national survey. Mental health experts thought that the book provides sound advice about how to communicate more effectively with children. The advice is practical, extremely easy to understand, and provides a climate for replacing yelling and pleading with cooperation.

♦   *Living with Children* (3rd ed., 1987) by Gerald Patterson. Champaign, IL: Research Press.

Living with Children presents a behavior modification approach to disciplining children. Author Gerald Patterson, Ph.D., is a well-known behaviorist and a professor of psychology at the University of Oregon.

Living with Children has an unusual style for self-help books. It is written in a programmed instruction format that makes the material easy to learn, according to Patterson. In this approach, the main ideas are broken down into small units or items. Parents are asked to respond to the items actively rather than just read them.

Four sections tell parents how learning takes place, how to change undesirable behavior, how normal children have normal problems, and what the problems of more seriously disturbed children are like. Patterson explains how reinforcement works and the importance of rewarding children immediately. Parents learn to develop a plan for changing their child's undesirable behavior. They begin by observing and recording the child's behaviors, detecting what led up to the behaviors and what followed them as well as how they the parents responded when the child behaved in undesirable ways. Parents then learn to respond to the child's behaviors differently than they have in the past. Time out (short for "time out for positive reinforcement") figures prominently in replacing the child's negative behaviors with positive ones.

Living with Children made the Diamonds in the Rough category. Several of the respondents said that Patterson's exercises are easy for parents to follow. They also commented that his book is simple but powerful in helping parents replace children's undesirable behaviors with desirable ones by rearranging the way they respond to the child.

♦   *Positive Discipline* (2nd ed., 1987) by Jane Nelson. New York: Ballantine.

Positive Discipline, first published in 1981 and revised in 1987, presents a strategy for disciplining children. Author Jane Nelson, Ed.D., has an extensive background in counseling. She also is the mother of seven children.

Positive Discipline was written to help both parents and teachers better understand children and discipline them so that they can learn to be self-disciplined and responsible. Nelson contrasts positive discipline ("Together we will decide on rules for our mutual benefit") with strictness ("These are the rules by which you must abide, and this is the punishment you will receive for violation of those rules"). Basing her discipline recommendations heavily on the view of psychology proposed by Alfred Adler (and Rudolph Dreikurs), the author roots the positive discipline approach in the following basic concepts:

- Children are social beings.
- Behavior is goal oriented.
- The child's primary goal is to belong and be significant.
- A misbehaving child is a discouraged child.
- Children have a sincere regard for their "fellowpersons."
- Children share equality with parents and teachers.
- Make sure the message gets through.

Nelson advises that when children do misbehave, parents should not overpunish them because it causes children to resent parents. She says that misbehavior should have logical consequences, but the consequences should always take the direction of encouragement and redirection. Mutual respect is emphasized and weekly family meetings (in the case of teachers, class meetings) are strongly recommended.

Positive Discipline made the Diamonds in the Rough category. Several mental health professionals applauded Nelson's positive strategy for handling discipline, stating that this approach eliminates guilt and recrimination. They also said that in this approach children are able to maintain their self-respect and understand that parents and teachers love and accept them.

♦ *The Preschool Years* (1988) by Ellen Gallinsky and Judy David. New York: Times Books.

The Preschool Years describes normal child development in the 3 to 5 years age period and provides suggestions for parents about how to cope with specific problems in this period of development. Author Ellen Gallinsky is copresident of the Family and Work Institute in New York City and is also on the staff of Bank Street College in New York City. She has been president of the prestigious National Association for the Education of Young Children. Coauthor Judy David, Ed.D., is a research associate with Gallinsky at the Family and Work Institute and Bank Street College.

The Preschool Years presents a wealth of information about the preschool years and serves as an excellent resource guide for children's growth and development during this time frame. Gallinsky and David sort through what researchers have found out about children's development and make practical suggestions for parents based on the research. They present a range of helpful strategies for solving children's everyday problems in the preschool years.

The Preschool Years contains eight long chapters that are full of examples of young children's interchanges with parents, teachers, and peers. The chapters focus on discipline, learning and growth, at-home and away-from-home routines, happy and sad times, family relationships, family work, work and family life, and schools and child care. The format consists of questions that are most often asked by parents of preschoolers followed by answers. Nearly 500 pages provide comprehensive answers to these questions that range from setting limits to how to talk to the child's teacher.

The Preschool Years was placed in the Diamonds in the Rough category in the national survey. The mental health professionals felt that Gallinsky and David have compiled an impressive resource guide for parents that will help them deal more effecively with their preschool child. This book contains far more specific advice about the preschool years than any other self-help book in the national survey. Well-known pediatrician T. Berry Brazelton commented that *The Preschool Years* gives parents an understanding of what they are going through and step-by-step instructions on how to help their young children develop more competently.

NEUTRAL

★ ★ ★   *The Father's Almanac* (1980) by S. Adams Sullivan. Garden City, NY: Doubleday.

The Father's Almanac is a guide for the day-to-day care of children written primarily for fathers. Author S. Adams Sullivan has worked as schoolteacher and editor.

The Father's Almanac begins before the child is born and includes a discussion of childbirth classes. The father's role at birth and infancy is chronicled, as is the father's relationship with the child during the preschool years. The traditional role of the father is emphasized by Sullivan. For example, one chapter is devoted to "Daddy's Work," which describes how business travel or commuting cuts into the father's available time for his children. Another chapter stresses the importance of the father being supportive of the mother. Other chapters focus on the father's play with children, building things with them, learning with them, and hints about photographing the family.

The Father's Almanac received a 3-star Neutral rating in the national survey. The book includes a great deal of practical advice for helping fathers to interact with their young children effectively. While much of the book is geared toward traditional fathers in "intact," never-divorced families, the numerous suggestions for projects, short trips, and activities can benefit divorced fathers as well.

★ ★ ★   *How to Discipline Your Six- to Twelve-Year-Old without Losing Your Mind* (1991) by Jerry Wyckoff and Barbara Unell. New York: Doubleday.

As its title suggests, this book falls into the category of discipline techniques for parents. Author Jerry Wyckoff, Ph.D., is a family therapist who specializes in parent–child relationships. He is a professor of human development at Ottawa (Kansas) University and also in private practice. Coauthor Barbara Unell is the cofounder and editor of *Twins* magazine and hosts a daily parenting information show on the Associated Press Radio Network.

The authors define discipline as a teaching system that leads to orderliness and control. They state that discipline is not a punishment system that is designed to break a child's spirit and individuality. Chapters focus on such topics as social problems, school problems, noise, children wanting their own way, irresponsibility/disorganization, sleeping/eating/hygiene problems, self-image problems, and activities. Each chapter begins with the statement of a problem followed by a brief description of how the problem could be prevented. Then the authors tell parents how to solve the problem. A "what not to do" section is also included.

How to Discipline Your Six- to Twelve-Year-Old Child without Losing Your Mind received a 3-star Neutral rating in the national survey. Although the book's title indicates that it is about discipline, in reality the book is a general parenting guide that provides suggestions for how to prevent or solve typical childhood problems. The mental health professionals felt that the authors do a good job of providing parents with concrete advice in an easy-to-read format.

WORTH A FURTHER LOOK

◑ ◑   *The Drama of the Gifted Child* (1981) by Alice Miller. New York: Basic Books.

The Drama of the Gifted Child is about how disturbed parent–child relationships negatively affect children's development. The book was originally published in German as *Prisoners of Childhood*. Author Alice Miller, M.D., is a Swiss psychoanalyst.

In *The Drama of the Gifted Child*, Miller tries to get parents to recognize the dangers of misusing their power. The title of the book is somewhat misleading in that "gifted" here does not mean talented in ability or intellect; rather, it means sensitive and alert to the needs of others, especially to the feelings and needs of parents. As a result of parents' unintentional or unconscious manipulation of them, gifted children's feelings are stifled. While gifted children become well-behaved, reliable, empathic, and understanding in order to keep their parents happy, they end up never having experienced childhood at all.

Miller believes that gifted children's sensitivity, empathy, and unusually powerful emotional antennae predispose them to be used by people with intense narcissistic needs (the term "naricissism" is derived from the legend of Narcissus, who fell in love with his beautiful, perfect image, never seeing the other parts of his life and never being sensitive to the needs of others). Miller argues that narcissistic individuals do not experience genuine feelings, and ultimately they destroy the authentic experiencing of genuine feelings in their children. Miller's comments are especially directed at adults whose narcissistic parents misused their power.

The Drama of the Gifted Child was positively rated but by only 5 respondents. The few mental health professionals who did evaluate the book felt that it is beautifully written and can help "gifted" readers to gain insight into their own feelings.

◗ ◗ *Solve Your Child's Sleep Problems* (1985) by Richard Ferber. New York: Simon & Schuster.

Solve Your Child's Sleep Problems helps parents to solve their children's sleep problems. Author Richard Ferber, M.D., is director of the Sleep Lab and the Center for Pediatric Sleep Disorders at Children's Hospital (one of Harvard University Medical School's teaching hospitals) in Boston, Massachusetts. Ferber also teaches at Harvard and is a pediatrician.

This book is divided into five parts: Part I, Your Child's Sleep; Part II, The Sleepless Child; Part III, Sleep Rhythm Disturbances; Part IV, Interruptions during Sleep; and Part V, Other Problems (such as snoring and head banging). An appendix provides suggestions for further reading, such as children's books on bedtime, sleep, and dreams, as well as information about organizations that help parents who have children with sleep problems.

Ferber begins by offering tired, frustrated, and possibly even angry parents some hope for remedying their child's sleep problems. Children's stages of sleep are outlined, along with suggestions for developing good sleep patterns in children. Chapter 5 is especially good; it alone will solve many children's sleep problems. In this chapter, the author tells parents that the key problem in sleep disorders is what their children associate with falling asleep. He provides a step-by-step plan for parents that will help their children sleep through the night. Additional strategies are given for feeding problems during the night, colic, and bedwetting. More serious sleep problems, such as sleep apnea (when breathing stops during sleep), narcolepsy (irresistable urge to fall asleep), and night terrors, are described in depth.

Solve Your Child's Sleep Problems was rated very positively in the national survey but by fewer than 10 respondents, hence its relegation to the Worth a Further Look category. This is an excellent self-help book for parents whose child has a sleep problem. Ferber's writing is clear and his prescriptions are humane and wise. If you are a parent with a child who has a sleep problem, read this book!

❶ ❶ *Good Behavior: Over 1200 Sensible Solutions* (1987) by Stephen Garber, Marianne Garber, and Robyn Spizman. New York: Villard.

Good Behavior is a resource for parents to consult when their children encounter problems as they age from birth to 12 years of age. Author Stephen Garber, Ph.D., is a clinical psychologist who has worked with children with a variety of learning and behavioral problems. He is in private practice with his wife, Marianne Garber, Ph.D., an education consultant, researcher, and reading specialist, and codirector of the Atlanta Hyperactivity Clinic. Coauthor Robyn Spitzman is a former elementary school art teacher.

Good Behavior is subtitled *Over 1,200 Sensible Solutions to Your Child's Problems from Birth to Age Twelve.* It takes 17 chapters—more than 500 pages—to communicate these 1,200 solutions. The topics include basic techniques of discipline, elimination problems, tantrums, school and learning problems, nervous habits, fears, and how to find professional help. The book is encyclopedic in its coverage of childhood problems, and it has more material about school-related problems, attention deficit disorder, and learning disabilities than most general books on parenting and children's development.

Good Behavior received a very high positive rating in the national survey but was evaluated by only eight respondents. The book is extremely well organized and contains good advice for parents. The authors state that their book is designed to be read from beginning to end, but most parents will benefit from its use as a resource guide.

◑ ◑   *Systematic Training for Effective Parenting* (3rd ed., 1976) by Don Dinkmeyer and Gary McKay. Circle Pines, MN: American Guidance Service.

Systematic Training for Effective Parenting is the accompanying text for the STEP (Systematic Training for Effective Parenting) program that has trained thousands of parents across the country to become more effective communicators with their children. Author Don Dinkmeyer, Ph.D., is president of the Communication and Motivation Training Institute in Coral Springs, Florida, and coauthor Gary McKay, Ph.D., is president of an institute with the same name in Tucson, Arizona. Both authors are clinical members of the American Association of Marriage and Family Therapy.

Dinkmeyer and McKay believe that democratic child rearing is the best strategy for parents. In this strategy, both parent and child are socially equal in the family and mutually respect each other. The authors explain why children misbehave (to get attention, achieve power, mete out revenge, or display inadequacy). They suggest family activities and encourage parents to develop parenting goals. Parents are told how to get in touch with their own emotions and understand their children better. Encouragement, communication skills, and discipline methods that develop responsibility are advocated. One chapter is exclusively devoted to the family meeting, in which all members of the family have an equal opportunity to discuss issues of concern. Every chapter includes a guide for parents to use in constructing goals for improving family relationships.

Systematic Training for Effective Parenting received a very high positive rating but was evaluated by only eight respondents. The book is rather brief (less than 100 pages) and is somewhat sketchy without the accompanying parenting course that it is designed to supplement. The authors' approach is similar to that taken by Rudolph Dreikurs (*Children: The Challenge*), Thomas Gordon (*Parent Effectiveness Training*), and Jane Nelson (*Positive Discipline*). Several mental health professionals mentioned that the exercises and goal-setting strategies in *Systematic Training for Effecive Parenting* are especially effective, but that the depth and extensive examples in Dreikurs's, Gordon's, and Nelson's books make them more attractive on their own. The best use of *Systematic Training for Effecive Parenting* is in conjunction with the parent training workshops developed by the authors.

◑ ◑   *Dr. Mom* (1986) by Marianne Neifert. New York: G. P. Putnam's Sons.

Dr. Mom is a resource guide for parents that focuses on children's health and development from birth to five years of age. Marianne Neifert, M.D., has an incredible background. In seven calendar years, she finished college, graduated from medical school, completed a pediatric residency, and gave birth to five children! She is currently a pediatrician and professor at the University of Colorado Medical School and also is medical director of the lactation program at AIM St. Luke's Hospital in Denver. She writes a column for *McCall's* magazine and has cowritten two books on breast feeding.

Dr. Mom is an A to Z encyclopedic guide (more than 500 pages) on childhood illnesses, children's day-to-day experiences and development, and emergency care from birth to five years of age. Topics range through understanding medical symptoms, basic baby care, discipline, breast vs. bottle feeding, toilet training, day care, and nonsexist child rearing.

Dr. Mom is a comprehensive guide to the practical aspects of parenting infants and young children. The book includes far more information on the infant years (first two years of life) than the early childhood years (from three through five years). And the book is stronger on pediatric illness and how to take care of babies' needs than psychological advice and communication strategies for parents.

◗ ◗   *Raising Black Children* (1992) by James P. Comer and Alvin E. Poussaint. New York: Plume.

Raising Black Children is written by two highly respected experts on black children—James Comer and Alvin Poussaint, professors of psychiatry at Yale and Harvard, respectively. Comer and Poussaint argue that black parents face additional difficulties in raising emotionally healthy children because of ethnic minority and income problems. Comer and Poussaint's guide contains almost 1,000 child-rearing questions they have repeatedly heard from black parents across the income spectrum. Among the issues on which they advise black parents are how to improve the black child's self-esteem and identity, how to confront racism, how to teach their children to handle anger, conflict, and frustration, and how to deal with the mainstream culture and still retain a black identity.

This is an excellent self-help book for black parents that includes pertinent suggestions that are not found in most child-rearing books. Virtually all other child-rearing books are written for white, middle-class parents and do not deal with many of the problems faced by black parents, especially black parents form low-income backgrounds.

◗◗   *The Measure of Our Success: A Letter to My Children and Yours* (1992) by Marian Wright Edelman. Boston, MA: Beacon Press.

Marian Wright Edelman founded the Children Defense Fund in 1973 and for more than two decades has been working to advance the health and well-being of America's children and parents. This slim volume begins with a message to her oldest son, Joshua, 22. In that message and throughout the book, Edelman conveys that parenting and nurturing the next generation is the most important function of a society and that we need to take it more seriously than we have in the past. High on her recommended list is the belief that there is no free lunch—don't feel entitled to anything you don't sweat and struggle for. She also warns against working only for money or for power because they won't save your soul, build a decent family, or help you sleep at night. She also tells her son to remember that his wife is not his mother or his maid. And Edelman admonishes our society for not developing better safety nets for children and not being the caring community that children and parents need.

Edelman's book stimulates thought about what kind of nation we want to be, what kind of values mean the most to us, and what we can do to improve the health and well-being of our nation's children and parents.

◖ ◖   *Touchpoints* (1992) by T. Berry Brazelton. Reading, MA: Addison-Wesley.

Touchpoints is parenting self-help writer T. Berry Brazelton's latest book, published after the national self-help survey was conducted. From fetus to first grade, Brazelton focuses on the concerns and questions that parents have about children's feelings, behavior, and development. The title *Touchpoints* is derived from Brazelton's belief that there are universal spurts of development and trying times of adaptation throughout childhood. Section I portrays development from fetus through three years; Section II describes a number of challenges to development—from allergies to toilet training; and Section III focuses on important social agents in children's development, such as fathers, mothers, grandparents, caregivers, and doctors.

Touchpoints has some pluses compared with Brazelton's earlier books. In *Touchpoints* Brazelton gives more attention to fathers and other socializing agents in children's development—grandparents and caregivers, for example. This is an excellent self-help book for parents.

CONCLUSIONS

In summary, we recommend:

- For parents who want to learn about the normal course of child development and how to cope with problems through the childhood years:

  ★★★★★ *To Listen to a Child* by T. Berry Brazelton

  ★★★★ *Your Baby and Child* by Penelope Leach

  ◑◑ *Good Behavior* by Steven Garber, Marianne Garber, and Robyn Spitzman

  ◑◑ *Dr. Mom* by Marianne Neifert

  ◑◑ *Touchpoints* by T. Berry Brazelton

- For parents of toddlers:

  ★★★★★ *Toddlers and Parents* by T. Berry Brazelton

- For parents of preschoolers:

  ◆ *The Preschool Years* by Ellen Gallinsky and Judy David

- On general parenting skills and better communication with children:

  ★★★★★ *Between Parent and Child* by Haim Ginott

  ★★★★★ *Parent Effectiveness Training* by Thomas Gordon

  ◆ *How to Talk So Kids Will Listen and How to Listen So Kids Will Talk* by Adele Faber and Elaine Mazlish

  ◑◑ *The Measure of Our Success* by Marian Wright Edelman

- On effective discipline for children:

  ★★★★★ *Children: The Challenge* by Rudolph Dreikurs

  ◆ *Living with Children* by Gerald Patterson

  ◆ *Positive Discipline* by Jane Nelson

  ◆ *How to Discipline Your Six- to Twelve-Year-Old Without Losing Your Mind* by Jerry Wyckoff and Barbara Unell

- On the status of childhood in America and the problem of children growing up too soon:

  ★★★★★ *The Hurried Child* by David Elkind

(cont.)

CONCLUSIONS *(Continued)*

- For fathers who want to participate more actively in their children's lives:

  ★★★   *The Father's Almanac* by S. Adams Sullivan

- On the effect of emotionally unavailable, narcissistic parents on children's development:

  ◗◗   *The Drama of the Gifted Child* by Alice Miller

- On sleep problems:

  ◗◗   *Solve Your Child's Sleep Problems* by Richard Ferber

- For African-American parents:

  ◗◗   *Raising Black Children* by James Comer and Alvin Poussaint

---

CHAPTER ELEVEN

Codependency and Recovery

Ten years ago the term "codependency" did not exist. In just a few short years it has become a household word. It's hard to escape hearing someone talking or writing about it—in magazines, on TV talk shows, in self-help groups, and, of course, in self-help books. Some bookstores now even have a codependency section.

Codependency has become a national phenomenon, but just what is it? Codependency originally referred to the problems of people married to alcoholics, but it spread rapidly to include a host of other circumstances. Agreement on a precise definition of codependency has not been forthcoming, although Melodie Beattie, one of the leaders of the codependency movement, says that a codependent person is someone who has let another person's behavior affect him or her and who is obsessed with controlling that person's behavior. Many people fit under the umbrella of this definition. Beattie agrees, saying that codependency is *anything* and *everyone* is codependent.

What most disciples of codependency do agree on is that the number of women who are codependent is staggering. And they agree that women who are codependent have low self-esteem, grew up in a dysfunctional family, and need to focus more on their own inner feelings instead of catering to someone else's needs. In the language of codependency, many women stay with an unreliable partner, usually a male, because they are addicted to the relationship dynamics of being subservient to a male. Recommended therapy strategies for codependent people include a spiritually-based Twelve-Step program similar to that developed by Alcoholics Anonymous and Al-Anon.

Codependency is a highly controversial concept, and its therapeutic approach to helping people cope more effectively with problems has its enthusiastic supporters and its critical detractors. Codependency Anonymous is one of the most rapidly growing self-help support groups in the

United States. Advocates of the approach believe that codependency helps to explain women's emotional problems better than any approach that has come along in years. Until they learn about the nature of codependency, say endorsers of the concept, codependents are not aware of why they got into these troubled relationships in the first place or why they are still in them. By reading a codependency self-help book and/or seeing a codependency therapist, codependents learn about what codependency is, develop insight about their own codependent status, and acquire the courage to break free from their codependency addiction.

Not long after the concept of codependency emerged, critics began attacking it. The critics included some highly respected mental health professionals. UCLA psychologist Jacqueline Goodchilds, Ph.D., says that codependency's emphasis on inner feelings and higher powers underestimates the importance of social influences in people's lives. For example, she says that psychologists know that children and finances influence women's self-esteem, but codependency doesn't deal with them. Highly respected therapist and self-help author Harriet Lerner also comments that the codependency concept describes codependent people as sick and diseased, without considering the larger social world in which they are embedded. Lerner also believes that codependency places too much blame on a woman for her husband's problems; the husband is usually not considered as responsible for his abusive, violent, and rotten behavior in the codependency framework. New York psychologist Leonore Tiefer argues that the vagueness of codependency concepts makes it easy for just about anyone to have at least one of the symptoms, which she says, is a perfect formula for a best-selling, but not necessarily good, self-help book. And in a paper recently presented at the American Psychological Association in 1992, therapist Alice Lawler labeled codependency "the women's disease of the decade" because codependency attributes women's problems to women themselves rather than where the blame should be placed—the culture in which we live. Other critics say that codependency doesn't in any way address the individual perturbations that punctuate each of our lives, but rather it fits every person's unique and personal woes into a label—codependency—that describes a problem that is common to just about everyone. Yet another criticism of many mental health professionals is that despite the success of Twelve-Step programs with many alcoholics, transporting the Twelve-Step recovery program and its abdication of power and control to a higher deity to relationship problems doesn't work effectively. Rather, say the mental health critics, we should foster in people a greater sense of taking control of their lives when they have relationship problems.

Of the many self-helps books on codependency, five were evaluated by enough respondents to be included in the final ratings in the nation-

---

Codependency
BOOK RATINGS IN THE NATIONAL SURVEY

Neutral	★★★ *Codependent No More* by Melodie Beattie
	★★★ *Beyond Codependency* by Melodie Beattie
Not Recommended	★★ *How to Break Your Addiction to a Person* by Howard Halpern
	★ *Love Is a Choice* by Robert Helmfelt, Frank Minirth, and Paul Meier
	★ *Co-Dependence: Healing the Human Condition* by Charles Whitfield

---

al survey: *Codependent No More* by Melodie Beattie; *How to Break Your Addiction to a Person* by Howard Halpern; *Beyond Codependency* by Melodie Beattie; *Love Is a Choice* by Robert Helmfelt, Frank Minirth, and Paul Meier; and *Codependency: Healing the Human Condition* by Charles Whitfield.

NEUTRAL

★ ★ ★ *Codependent No More* (1987) by Melodie Beattie. New York: Harper & Row.

Codependent No More is Melodie Beattie's personal narrative about being addicted to a certain type of relationship and how she recovered from it. In addition to describing her own personal struggles, she discusses the nature of codependency and how to recover from it. Beattie is a recovering chemical abuser and self-described codependent person; the book lists no mental health training or affiliations.

Codependent No More is subtitled *How to Stop Controlling Others and Start Caring for Yourself.* Beattie estimates that upwards of 80 million Americans are emotionally involved with an addict or are addicted themselves, not necessarily to alcohol or drugs but also to sex, work, food, or shopping. What kind of characteristics do codependents have? Beattie says that they are sufferers who feel anxiety, pity, and guilt when other people have a problem and that they overcommit themselves. Codependents have a history of taking care of others but not themselves, she says.

How do codependents get out of this relationship mess? Beattie endorses insight about the nature of codependent relationships and a version of the spiritually based Twelve-Step recovery popularized by Alcoholics Anonymous and other alcohol addiction recovery programs, such as Al-Anon. A basic theme of Beattie's recovery strategy is to begin having a love affair with yourself instead of with someone else to whom you have given too much.

Codependent No More received a 3-star Neutral rating in the national survey. Some respondents called it a great book, others an awful book. Beattie has become the queen of the codependency movement, and this book is the bible of it. *Codependent No More* was on *The New York Times* best-seller list for 115 weeks and has sold upwards of 4 million copies since its 1987 publication. Beattie enthusiasts say that her book and the concept of codependency have thrown a lifeline to millions of people who were adrift in addictive relationships. Her detractors list all of the criticisms of the codependency concept we have already cited. One critic said that she couldn't imagine that anyone looking for help would find it in this book.

★ ★ ★   *Beyond Codependency* (1989) by Melodie Beattie. New York: Harper & Row.

Beyond Codependency is the sequel to Beattie's *Codependent No More.* In *Codependent No More*, Beattie describes the self-sabotaging behavior patterns of codependency in which the codependent person overcares for an unreliable, addictive person. In *Beyond Codependency*, Beatty spends more time addressing healthy recovery, the role of recycling (falling into old bad habits) in recovery, and how positive affirmations can counter negative messages. As in *Codependent No More*, in *Beyond Codependency* Beattie advocates a Twelve-Step program to recovery that is based on AA and Al-Anon's programs. A number of testimonials from people who have used this method to break away from an addictive relationship are liberally interspersed throughout the book.

Beyond Codependency received a 3-star Netural rating in the national survey. Virtually the same plaudits and criticisms that characterize reviews of Beattie's *Codependent No More* apply to *Beyond Codependency* as well.

NOT RECOMMENDED

★ ★   *How to Break Your Addiction to a Person* (1982) by Howard Halpern. New York: McGraw-Hill.

How to Break Your Addiction to a Person actually preceded the coinage of the term codependency. Although the word does not appear in the title or anywhere in the book, the book includes some codependency ideas. Author Howard Halpern, Ph.D., has been a psychotherapist for more than three decades.

The book is divided into three parts that address the basis of relationship addiction, how it works, and how to break out of it. Halpern believes that people remain in bad relationships for three reasons: it's practical; they have certain beliefs that keep them from leaving the relationship; and they have a deep-seated hunger for attachment. He places the most emphasis on hunger for attachment. To break away from an addictive relationship, Halpern recommends keeping a detailed diary, doing a cost/benefit analysis, and developing a network of friends who can provide moral support during withdrawal. The book differs from other books in the codependency category in that it does not describe a spiritually based Twelve-Step program or healing from within as recovery strategies. Indeed, an argument could be made that without those two ingredients, Halpern's book is about relationship addiction, not codependency.

How to Break Your Addiction to a Person received a 2-star Not Recommended rating in the national survey. Endorsers of Halpern's book say that he offers good practical advice for getting out of an addictive relationship. Critics believe that the book falls into the trap of not adequately recognizing people's personal and unique lives.

★ *Love Is a Choice* (1989) by Robert Helmfelt, Frank Minirth, and Paul Meier. Nashville, TN: Thomas Nelson.

Love Is a Choice is a codependency book that emphasizes the spiritual and emotional dimensions of being addicted to another person. Author Robert Helmfelt, Ed.D., is a therapist who specializes in the treatment of chemical dependency, codependency, and compulsive disorders. Frank Minirth and Paul Meier, both M.D.s, founded the Minirth–Meier Clinic in Dallas, Texas, which is one of the largest psychiatric clinics in the world. Helmfeldt is affiliated with the Minirth–Meier clinic. Minirth and Meier, who also have degrees from Dallas Theological Seminary, have written a number of other self-help books.

Love Is a Choice is divided into five main parts: Part I, What Codependency Is; Part II, The Causes of Codependency; Part III, Factors That Perpetuate Codependency; Part IV, Codependency in Interpersonal Relationships; and Part V, The Ten Stages of Recovery. In the final section, the authors place special emphasis on perceiving God's unconditional love as the solution to one's need for deep emotional bonds and love.

Love Is a Choice received a 1-star Not Recommended rating in the national survey. Only people with a strong spiritual bent will be attracted to the book. Criticisms of the codependency concept in general apply here, as well.

★ *Co-Dependence: Healing the Human Condition* (1991) by Charles Whitfield. Deerfield Beach, FL: Health Communications.

Co-Dependence: Healing the Human Condition focuses on the nature of codependent relationships and how to break free of them. Author Charles Whitfield, M.D., is a therapist in private practice in Baltimore, Maryland.

This book purports to offer a "new paradigm" for helping people heal their codependent relationship(s). According to Whitfield, the old paradigm (model) is based on the belief that there is a separate cause for each illness that befalls human beings and that the cause is usually biological or psychological in nature. Whitfield's new paradigm acknowledges multiple levels of causes that are physical, mental, emotional, and spiritual in nature. Whitfield says that codependency plays a major role at all levels of human problems.

Co-Dependence: Healing the Human Condition received a low 1-star Not Recommended rating, barely escaping the Strongly Not Recommended category. The consensus of the mental health professionals in the national survey was that this is not a good self-help book. Critics especially faulted the author's presentation, saying that it is unorganized.

CONCLUSIONS

Codependency is a highly controversial concept in the mental health field. None of the codependency books in the national survey made the Strongly Recommended, Recommended, or Diamonds in the Rough lists. The ratings of the codependency books—especially Melodie Beattie's books—varied extensively. Some of the mental health professionals enthusiastically endorsed her books, but these positive ratings were counterbalanced by a number of very negative ratings. Indeed, in the section of the national survey where the best five and the worst five self-help books were to be listed, codependency books showed up on the "best" lists of some experts and on the "worst" lists of others. On more lists than not, however, the codependency books were rated as the worst rather than the best self-help books of all. A common statement in the slot for the worst self-help book was "All of the codependency books." On the other hand, none of the codependency books received the Strongly Not Recommended, negative average rating because every codependency book had at least a few strong advocates.

Readers who want to learn more about the nature of codependency and strategies codependency therapists recommend for recovering from a codependent relationship might want to read one of Melody Beattie's books. However, the consensus of mental health professionals in the national survey was that the following books are more helpful to people with relationship problems:

- *The Courage to Heal* by Ellen Bass and Laura Davis (Chapter 2)

- *The Dance of Anger* by Harriet Lerner (Chapter 6)

- *Your Perfect Right* by Robert Alberti and Michael Emmons (Chapter 8)

- *You Just Don't Understand* by Deborah Tannen (Chapter 12)

- *The Dance of Intimacy* by Harriet Lerner (Chapter 22)

- *The Battered Woman* by Lenore Walker (Chapter 2)

For criticism of the codependency concept, see Carol Tavris's book, *The Mismeasure of Woman* (Chapter 33)

CHAPTER TWELVE

Communication

We get things done by talking with family, friends, colleagues, and neighbors. When someone doesn't quite grasp what we are saying, we often let it go, the talk continues, and nobody pays much attention. But some conversations have important outcomes that hinge on the effectiveness of the conversation—a job interview, a business meeting, a marriage proposal. In these circumstances, ineffective communication can have serious negative consequences: we don't get the job, don't convince our business colleague our ideas are worth adopting, and are turned down for marriage.

Sometimes strained conversations reflect real differences between people—they are angry with each other; one person is a liberal, the other a conservative; and so on. On many occasions, though, strained conversations develop when people simply are miscommunicating. Their conversations could easily be improved by understanding the nature of interpersonal communication.

The topic of self-help books on communication can be grouped in seven categories: broad-based discussion of communication skills; conversation skills; female–male communication; negotiating agreements; nonverbal communication; communication skills in families; and confession.

Four books that provide a broad understanding of communication skills made the national survey's final ratings: *People Skills* by Robert Bolton; *Coping with Difficult People* by Robert Bramson; *Games People Play* by Eric Berne; and *Stop! You're Driving Me Crazy* by George Bach and Ronald Deutsch. A fifth book was positively rated but fewer than 10 times: *Messages* by Matthew McKay, Martha Davis, and Patrick Fanning. This book is discussed in the Worth a Further Look section.

Two books that emphasize conversation skills were rated in the national survey: *That's Not What I Meant!* by Deborah Tannen and *The Talk Book* by Gerald Goodman and Glenn Esterly.

One book that focuses on female–male communication was rated: *You Just Don't Understand: Women and Men in Conversation* by Deborah Tannen.

One book that tells people how to negotiate agreements was rated: *Getting to Yes* by Roger Fisher and William Ury.

One book that focuses exclusively on nonverbal communication made the final ratings: *Body Language* by Julius Fast.

No books that stress communication skills in families made the final ratings, but one book — *Peoplemaking* by Virginia Satir — is reviewed in the Worth a Further Look section. Other books that emphasize family communication patterns are evaluated in Chapter 19, The Family.

One book that underscores the importance of confession in coping and healing was rated: *Opening Up* by James Pennebaker.

Communication
BOOK RATINGS IN THE NATIONAL SURVEY

Strongly Recommended	★★★★★	*You Just Don't Understand* by Deborah Tannen
Recommended	★★★★	*Getting to Yes* by Roger Fisher and William Ury
	★★★★	*People Skills* by Robert Bolton
Diamonds in the Rough	◆	*The Talk Book* by Gerald Goodman and Glen Esterly
Neutral	★★★	*That's Not What I Meant!* by Deborah Tannen
	★★★	*Opening Up* by James Pennebaker
	★★★	*Coping with Difficult People* by Robert Bramson
	★★★	*Games People Play* by Eric Berne
	★★★	*Stop! You're Driving Me Crazy* by George Bach and Ronald Deutsch
Not Recommended	★	*Body Language* by Julius Fast

STRONGLY RECOMMENDED

★ ★ ★ ★ ★   *You Just Don't Understand: Women and Men in Conversation* (1990) by Deborah Tannen. New York: Ballantine.

As its title implies, *You Just Don't Understand: Women and Men in Conversation* is about how women and men communicate—or all too often miscommunicate—with each other. *You Just Don't Understand* reached number one on a number of best-seller lists and as we write, this book continues to be on *The New York Times* best-seller list. Author Deborah Tannen, Ph.D., is a professor of linguistics at Georgetown University and an internationally recognized expert on communication in interpersonal relationships.

Tannen shows that friction between women and men in conversation often develops because as girls and boys they were brought up in two virtually distinct cultures and continue to live in those two very different cultures. The two gender cultures are rapport talk (female culture) and report talk (male culture). Rapport talk is the language of conversation and a way of establishing connections and negotiating relationships, which women feel more comfortable doing. Report talk is public speaking, which men feel more comfortable doing. Women enjoy private speaking, talk that involves discussing similarities and matching experiences. Men are more likely to want to hold center stage through story telling, joking, or giving information. It is men's lack of interest in rapport talk that bothers many women.

Tannen illustrates the miscommunication in male–female relationships through several cartoons about a husband and wife at the breakfast table. For example, in one, the husband opens a newspaper and asks his wife, "Is there anything you want to say to me before I begin reading the newspaper?" The reader knows there isn't but that as soon as he starts reading the newspaper, she will think of something to say. This cartoon highlights the difference in what women and men think talk is for: To him, talk is for information, so when his wife interrupts his reading, it must be to inform him of something he needs to know. For him, she might as well tell him what she thinks he needs to know before he starts reading. But for her, talk is for interaction and connection. She believes that talking is a way to show involvement, listening a way of showing caring and interest.

Tannen says that the difference between public speaking (report talk) and private speaking (rapport talk) can be understood in terms of status and connection. It is not surprising that many women are more comfortable talking when they feel safe and connected, among friends and equals, while men feel more comfortable talking when there is a need to establish and maintain their status in a group. But the situation is more complex. What seems like a status bid could be intended as a bid for closeness, and what seems like distancing may be intended to avoid the appearance of pulling rank. Harmful and unjustified misinterpretations might be avoided by understanding the conversational styles of the other gender.

The problem, then, may not be an individual man or even men's styles but the difference between women's and men's styles, says Tannen. If so, both women and men need to make adjustments. In the public context, a woman can push herself to speak up without being invited or begin to speak at even the slightest pause in talk. Men can learn that women are not accustomed to speaking up in groups. They can make women feel more comfortable by warmly encouraging and allowing them to speak rather than hogging public talk for themselves.

In private talk—rapport talk—understanding women's and men's different views can detoxify the situation. A woman can observe a man's motivation for reading the newspaper at the breakfast table and not interpret it as rejection of her or a failure in their relationship. And a man can understand a woman's motivation for talk without interpreting it as an unreasonable demand or manipulative attempt to prevent him from doing what he wants to do.

You Just Don't Understand is an excellent self-help book. It received the 5-star Strongly Recommended rating in the national survey. Tannen's book has been especially taken up by women, who after reading the book, want their husband or male partner to read it too. Prior to Tannen's analysis, the common way to explain communication problems between women and men was to resort to blaming men's desire to dominate women. Tannen presents a more balanced approach to female–male communication problems by focusing on the different ways females and male communicate, and a more positive approach by emphasizing that women and men can get along better by understanding each other's different styles.

Tannen's book is well written, well researched, and entertaining. Human sexuality expert Bernie Zilbergeld said that Tannen has a keen sense for the ways in which talk gets us into trouble and that people who read his book will recognize their own conversations and misunderstandings on virtually every page. Maggie Scarf, a leading authority on intimate relationships, commented that anyone who wants to understand what the stranger on the opposite side of the bed is actually saying should consult this witty and sophisticated book.

RECOMMENDED

★ ★ ★ ★   *Getting to Yes: Negotiating Agreement without Giving In* (1981) by Roger Fisher and William Ury. New York: Penguin.

Getting to Yes explains how to effectively negotiate personal and professional disputes. Author Roger Fisher teaches negotiation at Harvard Law School and has practiced law in Washington, D.C. Coauthor William Ury has been Associate Director of the Harvard Negotiation Project. Both authors have conducted many negotiation workshops.

Getting to Yes offers a concise (the book is only about 150 pages long), step-by-step method for arriving at mutually acceptable agreements in many different types of conflict—whether the conflict is between parents and children, neighbors, bosses and employees, customers and business managers, tenants and landlords, or diplomats. Fisher and Ury describe how to

- separate people from the problem
- emphasize interests, not positions
- develop precise goals at the outset of negotiations
- work together to establish options that will satisfy both parties
- negotiate successfully with opponents who are more powerful, refuse to play by the rules, or resort to "dirty tricks"

Getting to Yes is based on the method of principled negotiation developed as part of the Harvard Negotiation Project. This method helps people evaluate issues based on their merits instead of regressing to a haggling process in which each side says what it will and won't do. It teaches negotiators to look for mutual gains whenever possible. If interests conflict, they can insist that the result be based on some fair standards. The method of principled negotiation is hard on the merits of the issues, soft on the people. It uses no tricks and no posturing. Negotiators get what they are entitled to and still stay decent, and they are protected against people who try to take advantage of them.

Getting to Yes received a 4-star Recommended rating in the national survey. Although written more than a decade ago, the book remains one of the best easy-to-read resources for learning how to negotiate effectively in a wide range of situations. Economics giant John Kenneth Galbraith said *Getting to Yes* is by far the best book he has ever read about negotiation and that it can be equally effective for people who want to keep their friends, property, income, and peace among nations.

★ ★ ★ ★   *People Skills* (1979) by Robert Bolton. New York: Touchstone.

People Skills provides a broad overview of communication skills in many different contexts. Author Robert Bolton, Ph.D., is president of Ridge Consultants in Cazenovia, New York, a firm that specializes in improving human communication.

People Skills is divided into four main parts. Part I, the Introduction describes a number of skills for bridging gaps in interpersonal communication and barriers to communicating effectively; Part II, Listening Skills explains how listening is different from merely hearing, how to develop the important skill of reflective listening, and how to read body language; Part III, Assertion Skills outlines a number of valuable techniques to help you become more assertive in relationships, and Part IV, Conflict Management Skills discusses how to effectively manage conflict in many different circumstances.

People Skills lists five important sets of skills that encourage more satisfying interpersonal relationships:

- *Listening skills* help you understand what other people are saying. You learn to respond so that other people feel that their problems and feelings have been understood. Using listening skills encourages other people to solve their problems without depending on you.
- *Assertion skills*, involving both verbal and nonverbal behaviors, enable you to maintain respect, satisfy your needs, and defend your rights without dominating, manipulating, abusing, or controlling others.
- *Conflict–resolution skills* help you deal with the emotional turbulence that often accompanies conflict.
- *Collaborative problem-solving skills* are a way of resolving conflicting needs that satisfies all parties.
- *Skill selection* enable you to decide which communication skills to use in different situations.

People Skills received a 4-star Recommended rating in the national survey. It was the highest-rated book that describes a broad range of communication skills and situations. Many books on communication skills have been written since Bolton's book was published in 1981, in response to people's increasing awareness of the importance of communication in their lives. However, a number of the mental health professionals concluded that *People Skills* is still the best easy-to-read general introduction to communication skills in the self-help market.

DIAMONDS IN THE ROUGH

♦ *The Talk Book: The Intimate Science of Communicating in Close Relationships* (1988) by Gerald Goodman and Glenn Esterly. New York: Ballantine.

The Talk Book is about ways to improve talk in face-to-face communication. Author Gerald Goodman, Ph.D., is a professor of psychology at UCLA and a well-known expert on communication skills. Glenn Esterly is a professional writer.

According to Goodman and Esterly, talk is an essential tool for ensuring the success and growth of all close relationships. If people don't know how to use talk to benefit themselves, the cost can be high. *The Talk Book* describes six communication tools that contribute to using talk more effectively: disclosures, reflections, interpretations, advisements, questions, and silences. These talk tools fashion most of the meaning that bounces back and forth in everyday conversation. Understood well, they can help improve close relationships.

Goodman and Esterly's book is divided into two main parts. Part I, The Intimate Science Explained, explores the inner workings of person-to-person talk. Natural conversations are used to illustrate events, habits, and hidden rules that go unnoticed in the flow of conversation. Part II, The Intimate Science Mastered, tells how to initiate self-change and improve talk. Readers learn talk skills and how to diagnose bad habits and apply what they learn to real-life situations. Each chapter in Part II ends with a "Practicing" section that includes several tested methods for improving mastery of talk and making sense of another person's talk. A helpful appendix lists who's who in the talk business and what to read beyond *The Talk Book*.

The Talk Book made the Diamonds in the Rough category in the national survey; it was rated positively but by too few people to reach the 4-star or 5-star categories. This is a solid book on conversation skills written by a leading expert. M. Brewster Smith, former president of the American Psychological Association, said that *The Talk Book* is good psychology and a fine gift to humanity. *The Talk Book's* main drawbacks are its length (almost 400 pages of small type) and encyclopedic tendencies (it covers an extensive number of ideas, each in great depth, and is boring reading in places).

NEUTRAL

★ ★ ★   *That's Not What I Meant!: How Conversational Style Makes or Breaks Relationships* (1986) by Deborah Tannen. New York: Ballantine.

That's Not What I Meant! provides a broader understanding of the inner workings of conversation than Tannen's earlier-reviewed book, *You Just Don't Understand*, which focuses on how females and males communicate and miscommunicate. Tannen believes that different conversational styles are at the heart of miscommunication. In *That's Not What I Meant!* conversational confusion between the sexes is only part of the picture. Tannen shows that growing up in different parts of the country, having different ethnic and social class backgrounds, being of different ages, and having different personality traits all contribute to different conversational styles that can cause disappointment, hurt, and misplaced blame.

That's Not What I Meant! is divided into four main parts. Part I, Linguistics and Conversational Style, describes different types of conversational styles and different conversational signals and devices. Part II, Conversational Strategies, discusses why we don't say what we mean, how to use framing and reframing in conversation, and the role of power and solidarity in conversation. Part III, Talking at Home: Conversational Style in Close Relationships, covers why things often get worse in intimate conversations, how women and men communicate differently, and the problems of criticism in intimate conversation. Part IV, What You Can and Can't Do with Conversational Style, summarizes the main points already discussed in the book and shows how knowledge and understanding of conversational styles can go a long way toward solving communication problems.

That's Not What I Meant! received a 3-star Neutral rating in the national survey, just missing the 4-star Recommended rating. This is a good self-help book that provides a rich understanding of how conversational styles make or break relationships. Jeremy Campbell, author of *Grammatical Man*, said that Tannen shows us why conversations—and consequently friendships, marriages, and even jobs—can break down even with the best intentions and how understanding conversational skills can rescue us.

Why was Tannen's *You Just Don't Understand* given a 5-star rating and her *That's Not What I Meant!* only a 3-star rating? *You Just Don't Understand* is about a very contemporary topic that touches the nerves of many people in our world—females and males in conversation. It stands alone as *the* book to read on how to understand and improve female–male conversation. *You Just Don't Understand* includes more basic information about communication skills in general that are also covered in other books, although Tannen does a better job of describing these skills than most other authors.

★ ★ ★   *Opening Up: The Healing Power of Confiding in Others* (1990) by James Pennebaker. New York: Avon.

Opening Up, as its subtitle says, is about the healing power of confiding in others. Author James Pennebaker, Ph.D., is a professor of psychology at Southern Methodist University and an internationally recognized authority in the field of health psychology and stress.

Pennebaker's book deals with the following issues:

- Why suppressing inner turmoil has a devastating effect on health
- How long-buried childhood traumas can cause lifelong illness
- How denial of mental pain can cause physical pain
- Why talking about or writing about troubling thoughts protects us from the internal stresses that cause physical illness

Pennebaker's advice is not based just on his own opinions. For more than a decade he has studied thousands of people in many different contexts to learn how their confession of troubling thoughts, feelings, and experiences benefits their physical and mental health. What is surprising about Pennebaker's findings is that the benefits of confession occur whether you tell your secrets to someone else or simply write about them privately.

Pennebaker is especially adept at pinpointing how the hard work of inhibiting troublesome thoughts and feelings gradually undermines the body's defenses. Inhibition can cause problems in the immune system, heart and vascular system, and even the biochemical workings of the brain and nervous system. In short, excessive holding back of thoughts, feelings, and behaviors can place us at risk for both major and minor illnesses. By contrast, confronting our deepest thoughts and feelings can have remarkable short-term and long-term health benefits.

Opening Up received a 3-star Neutral rating in the national survey, almost making the 4-star Recommended category. The book is not yet well known; it was rated by only 18 respondents. Several mental health experts found Pennebaker's book excellent. Daniel Wegner, author of *White Bears and Other Unwanted Thoughts*, said that *Opening Up* throws open new doors of understanding and offers new hope for gaining control of our lives. Robert Ornstein, coauthor of *Healthy Pleasures*, commented that if followed, Pennebaker's strategies could change the lives of millions of people.

★ ★ ★   *Coping with Difficult People* (1981) by Robert Bramson. New York: Dell.

Coping with Difficult People explains how to deal with the troublemakers in life, both at home and at work. Author Robert Bramson, Ph.D., received his doctorate from the University of California at Berkeley and is a well-known management consultant to many businesses, including IBM and Bank of America.

Bramson describes and presents strategies for coping with the following types of difficult people:

- *The Hostile Aggressive,* who bullies by bombarding, making cutting remarks, or throwing tantrums
- *The Complainer,* who gripes incessantly but never gets any closer to solving the problem
- *The Silent Unresponsive,* who is always reasonable, sincere, and supportive to your face but never comes through
- *The Negativist,* who responds to any proposal with statements like "It will never work"
- *The Know-It-All,* who is confident that he or she knows everything there is to know about anything worth knowing
- *The Indecisive,* who delays any important decision until the outcome is certain to be what he or she wants and refuses to let go of anything until it's perfect—which is never

Bramson outlines a six-step plan to cope with any of these people and make life less stressful:

1. Assess your situation
2. Stop wishing that the difficult person was different
3. Put some distance between you and the difficult behavior
4. Form a plan for interrupting the interaction
5. Put your strategy into action
6. Monitor your progress and modify your plan as appropriate

Coping with Difficult People received a 3-star Neutral rating in the national survey. The book is entertaining reading, and the author uses a lot of catchy labels to get his points across and grab the reader's attention, such as describing the Know-It-Alls as bulldozers and balloons and Hostile–Aggressives as Sherman tanks, snipers, and exploders. Written over a decade ago, *Coping with Difficult People* has been successful, with sales of more than 500,000 copies. The mental health experts in the national survey recommended the book for improved understanding of people in work settings rather than family settings; since the author's background is in managerial consulting, many of the examples naturally come from work settings.

★ ★ ★   *Games People Play* (1964) by Eric Berne. New York: Grove
Press.

Eric Berne, M.D., was the founder of transactional analysis, an approach
to understanding interpersonal relationships that emphasizes communication patterns. Berne was a practicing psychiatrist in Carmel, California. He died in 1970.

According to Berne, people tend to live their lives by playing out
"games" in their interpersonal relationships. People Play games to
manipulate others, avoid reality, and conceal ulterior motives. Berne analyzes thirty-six different games, which he divides into seven main
categories:

- *Life games*, which pervade every person's behavior
- *Marital games*, which partners may use to maintain a frustrating
  and unrewarding life
- *Sexual games*, in which one person provokes sexual reactions in
  another and then acts like an innocent victim
- *Party games*, which are highly social and include perpetual gossip
- *Consulting room games*, played by a patient with a doctor to avoid
  cure (as in psychiatry)
- *Underworld games*, most often played for material gain but can
  be played for psychological gain
- *Good games*, which involve social contributions that outweigh
  the complexity of underlying motivation and manipulation

Berne's book is divided into three main parts. In Part I, Analysis of
Games, the nature of transactional analysis and game playing is presented. Part II, A Thesaurus of Games, extensively describes the seven types
of game playing. In Part III, Beyond Games, the significance of games
in people's lives is evaluated and ways to break free from destructive game
playing are outlined. Too many of life's games are vacuous and deceitful, undermining genuine intimacy and effective communication. Berne
argues that the way out of destructive game playing is to become aware
of its harmful effects.

Games People Play received a 3-star Neutral rating in the national
survey. Some mental health experts described the book as a classic in
the self-help field. It has been a huge best seller and was one of the most
frequently rated books in the national survey: 350 respondents evaluated it. On the positive side, Berne's book singles out an important dimension of communication that had not before been detected as critical to
intimate relationships—game playing. Anyone who reads *Games People Play* will find numerous examples that apply to their own lives. And

Berne connects with readers through catchy, witty writing that produces good theater. You can read about the sweetheart, the threadbare, the rapo, the schlemiel, the stocking game, the wooden leg, and the sywmd (see what you made me do). According to human adjustment expert Wayne Weiten, Berne's analysis of games is shrewd and discerning. Other mental health professionals asserted that *Games People Play* cuts through our social façades and help us clearly see the flaws in our communication with each other. Although almost three decades old, some counselors continue to strongly recommend *Games People Play* to their clients who are having communication problems and use Berne's transactional analysis approach in their practice.

Although it still has its disciples, *Games People Play* is not nearly as popular as it was two and three decades ago. Some critics think that Berne overdramatizes the role of game playing in intimate relationships. They believe that there is a lot more to intimate communication than game playing. Other critics don't like the parent–adult–child aspect of Berne's transactional analysis approach. The critics also point out that the age of *Games People Play* shows in its assumption that all people adopt traditional male and female orientations. When Berne wrote *Games People Play*, there were few assertive women and men were not supposed to be nurturant. The gender times have changed, and books such as Deborah Tannen's *You Just Don't Understand* provide analysis of gender's role in contemporary interpersonal communication.

★ ★ ★   *Stop! You're Driving Me Crazy* (1979) by George Bach and Ronald Deutsch. New York: Berkley.

Stop! You're Driving Me Crazy covers a broad array of communication strategies to help, in the authors' words, "keep the people in your life from driving you up the wall." George Bach was one of the earlier pioneers in group psychotherapy. He conducted an extensive number of workshops and seminars at the Bach Institute in Los Angeles. Ronald Deutsch is a professional writer.

    Stop! You're Driving Me Crazy spells out Bach's catchy concept of "crazymaking." Crazymaking describes a wide variety of harmful communication patterns that are passive–aggressive in nature. Passive–aggressive individuals consciously like, love, or at least respect each other but unconsciously undermine rather than build up the morale and mental well-being of a friend, lover, or spouse. Some examples of passive–aggressive crazymaking:

- A husband stirs up a screaming fight, then wants to make passionate love.

- A boss gives an employee a promotion, then says, "You're worthless."
- A young woman tells her mother that she is on a crash diet, and a day later her mother brings her a chocolate cake.

Stop! You're Driving Me Crazy helps you to identify, cope with, and eliminate such crazymaking techniques.

This book was on the borderline between 2 and 3 stars and just managed the 3-star Neutral rating. *Stop! You're Driving Me Crazy* was one of the early success stories in the communication category of self-help books, achieving best seller status in the early 1980s. In recent years its popularity has waned. Several mental health experts criticized the book for being too sensational, gender-biased, and difficult to read in places.

NOT RECOMMENDED

★   *Body Language* (1970) by Julius Fast. New York: Pocket Books.

Body Language explains how our bodies communicate information to others and how we can read the body language of others to our advantage. This very popular book has sold more than 3 million copies. The book lists no professional mental health affiliation for author Julius Fast.

Body Language includes discussion of how we unconsciously give communication signals with our body, how we handle territorial space and what we do when others invade it, how men wear their masks, and the role of touch in communication, how body postures communicate information, and the language of the legs.

This book received a 1-star Not Recommended rating in the national survey. Critics felt that some of the information about basic aspects of body language was beneficial but was overshadowed in too many places by sensational comments and sexism. The book gets off to a wrong start on the cover, which shows a woman sitting in a chair, accompanied by such questions as "Does her body say that she's a loose woman?" It ends on a wrong note, as well, with the following statement on the back cover: "Read *Body Language* so that you can penetrate the personal secrets of both intimates and total strangers." Better to read one of the general approaches to communication skills. Robert Bolton's *People Skills*, for example, has a chapter on nonverbal communication skills that is a much less sexist, less sensationalized account of body language. The next book we review—*Messages*— also has a good discussion of how to read body language.

WORTH A FURTHER LOOK

❍ ❍ *Messages: The Communication Skills Book* (1983) by Matthew McKay, Martha Davis, and Patrick Fanning. Oakland, CA: New Harbinger.

Messages: The Communication Skills Book is a broad-based approach to improving communication skills. Matthew McKay, Ph.D., is a founding director of Haight-Ashbury Psychological Services in San Francisco. He is also co-author of the positively reviewed book *The Relaxation and Stress Reduction Workbook* (Chapter 26). Martha Davis, Ph.D., is a psychologist with Kaiser Permanente Medical Center in Santa Clara, California and is a coauthor of *The Relaxation and Stress Reduction Workbook.* Patrick Fanning is a professional writer.

Messages is divided into six main parts. Part I, Basic Skills, focuses on improving listening skills, self-disclosure, and expressing, and Part II, Advanced Skills, discusses body language, hidden messages, transactional analysis, and verbal communication. Part III, Conflict Skills, describes assertiveness training, fair fighting, and negotiation. Part IV, Social Skills, deals with judging people and making contact more easily. Part V, Family Skills, which focuses on sexual communication, parent effectiveness, and family communication, is balanced by Part VI, Public Skills, which focuses on strategies for effective communication in small groups and in front of audiences.

Messages was positively rated in the national survey but by only 5 respondents, who thought that the book provides a good overview of the basic books on communication. *Messages* is more closely aligned with the way many courses on introductory communication skills are taught at colleges and universities. Well-known family therapist Virginia Satir gave *Messages* a positive review, calling it a comprehensive handbook of personal communication that is enthusiastic about getting people to improve their skills.

❍ ❍ *Peoplemaking* (1972) by Virginia Satir. Palo Alto, CA: Science and Behavior Books.

Peoplemaking is a book about how to improve communication with a select group of people in your life—family members. Author Virginia Satir is a pioneer and leading figure in the field of family therapy.

Satir believes that all of the ingredients in a family that count can be changed and improved: individual self-worth, communication, the family system, and rules. By reading *Peoplemaking,* couples can learn better communication skills, parents can learn to improve their communication with their children, single parents and stepparents can learn ways to cope with the special issues in their families, and individuals can learn how to communicate more effectively with extended family members.

Satir's book was positively rated in the national survey but by only seven respondents. The book is now more than two decades old and was more popular in the 1970s. It still contains some valuable advice, especially for couples who want to communicate more effectively and for parents who want to communicate more effectively with their children.

CONCLUSIONS

In summary, we recommend:

- On a wide range of communication skills:

  ★★★★ *People Skills* by Robert Bolton

  ◑◑ *Messages* by Matthew McKay, Martha Davis, and Patrick Fanning

- For improving conversation skills:

  ◆ *Talk Book* by Gerald Goodman and Glen Esterly

  ★★★ *That's Not What I Meant!* by Deborah Tannen

- For improving female–male communication:

  ★★★★

  ★ *You Just Don't Understand* by Deborah Tannen

- On negotiating agreements:

  ★★★★ *Getting to Yes* by Roger Fisher and William Ury

- On the healing power of confiding in others:

  ★★★ *Opening Up* by James Pennebaker

- For improving family communication:

  ◑◑ *Peoplemaking* by Virginia Satir

CHAPTER THIRTEEN

Death, Dying, and Grief

Famous therapist Erich Fromm once commented that "man is the only animal that finds his own existence a problem he has to solve and from which he cannot escape." He went on to say that "in the same sense man is the only animal who knows he must die." Our life does ultimately end, the point at which Italian playwright Salvadore Quasimodo says, "Each of us stands alone at the heart of the earth pierced through by a ray of sunlight, and suddenly it is evening." At last, years do steal us from ourselves and from our loved ones.

Compared to people in many other cultures around the world, Americans are death avoiders and death deniers. Although each of us must face our own death and the loss of loved ones, we are rarely prepared to cope with the overwhelming emotions and upheavals that fear, despair, and grief bring into our lives. Because we are such a death-avoiding and death-denying culture, many people might expect this chapter to be depressing. We think you will not find that to be the case. Self-help writers who dispense advice for how to cope with the sadness of one's own death or the death of a loved one balance the sadness with love, support, and spiritual healing. For people who have lost a loved one, recovery, growth, and the expectation that survivors at some point in the future will feel better than they do now are frequent themes.

Topics of self-help books on death, dying, and grief can be grouped in the following categories: coping with loss of any kind, including death; coping with impending death (one's own or someone else's); grief in general, including its stages and recovery; grieving over the death of a child; grieving over the death of a spouse; helping children cope with grief; suicide; and spiritually-based approaches.

Coping with loss of any kind (including death) is the topic of two books rated in the national survey: *How to Survive the Loss of a Love*

Death, Dying, and Grief
BOOK RATINGS IN THE NATIONAL SURVEY

Stongly Recommended	★★★★★	*How to Survive the Loss of a Love* by Melba Colgrove, Harold Bloomfield, and Peter McWilliams
Recommended	★★★★	*How to Go on Living When Someone You Love Dies* by Therese Rando
	★★★★	*Learning to Say Good-By* by Eda LeShan
	★★★★	*Talking about Death* by Earl Grollman
Diamonds in the Rough	◆	*When Bad Things Happen to Good People* by Harold Kushner
	◆	*Recovering from the Loss of a Child* by Katherine Donnelly
	◆	*Helping Children Grieve* by Theresa Huntley
	◆	*Living through Personal Crisis* by Ann Stearns
	◆	*Sudden Infant Death* by John DeFrain, Linda Ernst, Deanne Jakub, and Jacque Taylor
	◆	*Up from Grief* by Bernadine Kreis and Alice Pattie
Neutral	★★★	*On Death and Dying* by Elisabeth Kübler-Ross
	★★★	*The Enigma of Suicide* by George Colt
	★★★	*The Widow's Handbook* by Charlotte Foehner and Carol Cozart
Strongly Not Recommended	†	*Widowed* by Joyce Brothers
	†	*Final Exit* by Derek Humphrey

by Melba Colgrove, Harold Bloomfield, and Peter McWilliams and *Living Through Personal Crisis* by Ann Stearns.

Only one book rated in the national survey deals with impending death: *On Death and Dying* by Elisabeth Kübler-Ross.

Two books focus on the general process of grief, its stages and recovery from it: *How to Go on Living when Someone You Love Dies* by Therese Rando and *Up from Grief* by Bernadine Kreis and Alice Pattie. A third

book—*The Grief Recovery Handbook* by John James and Frank Cherry—
is evaluated in Worth a Further Look.

Grieving over the death of a child is the topic of two books: *Recovering from the Loss of a Child* by Katherine Donnelly and *Sudden Infant Death* by John DeFrain, Linda Ernst, Deanne Jakub, and Jacque Taylor. A third book—*The Bereaved Parent* by Harriet Schiff—is profiled in Worth a Further Look.

Grieving over the death of a spouse is addressed by two books: *The Widow's Handbook* by Charlotte Foehner and Carol Cozart, and *Widowed* by Joyce Brothers.

Three books examine how to help a child cope with grief: *Learning to Say Good-By* by Eda LeShan, *Talking about Death* by Earl Grollman, and *Helping Children Grieve* by Theresa Huntley.

Suicide is the focus of two books: *The Enigma of Suicide* by George Colt and *Final Exit* by Derek Humphrey.

One spiritually based book on death, dying, and grief is evaluated: *When Bad Things Happen to Good People* by Harold Kushner. One spiritually based book is also profiled in the Worth a Further Look category: *A Grief Observed* by C. S. Lewis.

STRONGLY RECOMMENDED

★ ★ ★ ★ ★   *How to Survive the Loss of a Love* (2nd ed., 1991) by Melba Colgrove, Harold Bloomfield, and Peter McWilliams. Los Angeles, CA: Prelude Press.

How to Survive the Loss of a Love provides suggestions for coping with the loss of a loved one, through death or otherwise. Author Melba Colgrove, Ph.D., has a background in counseling and education and currently is on the staff of Waterford Family Counseling in Waterford, Michigan. Harold Bloomfield, M.D., is a psychiatrist in private practice in Del Mar, California. He also is the author of other self-help books, such as *Making Peace with Your Parents* (evaluated in Chapter 4, Adult Development). Peter McWilliams is a poet whose work was the inspiration for *How to Survive the Loss of a Love*. He has written a number of books on topics ranging from meditation to personal computers.

Since the first edition of this book appeared in 1976, the authors have experienced, between them, the death of a parent, a major stroke, two serious car accidents, a bankruptcy, a lawsuit, and an impending divorce. Consequently the authors view loss broadly. They subdivide loss into four categories: obvious losses, such as death of a loved one, divorce, robbery, and rape; not-so obvious losses, such as moving, loss of a long-term goal, and success (loss of striving); loss related to age, such as leaving home, loss of "youth," loss of hair, and menopause; and limbo losses, such as awaiting medical tests, going through a lawsuit, and dealing with having a loved one "missing in action."

The presentation in *How to Survive the Loss of a Love* is unusual for a self-help book. Poetry, common sense, and psychologically based advice are interwoven throughout more than a hundred very brief topics that are organized according to the categories of understanding loss, surviving, healing, and growing. The topics include it's OK to feel, tomorrow will come, seek the comfort of others, touching and hugging, do the mourning now, when counseling or therapy might be helpful, nutrition, remaining distraught is no proof of love, pray, meditate, contemplate, keep a journal, take stock of the good, and your happiness is up to you.

How to Survive the Loss of a Love received a 5-star Strongly Recommended rating in the national survey. This has been a highly successful book, selling more than 2 million copies. The content is clear, succinct, and helpful, and it covers a vast range of situations involving loss. Among the many positive comments about *How to Survive the Loss of a Love* from mental health professionals is that it is the perfect book to keep handy for use as a guide when help is needed. This is a very good self-help book that can help people cope with many different types of loss.

RECOMMENDED

★ ★ ★ ★   *How to Go on Living When Someone You Love Dies* (1991) by Therese Rando. New York: Bantam.

How to Go on Living When Someone You Love Dies, originally published as *Grieving* in 1988, advises people about ways to grieve effectively when someone they love dies. Author Therese Rando, Ph.D., is a clinical psychologist and the director of a multidisciplinary team that provides therapy and consultation about loss and grief to clients. She has also developed a program for training hospice nurses that has been widely used throughout the United States.

Rando believes that there is no wrong or right way to grieve because people are so different. She describes a variety of ways to grieve and encourages readers to select the best coping strategy for them.

How to Go on Living When Someone You Love Dies is divided into five main parts. Part I, Learning about Grief, identifies what grief is, how it affects people, what factors influence grief, and how women and men experience grief differently. Part II, Grieving Different Forms of Death, explains how grief often varies depending upon what caused the death.

Part III, Grieving and Your Family, addresses the inevitable family reorganization following a family member's death and how to cope with the death of specific family members—spouse, adult loss of a parent, adult loss of a sibling, and loss of a child. Part IV, Resolving Your Grief, offers specific recommendations for getting through bereavement rituals and funerals, including information about funeral arrangements and talking about loss to others. Part V, Getting Additional Help, explains how to find effective professional and self-help group and book assistance.

How to Go on Living When Someone You Love Dies received a 4-star Recommended rating in the national survey. Its average rating was high enough to make it a 5-star book, but it wasn't evaluated by enough respondents (31). This is an excellent self-help book for learning how to cope with the death of a loved one. There are no pat, overgeneralized suggestions for how to grieve. Rando covers a variety of grief circumstances and dispenses easy-to-understand, practical advice for each.

★ ★ ★ ★   *Learning to Say Good-By* (1976) by Eda LeShan. New York: Macmillan.

Learning to Say Good-By was written to help children cope with the death of a parent. Eda LeShan is a well-known educator, family counselor, and self-help book author (see *It's Better to Be Over the Hill than Under It* in Chapter 5, Aging).

LeShan believes that children are resilient and can live through *anything* as long as they are told the truth and are allowed to share with loved ones the natural feelings people have when they are suffering. The book is a "letter" to children from LeShan, and it helps children to understand what they are probably feeling, what their surviving parent is probably feeling, and why family members are behaving so strangely. Topics addressed include what happens immediately following a parent's death, feelings of grief, recovering, and how death teaches us about life. Although written for children, *Learning to Say Good-By* can help a surviving parent to better understand children's feelings during this time of emotional upheaval.

Learning to Say Good-By received a 4-star Recommended rating in the national survey. In our death-denying and death-avoiding culture, LeShan's message is an important one: Children should be allowed to see our grief at death and should have the privilege of expressing their own grief at their own time. LeShan is an excellent writer and she sensitively communicates with children in *Learning to Say Good-By*. This is an excellent book for children who experience the death of a parent. Like *How to Go on Living When Someone You Love Dies*, the average rating of *Learning to Say Good-by* was high enough for the 5-star category, but it was not rated by enough respondents (52).

★ ★ ★ ★   *Talking about Death: A Dialogue between Parent and Child*
(rev. ed., 1976) by Earl Grollman. Boston, MA: Beacon Press.

Like *Learning to Say Good-By, Talking about Death* helps children cope
with the death of a loved one. Author Earl Grollman is the rabbi of Beth
El Temple Center, Belmont, Massachusetts. He is the author of a number of other self-help books on parent–child communication and death.

Talking about Death is a brief book (under 100 pages) that is appropriate for children of all faiths. It consists of dialogues between parents and children and is divided into two main parts, The Children's
Read-Along, which uses simple language so that even five- to nine-year-
olds can understand the messages about death and dying, and The Parent's Guide to Talking About Death, which provides answers for children's anticipated questions about death. Throughout *Talking about
Death*, parents are urged to be straightforward with their children and
are also helped to come to terms with their own feelings of loss.

Talking about Death received a 4-star Recommended rating in the
national survey. Like the other 4-star books in the death, dying, and grief
category, its average rating was high enough to be a 5-star book, but it
was rated by too few respondents (40).

DIAMONDS IN THE ROUGH

◆   *When Bad Things Happen to Good People* (1981) by Harold Kushner. New York: Schocken Books.

When Bad Things Happen to Good People provides a spiritual perspective on death, dying, and grief. Author Harold Kushner is the rabbi of
Temple Israel in Natick, Massachusetts.

Kushner wrote this book after his teenage son died from a rare disease. However, the book does not solely address parents' bereavement.
It tackles an ancient question: If there is a God who is just and all-
powerful, why does He cause good people to suffer? Western religions
have three conventional explanations for such tragedies: they are God's
punishment for sins; God is teaching us a lesson; they are part of some
divine plan that is beyond human comprehension. Kushner's choice is
to strip God of His omnipotence in order to be able to continue to see
Him as good. For Kushner, God is unable to prevent the misfortunes of
good people, but He can give us strength to bear them.

When Bad Things Happen to Good People was rated very positively but by fewer than 30 respondents (24), so it was placed in the Diamonds in the Rough category. The well-known authority on death and

dying Elisabeth Kübler-Ross said that *When Bad Things Happen to Good People* is a moving and humane approach to understanding life's trage-dies. Norman Vincent Peale, well-known theologian and positive think-ing advocate, commented that this is a book that all humanity needs and that it helps people to understand and cope with the painful vicissi-tudes of life.

♦ *Recovering from the Loss of a Child* (1982) by Katherine Donnelly. New York: Macmillan.

Recovering from the Loss of a Child tells parents and other family mem-bers how to cope with the death of a child. Author Katherine Donnelly is a professional writer who lives in New York City.

This book features excerpts from interviews with parents and si-blings of children who died through illness, accident, and suicide. It is divided into two main parts. Part I describes family members' and friends' experiences with grief; Part II is devoted to organizations that help bereaved families, from the American Association for Marriage and Fam-ily Therapy to Gold Star Mother to Sudden Infant Death Syndrome groups, and it lists the organizations and their addresses by state. A bas-ic theme of the book is that the loss of a child of any age is a tragic oc-currence and a terrible loss for all members of the family.

The mental health professionals' ratings in the national survey place *Recovering from the Loss of a Child* in the Diamonds in the Rough category. The book's supporters said that the authors present a sensitive portrayal of a family's struggle to cope with the loss of a child; they also commented positively about the book's extensive list of support organi-zations. Critics said that the book leans too heavily on tragic case histo-ries and quotations from bereaved parents. They faulted the book's lack of depth and originality, and some mental health experts questioned the validity of the advice dispensed. For example, can parents truthfully promise a frightened surviving son that the death of a sibling "occurred for a specific reason and will not happen to him, his parents, or to his older brothers and sisters"?

♦ *Helping Children Grieve* (1991) by Theresa Huntley, Minneapolis, MN: Augsburg Fortress.

Helping Children Grieve, as the title suggests, is about helping children cope with death—their own and the death of a loved one. Theresa Hunt-ley is employed as a prenatal counselor at the Minneapolis Seton Center. She also has worked for two hospitals as a registered nurse in pediatrics and a children's loss and grief specialist.

Helping Children Grieve presents a developmental approach to helping children cope with death. Huntley begins by discussing how children under 3 years of age understand death. She then describes how death is perceived by children in the age periods from 3 to 6 years, 6 to 10 years, 10 to 12 years, and early and late adolescence. Huntley says that children of different ages have different thoughts about the nature of death. For example, toddlers come to understand death as an extension of "all gone," while 10-year-olds often view a loved one's death as a punishment for some misdeed.

Advice is given on how to talk about death with children, and common behaviors and feelings children show when faced with death are discussed. Among the common behaviors and feelings are denial, panic, anger, guilt, regression, hyperactivity, and withdrawal. Adults are advised to encourage children to ask them questions about death and to answer these questions as honestly as possible. Fears of the dying child are presented, as are ways for adults to care for the dying child's basic emotional needs.

Helping Children Grieve was placed in the Diamonds in the Rough category. Huntley gives adults sound, clear advice about helping children cope with their own death or the death of a loved one.

◆   *Living through Personal Crisis* (1984) by Ann Stearns. Chicago: The Thomas More Press.

Living through Personal Crisis provides advice about coping with many different kinds of loss, especially the death of a loved one. Author Ann Stearns has a doctorate in clinical psychology from Union Graduate School. She is a professor of psychology at Essex Community College in Baltimore, Maryland, and is a member of the Family Practice Training Program at Franklin Square Hospital.

Using case studies to document her ideas, Stearns stresses that it is common for the bereaved to blame themselves and that the grieving person will undoubtedly experience such physical symptoms as aches and pains or eating and sleeping problems. Stearns advises readers not to hide their feelings but to get them out in the open, to be good to themselves, and surround themselves with caring, sensitive people.

Stearns suggests when to seek professional help, how to find it, and how to evaluate progress. She closes the book with the image of a bird rising from the ashes as a metaphor for successfully overcoming the sense of loss, but she reminds readers that their scars will never completely disappear. An appendix answers commonly asked questions about grieving.

Living through Personal Crisis made the Diamonds in the Rough category. Several mental health professionals felt that Stearns's book provides a good overview of how grief works in variety of loss circumstances (loss of limb, rape, loss of personal possessions in a fire, as well as the loss of a loved one through death).

♦ *Sudden Infant Death: Enduring the Loss* (1991) by John DeFrain, Linda Ernst, Deanne Jakub, and Jacque Taylor. Lexington, MA: D. C. Heath.

Sudden Infant Death focuses on how to cope with the death of a child through sudden infant death syndrome (SIDS). Author John DeFrain, Ph.D., is a professor of family science at the University of Nebraska—Lincoln; Linda Ernst, Ph.D., is a professor of family life at the University of Minnesota—St.Paul and St. Olaf's College; Deanne Jakub, M.S., is an adoption and unplanned pregnancy counselor for the Lutheran Family Services in Omaha, Nebraska; and Jacque Taylor, M.S., is director of the Office on Family Violence and Sexual Assault in Riverton, Wyoming.

SIDS is a condition that occurs when an infant stops breathing, usually during the night, and dies suddenly without apparent cause. SIDS is the major cause of infant death from birth to 1 year of age, claiming as many as 10,000 infants per year in the United States alone. The tragic loss of a baby to SIDS affects families in many ways, and it is the authors' intention to help these families recapture the meaning and direction of their lives. The book's contents are based on interviews with 392 mothers, fathers, and siblings who have directly experienced the devastation of SIDS.

Sudden Infant Death recounts stories of "the day the baby died" and how parents mistakenly feel an overwhelming sense of guilt that their baby died of neglect. Grief symptoms, effects of SIDS on marital relationships, and the suffering of grandparents are also covered. Suggestions for how friends and family members can be supportive during this difficult time are given. The fear of having another child and having it die is dealt with at length.

Sudden Infant Death was placed in the Diamonds in the Rough category. Some mental health experts believed that the book provides extensive knowledge about SIDS and that the many personal stories can help family members who experience SIDS themselves understand and cope better with their own situation. The book also is helpful to friends of a family who experience SIDS, providing them with knowledge of SIDS and support strategies.

◆   *Up from Grief* (1969) by Bernadine Kreis and Alice Pattie. Minneapolis, MN: Winston Press.

Up from Grief provides advice about coping with the death of another person. Bernadine Kreis is a free-lance writer and Alice Pattie is a program supervisor for the elderly on Long Island in New York.

Following the loss of her husband, father, and mother, Kreis tried to sort out her feelings of bereavement in the hope that others might benefit from her experience and the experiences of others on the way "up from grief." She and coauthor Alice Pattie interviewed approximately 500 people to discover what happens to people when a close friend or relative dies. *Up from Grief* discusses three stages of grief—shock, suffering, recovery—with most attention given to recovery. Interviews with six clergyman are reported toward the end of the book.

Up from Grief barely made the Diamonds in the Rough category. Mental health professionals who like the book said that it is filled with anecdotes from individuals and professionals that can help people cope with grief in their own life. However, the consensus of mental health experts in the national survey was that *How to Go On Living When Someone You Love Dies* by Therese Rando is a better choice.

NEUTRAL

★ ★ ★   *On Death and Dying* (1969) by Elisabeth Kübler-Ross. New York: Macmillan.

On Death and Dying is an extremely well-known book about how to cope when facing one's own death and about the stages dying people go through. Author Elisabeth Kübler-Ross, M.D., is a psychiatrist and has been the medical director of the Family Service and Mental Health Center of South Cook County in Illinois.

In the 1960s, Kübler-Ross and her students studied terminally ill patients to learn how they faced and coped with the crisis of their own impending death. Kübler-Ross and her staff interviewed 200 of these patients, focusing on them as human beings rather than bodies to be treated. Kübler-Ross concluded that people go through five stages as they face death:

1. Denial and isolation: The person denies that death is really going to take place.
2. Anger: The dying person's denial can no longer be maintained and gives way to anger, resentment, rage, and envy.

3. Bargaining: The person develops the hope that somehow death can be postponed or delayed.
4. Depression: The person accepts the certainty of death but is unhappy about it.
5. Acceptance: The person develops a sense of peace about accepting the inevitable and often wants to be left alone.

Kübler-Ross presents the five stages of dying in considerable detail and then discusses the effects of impending death on the dying person's family. Suggestions for therapy with the terminally ill are included.

On Death and Dying received a 3-star Neutral rating in the national survey, just missing the 4-star Recommended category. The book was one of the most frequently rated in the entire survey: 355 mental health professionals evaluated it. The book's enthusiasts said that Kübler-Ross's book is a classic in the field of death and dying and that her approach has helped millions of people cope effectively with impending death. Critics of the book said that no one has been able to confirm that people go through the stages of dying in the order Kübler-Ross proposes. Kübler-Ross herself feels that she has been misinterpreted, saying that she never intended the stages to be taken as an invariant sequence of steps toward death, although she also says that in her experience, most dying people go through the stages in the order she presents them. Other critics commented that she later discredited herself with her support of the existence of the near-death experience.

★ ★ ★   *The Enigma of Suicide* (1991) by George Colt. New York: Summit Books.

The Enigma of Suicide deals with a number of aspects of suicide. Author George Colt is a staff writer for *Life* magazine.

Colt's book is based on interviews with several hundred people who attempted suicide, are the survivors of suicide victims, or are mental health professionals who treat suicidal cases. Colt also examines contemporary medical and psychological research on suicide, as well as the poetry and prose of suicidal writers, in search of clues to the causes of suicide, its effects on friends and families, how to recognize indicative behavior and prevent suicide, and how survivors can cope in its aftermath.

This lengthy book (almost 600 pages) is divided into six main parts that explore adolescent suicide, the history of suicide, the range of self-destructive behaviors, prevention, the right-to-die movement, and the experiences of survivors. Personal narratives are interwoven throughout the book.

The Enigma of Suicide received a 3-star Neutral rating in the national survey. The book was published just before the survey was conducted and was rated by only 13 respondents. *The Enigma of Suicide* is exhaustive, which is both a strength and a weakness. The strength lies in the coverage of a wide range of important issues related to suicide, the weakness in an almost unwieldy volume. For any reader willing to plow through its many pages, the result will be extensive knowledge about suicide.

★ ★ ★   *The Widow's Handbook* (1988) by Charlotte Foehner and Carol Cozart. Golden, CO: Fulcrum.

The Widow's Handbook gives recommendations on how to cope with the death of a husband. Authors Charlotte Foehner and Carol Cozart both are widows with children.

Following the deaths of their husbands, Foehner began studying financial investment and tax preparation and Cozart started her first full-time job. While *The Widow's Handbook* provides some emotional support for widows, offers suggestions for rearing children, tells widows how to care for themselves, and discusses changes in relationships, the book's main emphasis is on financial and procedural issues widows are likely to encounter. How to make funeral arrangements, how to select an attorney and a financial advisory team, an executor's duties, how to file claims for life insurance and survivor benefits, how to get credit and checking accounts in order, and how to maintain a house and car are some of the practical topics that are covered. The authors include sample letters widows need to write and frequently examine questions that crop up in a widow's life.

The Widow's Handbook received a 3-star Neutral rating in the national survey. The book is very good at what it attempts—providing widows with sound advice about financial and procedural matters—but it includes only minimal advice about the psychological and emotional dimensions of coping with the loss of a husband.

STRONGLY NOT RECOMMENDED

†   *Widowed* (1990) by Joyce Brothers. New York: Simon & Schuster.

Widowed is a personal account of coping with the death of a husband. Joyce Brothers, Ph.D., is a well-known media psychologist and self-help book author. She formerly taught at Hunter College and Columbia University in New York City.

Joyce Brothers's husband of more than 30 years, Milton Brothers, died of cancer in 1989. She tells the story of how she coped with the despair and loneliness that ensued and how she gradually put the pieces of her life back together.

Widowed is divided into three parts. Part I, From Wife to Widow, recounts the history of the Brothers's marriage, her husband's struggle with cancer, and his eventual death. Part II, Through the Tunnel of Grief, chronicles her grief and recovery. And Part III, What Everyone Should Know About Grief, offers advice to anyone who has lost a loved one, with special attention given to widows and widowers.

Widowed was given a negative average rating by the mental health professionals in the national survey, placing it in the Strongly Not Recommended category. Critics of the book said that Brothers's ordeal was neither especially intense nor trenchant and would probably not have merited publication had the widow not been famous. They also commented that her account says little that has not already been said in the memoirs of other widows.

† *Final Exit: The Practicalities of Self-Deliverance and Assisted Suicide for the Dying* (1991) by Derek Humphrey. Eugene, OR: The Hemlock Society.

Final Exit deals with a specific aspect of suicide: telling people who are dying how to commit suicide themselves or assisting in another dying person's voluntary death. Derek Humphrey was a journalist in England and the United States before founding the Hemlock Society in 1980 in California after he assisted his first wife to escape a lingering death from cancer by taking her own life. Humphrey has written or been coauthor of ten books on civil liberties, racial integration, and voluntary euthanasia. From 1988 to 1990, he was president of the World Federation of Right to Die Societies and still serves on the board.

Final Exit is subtitled *The Practicalities of Self-Deliverance and Assisted Suicide for the Dying*. The book advocates suicide as the most adaptive course for escaping the pain and emotional difficulties of lingering death. Humphrey uses charts to inform readers about lethal dosages for 18 prescription drugs, primarily pain killers and sleeping pills; offers advice on asphyxiation by plastic bag or auto exhaust; and discusses the use of cyanide. Specific recommendations are made about the details of suicide or assisting someone else in suicide. For example, Humphrey writes that mixing pills with yogurt or pudding prevents vomiting or passing out before a lethal dose is reached. He also says not to turn off a telephone answering machine because changes in habits alert others that something is different. He advises family members not to give direct assistance because they risk prosecution. And he also tells heirs to object to an autopsy.

Final Exit was the lowest-rated book in the Death, Dying, and Grief category; it received a negative average rating, placing it in the Strongly Not Recommended category. *Final Exit* is highly controversial and touches on ethical issues that have been debated by philosophers, poets, health professionals, and lay people. Is assisted suicide an evil killing act or a loving merciful act? Humphrey states that assisting people who have a terminal illness and are suffering unbearable pain to die with dignity is loving and merciful. Critics, however, say that Humphrey is naive to assume that assisted suicide will occur only with the terminally ill. Some families have even accused Humphrey of causing a healthy family member's suicide. The consensus of the mental health professionals in the national survey was that *Final Exit* is a harmful self-help book because it doesn't adequately take into account the psychological consequences for survivors and potential abuses by depressed persons who are not terminally ill.

WORTH A FURTHER LOOK

◐ ◐   *The Bereaved Parent* (1977) by Harriet Schiff. New York: Crown.

The Bereaved Parent provides advice for parents about how to cope with the death of their child. Harriet Schiff's son died at the age of 10 and she and her husband were comforted by no one at the time. She wrote this book to offer guidance and support to other parents of a child who dies.

Schiff begins *The Bereaved Parent* by recounting her experience with her son's death, then quickly moves on to describe what parents feel when a child dies and explains how important it is for them to get support from other parents. Schiff weaves her own experiences with those of other parents in descriptions of the funeral process, the development of grief over time, the guilt and powerlessness parents often feel, the effects on a marriage and surviving siblings, communication, and getting on with life.

The Bereaved Parent received very high positive ratings but was rated by only a five respondents, hence its relegation to Worth a Further Look. Mental health professionals who like the book, including death and dying expert Elisabeth Kübler-Ross, said that it provides good advice, support, and reassurance for bereaved parents.

○ ○   *The Grief Recovery Handbook: A Step-By-Step Program for Moving Beyond Loss* (1988) by John James and Frank Cherry. New York: Harper & Row.

The Grief Recovery Handbook describes how to deal with the death of a loved one. It is written from the perspective of two people who have endured considerable personal loss. Coauthors John James and Frank Cherry are cofounders of the Grief Recovery Institute, have backgrounds in counseling and education, and conduct seminars for grief recovery outreach programs across the United States and Canada.

This book presents a step-by-step recovery plan that has helped many people recover from significant loss. The plan is based on the belief that grief is not well understood and is often neglected. The authors stress that grieving is a growth process.

The book is divided into three main parts. In Part I, the acceptance of devastating grief is presented as a positive reaction to loss that prepares the griever for recovery. In Part II, the authors advocate choosing to grow through grief rather than shutting it out or seeking short-term, ineffective relief. Part III lists the five stages in recovering from grief: gaining awareness, accepting responsibility, identifying recovery communications, taking action, and moving beyond loss.

The Grief Recovery Handbook was positively rated in the national survey but by only six respondents. It provides considerable insight into expressing and coping with feelings in the aftermath of the death of a loved one.

○●   *A Grief Observed* (1961) by C. S. Lewis. New York: The Seabury Press.

A Grief Observed is a spiritual account of one person's experience with grief following the death of a spouse. C. S. Lewis was a professor at Cambridge University in England. He was an essayist and wrote a number of other books, such as *Miracles, The Great Divorce,* and *Mere Christianity.*

This very brief volume (only 60 pages) describes Lewis's grief following the death of his wife from cancer. Originally published under the pseudonym of N. W. Clerk just before Lewis's own death, *A Grief Observed* reveals the inner turmoil of his grief. The author says that he wrote these memoirs as a "defense against total collapse, a safety valve."

A Grief Observed received a positive rating in the national survey but was evaluated by only five respondents. The book is a unique account of a profound human experience from the spiritual perspective of a gifted writer. It offers no advice for recovery but rather presents a moving description of human vulnerability and powerful emotions.

CONCLUSIONS

In summary, we recommend:

- On coping with loss of any kind, including death:

  ★ ★ ★ ★ ★   *How to Survive the Loss of a Love* by Melba Colgrove, Harold Bloomfield, and Peter McWilliams

- On coping with impending death (your own or someone else's):

  ★ ★ ★   *On Death and Dying* by Elisabeth Kübler-Ross

- On how to grieve, the stages of grief, and recovery from grief:

  ★ ★ ★ ★ ★   *How to Go on Living When Someone You Love Dies* by Therese Rando

- On grieving over the death of a child:

  ◗◗   *The Bereaved Parent* by Harriet Schiff

- On sudden infant death syndrome:

  ◆   *Sudden Infant Death* by John DeFrain, Linda Ernst, Deanne Jakub, and Jacque Taylor

- For widows who need financial and procedural advice:

  ★ ★ ★   *The Widow's Handbook* by Charlotte Foehner and Carol Cozart

- On helping a child cope with grief:

  ★ ★ ★ ★   *Learning to Say Good-By* by Eda LeShan

  ★ ★ ★ ★   *Talking about Death* by Earl Grollman

  ◆   *Helping Children Grieve* by Theresa Huntley

- On the causes of suicide and its prevention:

  ★ ★ ★   *The Enigma of Suicide* by George Colt

- A spiritually-based approach to death, dying, and grief:

  ◆   *When Bad Things Happen to Good People* by Harold Kushner

  ◆   *A Grief Observed* by C. S. Lewis

CHAPTER FOURTEEN

Depression

In our stress-filled world, *depression* is a frequently used term. When someone asks you what is wrong as they look at your gloomy face, you might respond, "I feel depressed—about myself, about my life." Everyone is down in the dumps some of the time, but most people, after a few hours, days, or weeks, snap out of their despondent mood and begin again to cope effectively with life's stresses. However, some people are not as fortunate. They have major depression, a mood disorder that involves feeling deeply unhappy, demoralized, self-derogatory, and bored. When people have major depression, they often do not feel physically well, lose stamina, have a poor appetite, are listless, and are unmotivated. Major depression is so common in the United States that it has been called the common cold of mental disorders. More than 250,000 people are hospitalized every year for the disorder. Students, housewives, executives, laborers—no one is immune to depression, not even F. Scott Fitzgerald, Ernest Hemingway, Abraham Lincoln, or Winston Churchill, all of whom experienced major depression.

While major depression is the most common mood disorder, some people also experience bipolar disorder, characterized by extreme mood swings between depression and mania. In the mania phase, people are exuberant, have tireless stamina, and tend toward excess.

Just as with anxiety, controversy swirls about whether depression is psychologically and experientially determined and therefore capable of being treated through psychotherapy or is biologically determined and thus can be treated only with drug therapy.

The widely varying topics of self-help books on coping with depression fall in seven different categories: cognitive therapy approaches to treatment; behavioral approaches to treatment; biological and drug-based approaches to treatment; dysthymic disorder (a long-lasting, relatively

---

Depression
BOOK RATINGS IN THE NATIONAL SURVEY

Strongly Recommended	★★★★★	*Feeling Good* by David Burns
	★★★★★	*The Feeling Good Handbook* by David Burns
	★★★★★	*Cognitive Therapy and the Emotional Disorders* by Aaron Beck
Neutral	★★★	*Getting Un-Depressed* by Gary Emery
	★★★	*How to Cope with Depression* by Raymond DePaulo and Keith Ablow
	★★★	*When the Blues Won't Go Away* by Robert Hirschfeld
	★★★	*From Sad to Glad* by Nathan Kline
Not Recommended	★★	*You Mean I Don't Have to Feel This Way!* by Colette Dowling
	★★	*Happiness Is a Choice* by Frank Minirth and Paul Meier
	★	*The Good News about Depression* by Mark Gold

---

mild form of depression); women and depression; spiritual/emotional approaches to treatment; and seasonal depression.

Three books in the survey advocate a cognitive therapy approach to depression: *Feeling Good: The New Mood Therapy* by David Burns; *The Feeling Good Handbook* by David Burns; and *Cognitive Therapy and the Emotional Disorders* by Aaron Beck. A fourth book—*How to Stubbornly Refuse to Make Yourself Miserable About Anything, Yes, Anything!* by Albert Ellis—is profiled in Worth a Further Look.

No books on the behavioral approach to depression made the final ratings. However, the behavioral approach of Peter Lewinsohn and his colleagues, presented in *Control Your Depression*, is reviewed in Worth a Further Look section.

Four books take a biological and drug-based approach to depression: *How to Cope with Depression* by J. DePaulo and Keith Ablow, *From Sad to Glad* by Nathan Kline, *You Mean I Don't Have to Feel This Way!* by Colette Dowling, and *The Good News About Depression* by Mark Gold.

One book in the survey evaluates dysthymic disorder: *When the Blues Won't Go Away* by Robert Hirschfeld.

One book about depression is written exclusively about women and depression: *Getting Undepressed* by Gary Emery.

One book describes an emotional/spiritually based approach to depression: *Happiness Is a Choice* by Frank Minerth and Paul Meier.

One book focuses on a specific type of depression—seasonal depression: *Seasons of the Mind* by Norman Rosenthal.

STRONGLY RECOMMENDED

★ ★ ★ ★ ★   *Feeling Good: The New Mood Therapy* (1980) by David Burns. New York: Signet.

Feeling Good is a cognitive therapy appproach to coping with depression. Author David Burns, M.D., is a clinical psychiatrist, teacher, and researcher at the Presbyterian Medical Center of Philadelphia.

The cognitive therapy approach Burns describes was developed by psychiatrists at the University of Pennsylvania School of Medicine, led by Aaron Beck, who was Burns's teacher. Cognitive therapists believe that people become depressed because of their faulty thinking, which triggers self-destructive moods. The faulty thinking includes automatic negative thoughts, self-defeating statements that people often make when they enounter problems. Examples of faulty automatic negative thoughts include all-or-nothing thinking (if a situation is anything less than perfect, it is a total failure), discounting the positive (positive experiences "don't count"), jumping to conclusions (making negative interpretations when there are no facts to support them), magnification (exaggerating the importance of problems and shortcomings), and personalization and blame (taking personal responsibility for events that aren't entirely under your conrol).

Cognitive therapists like Burns argue that the key to coping with depression is identifying and restructuring faulty negative thinking. In *Feeling Good*, Burns outlines techniques people can use to identify and combat the false assumptions that underlie faulty negative thinking.

Feeling Good is divided into seven main parts. Part I, Theory and Research, is a journey through the development of the cognitive therapy approach and why it is superior to the psychodynamic approach, how to diagnose your moods, and why you feel the way you think. Part II, Practical Applications, provides insight into how to start building self-esteem, how to stand up for your rights when you are unjustly criticized, how to cope with anger, and how to defeat guilt. Part III, Realistic Depressions, distinguishes between normal bouts of sadness and serious depression. Part IV, Prevention and Personal Growth, explores how to cope with depression related to approval, love, work, and perfectionism. Part V, Defeating Hopelessness and Suicide, examines the nature of suicide and explains why the best choice is to live. Part VI, Coping with the Stresses and Strains of Daily Living, includes Burns's revelations of instances in which he succumbed to depression (sometimes after sessions with thorny patients) and had to prescribe cognitive therapy for himself. Part IV, The Chemistry of Mood, presents a consumer's guide to antidepressant drug therapy.

Feeling Good is peppered with self-assessment tests, self-help forms, and charts. The self-assessment techniques include the widely used Beck Depression Inventory, an anger scale, and a dysfuntional attitude scale. The self-help forms and charts include a daily record of dysfunctional thoughts, an antiprocrastination sheet, a pleaure-predicting sheet, an anger cost/benefit analysis, and an antiperfection sheet.

Feeling Good was the highest-rated book in the depression category of the national survey, receiving the 5-star Strongly Recommended rating. This is an outstanding self-help book that has sold more than two million copies since its publication in 1980. Burns's easy-to-read writing style, extensive use of examples and charts, and enthusiasm give readers a clear understanding of cognitive therapy and the confidence to try out its techniques. The pioneer of the cognitive therapy approach to depression, Aaron Beck, is laudatory in his praise of *Feeling Good* in a preface to the book. Beck says that readers of this book should be able to apply to their own problems the techniques he and other cognitive therapists have successfully used with their patients.

★ ★ ★ ★ ★   *The Feeling Good Handbook* (1989) by David Burns. New York: Plume.

The Feeling Good Handbook is Burns's sequel to *Feeling Good*. Burns says that one of the most exciting developments since the publication of *Feeling Good* in 1980 is the discovery that cognitive therapy, which he calls the new mood therapy, can help people with an entire range of mood problems they encounter in their everyday lives. These include feelings of insecurity and inferiority, procrastination, guilt, stress, frustration, and irritability. In *The Feeling Good Handbook* Burns explains why we are plagued by irrational worries and how to conquer our worst fears without having to rely on addictive tranquilizers or alcohol. Burns also describes another important application of cognitive therapy in recent years—to problems in personal relationships especially marital and couple relationships.

The Feeling Good Handbook is scheduled, and the reader is asked to complete a number of self-assessment tests once a week, just as Burns's patients do, to monitor progress. The tests ask about thoughts, feelings, and actions in a variety of circumstances that typically make people angry, sad, frustrated, or anxious. Then Burns suggests new and different ways to communicate or think about the circumstances.

The Feeling Good Handbook is divided into six main parts. Part I, Understanding Your Moods, shows readers how to change the way they feel, how to measure their moods, how to diagnose their moods, and whether they should change the way they feel. Part II, Feeling Good About Yourself, discusses how to conquer depression and build self-esteem, and Part III, Feeling Confident, outlines how to conquer anxiety, fears, and phobias. Part IV, Feeling Good Together, evaluates how to strengthen relationships through improved communication. Part V, Mood-Altering Medications, describes mood-altering drugs, and Part VI, For Therapists (and Curious Patients) Only, suggests ways of dealing with difficult patients..

In summary, there are three main differences between *The Feeling Good Handbook* and *Feeling Good: The New Mood Therapy*. *The Feeling Good Handbook* covers a wider array of problems (anxiety and relationships as well as depression), it includes daily logs to fill out, and it was written almost a decade later and thus presents more recent developments in cognitive therapy.

The Feeling Good Handbook was rated very positively in the national survey; it was a 5-star Strongly Recommended book. It can be used as an adjunct to *Feeling Good* by people who want to learn how to cope with depression. Cognitive therapy pioneer Albert Ellis said that *The Feeling Good Handbook* carries the very useful ideas of *Feeling Good* into a number of other important areas of life. Marvin Goldfried, Professor of Psychiatry at the State University of New York at Stony Brook, commented that Burns has written an invaluable guide to dealing with fears, anxieties, panic attacks, procrastination, and communication problems.

★ ★ ★ ★ ★   *Cognitive Therapy and the Emotional Disorders* (1976) by Aaron Beck. New York: International Universities Press.

Cognitive Therapy and the Emotional Disorders, as the title implies, presents a cognitive therapy approach to depression and other emotional disorders. Author Aaron Beck, M.D., pioneered the cognitive therapy approach to depression. He is a professor of psychiatry at the University of Pennsylvania School of Medicine.

Beck describes the cognitive triad that consists of negative thoughts about the self, about ongoing experience, and about the future. Depressive individuals' negative thoughts about the self are beliefs that they are defective, worthless, and inadequate. Negative thoughts about ongoing experience are interpretations that what happens is bad. Negative thoughts about the future view the future as hopeless.

Beck believes that systematic errors in logical thinking, each of which darkens the person's experiences, produce depression. These errors include drawing a conclusion when there is little or no evidence to support it; focusing on an insignificant detail while ignoring the more important features of a situation; drawing global conclusions about worth, ability, or performance on the basis of a single fact; magnifying small bad events and minimizing large good events; and incorrectly engaging in self-blame for bad events.

Beck's cognitive therapy attempts to counter these distorted thoughts. People are taught to identify and correct the flawed thinking and are trained to conquer problems and master situations they previously thought were insurmountable. *Cognitive Therapy and the Emotional Disorders* describes Beck's approach to depression in considerable detail and includes applications to other disorders—anxiety, fears, obsessions, and psychosomatic disorders—as well.

Cognitive Therapy and the Emotional Disorders received a 5-star Strongly Recommended rating in the national survey. Respected cognitive behavior therapist Michael Mahoney said that Beck's book is an important book, practically and theoretically. As was Beck's other 5-star book—*Anxiety Disorders and Phobias*—which was profiled in Chapter 7, *Cognitive Therapy and the Emotional Disorders* was written primarily for a professional rather than a self-help audience. Many of the ideas in Beck's book are presented in a much easier-to-read fashion in Burns's *Feeling Good* and *The Feeling Good Handbook*. *Cognitive Therapy and the Emotional Disorders* appeals primarily to the professional clinical community and to the very knowledgeable, intellectually challenged lay person.

NEUTRAL

★ ★ ★   *Getting Un-Depressed: How a Woman Can Change Her Life through Cognitive Therapy* (rev. ed., 1988) by Gary Emery. New York: Touchstone.

Getting Un-Depressed is a cognitive therapy approach for women in coping effectively with depression. Author Gary Emery, Ph.D., trained under Aaron Beck at the University of Pennsylvania School of Medicine. He is director of the Los Angeles Center for Cogniive Therapy and a professor in the Department of Psychiatry at UCLA.

A man's lifetime risk of developing major depression is about 10%.

The risk is much greater for women—almost 25%. In fact, the most common psychiatric diagnosis for both black and white women is depression. Men and women often get depressed for different reasons—men for career problems and loss of sexual prowess, women for relationship problems (i.e., difficulties with boyfriends, husbands, parents, and children).

Emery explains at the beginning of the book what depression is and how cognitive therapy can help. Then he describes how women can get immediate relief from their symptoms (inactivity, negative feelings, thinking problems, and physical problems) and improve their state of mind. Next, the author focuses on ways to overcome common complications of depression (weight gain, alcohol and drug dependency, and relationship problems). After this, women learn that they can avoid future depression by working on the psychological causes of depression, which according to Emery are underlying negative beliefs and ineffective ways of handling stress. Finally, Emery outlines how women can lead more self-reliant and self-directed lives.

Getting Un-Depressed received a 3-star Neutral rating in the national survey, just missing the 4-star Recommended rating. According to Aaron Beck in a preface to *Getting Un-Depressed,* most popular books on depression merely describe the problem. Beck says that Emery's book is unique in clearly spelling out proven techniques that have been used to help women overcome depression. Alan Roberts, Ph.D., of the Scripps Clinic and Research Foundation, commented that *Getting Un-Depressed* is the only self-help book he has ever recommended to his clients.

★ ★ ★   *How to Cope with Depression* (1989) by Raymond DePaulo and Keith Ablow. New York: McGraw Hill.

How to Cope with Depression is subtitled *A Complete Guide for You and Your Family,* but it is primarily about the biological causes of depression and the treatment of depression through drug therapy. Author Raymond DePaulo, M.D., is director of The Center for Affective Disorders at the Johns Hopkins Hospital in Baltimore, Maryland. Coauthor Keith Ablow, M.D., is a physician and journalist who graduated from the Johns Hopkins Medical School.

How to Cope with Depression is divided into four main parts. Part I, Depression: What We Know, defines depression and bipolar disorder (the authors call it manic-depressive illness) and describes the causes of depression as biological. Part II, The Experience of Depression, portrays the nature of depression from the perspective of the patient, the family, and the physician. Part III, The Four Perspectives of Depression, evaluates the disease perspective, the personality perspective, the behavior perspective, and the life story perspective, and Part IV, Current Treatments, persents the authors view of how depression should be treated.

How to Cope with Depression received a 3-star Neutral rating in the national survey. It was not widely known: only 20 respondents evaluated it. The title of the book not-withstanding, the book is less a guide to coping with depression than a primer on possible causes, treatments, and professional perspectives. The authors make clear their own view: Depression is a physical disease with genetic, biological causes that can be successfully treated only through drug therapy. Other therapies are given token discussion and are said to be useful only as supplements to drug therapy. Cognitive therapy is inappropriately discussed under behavior therapy, given a scant several pages of coverage, and then dismissed. Hence, the subtitle of the book, *A Complete Guide*, is a misnomer.

The book provides an excellent portrayal of the biological, drug-based therapy approach to depression. Because clinical and counseling psychologists do not have medical degrees, they cannot use drug therapy with their clients, while psychiatrists, who have a medical background, can. Had more psychiatrists been in the national survey, *How to Cope with Depression* would undoubtedly have been given higher marks. For example, Carol Nadelson, M.D., past president of the American Psychiatric Association, said that *How to Cope with Depression* provides a wealth of information on the conceptualization, diagnosis, and treatment of depression and offers hope to those affected.

★ ★ ★   *When the Blues Won't Go Away* (1991) by Robert Hirschfeld. New York: Macmillan.

When the Blues Won't Go Away is about one form of depression—dysthymic disorder—that is long lasting and relatively mild. Robert Hirschfeld, M.D., is a psychiatrist who is professor and chair of the Department of Psychiatry and Behavioral Sciences at the University of Texas Medical Branch at Galveston. He has published numerous research papers on depression and is recognized as a leading authority on the treatment of depression.

In the first several chapters, Hirschfeld describes the rut that people with dysthymic disorder (DD) get themselves into and what they do to stay in that rut. Many characteristics of DD resemble those of major depression, but DD's symptoms are less severe and usually longer lasting. A person who has been a blue mood most of the time for two years or more, and the mood has not lifted for more than two months at a time, probably has DD. Most DD sufferers have difficulty pinpointing why they are down in the dumps all the time. DD involves the way people think, feel, act, and relate to other people. People with DD continue to function at home and work but not at the level they once did. A recent study conducted by the National Institute of Mental Health found that approximately 3 to 5% of Americans suffer from this disorder.

Most of Hirschfeld's book is devoted to getting rid of dysthymic disorder. Hirschfeld does an excellent job of presenting a variety of strategies to help people overcome the blues. He says that DD—and any long-lasting blue mood, for that matter—can be overcome in a short period of time. The author outlines self-help strategies and therapies that are tailor-made for such problems. He also discusses helpful antidepressant medications; and he shows how a combination of drug therapy and psychotherapy/self-help can be effective.

When the Blues Won't Go Away received a 3-star Neutral rating in the national survey. The book came out just before the survey was conducted, so only a small number of mental health profesionals rated the book (13). We believe that *When the Blues Won't Go Away* provides a well-balanced analysis of a specific type of depression—long-lasting, relatively mild depression.

★ ★ ★   *From Sad to Glad* (1974) by Nathan Kline. New York: G. P. Putnam's Sons.

From Sad to Glad is about the biological basis of depression and its treatment through drug therapy. Author Nathan Kline, M.D., has been a professor of psychiatry at Columbia University College of Physicians and Surgeons, and he has been on the staffs of several prestigious psychiatric hospitals. In the 1960s and 1970s, Kline was a pioneer in the use of antidepressant drugs for reducing depression. At the time his book was published, Kline estimated that he had treated one of every ten thousand New Yorkers!

In *From Sad to Glad*, Kline outlines the social history of depression, the chemical processes in the brain involved in depression, and the misapplications of psychoanalytic methods.

From Sad to Glad just barely received a 3-star Neutral rating in the national survey. Critics said that the book is seriously dated and is of only historical interest.

NOT RECOMMENDED

★ ★   *You Mean I Don't Have to Feel This Way?* (1991) by Colette Dowling. New York: Charles Scribner & Sons.

You Mean I Don't Have to Feel This Way? is a depression book that emphasizes the biological basis of depression and its treatment through drugs. Author Colette Dowling is a professional writer and is also the author of *The Cinderella Complex.*

Dowling argues that depression, as well as panic disorder, addictions, and a host of other mental disorders, are due not to disturbing childhood experiences or to psychological weaknesses but rather to biochemical changes in the brain. She presents research on brain chemistry to document that a lack of serotonin—a natural "feel-good" chemical—is the culprit in an array of mental disorders. She says that alcoholics are attempting to replace the missing chemical and can be helped more by drug therapy than by the AA Twelve-Steps or other nonmedical treatments. Similarly, according to Dowling, people with chronic depression and anxiety can be cured by taking antidepressant drugs. Dowling witnessed the development of severe depression in both her husband and her daughter and saw them both successfully overcome depression through drug therapy.

You Mean I Don't Have to Feel This Way? received a 2-star Not Recommended rating in the national survey. Several of the mental health professionals commented that while antidepressant drugs have helped many people cope with depression, they are not the panacea Dowling thinks they are. They also stressed that the evidence for lack of the neurotransmitter serotonin as the cause of depression and a host of other mental disorders is not nearly as strong as Dowling leads readers to believe.

★ ★   *Happiness Is a Choice* (1978) by Frank Minerth and Paul Meier. Grand Rapids, MI: Baker Book House.

Happiness Is a Choice is the only book in the depression category of the national survey that advocates an emotional/spiritual approach to coping with depression. Authors Frank Minerth, M.D., and Paul Meier, M.D., are psychiatrists in Richardson, Texas, where they treat depressed clients at the Richardson Medical Center. They have written or cowritten a number of other books on a wide range of mental health problems.

Happiness Is a Choice is a blend of psychiatry and conservative religion. The book is divided into three main parts: Part I, What Is Depression?; Part II, What Causes Depression?; and Part III, How Can One Overcome Depression? Minerth and Meir conclude that the best way to get rid of depression is through religious means. They begin a list of steps to take in overcoming depression with "Commit your life daily to the purpose of glorifying Jesus Christ." The other six steps are also religion-based.

Happiness Is a Choice received a 2-star Not Recommended rating in the national survey. Critics of the book said that the psychiatric part of the book is impoverished and dated. The book appeals only to individuals with a Christian orientation. Several mental health professionals also commented that the step-by-step guide to counseling depressed persons could be dangerous in the hands of overly zealous, untrained religious counselors.

★ *The Good News about Depression: Cures and Treatments in the New Age of Psychiatry* (1986) by Mark Gold. New York: Villard.

The Good News about Depression is about the biological basis of depression and its treatment through drug therapy. Mark Gold, M.D., is a psychiatrist and Director of Research at Fair Oaks Hospital in Summit, New Jersey, and Delray Beach, Florida.

Subtitled *Cures and Treatments in the New Age of Psychiatry*, *The Good News about Depression* describes new insights in medical diagnosis and treatment of depression. The book is divided into five main sections. The titles of the first two parts speak for themselves: Part I, What Is a Psychiatrist? and Part II, Diagnosis and Misdiagnosis. Part III, Depression Is . . . , discusses alternative interpretations of depression's nature and concludes that it is a disease that is usually best treated by drug therapy. Part IV, The State of the Art: Treatment of Depression in Psychiatry's New Age, provides details about biological and psychotherapy approaches to depression, and Part V, The Chosen, analyzes the nature of depression and its treatment in women, children, and the elderly.

While Gold comes across strongly in favor of drug therapy in the treatment of depression, he does acknowledge the effective role that cognitive therapy or interpersonal therapy can play in helping people cope with depression. He states that even in cases of severe depression, a combination of drug therapy and cognitive or interpersonal therapy is more effective in treating depression than drug therapy alone.

The Good News about Depression received a 1-star Not Recommended rating in the national survey. The 1-star rating is not surprising and is consistent with the clinical and counseling psychologists' ratings of other self-help books that emphasize the biological basis of mental disorders and their treatment through drug therapy. Had more psychiatrists been included in the national survey, *The Good News about Depression* undoubtedly would have received a higher rating. The book actually does a better job of providing a well-rounded presentation of drug therapy and psychotherapy (cognitive and interpersonal) in the treatment of depression than the other two biologically oriented books in this category—*How to Cope with Depression* and *You Mean I Don't Have To Feel This Way?*.

WORTH A FURTHER LOOK

❑ ❑   *Control Your Depression* (revised and updated, 1986) by Peter
Lewinsohn, Ricaardo Muñoz, Mary Ann Youngren, and Antonette
Zeiss. Englewood Cliffs, NJ: Prentice-Hall.

Control Your Depression presents a view of helping people cope with
depression that is different from that of any of the other books in this
category—the behavioral approach. Lead author Peter Lewinsohn, Ph.D.,
is a clinical psychologist and a professor of pschology at the University
of Oregon. All of the other authors are also clinical psychologists.

Control Your Depression explains how to reduce depression through
self-control techniques, relaxation training, pleasant activities, planning
ahead, modifying self-defeating thinking patterns, and other be-
havioral/cognitive strategies. Dozens of examples illustrate how to gauge
progress, maintain the gains made, and determine whether further help
is needed. The book is divided into three main parts: Part I describes how
people think when they are depressed; Part II presents a host of strategies for controlling depression, including step-by-step methods, and Part
III is about ensuring success.

Control Your Depression was positively rated but by only four
respondents. The cognitive therapy strategies advocated by Burns and
Beck in their self-help books have generally been more effecive in treating depression than the behavioral approach advocated by Lewinsohn
and his colleagues. And for severe depression, a combination of drug therapy and cognitive or interpersonal therapy has been found to be more
effective. Nonetheless, Lewinsohn'a behavioral approach (which contains
some cognitive components, such as modifying self-defeating thinking
patterns) has been successful in treating some individuals with less severe forms of depression.

❑ ❑   *How to Stubbornly Refuse to Make Yourself Miserable about
Anything, Yes, Anything!* (1988) by Albert Ellis. New York: Carol
Publishing.

*How to Stubbornly Refuse to Make Yourself Miserable about Anything,
Yes, Anything!* presents a cognitive therapy approach to coping with
depression. Author Albert Ellis, Ph.D., is a well-known clinical psychologist, who, along with Aaron Beck, has been a pioneer in developing the
cognitive therapy approach to the treatment of mental disorders. Ellis
is the founder of the Institute for Rational Emotive Therapy in New York
City.

Ellis contends that people create their own feelings and choose to
think and feel in self-harming ways. In Ellis's view, the way to escape

this trap is to apply the principles of rational emotive therapy (RET), which Ellis developed. The book is organized in 14 chapters, most of which are insights based on rational emotive therapy. Ellis describes the ABCs of RET, showing how Activating Events (A) in life do not mainly or directly cause emotional Consequences (C). Rather, one's Belief System (B) is at fault, and that is what has to be changed to cope effectively with depression. In rational emotive therapy, disputation (D) takes place: irrational beliefs are disputed or contested by the therapist. Following disputation comes improved functioning Effects (E). The book is filled with examples of how RET can be used to help people reduce their depression.

How to Stubbornly Refuse to Make Yourself Miserable about Anything, Yes, Anything! was positively rated but by very few respondents. Some of the mental health professionals said that Ellis's approach is very effective and that they have used it successfully in treating depressed clients.

CONCLUSIONS

In summary, we recommend:

- On coping effectively with depression through nonmedical, psychological means:

    ★★★★★ *Feeling Good* by David Burns

    ★★★★★ *The Feeling Good Handbook* by David Burns

    ◑◑ *Control Your Depression* by Peter Lewinsohn and others

    ◑◑ *How to Stubbornly Refuse to Make Yourself Miserable About Anything, Yes, Anything!* by Albert Ellis

- For women who want to reduce their depression:

    ★★★ *Getting Un-Depressed* by Gary Emery

- On the biological basis of depression and its treatment through drug therapy:

    ★ *The Good News about Depression* by Mark Gold

- For people who have had the "blues" for several years, any of the above books plus

    ★★★ *When the Blues Won't Go Away* by Robert Hirschfeld

CHAPTER FIFTEEN

Dieting and
Weight Loss

Even ancient Romans were known to starve themselves, but never before have so many people, especially women, spent so much time, energy, and money on their weight. Since its inception in 1963, Weight Watchers alone has enrolled more than 15 million members. And hundreds of self-help books that recommend strategies for losing weight reflect our national obsession with being thin, or at least thinner than we are. Some books that encourage dietary modifications combined with exercise are based on sound nutritional and health principles. However, many books that are aimed directly at weight loss itself are based on a gimmick, some quick fix for obesity, that is either nutritionally unsound or impossible to follow for any length of time or both. As you read about the dieting and weight loss book ratings, keep in mind that they were made by mental health professionals who sometimes counsel individuals who want to lose weight, not by nutritionists or physicians who specialize in weight loss.

The dieting and weight loss books were that were rated in the national survey focused on six topics: women and weight loss; nutritionally balanced eating programs that focus on weight loss and involve highly structured plans; behavior modification strategies that advocate a change in life style as the best way to achieve and maintain weight loss; health and physical fitness; vegetarian diets; and quick-fix diets.

Two books were rated that focus on women and weight loss: *Fat Is a Feminist Issue* by Susie Orbach and *The 35 Plus Diet for Women* by Jean Spodnik and Barbara Gibbons.

One book focuses on a nutritionally balanced eating plan: *The Diet Center Program* by Sybil Ferguson.

No books on behavior modification and weight loss made the final ratings, but two books on this topic — *LEARN Program for Weight Con-*

trol by Kelly Brownell and *Diets Still Don't Work* by Bob Schwartz—are evaluated in the Worth a Further Look section.

Three books place their main emphasis on health and physical fitness: *The New Fit or Fat* by Covert Bailey; *The Pritikin Program for Diet and Exercise* by Nathan Pritiken; and *One Meal at a Time* by Martin Katahn.

One book emphasizes a vegetarian diet for weight loss: *Diet for a Small Planet* by Frances Lappe.

Six books fall into the category of quick-fix diet books: *The T-Factor Diet* by Martin Katahn; *The Rotation Diet* by Martin Katahn; *Dr. Atkins' Diet Revolution* by Robert Atkins; *Dr. Abravanel's Anti-Craving Weight-Loss Diet* by Elliot Abravanel and Elizabeth King; and *The Carbohydrate Addict's Diet* by Rachael and Bob Heller; and *The Beverly Hills Diet* by Judy Mazel and Susan Schultz.

Dieting and Weight Loss
BOOK RATINGS IN THE NATIONAL SURVEY

Diamond in the Rough	♦	*Fat Is a Feminist Issue* by Susie Orbach
Neutral	★★★	*The New Fit or Fat* by Covert Bailey
Not Recommended	★★	*Diet for a Small Planet* by Frances Lappe
	★	*The Pritikin Program for Diet and Exercise* by Nathan Pritikin
	★	*One Meal at a Time* by Martin Katahn
Strongly Not Recommended	†	*The T-Factor Diet* by Martin Katahn
	†	*The Rotation Diet* by Martin Katahn
	†	*The Diet Center Program* by Sybil Ferguson
	†	*The 35-Plus Diet for Women* by Jean Spodnik and Barbara Gibbons
	†	*Dr. Atkins' Diet Revolution* by Robert Atkins
	†	*Dr. Abravanel's Anti-Craving Weight-Loss Diet* by Elliot Abravanel and Elizabeth King
	†	*The Carbohydrate Addict's Diet* by Rachel Heller and Richard Heller
	†	*The Beverly Hills Diet* by Judy Mazel and Susan Schultz

DIAMONDS IN THE ROUGH

◆ *Fat Is a Feminist Issue* (2 vols., 1982) by Susie Orbach. New York: Berkley Books.

Fat Is a Feminist Issue is a psychological exploration of why so many women are compulsive overeaters rather than a diet book per se. Susie Orbach is a psychotherapist who co-founded the Women's Therapy Center and the Women's Therapy Institute in New York. She has worked with hundreds of women to help them cope with their eating problems and has conducted postgraduate training on diet and weight loss with psychotherapists.

Fat Is a Feminist Issue is published in two volumes. In Volume I, Orbach states that because compulsive overeating is primarily a woman's problem, it may have something to do with being a female in today's society. Examining compulsive overeating from a psychoanalytic perspective, Orbach believes that being fat serves a number of purposes for women: It prevents them from being perceived as sex objects, expresses anger they have been conditioned to deny, or reflects problems of separation from their mothers. Orbach suggests that a woman's body is not her own; it is prey for the fashion and diet industries, which set unrealistic expectations for women. Orbach presents a program to help women learn the difference between hunger, boredom, and loneliness and to show them how to satisfy their hunger rather than more profound longings.

Volume II is part sequel, part workbook on how to put into practice the ideas described in Volume I. Both are based on the belief that once women understand and come to grips with their real problems, they will usually lose weight.

Fat Is a Feminine Issue was positively rated but by only 16 respondents, so it was placed in the Diamonds in the Rough category. The small number of mental health professionals who evaluated *Fat Is a Feminine Issue* felt that Orbach gives important insights into the nature of obesity and the psychological underpinnings of compulsive overeating. However, critics pointed out several minor flaws in her arguments. For example, she equates fatness with compulsive overeating, whereas the two can be entirely different conditions. She also may have overstated the feminist viewpoint: Insecurity is not exclusively a female issue. Nonetheless, *Fat Is a Feminist Issue* is one of the few self-help books that received a positive rating in the national survey in the dieting and weight loss category.

NEUTRAL

★ ★ ★   *The New Fit or Fat* (rev. ed., 1991) by Covert Bailey. Boston: Houghton Mifflin.

The New Fit or Fat describes ways to become healthy by developing better diet and exercise routines. Covert Bailey has a Master of Science degree in nutritional biochemistry from MIT. He heads the Bailey Fit-or-Fat Center in Oregon and conducts Bailey Seminars nationwide. He has also written *The Fit or Fat Target Diet* and *Fit or Fat for Women,* which addresses women's special weight and fitness problems.

Bailey argues that the basic problem for overweight people is not losing weight, which fat people do periodically, but in gaining weight, which fat people do more easily than those with a different body chemistry. He explores the way our body stores fat and analyzes why crash diets don't work. He explains the relation between fat metabolism and weight, concluding that the ultimate cure for obesity is aerobic exercise coupled with a sensible, low-fat diet.

Originally published in 1977 as *Fit or Fat,* the 1991 edition is greatly expanded with new information on fitness life styles and recent scientific advances. A new chapter answers readers' most frequently asked questions about Bailey's views on diet and exercise. A new section suggests strategies for getting started.

The New Fit or Fat received a 3-star Neutral rating in the national survey. The book offers solid, no-nonsense advice about how to lose weight and become more physically fit and deservedly was the highest-rated book on diet and weight loss. Why did it get only 3-stars in the national survey? Enough mental health experts said that *all* diet and weight loss books are terrible! Thus, the book unfortunately got lumped in with other diet books, many of which are not beneficial. We believe that this is a good self-help book on diet, weight loss, and developing a fit life style.

NOT RECOMMENDED

★ ★   *Diet for a Small Planet* (20th Anniversary Edition, 1991) by Frances Lappe. New York: Ballantine.

Diet for a Small Planet presents a political, vegetarian approach to dieting and weight loss. Author Frances Lappe founded the Institute for Food and Development Policy in San Francisco in 1975. The recurrent theme of her work at the institute is that the worldwide problem of hunger is not a scarcity of food but a scarcity of democracy. In 1987 she received the Right Livelihood Award from the Swedish parliament for her work as an activist against hunger and economic injustice.

The 20th Anniversary Edition of *Diet for a Small Planet* contains a new introductory chapter and reflects Lappe's continued study of world food problems. She believes that the global system of food production and distribution is grossly inequitable. She assails America's reliance on grain-fed beef as a primary protein source due to the protein energy required to feed livestock. She thinks we should omit meat from our diets for both nutritional and political reasons.

Although there is a loud political overtone to *Diet for a Small Planet,* a large part of the book is devoted to ways in which the reader can eat a high-protein, meatless diet that relies on dairy products, fish, nuts, and eggs as sources of protein. Meatless recipes make up nearly half of the book, and many charts and tables are included to illustrate the benefits of a vegetarian way of life.

Diet for a Small Planet received a 2-star Not Recommended rating in the national survey. Several mental health professionals said that Lappe's arguments for a meatless diet are persuasive. To someone considering going on a vegetarian diet, *Diet for a Small Planet* should be of interest. And Lappe's perspective on food production and consumption in the United States is intriguing. The book's low rating is partly due to it being lumped together with other diet books by the mental health professionals who said that all books in this category are worthless.

★   *The Pritikin Program for Diet and Exercise* (1979) by Nathan Pritikin. New York: Bantam.

The Pritikin Program for Diet and Exercise addresses incorporating diet into a life style program of becoming healthy and physically fit. Author Nathan Pritikin, a nutritionist, was the founder of the Longevity Center and the Pritikin Research Center in the Los Angeles area.

This book is based on the famous Pritikin diet plan that is designed to help people lower cholesterol and lose weight. The plan recommends a diet of no more than 10% fat, forbids sodium and sweeteners, and suggests 1000 to 1200 calories per day. The book contains more than 100 pages of recipes to help dieters stay on the program. Pritikin also strongly advocates exercise—walking or jogging—to accompany the eating plan. The author cautions that the plan is recommended only for individuals in good physical health.

The Pritikin Program for Diet and Exercise was given a 1-star Not Recommended rating in the national survey, even though the book has sold millions of copies since its publication in 1979. The diet is extreme—some have even called it grim. It is virtually impossible to follow when you are away from home. One critic said that when he over-indulges, he often takes this book off the shelf for a "bit of self-flagellation." The critic goes on to say that the diet is basic, if not sermonizing.

A new Pritikin-based book was written by Pritikin's son, Robert, who currently is director of the Pritikin Longevity Center. Although it gives brief advice about engaging in exercise and reducing stress, the bulk of *The New Pritikin Program* contains basically the same messages as the father's 1972 book.

★   *One Meal at a Time: Step-By-Step to a Low-Fat Diet for a Happier, Healthier, Longer Life* (1991) by Martin Katahn. New York: W. W. Norton.

One Meal at a Time focuses on weight loss. It is the latest in a series of weight loss books written by Martin Katahn, Ph.D., formerly director of the weight loss management program and a professor of clinical psychology at Vanderbilt University.

One Meal at a Time, despite its similar title, is not fashioned after the Alcoholics Anonymous slogan "One day at a time." Rather, *One Meal at a Time* is a learning process that tackles, in this order, breakfast, lunch, dinner, and snacks. There is nothing to count except grams of fat in your diet. Katahn provides several menus, offers recipes and food tables that reflect the plan's strategy, gives tips for eating out, and includes a chapter on feeding your children. Physical activity is also recommended.

One Meal at a Time received a 1-star Not Recommended rating in the national survey, the highest rating of the quick-fix diet books. The content of *One Meal at a Time* is similar to that of Katahn's earlier *The T-Factor Diet*, although the writing is clearer. Katahn's diet recommendations in *One Meal at a Time* are not harmful; indeed, they fall within accepted nutritional guidelines and, when followed, do help people to lose weight—short-term. And therein lies the rub. As with so many diet plans that require a rather rigid format, it is very difficult to stay on the *One Meal at a Time* plan over the long term and maintain weight loss. Also, the number of pages devoted to physical activity and exercise is minimal.

STRONGLY NOT RECOMMENDED

†   *The T-Factor Diet* (1989) by Martin Katahn. New York: W. W. Norton.

The T-Factor Diet is similar to Katahn's *One Meal at a Time*. The "T" factor in *The T-Factor Diet* is thermogenesis, which is the burning of calories for energy, a process that requires as fuel a mixture of fats and nonfats. Katahn believes that we can use thermogenesis to lose weight even without counting calories by cutting down on the fat in our diet and going on a low-intensity aerobic exercise program. The book is filled with charts, tables, and recipes that show how to reduce the amount of fat in the diet.

The T-Factor Diet was given a negative average rating in the national survey, placing it in the Strongly Not Recommended category. As in *One Day at a Time*, Katahan's advice in *The T-Factor Diet* will help people to lose weight short-term and is nutritionally sound. However, maintaining weight loss over any extended period of time with this diet is unlikely. Also, the writing in *The T-Factor Diet* vacillates between *Family Circle* homemaker style and technical academic style.

† *The Rotation Diet* (1986) by Martin Katahn. New York: W. W. Norton.

The Rotation Diet was Katahn's first major entry in the diet self-help market. The diet is based on one the author used earlier in his life to shed 75 pounds. Katahn tells you that you can expect to lose two-thirds of one pound to one pound a day on the diet. The diet plan alternates caloric intake over a three-week period. Women are permitted 600 calories for three days, 900 for four days, 1,200 the following week, then the first week is repeated. For men, the rotation is 1,200/1,500/and 1,800. The dieter must then stop for at least one week to prevent the metabolic changes that predispose the dieter to regain weight. The diet is accompanied by an activity plan that allows choices between walking, jogging, cycling, and other aerobic activities.

The Rotation Diet received a negative average rating in the national survey, placing it in the Strongly Not Recommended category. This was Katahn's first and worst book, according to critics. They stress that *The Rotation Diet,* while not harmful, is a not a realistic long-term eating plan.

† *The Diet Center Program: Lose Weight Fast and Keep It Off Forever* (rev. ed., 1990) by Sybil Ferguson. Boston: Little, Brown.

The Diet Center Program focuses on how to lose weight. Author Sybil Ferguson is the founder of Diet Center. Ferguson developed the Diet Center's plan to end her personal 18-year ordeal with excess weight, and it has grown into a worldwide program for dieters.

This book contains the step-by-step program followed by people who attend a Diet Center. Ferguson believes that obesity is a chronic, incurable illness that can be controlled by eating the proper foods. She gives tips for food preparation and menu planning, basic recommendations for physical activity, and information concerning emotional issues related to dieting. The diet plan is nutritionally balanced and includes nutrition education, behavior modification, and sensible physical activity and exercise.

The Diet Center Program received a negative average rating, relegating it to the Strongly Not Recommended category. Critics say that the diet recommendations are basically sensible, and they applaud the nutritional balance of the program. However, they say that the diet plan is complicated and requires strict adherence in order for it to work. As with most other diet plans, exercise is recommended but gets minimal attention in relation to food.

† *The 35-Plus Diet for Women* (1987) by Jean Spodnik and Barbara Gibbons. New York: Harper & Row.

The 35-Plus Diet for Women, is designed to help women over the age of 35 lose weight. Author Jean Spodnik is the lead clinical dietician at the Kaiser Permanente offices in Cleveland, Ohio. Coauthor Barbara Gibbons is a columnist and author of *The Slim Gourmet, Lean Cuisine,* and other cookbooks—and she has maintained an 80-pound weight loss.

The authors contend that the physiological changes in metabolism and water retention in women over the age of 35 causes problems in losing weight. They recommend a nutritionally balanced diet high in fiber, low in cholesterol, and low in fat eaten in small servings at regular intervals. Calcium-rich foods and bone-strengthening exercises are advocated to prevent osteoporosis.

The 35-Plus Diet for Women is divided into two main parts. The first half of the book presents the rationale for this eating plan and discusses why women over the age of 35 have problems in losing weight. The second half of the book contains sample menus and recipes to be used on this diet.

The 35-Plus Diet for Women received a negative average rating, which places it in the Strongly Not Recommended category. Critics comment that intermingled with some good advice for women over 35 are lapses into the kind of hype associated with fad diets. The crash course in nutrition is overly simplistic and would have been improved by diagrams or charts.

† *Dr. Atkins' Diet Revolution* (1972) by Robert Atkins. New York: M. Evans.

Dr. Atkins' Diet Revolution focuses on how to lose weight. Robert Atkins, M.D., is a cardiologist in private practice.

Atkins contends that weight loss has little to do with fat intake. He believes that people can burn off fat while eating luxuriously. The key is a 14-day induction diet in which almost all carbohydrates are banned, forcing the body into a fat-burning process called ketosis. Atkins recommends eating red meat and bacon, and eggs for breakfast. He also suggests supplementary vitamins to take up any nutritional slack. The author recognizes that this is not a long-term eating plan.

Dr. Atkins' Diet Revolution received a negative average rating in the national survey, placing it in the Strongly Not Recommended category. The book sold millions of copies in the 1970s when it first came out and created a stir in the medical community. Critics questioned the soundness of the eating plan because ingestion of large quantities of protein can be extremely harmful to people with kidney or liver problems.

A revision of Atkins's book was recently published in 1992: *Dr. Atkins' New Diet Revolution*. While the revised edition focuses more on health matters than did its predecessor, its poorly conceived nutritional recommendations remain virtually intact. Avoid it.

† *Dr. Abravanel's Anti-Craving Weight-Loss Diet* (1990) by Elliot Abravanel and Elizabeth King. New York: Bantam.

Dr. Abravanel's Anti-Craving Weight-Loss Diet focuses on how to lose weight. Elliot Abravanel, M.D., is a physician who developed the Skinny School clinics. Abravanel first created the clinics in Los Angeles and they now are located in 50 cities in the United States. Elizabeth King helped Abravanel develop the Skinny School clinics.

The book's main premise is that the intense cravings we sometimes get for certain foods, such as sweets and starches or greasy and salted foods, cause efforts at weight loss to fail. Readers take a quiz to determine their cravings, then based on their answers learn about the best diet for themselves. Abravanel's system is based on a theory that states that people don't really crave food, they crave the "M" state, a feeling of tranquil alertness that can be achieved only by transcendental meditation.

Dr. Abravanel's Anti-Craving Weight-Loss Diet did not fare well in the national survey, receiving a low negative average rating and Strongly Not Recommended status. Some mental health professionals labeled the diet a nuisance and questioned the recommended dosages of over-the-counter phenylpropanolmine and appetite suppressants as well as vitamin and mineral shots intended to help burn fat from specific locations, such as the buttocks and thighs. The book also includes hard sells for Abravanel's line of minerals and food supplements. And the "M" state/food connection described as the theoretical basis for the diet strategy is hazy at best.

† *The Carbohydrate Addict's Diet* (1991) by Rachael Heller and Richard Heller. New York: Dutton.

The Carbohydrate Addict's Diet is another in the long list of books that recommend quick fixes to lose weight. Author Rachael Heller, Ph.D., is a research and health psychologist at both Mt. Sinai School of Medicine and the Graduate Center of the City University of New York. Richard Heller, Ph.D., is a professor at the Mt. Sinai School of Medicine and a professor of biology at the City University of New York. The Hellers are codirectors of the Carbohydrate Addict's Center in New York.

This low-carbohydrate diet was designed to treat hyperinsulnemia, a condition in which normal carbohydrate consumption produces increased hunger rather than satisfaction. The diet plan basically consists of eating two low-carbohydrate meals per day and one "reward" meal that is rich in carbohydrates (bread, rice, pasta, potatoes, chocolate, fruit, cake, potato chips, and the like). The diet was derived from an eating plan in which Rachael Heller would not eat at all during the day and then would eat whatever she wanted for dinner, resulting in a 150-pound weight loss. The book includes several recipes that fit their diet plan.

The Carbohydrate Addict's Diet Plan did not fare well in the national survey, receiving a low-negative average rating that categorized it as Strongly Not Recommended. The Hellers claim that their diet has an 80% success rate with their Carbohydrate Addict Center clients and that their program reduces, and even eventually eliminates, your craving for carbohydrates. Critics questioned how healthy this diet is for most people.

† *The Beverly Hills Diet* (1981) by Judy Mazel. New York: Macmillan.

The Beverly Hills Diet is another quick-fix diet plan. Author Judy Mazel is described by *New West* magazine as the "nutrition magician and diet guru" of Los Angeles, and this comment is included on the cover of the book. No professional background, training, or affiliation is listed.

The basic theme of *The Beverly Hills Diet* is that weight can be lost quickly by eating a diet that consists mainly of fruits. The argument is that fruits are about 90% water and only about 50 to 100 calories per serving. The first week is fruit only—up to five pounds of grapes a day, says Mazel. So is the second week up until day 11, when a few bagels or slices of bread and three ears of corn on the cob are added. By the end of the third week, a steak is permitted, along with continued bushels of fruit. In weeks four and five, more varieties of foods are added, but the overall diet is still mainly fruits. Week six provides specific requirements for which fruit and how much, but by now, says Mazel, anything else can be eaten with no weight gain.

The Beverly Hills Diet received an extremely low negative rating in the national survey; it was the lowest rated of all the books on diet and weight loss. Mark Hegsted, Associate Director of Research at the Harvard Medical School, said that an all-fruit diet makes no nutritional sense at all and that staying on it long enough will lead to serious malnourishment. He also severely criticizes Mazel for including comments on virtually every page that are nutritionally wrong. Enough said.

WORTH A FURTHER LOOK

◑ ◑   *The LEARN Program for Weight Control* (1988) by Kelly Brownell. Dallas: American Health Publications.

The LEARN Program for Weight Control advocates a change in life style in order to lose weight. Author Kelly Brownell, Ph.D., is a highly respected authority on dieting and eating disorders. He is currently a professor of psychology at Yale University and codirector of the Yale Center for Eating and Weight Disorders. He has written a number of academic books on nutrition and eating behavior and published more than 90 papers in scientific journals. He is a past president of the Society of Behavioral Medicine.

LEARN stands for Life style, Exercise, Attitudes, Relationships, and Nutrition. Brownell weaves his LEARN program through 16 lessons that guide effective, medically sound weight loss. The LEARN program promises an average weight loss of 20 to 25 pounds, translating into a 1 to 2-pound weight loss each week for 1 to 20 weeks the program usually lasts.

A Self-Assessment Questionnaire and homework assignment accompany each of the sixteen lessons. These exercises show which techniques are working and how much progress has been made. Brownell teaches when, how, and why habits occur and how to change them. He believes that the new habits the program instills encourage a new life style and thus have a good probability of being maintained over the long term.

The LEARN Program for Weight Control was rated very positively by the few mental health professionals who evaluated it. They were enthusiastic about Brownell's approach, saying that it is an excellent strategy for weight loss that has a much better chance of helping people lose weight and maintain the weight loss than the quick-fix diet books that were negatively rated in the national survey. Brownell's book contains no gimmicks, no quick fixes, and no false promises. Rather, readers are encouraged to alter their exercise, life style, and eating patterns in order to lose weight and keep it off. The book is also clear, well written, and well organized. Clearly, based on the ratings of the mental health professionals, good self-help books on dieting are few and far between, and *The LEARN Program for Weight Control* is one of them.

The one problem for self-help readers is that Brownell's book is hard to obtain. For all of its good qualities, this diet workbook unfortunately has not reached the shelves of bookstores. It is available in some libraries and can be obtained by contacting the LEARN Education Center, 1555 W. Mockingbird Lane, Dallas, TX 75325; phone 800-736-7323.

◑ ◑   *Diets Still Don't Work* (1990) by Bob Schwartz. Houston: Breakthru Publishing.

Diets Still Don't Work emphasizes that the best way to lose weight is to change your life style rather than focusing on diet alone, especially a quick-fix diet. Author Bob Schwartz owns a chain of health spas in the southwestern United States. For years he struggled to lose 20 to 40 pounds without success until he discovered a way to be "naturally thin" without dieting.

Initially published as *Diets Don't Work* in 1982, *Diets Still Don't Work* is divided into three main parts. Part I, The Truth About Dieting, explains why diets don't work, with special attention to the yo-yo weight loss/weight gain cycles that so many overweight people experience. Part II, How To Dismantle the Diet Mentality, explores the reasons people overeat, how thin people think and eat differently than fat people, and factors anyone should consider in making the choice of being fat or thin. Part III, Living the Naturally Thin Life, describes and explains the physical and psychological breakthroughs in life style that lead to weight loss.

Diets Still Don't Work was very positively rated in the national survey but by only five respondents. The book's enthusiasts applauded its solid advice about why diets don't work and its recommendations for a change in life style instead of a quick-fix, gimmicky diet. This book merits more attention than it has received.

CONCLUSIONS

In summary, we recommend:

- On losing weight and maintaining the weight loss by changing life style:

  ★★★ *The New Fit or Fat* by Covert Bailey

  ◑◑ *The LEARN Program for Weight Control* by Kelly Brownell

  ◑◑ *Diets Still Don't Work* by Bob Schwartz

- On the cultural and psychological underpinnings of women's weight loss problems:

  ◆ *Fat Is a Feminist Issue* by Susie Orbach

CHAPTER SIXTEEN

Divorce

Divorce has become epidemic in our culture. Until recently, it was increasing annually by 10 percent, although its rate of increase is now slowing. For those who divorce, separation and divorce are complex and emotionally charged. The stress of separation and divorce places men, women, and children at risk for psychological and physical difficulties. Separated and divorced men and women have higher rates of psychiatric disorders, admission to mental health hospitals, and depression. Many separations and divorces immerse children in conflict, and as a consequence the children are more likely to have school-related problems, especially at the beginning of the separation and divorce.

Self-help books on divorce fall into four main categories: for divorced or divorcing parents; for the children of divorced or divorcing parents; for divorced or divorcing adults in general; and child custody.

Three books for divorcing or divorced parents were rated in the national survey: *Growing Up with Divorce* by Neil Kalter; *Second Chances* by Judith Wallerstein and Sandra Blakeslee; and *Going It Alone* by Robert Weiss. A fourth book—*The Parents Book about Divorce* by Richard Gardner—is evaluated in the Worth a Further Look section.

Three books for children of divorced or divorcing parents made the final ratings: *The Boys and Girls Book About Divorce* by Richard Gardner; *Dinosaurs Divorce* by Laurene Brown and Marc Brown; and *How It Feels When Parents Divorce* by Jill Krementz.

One book for divorcing or divorced adults in general was rated: *Creative Divorce* by Mel Krantzler. A second book—*Rebuilding When Your Relationship Ends* by Bruce Fisher—is profiled in Worth a Further Look.

No books on child custody made the final ratings. However, one book that came out after the survey was completed—*The Custody Revolution* by Richard Warshak—is described in the Worth a Further Look category.

Divorce
BOOK RATINGS IN THE NATIONAL SURVEY

Strongly   ★★★★★ *The Boys and Girls Book about Divorce*
Recommended   by Richard Gardner

Recommended   ★★★★ *Dinosaurs Divorce* by Laurene Brown and
                              Mark Brown

                  ★★★★ *How It Feels When Parents Divorce* by
                              Jill Krementz

                  ★★★★ *Growing Up with Divorce* by Neil Kalter

Neutral   ★★★ *Second Chances* by Judith Wallerstein
                              and Sandra Blakeslee

                  ★★★ *Going It Alone* by Robert Weiss

                  ★★★ *Creative Divorce* by Mel Krantzler

STRONGLY RECOMMENDED

★ ★ ★ ★ ★   *The Boys and Girls Book about Divorce* (1983) by Richard
Gardner. Northvale, NJ: Jason Aronson.

The Boys and Girls Book about Divorce is written for children to help
them cope with their parents' separation and divorce. Author Richard
Gardner, M.D., is a widely respected psychiatrist and a professor in the
Department of Child Psychiatry at Columbia University College of Physicians and Surgeons.

The Boys and Girls Book about Divorce is appropriate for children
of average or better intelligence 10 to 12 years of age or older. Most of
what Gardner tells children in the book comes from his therapy experiences with divorced children. Gardner talks directly to children about
their feelings after the divorce, who is and is not to blame for the divorce,
parents' love for their children, and how to handle their angry feelings
and their fear of being left alone. Then he tells children about how to
get along better with their divorced mother and their divorced father.
Gardner also covers the important topic of how to get along with parents who live apart, sensitively handling such difficult issues as playing
one parent against the other and what to do when parents try to use the
child as a tool or weapon. How children can cope effectively in stepfamilies is briefly touched on, and a final chapter explains to children what
to expect if they have to see a therapist.

The Boys and Girls Book about Divorce received a 5-star Strongly Recommended rating in the national survey. This is a very good self-help book for children 10 to 12 years of age or older in divorced or divorcing families. Gardner's extensive therapy experiences with children of divorce serve as an excellent resource for communicating to children how to cope effectively with their changing family situation. The book is written at an appropriate reading level for its intended audience. A number of cartoonlike drawings add to the book's appeal for children.

The Boys and Girls Book about Divorce was first published in 1970. In the ensuing years, it has been the most widely recommended book by therapists for children of divorce. Famous child development expert Louise Bates Ames was especially laudatory in her praise of Gardner's book, saying that it provides children with an understanding of their fears, anxieties, and sorrows and assures them that they are not unique in experiencing such feelings. Bates also says that *The Boys and Girls Book about Divorce* gives children excellent advice on how to cope effectively with this traumatic event in their lives. Gardner's book was the first book on divorce written expressly for children. It has survived the test of time and remains a superb resource for divorced or divorcing parents to give to their 10- to 12-year-old or older children to read.

RECOMMENDED

★ ★ ★ ★ *Dinosaurs Divorce: A Guide for Changing Families* (1986) by Laurene Brown and Marc Brown. Boston: Little, Brown.

Dinosaurs Divorce, like *The Boys and Girls Book about Divorce,* was written for children living in divorced families. *Dinosaurs Divorce* grew out of the Browns' experiences with divorce as parent and stepparent, and for Laurene, as a child herself.

Dinosaurs Divorce is a 30-page, full-color picture book that takes children through the experience of divorce in a dinosaur family. The topics covered include why parents divorce, how children feel when their parents divorce, what happens after the divorce, what it's like to live with one parent, what it's like to visit the other parent, having two homes, celebrating holidays and special occasions, telling friends, meeting parents' new friends, and having stepsisters and stepbrothers.

Dinosaurs Divorce received a 4-star Recommended rating in the national survey. Its average rating was high enough for 5-stars but it was not evaluated by enough respondents to be placed at that level. The book is simple and easy for children to understand. Much of it can be read and understood by children who are in elementary school. Parents can read and discuss the pictures and words with younger children. Several of the mental health professionals said that they highly recommend the book for children of divorced parents. They commented that *Dinosaurs Divorce* helps children to understand many new experiences and difficulties that divorce brings to children's lives. They also mentioned that the authors suggest simple, positive ways to handle these circumstances.

★ ★ ★ ★   *How It Feels When Parents Divorce* (1984) by Jill Krementz. New York: Knopf.

How It Feels When Parents Divorce presents 19 children's experiences with the divorce of their parents. Author Jill Krementz is a professional writer and photographer who lives in New York City.

Krementz interviewed and photographed 19 children aged 7 to 16, from divorced families. The title of each of the chapters is a child's name. Each chapter opens with a full-page photograph of the child followed by the child's experience in a divorced family. The children talk about the changes in their lives, their hurt, the confusion they had to cope with, and the knowledge they gained. The book is mainly geared toward children and adolescents—it is at about the same reading level as Gardner's book, *The Boys and Girls Book about Divorce*—although divorced parents can also benefit from the children's descriptions of their experiences. The children's stories reflect their vulnerability and resilience. Thirteen-year-old Zach comments, "It's very sad and confusing when your parents are divorced." Ten-year-old Jimmy, whose mother once stole him away from his father, says, "When I think back over the past eight years, it seems as if I was just in one court and out the other, and half the time I didn't know what was going on." Eight-year-old Lulu reflects, "I suppose they needed the divorce to be happy, but there were times when I thought it was stupid and unfair and mean to me."

How It Feels When Parents Divorce received a 4-star Recommended rating in the national survey. Many mental health professionals found it a good self-help book for older children and adolescents. By listening to the sincere commentaries of their peers in divorced families, children can learn what has helped them and apply the knowledge to their own lives. Esteemed child developmentalist T. Berry Brazelton commented that this is a beautiful book that all parents and children in divorced families can benefit from reading.

★ ★ ★ ★   *Growing Up with Divorce* (1990) by Neil Kalter. New York: The Free Press.

Growing Up with Divorce is written for divorced parents and provides them with information to help their children avoid emotional problems.

Author Neil Kalter, Ph.D., is a highly respected clinical psychologist and Director of the Center for the Child and Family at the University of Michigan at Ann Arbor.

Growing Up with Divorce is especially designed to counteract the long-term effects of divorce on children, many of whom struggle with the emotional difficulties of divorce for years after the actual divorce itself. Kalter's book offers practical strategies for parents in helping children cope with the anxiety, anger, and confusion that can occur immediately or develop over a number of years.

Kalter shows how a child's level of psychological development influences the specific ways that he or she experiences, understands, and reacts to the stress of divorce. The author illustrates the separate problems and concerns of children of different ages and sexes at each stage of divorce. In-depth accounts of children's experiences in divorced families are given from infancy through adolescence.

Drawing on his extensive clinical background with divorced families, Kalter describes in considerable detail the kind of behavior parents can expect to see in their children and clearly explains how to detect signs of undue emotional distress. A wide variety of divorce circumstances are evaluated, including ongoing conflict between parents, joint custody, dating, and remarriage. Practical advice is given about how to minimize children's stress in each of these and many other situations, such as feeling caught by divided loyalties and coping with the dislocation of new household arrangements.

Kalter believes that rather than confronting children directly about their emotions, which usually causes children to retreat into silence, parents use an indirect communication strategy. He gives step-by-step instructions to parents about how to speak to their children in indirect and nonthreatening ways and tells them what to say in specific situations.

Growing Up with Divorce received a 4-star Recommended rating in the national survey. This was the highest-rated book for parents in the divorce category, almost making the 5-star Strongly Recommended rating. This is an excellent self-help book for divorced parents. Famous child-care expert Benjamin Spock commented that the book provides wise discussion of children's reaction to divorce at different ages and how to help them cope. Well-known pediatrician T. Berry Brazelton said that the book is very practical and helpful for parents, especially in its developmental approach. Divorce expert Robert Weiss recommends this book to all divorced parents and to all mental health professionals who help divorced parents and their children. And well-known authority on divorce Judith Wallerstein said that divorced parents who read Kalter's book will learn valuable strategies for comforting their children. We evaluate Wallerstein's own book on divorce next.

NEUTRAL

★ ★ ★   *Second Chances: Men, Women, and Children a Decade after Divorce* (1989) by Judith Wallerstein and Sandra Blakeslee. New York: Ticknor & Fields.

Second Chances is based on a long-term study of divorced couples and their children. Author Judith Wallerstein, Ph.D., is founder and executive director of the Center for the Family in Transition in Corte Madera, California, which counsels more divorcing families than any other agency in America. She is also the author (with Joan Kelly) of *Surviving the Breakup: How Children and Parents Cope with Divorce* (1980). Coauthor Sandra Blakeslee is a professional writer.

In *Surviving the Breakup*, Wallerstein and Kelly chronicled how sixty families fared five years after divorce. In *Second Chances*, Wallerstein and Blakeslee describe the reevaluation of 90% of the original sixty families at 10 years post divorce, with some analysis of their lives at the 15-year mark. Additional commentary is included about divorced families who are seen at the California-based clinic that Wallerstein directs.

Wallerstein and Blakeslee argue that divorce is emotionally painful and psychologically devastating for a rather large portion of children, even 10 to 15 years after the divorce takes place. In their view, divorced parents, struggling to meet their own needs, often fail to meet their children's needs; through their own instability and continuing conflict with each other, divorced parents add to the psychological burdens of their children. Interview excerpts are interwoven with clinical interpretations and research findings to tell the emotionally difficult story of the long-term negative effects of divorce on children.

Second Chances received a 3-star Neutral rating in the national survey, just missing the 4-star Recommended category. Some mental health professionals made positive comments about *Second Chances*, others criticized it. In general, the book received more favorable responses in the counseling and clinical community than in the scientific research community. Highly esteemed psychoanalytic theorist Erik Erikson called *Second Chances* a landmark book. Well-known feminist clinician and writer Nancy Chodorow commented that the book is a sobering, powerful contribution to understanding family life in general and divorce in particular. Respected self-help author Judith Viorst said *Second Chances* is deeply touching, immensely readable, and impressively researched.

Commentary from the scientific community was less glowing. Reviews of *Second Chances* in the authoritative journals of the American Psychological Association (*Contemporary Psychology*) and the American Sociological Association (*Contemporary Sociology*) criticized

Wallerstein's work on a number of grounds. Both marital therapy expert Howard Markman of the University of Denver and family sociologist Terry Arendell of Hunter College said that the study's methodological limitations are substantial. They believe that Wallerstein and Blakeslee overgeneralize findings and make statements that are unwarranted on the basis of the research data. Markman and Arendell especially criticized Wallerstein and Blakeslee for uniformily stamping the children of divorce as developmentally and emotionally handicappped.

★ ★ ★   *Going It Alone: The Family Life and Social Situation of the Single Parent* (1979) by Robert Weiss. New York: Basic Books.

Going It Alone is about the family life and social life of the single parent. Author Robert Weiss, Ph.D., is a professor of sociology at the University of Massachusetts in Boston and a lecturer at Harvard Medical School. Weiss is a recognized authority in the study of divorced families.

Based on interviews with approximately 200 single and married parents, *Going It Alone* covers a number of problems in single parent families. The single parents in Weiss's book include not only divorced parents but also those who have been widowed and those who have had children out of wedlock. In *Going It Alone*, women and men talk about organizing their households as single parents, raising children of different ages, their own social lives, and juggling commitments. The book also examines basic ideas about the nature of parenthood, the role of marriage in people's lives, and about social relationships in general.

Going It Alone received a 3-star Neutral rating in the national survey. Weiss does a good job of presenting a broad perspective of what living in a single-parent family is like. Well-known author Lillian Rubin (*Intimate Strangers*) commented that Weiss lays bare the issues and problems of "going it alone." One problem for self-help readers is the book's lack of practical advice about such important single-parent issues as money, working, child care, custody disputes, and the like. Female critics especially fault his failure to adequately consider undereducated, underpaid, and minority group women.

★ ★ ★   *Creative Divorce* (1973) by Mel Krantzler. New York: Signet.

Creative Divorce is about divorced individuals' opportunities for personal growth. Author Mel Krantzler has a Master's degree in rehabilitation counseling and has extensively counseled divorced adults.

At 50 years of age, Krantzler and his wife separated after twenty-four years of marriage. He describes his ordeal—self-pity, guilt, loneliness, and helplessness—and how it helped him to grow as a person. The author also draws on the experiences of his male and female clients. Krantzler considers divorce the "death" of a relationship, requiring a mourning period followed by reflective self-evaluation and planning. The self-destructive patterns that many divorced adults engage in are portrayed, as when men say they want companionship yet pursue women as sexual objects. While Krantzler's description of divorce is better when he dispenses advice for men, he is sympathetic to some of the problems divorced women face—economic difficulties, for example.

Creative Divorce received a 3-star Neutral rating in the national survey. The book was a best seller in the 1970s, but its popularity has declined since then. Well-known self-help author Eda LeShan called Krantzler's book "spectacular" in touching the right aspects of divorced adults' concerns. Several mental health professionals commented that Krantzler gives divorced adults hope that they will get their lives together and that something positive can come out of their divorce.

WORTH A FURTHER LOOK

◑ ◑   *The Parents Book about Divorce* (1977) by Richard Gardner. New York: Doubleday.

The Parents Book about Divorce is the sequel to *The Boys and Girls Book about Divorce,* a 5-star, Strongly Recommended book that was evaluated earlier in this chapter. Gardner provides advice to divorced parents about what to tell children, how to help children cope with the separation period, and the best strategies for dealing with children in the aftermath of divorce. Parents are advised about how to get effective counseling and legal assistance, determine custody, cope with unreasonable demands of the ex-spouse, deal with the new mate of an ex-spouse, reduce guilt, make visitation less stressful, introduce a new lover into the family routine, and not make the mistake of picking the wrong mate again.

The Parents Book about Divorce was positively rated in the national survey but by too few respondents to make a rating category. For the most part, this is a good self-help book for parents. Is is well-written, insightful, and includes a rich assortment of examples from divorced families. However, the book is more than 15 years old now and is dated in its handling of gender roles and sexual orientation.

◑ ◑   *Rebuilding: When Your Relationship Ends* (1981) by Bruce Fisher. San Luis Obispo, CA: Impact.

Rebuilding When Your Relationship Ends is designed to help adults put the pieces of their lives back together after they have become divorced.

Author Bruce Fisher, Ed.D., is a marriage and family therapist in Boulder, Colorado.

The heart of Fisher's book is the 15 topics he explains to help divorced adults build a new life. The steps are denial, loneliness, rejection/guilt, self-concept, grief, rebuilding friendships, feeling lovable, disentanglement, anger, sex, trust, leftovers, aliveness, singleness, and freedom. Each chapter ends with homework to help readers about the topic discussed.

Rebuilding When Your Relationship Ends was positively rated but by only 8 respondents. Well-known family therapist Virginia Satir commented that *When Your Relationship Ends* provides a practical and useful framework for divorced adults who want to cope more effecively with the stress of their divorced circumstance.

❍ ❍   *The Custody Revolution* (1992) by Richard Warshak. New York: Poseidon Press.

The Custody Revolution is about child custody after divorce. Author Richard Warshak, Ph.D., is a child clinical psychologist in private practice in Dallas, Texas. He specializes in psychotherapy with children of divorce and their parents, and he has conducted research on children in divorced families for more than a decade.

The Custody Revolution tells parents that the most difficult issue they face when they divorce is child custody. Warshak continually advises parents to consider the needs of children when dealing with custody issues. He encourages parents to create a family structure that assures the children that *they* have not been divorced, safeguarding their birthright to two parents. Warshak believes that fathers have often not been given adequate consideration in custody decisions. Based on his own research and that of others, as well as on his extensive clinical experience, he argues that special attention should be given to same-sex child–parent custody arrangements — fathers and sons, mothers and daughters. He marshals research and clinical evidence to support the idea that fathers can competently manage the responsibilities of single parenting.

The Custody Revolution reveals how father custody and joint custody can yield special benefits for children, especially boys. Warshak makes the case for more balance in custody decisions, more careful consideration of all the factors involved before awarding children to mothers. Warshak gives sensitive advice on ways to keep both parents positively involved in the child's life. He hopes that custody can be handled in a more civilized fashion than it has been in the past.

The Custody Revolution was published after the national survey of self-help books was conducted. This is bound to be a controversial book and will probably be appreciated more by fathers than by mothers. Fathers who already have custody of their children or parents who are contemplating divorce can benefit considerably from Warshak's commentary about first considering the needs of children instead of their own egocentric needs. This book is well-written and contains an abundance of clinical examples that provide insight about the emotional lives of children and their parents in divorced families.

CONCLUSIONS

In summary, we recommend:

- For young children in divorced families:

    ★★★★ *Dinosaurs Divorce* by Laurene Brown and Mark Brown

- For older children and adolescents in divorced families:

    ★★★★★ *The Boys and Girls Book about Divorce* by Richard Gardner

    ★★★★ *How It Feels When Parents Divorce* by Jill Krementz

- For divorced parents:

    ★★★★★ *Growing Up with Divorce* by Neil Kalter

- For divorced adults:

    ◗◖ *Rebuilding: When Your Relationship Ends* by Bruce Fisher

- On custody and how fathers can be effective single parents:

    ◗◖ *The Custody Revolution* by Richard Warshak

CHAPTER SEVENTEEN

Eating Disorders

We are a nation obsesessed with food, spending an extraordinary amount of time thinking about it, gobbling it, and avoiding it. Eating disorders include obesity and compulsive overeating, anorexia nervosa (the relentless pursuit of thinness through starvation), bulimia (a consistent binge-and-purge eating pattern), and a general obsession with weight or body image. Eating disorders are far more common in women than in men, the most extreme case being anorexia nervosa—about 95% of the cases are female.

Three types of books on eating disorders were rated in the national survey: books on compulsive overeating and binging; book on eating disorders and relationships; and spiritually based approaches to eating disorders.

Three books on compulsive overeating and binging were rated: *Why Weight?* by Geneen Roth, *You Can't Quit Eating until You Know What's Eating You* by Donna LeBlanc, and *Love Hunger* by Frank Minirth and others. A fourth book—*The Obsession* by Kim Chernin—is evaluated in the Worth a Further Look section.

Two books on eating disorders and relationships were rated: *Fat Is a Family Affair* by Judi Hollis and *When Food Is Love* by Geneen Roth.

And two books that present a spiritually based approach to eating disorders were rated: *Food for Thought* by the Hazelden Foundation and *The Love-Powered Diet* by Victoria Moran.

Eating Disorders

BOOK RATINGS IN THE NATIONAL SURVEY

Neutral	★★★ *Fat Is a Family Affair* by Judi Hollis
	★★★ *Why Weight?* by Geneen Roth
	★★★ *When Food Is Love* by Geneen Roth
	★★★ *Food for Thought* by the Hazelden Foundation
Not Recommended	★★ *You Can't Quit Eating until You Know What's Eating You* by Donna LeBlanc
	★ *Love Hunger* by Frank Minirth & others
Strongly Not Recommended	† *The Love-Powered Diet* by Victoria Moran

---

NEUTRAL

★ ★ ★   *Fat Is a Family Affair* (1985) by Judi Hollis. New York: Harper & Row.

Fat Is a Family Affair focuses on the role of close relationships in eating disorders. Author Judi Hollis, Ph.D., is a teacher and trainer in addiction counseling. She is a former compulsive overeater who founded the HOPE Institute for the family treatment of eating disorders.

Fat Is a Family Affair describes a number of eating disorders, including the binging and vomiting of bulimia, the starvation of anorexia nervosa, and compulsive overeating. Hollis recommends a Twelve-Step program as the best treatment of eating disorders. The book is divided into two main parts: Part I, The Weigh In and Part II, The Weigh Out. The Weigh In discusses how eating disorders evolve and provides a self-test to determine if you have an eating disorder. Hollis says that eating disorders involve a physiological disorder and a psychological obsession with food. Further, Hollis believes that most people with eating disorders are surrounded by 10 or 12 codependent people who, for reasons of their own, are enmeshed in trying to help or change the eating disorder but instead only perpetuate it.

The Weigh Out is written for both people with eating disorders and their families. The section begins with the assumption that the reader is a person with an eating disorder who has acknowledged his or her obsession with food and its dominance over his or her life. The principles of Overeaters Anonymous (modeled on the Alcoholics Anonymous principles) are presented, a Twelve-Step program is outlined, and the reader is encouraged to attend or start up an Overeaters Anonymous support group. Hollis gives many examples of the success stories of people who have followed her advice. Special attention is given to the family's role in eating disorders.

Fat Is a Family Affair received a 3-star Neutral rating in the national survey. Some mental health professionals liked Hollis's Twelve-Step approach and her codependency explanations. They also applauded her promotion of Overeaters Anonymous, which has helped many individuals learn to change their eating habits and not let food dominate their life. Critics didn't like the "preachy" tone of Hollis's book and the codependency explanations.

★ ★ ★   _Why Weight?: A Guide to Ending Compulsive Eating_ (1989) by Geneen Roth. New York: Plume.

Why Weight? provides an understanding of overeating and advice on how to change eating habits. Author Geneen Roth is a writer and a teacher. She founded the Breaking Free workshops that help people cope with eating disorders.

Roth overcame her own compulsive overeating several years ago. First, she put an end to constant dieting that only led to an inevitable weight gain. She eliminated her compulsive overeating by developing seven eating guidelines that form the core of her Breaking Free program:

- Eat only when you are hungry.
- Eat only when sitting down.
- Eat without distractions.
- Eat only what you want.
- Eat until you are satisfied.
- Eat in full view of others.
- Eat with enjoyment.

Why Weight? has 16 chapters, each with written exercises that help compulsive overeaters become aware of what they are doing, the emotional basis of overeating, how it would feel to be thin, how it really felt to diet and binge all those years, and how the overeater can learn to eat only when physically hungry. Each chapter also contains charts and lists that focus on what is eaten, why, when, and associated feelings with food. The book closes with practical advice about making it through the holidays and special occasions, as well as how to care for oneself without overeating.

Why Weight? received a 3-star Neutral rating in the national survey. The book is full of helpful exercises for overeaters, is psychobabble-free, and provides insights about the nature of eating problems.

★ ★ ★   *When Food Is Love* (1991) by Geneen Roth. New York: Dutton.

When Food Is Love explores the relation between eating disorders and close relationships. The book was written by Geneen Roth, the author of *Why Weight?*

Why Weight? is a practical guide for controlling the binge/diet cycle. *When Food Is Love* focuses on how family experiences as we are growing up contribute to the development of eating disorders. Roth reveals her own childhood abuses that led to compulsive overeating in adulthood and prevented her from having a successful intimate relationship with a man. According to Roth, similar patterns are found in people who are compulsive overeaters and lack intimacy in their life: excessive fantasizing, wanting what is forbidden, creating drama, the need to be in control, and the "one wrong move syndrome" (placing too much importance on doing the absolutely correct thing at this moment).

When Food Is Love received a 3-star Neutral rating in the national survey. The book's supporters said that Roth does a good job of explaining how inadequate close relationships and eating disorders are linked. Critics said that Roth does not adequately consider the biological and sociocultural factors that determine eating disorders. They also said that the book is too melodramatic in places.

★ ★ ★   *Food for Thought* (1980) by the Hazelden Foundation. New York: Harper & Row.

Food for Thought is subtitled *Daily Meditations for Dieters* and presents a spiritually based approach to coping with eating disorders. The Hazelden Foundation is based near Minneapolis and is known primarily for its alcohol treatment program. Other Hazelden books evaluated in the national survey include *Each Day a New Beginning* and *Touchstones*, both rated in Chapter 26, Relaxation, Meditation, and Stress.

Through short, daily meditations, *Food for Thought* offers encouragement for anyone who has ever tried to diet, people who overeat or have an eating disorder, and members of Overeaters Anonymous. Each day's brief reading addresses the concerns of people with eating disorders.

Food for Thought recieved a 3-star Neutral rating in the national survey. The book is especially designed for use by individuals who go to Overeaters Anonymous meetings and will have special appeal to individuals who want a spiritually-based approach to coping with an eating problem.

NOT RECOMMENDED

★★ *You Can't Quit Eating until You Know What's Eating You* (1990) by Donna LeBlanc. Deerfield Beach, FL: Health Communications.

You Can't Quit Eating until You Know What's Eating You is about compulsive overeating. Author Donna LeBlanc, M.Ed., is a counseler and former compulsive overeater who has worked with many clients to help them try to overcome their eating problems.

This book stresses that knowledge and understanding, not deprivation, produce long-term weight loss. It covers the nature of compulsive overeating, the psychological aspects of losing and putting on weight, how to deal with cravings, self-image and body-image, and the important influences of moods and emotions. The family's role and how to "reparent" the inner child are outlined (LeBlanc believes that within every compulsive overeater is a frightened inner child who desparately needs a loving, nurturant parent).

You Can't Quit Eating until You Know What's Eating You received a 2-star Not Recommended rating in the national survey. Critics said that while some of the author's advice is well founded, the inner child concept is not.

★ *Love Hunger: Recovery from Food Addiction* (1990) by Frank Minirth, Paul Meier, Robert Helmfelt, Sharon Sneed, and Don Hawkins. Nashville, TN: Thomas Nelson.

Love Hunger addresses binge eating and compulsive overeating as a codependency problem. Frank Minerth, M.D., and Paul Meier, M.D., founded the Minerth-Meier Clinic in Dallas, Texas, a psychiatric facility with branches throughout the United States. Both received degrees from Dallas Theological Seminary and have cowritten many other self-help books. Robert Helmfelt, Ed.D., specializes in the treatment of chemical dependency, codependency, and eating disorders. Sharon Sneed, Ph.D., is a registered dietician and a professor at the Medical University of South Carolina.

Love Hunger defines compulsive overeaters as people who are eating to satisfy emotional hungers—some of which they are aware of, others of which they are not. The authors show the connection between compulsive overeating and past and present close relationships. They believe that an overeater's natural hunger for love was probably thwarted in the past and give advice for how to free oneself from a codependent relationship with food. A ten-stage recovery program is presented. The preliminary steps necessary for successful dieting are spelled out, as well as meal plans and 140 recipes and food charts.

Love Hunger received a 1-star Not Recommended rating in the national survey. The consensus of the mental health professionals was that this is not a good self-help book and that better solutions for compulsive overeating can be found elsewhere.

STRONGLY NOT RECOMMENDED

† *The Love-Powered Diet* (1992) by Victoria Moran. San Rafael, CA: New World Library.

The Love-Powered Diet focuses on addiction to food and takes a Twelve-Step recovery approach. Author Victoria Moran, a contributing editor to *Victorian Times,* conducts workshops on the love-powered diet.

The Love-Powered Diet is one of a number of eating plans derived from the Alcoholics Anonymous and Overeaters Anonymous Twelve-Step recovery approach. Moran retains AA's spiritual emphasis on "letting go" and placing trust in the "God of your understanding." The approach is embellished with the transformative power of love. The author believes that healing from within involves letting go of willpower and replacing it with love's power. She argues that this strategy permits the freedom to adopt a new and healthier way of eating: eating appropriately and nutritionally is a form of self-love.

The specific diet that Moran recommends is called a "vegan" diet, and it consists only of plant foods—no meat, fish, eggs, or dairy products. The author touts this diet as love-powered, saying it is generous, delicious, and aesthetically pleasing. She also argues that it promotes health and normal weight, is economical, respects all life, and is environmentally sustainable.

The mental health experts in the national survey gave *The Love-Powered Diet* a negative rating, placing it in the Strongly Not Recommended category. They said that the book recommends a diet that is extreme and likely to be unsustainable by most human beings.

WORTH A FURTHER LOOK

◐◐ *Obsession* (1981) by Kim Chernin. New York: Harper & Row.

Obsession is about compulsive overeating and the sociopolitical issues associated with being thin. Author Kim Chernin is a free-lance editor, a writing consultant, and an instructor at the University of California at Berkeley. She serves as a consultant on eating disorders.

Chernin was a compulsive overeater herself and she recounts her own story about binging rather than dealing with her emotions. However, the book goes far beyond her personal narrative. She believes that since the cultural ideal for women in American society is to be thin, many women feel guilty about deriving any pleasure from eating. The result: Women diet compulsively every time they add an extra pound or two. Chernin says that the cultural ideal evolved from the masculine perception that a, large voluptuous body symbolizes power and danger. Women counteract this view by vigorously trying to control their own bodies. A lifelong obsession with food ensues. The author calls on literary sources, her own experiences, and testimonials from others as evidence that both anorexic and obese women share the same hostility, fear of sexuality, and uneasiness about women's roles.

Obsession received a positive rating in the national survey, but it was rated by only 5 respondents. The book's enthusiasts said that Chernin has provided an important analysis of the role that cultural and gender factors play in women's eating disorders. *Obsession* answers many of the questions posed by Susie Orbach's *Fat Is a Feminist Issue*, evaluated in Chapter 15, Dieting and Weight Loss. Critics said that in places Chernin is too histrionic and that she doesn't adequately address the biological basis of eating disorders.

CONCLUSIONS

In summary, we recommend:

- On the connection between close relationships and compulsive overeating:

  ★★★ *Why Weight?* by Geneen Roth

- On the contribution of cultural factors and gender roles to women's obsession with food:

  ❍❍ *Obsession* by Kim Chernin

- For a spiritually based approach to eating disorders:

  ★★★ *Food for Thought* by the Hazelden Foundation

CHAPTER EIGHTEEN

Exercise

In 1961, President John F. Kennedy offered the following message: "We are underexercised as a nation. We look instead of play. We ride instead of walk. Our existence deprives us of the minimum of physical activity essential for healthy living." Without question, people are jogging, cycling, and aerobically exercising more than they were in 1961, but far too many of us still fit that unflattering category of people known as "couch potatoes."

Most people are well aware that exercise benefits physical health but not as aware that it is also a plus for mental health. Exercise can improve self-esteem, lower anxiety, and reduce depression. How much exercise? Research on the benefits of exercise suggests that both moderate and intense exercise produce important physical and psychological gains. Some people enjoy rigorous, intense exercise, others more moderate exercise. The mental health benefits added to the physical health benefits make exercise one of life's most important activities. And it's never too late. Researchers are now showing strong benefits of exercise in the elderly.

Is exercise always good for a person? Almost always. Some people, though, become so compulsive about exercise that it is unhealthy. Activity disorder is an intense, driven, compulsive exercise pattern often combined with rigid dietary restrictions that can damage the person's body. People with this disorder tend to be high achieving, independent, and high in self-control and perfectionism. As with so many of life's journeys, too much of a good thing is not healthy.

The topics of books on exercise that made the final ratings in the national survey fall in four categories: aerobic exercise for men; exercise for women; running; and exercise for children.

One book on aerobic exercise for men was rated: *The New Aerobics* by Kenneth Cooper.

Exercise
BOOK RATINGS IN THE NATIONAL SURVEY

Strongly Recommended	★★★★★	*The New Aerobics* by Kenneth Cooper
Diamonds in the Rough	◆	*The New Aerobics for Women* by Kenneth Cooper and Mildred Cooper
Neutral	★★★	*Kid Fitness* by Kenneth Cooper
	★★★	*The Complete Book of Running* by James Fixx
Strongly Not Recommended	†	*The FAT-Burning Workout* by Joyce Vedral

---

Two books on exercise for women were rated: *The New Aerobics for Women* by Kenneth and Mildred Cooper and *The FAT-Burning Workout* by Joyce Vedral.

One book on running was rated: *The Complete Book of Running* by James Fixx.

One book on exercise for children was rated: *Kid Fitness* by Kenneth Cooper.

Another book—*Living with Exercise* by Steven Blair—is profiled in Worth a Further Look. It explores how to improve one's health through moderate physical activity.

STRONGLY RECOMMENDED

★ ★ ★ ★ ★   *The New Aerobics* (1970) by Kenneth Cooper. New York: Bantam.

The New Aerobics is the updated version of Kenneth Cooper's *Aerobics*, both of which lay out Cooper's age-adjusted recommendations for aerobic exercise. Author Kenneth Cooper, who has a medical degree and a Master's degree in public health, developed the concept of aerobic exercise. The aerobic exercise program recommended by Cooper in *The New Aerobics* has been adopted as the official exercise program of the United States Air Force, the United States Navy, and the Royal Canadian Air Force. Currently, Cooper directs the Aerobic Center and the Cooper Clinic in Dallas, Texas, elaborate facilities that house extensive and varied exercise programs, health testing, and research on aerobic exercise.

Just what is aerobic exercise? Aerobic exercise refers to sustained exercise—jogging, swimming, or cycling, for example—that stimulates heart and lung activity. Cooper's aerobic exercise program is medically sound and has been tested extensively on Air Force personnel and many others. The aerobics system is carefully planned to condition the heart, lungs, and body tissues of people who are either in fairly good health or poor health (the latter should have a physical checkup before beginning the program). The aerobics program uses common forms of exercise—walking, running, swimming, cycling, handball, squash, and basketball—to achieve the desired results.

Cooper developed a simple, easy-to-follow aerobics point system that is age-adjusted to the capabilities of men, women, and children. To begin, Cooper recommends taking a 12-minute fitness test to determine your current level of fitness. The test is simple: How far can you run or walk in 12 minutes? How far you can go in 12 minutes places you in one of five fitness categories from very poor to excellent. Then you embark on an aerobics exercise program based on your current fitness level. Four or five workouts a week—such as running 2 miles at about 10 minutes a mile or less—will get you aerobically fit. Recently, Cooper has pointed out that reducing health risks without being physically fit can be accomplished with a brisk half-hour walk four or five times a week. Cooper, now in his early sixties and still in great shape, has reduced his workouts as he has gotten older. He now jogs four or five times a week for 2 to 3 miles at about an 8-minute pace and lifts weights.

Much of the book consists of elaborate tables that spell out how many aerobic points you get for specific types and duration of exercise, along with how many points you should strive for per week based on your current level of fitness, your age, and your sex. A separate chapter deals with aerobic therapy for people with cardiovascular problems.

The New Aerobics received a 5-star Strongly Recommended rating in the national survey. This is an outstanding self-help book. It is research based and easy to read, and for people who are in poor or only fairly good physical shape, Cooper's recommended aerobic program will reap physical and psychological benefits. Kathie Davis, Director of the Assocation for Fitness Professionals, says that Kenneth Cooper was the first doctor to write and speak about the benefits of exercise and that he is responsible for getting thousands of people off their couches. Donald Cooper (no relation), M.D., comments that Kenneth Cooper has had more influence on getting America running than any other person. And his positive influence is international. In Brazil, when people go out to run they call it "doing the Cooper."

Another Cooper book that was written after *The New Aerobics* is

The Aerobics Program for Well-Being (1982). In *The Aerobics Program for Well-Being*, Cooper argues that to become physically fit a person doesn't have to run more than 15 miles a week. Anything more yields diminishing returns because of potential injuries.

DIAMONDS IN THE ROUGH

◆ *The New Aerobics for Women* (1988) by Kenneth Cooper and Mildred Cooper. New York: Bantam.

The New Aerobics for Women tailors Kenneth Cooper's aerobic exercise program to the capabilities and needs of women. Cooper is joined in the authorship of this book by his wife, Mildred.

The New Aerobics for Women is the revised edition of Cooper's 1972 book, *Aerobics for Women*. Far more research has been conducted on women's physical fitness and many women's life styles have dramatically changed since 1972. The Coopers incorporate these changes in their 1988 book.

The New Aerobics for Women is a comprehensive guide that is designed to help women become physically fit. It includes age-adjusted exercise programs that are tailored to a woman's life style and current level of physical fitness. Following are some of the topics covered in the book:

- Common misconceptions women have about exercise and how to correct them
- How to use the aerobic point system to chart their progress
- How to use aerobic exercise to combat fatigue and depression
- How aerobic exercise can prevent heart disease, osteoporosis, and other diseases and ailments

The New Aerobics for Women was placed in the Diamonds in the Rough category because it was rated very positively but by only 28 respondents. Its average rating was high enough for 5-stars. This is an excellent self-help book for women. The addition of Cooper's wife provides a woman's perspective on aerobic exercise, and the tailoring of the aerobic system to women is effectively carried out. This book can provide physical and mental health benefits for women who are in poor or only fairly good physical shape.

NEUTRAL

★ ★ ★ *Kid Fitness: A Complete Shape Up Program* (1991) by Kenneth Cooper. New York: Bantam.

Kid Fitness is Kenneth Cooper's recently published book on improving children's physical fitness. Cooper's concern about the declining fitness levels of today's children and youth motivated him to write this book, which is aimed at parents. Cooper tells parents how to help their children develop good exercise and eating habits. Parents learn how to motivate their children to exercise, how to test their fitness, and how to implement aerobic exercise programs to achieve physical fitness in their children. The book emphasizes nutrition more than Cooper's other aerobic books and includes 50 pages of diet recommendations and recipes for children, and it comes down hard on fast-food resturants and the high cholesterol and fat content of their food. Cooper also emphasizes the importance of family involvement in exercise, peer reinforcement, and sports participation. He says that schools have not done a good job in physical education. However, Cooper distinguishes between playing sports and being in good physical shape—some children who play sports are not aerobically fit. The book is filled with charts and exercises for children of different ages.

Kid Fitness received a 3-star Neutral rating in the national survey. The book was published just prior to the national survey and was rated by only 15 respondents. This is a good self-help book for parents who are concerned about their children's physical fitness. It is well-written, practical, and medically sound.

★★★ *The Complete Book of Running* (1977) by James Fixx. New York: Random House.

The Complete Book of Running is an encyclopedic volume that covers virtually every aspect of running. Author James Fixx was a runner and writer who lived in New York City.

Fixx begins with his own story. He was once overweight, tense, and smoked heavily. He began running to strengthen his legs after a recurring pulled muscle, and gradually he discovered that as his running prowess increased so did the physical and psychological benefits. Two years later he was winning 10-kilometer races, was 40 pounds lighter, and had quit smoking. He said he developed a stronger sense of controlling his life and could concentrate better and for longer periods of time. For more than 300 pages, Fixx cites studies and medical opinions on how running contributes to health, productivity, and well-being. Once Fixx has persuaded readers that running will reshape their bodies and their lives, he explains how to do it.

The Complete Book of Running received a 3-star Neutral rating in the national survey. Fixx does a commendable job of taking the nervous neophyte step-by-step from selecting the right running shoes to the ultimate euphoria of being in great physical shape. This is a good book on running, although Fixx glosses over the evidence that running too much can bring on a whole new set of aches and pains and that moderate exercise reaps the same physical and psychological effects. The book is much narrower than Cooper's aerobics books, which gives a choice among a number of different types of exercise.

STRONGLY NOT RECOMMENDED

† *The FAT-Burning Workout: From Fat to Firm in 24 Days* (1991) by Joyce Vedral. New York: Warner Books.

The FAT-Burning Workout is a quick-fix approach to weight loss through exercise for women. Author Joyce Vedral has a doctorate in English literature, has written other self-help books on exercise such as *The 12-Minute Total-Body Workout* and *Hardbodies,* and also has written numerous workout guides for parents and teenagers.

The FAT-Burning Workout is designed to help women burn fat, lose weight, and firm their muscles through regular brief and intense workouts. The book's cover states that Vedral will take you from fat to firm in just 24 days. Vedral argues that diets can help you lose weight, but they won't help you tone your body. You need something more: Vedral's fat-burning workout. Her fat-to-firm program uses 20 to 30 minute workouts using free weights and an exercise bench. A brief chapter on nutrition tells you how to develop a diet plan that will also help you to burn fat. The book includes a number of photographs of Vedral conducting the physical fitness exercises she recommends.

The FAT-Burning Workout received a negative average rating in the national survey, placing it on the Strongly Not Recommended list. The book's critics didn't like the quick-fix, gimmicky orientation and said that the book presents a very narrow approach to improving women's physical fitness and helping them lose weight. The mental health professionals in the national survey felt that Kenneth and Mildred Cooper's *New Aerobics for Women* presents a much more reasoned, well-balanced approach to women's physical fitness.

WORTH A FURTHER LOOK

❍ ❍ *Living with Exercise* (1991) by Steven N. Blair. Dallas: American Health Publishing Co.

Living with Exercise is about improving your health through moderate physical activity. Author Steven Blair has a doctorate in epidemiology.

He is director of epidemiology at the Institute for Aerobics Research in Dallas, Texas, and is a highly respected researcher in health behavior and sports medicine. He recently conducted research to show that moderate physical exercises increases the probability of living a longer life.

Living with Exercise focuses on helping inactive people to attain a moderate level of fitness by enaging in brief exercise sessions during the course of their daily lives. Blair explains how to overcome the psychological and physical roadblocks of beginning a fitness program and how to assess one's current level of fitness and commitment to making a change in life style. He explains how to seek opportunities to spend energy, evaluates the role of nutrition in fitness, advises maintain fitness over time, and includes information about exercise and fitness for children and youth.

Living with Exercise was published too late to be included in the national survey. It is an excellent self-help book for inactive people who want to reach a moderate rather than high level of fitness. The book is easy to read, the instructions are very clear, and the goals are reachable even by the most sedentary of people. Like Brownell's book on losing weight (Chapter 15), *Living with Exercise* is not available through bookstores. It can be ordered from the LEARN Education Center, 1555 W. Mockingbird Lane, Dallas, TX, 75325; phone: 800-736-7323.

CONCLUSIONS

In summary, we recommend:

- For men who want to become physically fit:

  ★★★★★   *The New Aerobics* by Kenneth Cooper

- For women who want to become physically fit:

  ◆   *The New Aerobics for Women* by Kenneth Cooper and Mildred Cooper

- For inactive people who want to become moderately fit:

  ❍❍   *Living with Exercise* by Steven Blair

- For parents who want to help their children become more physically fit:

  ★★★   *Kid Fitness* by Kenneth Cooper

CHAPTER NINETEEN

The Family

"A friend loves you for your intelligence, a mistress for your charm, but your family's love is unreasoning; you were born into it and are of its flesh and blood. Nevertheless, it can irritate you more than any group in the world," commented the French philosopher André Maurois. Families who do not function well together often foster maladjusted behavior on the part of one or more of their members.

In this chapter we limit our evaluation to general books on the family, especially those that examine how the family can be a source of problem behavior. Other chapters cover the family's role in a number of specific areas, abuse and recovery (Chapter 2), addiction and recovery (Chapter 3), child development and parenting (Chapter 10), divorce (Chapter 16), love, intimacy, and marriage (Chapter 22), stepfamilies (Chapter 31), and teenagers and parenting (Chapter 32).

The family books in the national survey can be divided into the following four categories: family systems approaches to solving family problems; book on adults who grew up in dysfunctional families; behavioral approaches to family problems; and books on competent families.

One book on the family systems approach made the final ratings: *The Family Crucible* by Augustus Napier and Carl Whitaker.

Two books for adults who grew up in dysfunctional families were rated: *Adult Children* by John Friel and Linda Friel, and *Bradshaw on the Family* by John Bradshaw.

One book that presents a behavioral approach for helping parents improve a child's behavior was rated: *Families* by Gerald Patterson.

And one book that explores what competent families are like was rated: *Back to the Family* by Ray Guarendi. Another book—*Familyhood* by Lee Salk—is profiled in Worth a Further Look.

Family

BOOK RATINGS IN THE NATIONAL SURVEY

Recommended	★★★★ *The Family Crucible* by Augustus Napier and Carl Whitaker
Diamonds in the Rough	◆ *Families* by Gerald Patterson
Neutral	★★★ *Back to the Family* by Ray Guarendi
	★★★ *Adult Children* by John Friel and Linda Friel
Not Recommended	★★ *Bradshaw on the Family* by John Bradshaw

RECOMMENDED

★★★★ *The Family Crucible* (1978) by Augustus Napier and Carl Whitaker. New York: Harper & Row.

The Family Crucible presents a family systems approach to solving family problems. August Napier, Ph.D., is a leading family systems therapist who has been on the faculty of the Department of Psychiatry at the University of Wisconsin Medical School for a number of years. Napier was trained by coauthor Carl Whitaker, M.D., a psychiatrist at the University of Wisconsin Medical School.

Family systems therapy has become increasingly popular in recent years. *The Family Crucible* describes in considerable detail what family systems therapy is and how it is conducted. In family systems therapy the family is viewed as a system of interacting individuals with different subsystems (husband–wife, sibling–sibling, mother–daughter, father–sibling–sibling, and so on). A basic theme of family system therapy is that most problems that seem to be the property of a single individual evolved from relationships within the family. Therefore, the best way to solve these problems is to work with the family rather than the individual. One person within the family may show some abnormal symptoms, but those symptoms are viewed in this approach as a function of family relationships.

Napier and Whitaker say that problem families have in common certain general patterns: acute interpersonal or intrapersonal stress; polarization (family members at odds with each other) and escalation (the conflict intensifies); triangulation (one member is the scapegoat for two other members who are in conflict but pretend not to be); blaming; diffusion of identity (no one is free to be autonomous); and fear of immobility, which Napier and Whitaker equate with fear of death (of the family).

The family systems therapist identifies how such problems are being played out by different family members and then tries to help them change their interaction patterns and relationships with each other. Napier and Whitaker describe in considerable detail how they used family systems therapy with a particular family — an angry adolescent and other angry and equally distressed family members.

The Family Crucible received a 4-star Recommended rating in the national survey. Many family therapists perceive this book to be one of the classics in family systems therapy. The extensive case study that is presented reveals how family systems therapy can succeed. The book is written mainly for a professional audience and is not really a self-help book, but self-help readers who are knowledgeable about therapy and who are intellectually challenged will enjoy this book.

DIAMONDS IN THE ROUGH

♦ *Families: Applications of Social Learning to Family Life* (rev. ed., 1975) by Gerald Patterson. Champaign, IL: Research Press.

Families presents parents with a behavioral approach to improving their children's behavior. Gerald Patterson is a well-known behaviorist who has been the director of the Oregon Behavioral Research Institute and is past president of the Association for the Advancement of Behavior Therapy.

Families describes behavior modification techniques that parents can use to correct children's problem behaviors. To begin, Patterson explains some important behavioral concepts like social reinforcers, aversive stimuli, and accidental training. Time-out procedures and behavioral contracts are integrated into a step-by-step reinforcement management program for parents to implement with their own children. Behavioral management strategies are also tailored to children with specific problems.

Families was placed in the Diamonds in the Rough category because it was positively rated but by only 12 respondents. Mental health professionals of a behavioral persuasion described this book as exceptionally good for parents who want to improve a child's behavior, especially that of a child who is aggressive and out of control. However, critics faulted Patterson for talking mainly to mothers and ignoring fathers and for focusing mainly on male children. Other critics said that improving a child's behavior involves reeducation of the family and is not as easy as early behavior modification enthusiasts thought (Patterson's *Families* was published in 1975). In the last two decades, researchers have found that changing a child's problem behavior often requires change not only on the part of the family but in other contexts as well, such as in the child's peer system and at school.

NEUTRAL

★ ★ ★   *Back to the Family* (1990) by Ray Guarendi. New York: Basic Books.

Back to the Family charts the characteristics of psychologically healthy families. Author Ray Guarendi, Ph.D., is a clinical psychologist who specializes in parenting and family issues.

Back to the Family is subtitled *How to Encourage Traditional Values in Complicated Times.* It is the result of a study sponsored by the Children's Hospital in Akron, Ohio. One hundred happy families were nominated by award winning educators in the National/State Teachers of the Year organization. Guarendi distilled information from interviews with the families and developed a how-to manual for parents who want to build a happy home. The interviews reveal how families can mature through good times and bad times and how parents in happy, competent families sifted through various types of child-rearing advice to arrive at the way they reared their own children. In some cases they agreed with the experts, in others they chose their own course.

Back to the Family received a 3-star Neutral rating in the national survey. The book's supporters said that, in a time when the family is under attack, Guarendi's approach of highlighting the strengths of happy, competent families can help families learn how to change for the better. However, one critic said that in spite of the author's good intentions, the book sounds like a combination revival meeting and talk-show parody. At times the book is inspirational, but families need more than a "pep talk" to solve their problems. Another critic commented that Guarendi's description of a model family lacks depth.

★ ★ ★   *Adult Children: The Secrets of Dysfunctional Families* (1988) by John Friel and Linda Friel. Deerfield Beach, FL: Health Communications.

Adult Children is primarily for adults who grew up in dysfunctional families and suggests what they can do about it to improve their lives. Author

John Friel, Ph.D., is a psychologist in private practice in St. Paul, Minnesota, and director of a codependency treatment program. Linda Friel is a codependency counselor.

Adult Children is modeled after the twelve-step program of Alcoholics Anonymous. It tries to shed light on why adults who grew up in dysfunctional families developed problems as adults—problems such as addiction, depression, compulsion, unhealthy dependency, stress disorders, and unsatisfying relationships. Five sections discuss who adult children are and what their symptoms are; family systems and how dysfunctional families get off track; how the dysfunctional family affects the child; a model of codependency; and recovery.

Adult Children barely received a 3-star Neutral rating, several mental health professionals liked the adult child approach of the book, in which people are encouraged to go back through their lives and search the psychological files of their families for clues to their current disordered lives. Critics of the book did not like the codependency approach of the authors and said that the authors' codependency model is very poorly defined. Critics also said that *Adult Children* might be appropriate for adults who grew up in an alcoholic family but that transporting concepts about that type of family to many other types is unwarranted.

NOT RECOMMENDED

★ ★ *Bradshaw on the Family* (1988) by John Bradshaw. Deerfield Beach, FL: Health Communications.

Bradshaw on the Family, like *Adult Children*, stresses that many types of adult problems are caused by growing up in a dysfunctional family. John Bradshaw was educated in Canada, where he studied for the Roman Catholic priesthood at the University of Toronto. He has a Master's degree in religion and philosophy. He joined a monastery at age 21 and stayed for nine and a half years. For the past two decades he has worked as counselor, theologian, management consultant, public speaker, and self-help book author.

Bradshaw on the Family is the outgrowth of a television series by the same name that Bradshaw narrated. He argues that the rules and attitudes that most of us learned while we were growing up are not the best and have caused innumerable problems and disorders in today's adults. Indeed, Bradshaw says that a stunning 96% of all families are emotionally impaired to some degree! The unhealthy rules have been handed down from generation to generation and ultimately have become ingrained in society at large. Bradshaw stresses that the society is sick because the family is sick, and he believes that the most common family illness of all is codependency.

How can adults break free from the shackles of a dysfunctional family upbringing? Bradshaw's road map for recovery has three stages:

1. Be willing to risk a new family of affiliation.
2. Break the original spell.
3. Adopt spiritual awakening and empowerment.

Bradshaw on the Family received a 2-star, Nor Recommended rating in the national survey. This was the most frequently rated family book in the survey, evaluated by 126 respondents. However, the consensus of the mental health professionals was that Bradshaw's dysfunctional-family/codependency approach to family problems has problems of its own. These problems are detailed in the profile of Bradshaw's book, *Healing the Shame that Binds You* in Chapter 2, Abuse and Recovery, and in a critique of codependency in Chapter 11, Codependency and Recovery. Critics especially fault Bradshaw for overgeneralizing family problems and spreading a net that is so broad that virtually everyone can say that they grew up in a troubled family. His critics also say that the quick-fix approach he advocates is overly simplistic, especially for people who have been seriously affected by long-term emotional problems. Yet other critics wonder if his parent blaming doesn't provide a convenient excuse for adults to avoid responsibility for their failures.

WORTH A FURTHER LOOK

◑ ◑   *Familyhood* (1992) by Lee Salk. New York: Simon & Schuster.

Familyhood is about the importance of the family in children's lives and about nurturing family values that matter. Lee Salk, Ph.D., was a clinical psychologist on the staff of the Department of Psychiatry at the New York Hospital—Cornell Medical Center. For more than two decades, he was a consultant to various institutions and clinics on child rearing and family issues. His column "You and Your Family" ran in *McCall's* magazine for 19 years. Salk wrote eight other books, including *What Every Child Would Like His Parents to Know*. He died in 1992.

Although the structure of families has changed enormously in recent years because of high divorce rates, increasing numbers of stepfamilies, and huge numbers of working mothers, Salk believes that the values the family cherishes most have not changed. Using results from a comprehensive family values survey, Salk describes how parents today still want their family members to provide emotional support for one another; want children to show respect for parents and believe that parents should also show respect for children; think that parents should show mutual respect for each other; believe that family members should take responsibility for their own actions; and think that family members should try to understand and listen to each other. Salk draws on his extensive background in counseling parents to provide advice on how to make the family a place where people care about each other and transmit important values.

Familyhood was published after the national survey was conducted. It is well-written and can especially benefit families searching for ways to instill positive values in their children, regardless of the family's structure.

CONCLUSIONS

In summary, we recommend:

- For a family systems therapy approach to solving family problems:

  ★★★★ *The Family Crucible* by Augustus Napier and Carl Whitaker

- For parents who want to instill positive values in their family:

  ◑◑ *Familyhood* by Lee Salk

CHAPTER TWENTY

Friendship, Loneliness,
and Single Adult Life

In this chapter we evaluate self-help books that explore three important aspects of people's social lives—friendship, loneliness, and single adult life. For many of us, finding a true friend is not an easy task. In the words of American historian Henry Adams, "One friend in life is much, two are many, and three hardly possible." While finding a true friend is often difficult, the power of friendship in making our life more enjoyable and meaningful is widely recognized. As Ralph Waldo Emerson said, "A man's growth is seen in the successive choirs of his friends."

Some of us are lonely. We may feel that no one knows us very well. We may feel isolated in the sense that we do not have anyone we can turn to in times of need or stress. The importance people attach to commitment in relationships and the decline in stable close relationships are among the reasons feelings of loneliness are common today.

The number of people in the United States who live a single adult life increased in the decades of the 1970s and 1980s and is expected to continue to increase at least through the end of the century. Many myths are associated with being single, ranging from "the swinging single" to the "desperately lonely, suicidal single." Most single adults, of course, are somewhere between these extremes.

The subjects of self-help books on friendship, loneliness, and single adult life can be divided into the following categories: intimacy and friendship; the benefits and rewards of friendship; how to meet people and make friends; how to overcome social isolation and shyness; and adjusting to living alone and single adult life.

One book in the national survey on intimacy and friendship was rated: *Intimate Strangers* by Lillian Rubin.

One book on the benefits and rewards of friendship was rated: *Just Friends,* also by Lillian Rubin.

Two books focus on how to meet people and make friends: *How to*

Friendship, Loneliness, and Single Adult Life
BOOK RATINGS IN THE NATIONAL SURVEY

Strongly Recommended	★★★★★	*Intimate Strangers* by Lillian Rubin
Recommended	★★★★	*Shyness* by Philip Zimbardo
	★★★★	*Intimate Connections* by David Burns
	★★★★	*Just Friends* by Lillian Rubin
Neutral	★★★	*Living Alone and Liking It* by Lynn Shahan
	★★★	*The Art of Living Single* by Michael Broder
Not Recommended	★★	*How to Start a Conversation and Make Friends* by Don Gabor
	★	*How to Win Friends and Influence People* by Dale Carnegie

Start a Conversation and Make Friends by Don Gabor and *How to Win Friends and Influence People* by Dale Carnegie.

Overcoming social isolation and shyness is addressed in two books: *Shyness* by Philip Zimbardo and *Intimate Connections* by David Burns.

Adjusting to living alone and single adult life are the main topics of two books: *Living Alone and Liking It* by Lynn Shahan and *The Art of Living Single* by Michael Broder.

STRONGLY RECOMMENDED

★ ★ ★ ★ ★   *Intimate Strangers* (1983) by Lillian Rubin. New York: Harper & Row.

Intimate Strangers focuses on intimacy and communication difficulties between women and men. Author Lillian Rubin, Ph.D., is a practicing psychotherapist. She also is a research associate at the Institute for the Study of Social Change at the University of California at Berkeley.

Rubin tackles a relationship problem that confronts many women and men—inability to develop a satisfying intimate relationship with each other. Rubin says that male/female differences in intimacy are related to the fact that it is primarily mothers who raise children and are the emotional managers in a family. Because girls identify with mothers and boys with fathers, females develop a capacity for intimacy and an interest in managing emotional problems but males do not. Rubin supports her ideas with a number of case studies derived from interviews with approximately 150 couples.

Many different dimensions of close relationships are analyzed in *Intimate Strangers*. Rubin especially provides detailed insights about the nature of intimacy and communication problems in sexual matters and in raising children. She concludes that the only solution to the intimacy gulf between females and males is for every child to be raised and nurtured by two loving parents, not just one (the mother), from birth on. That is, Rubin's culprit is the nonnurturant father, who, she says, has to change his ways and serve as a nurturant, intimate identification figure committed to managing emotional difficulties. Only then will boys have an opportunity to develop these important relationship qualities.

Intimate Strangers received a 5-star Strongly Recommended rating in the national survey. A number of mental health professionals thought that Rubin's thesis of the nonnurturing father is an important one and that it holds the key to unlocking the problems of relationship intimacy between women and men in adulthood. They believe that our relationships as adults would be much more satisfying if boys had nurturant, intimacy-oriented male models to identify with as they are growing up.

While this book is reviewed in this chapter, its contents certainly also apply to several other categories, such as communication (Chapter 12—where we evaluate Deborah Tannen's book, *You Just Don't Understand*, that focuses on female/male communication problems) and love, intimacy, and marriage (Chapter 22—where we review Harriet Lerner's book, *The Dance of Intimacy*, and Maggie Scarf's *Intimate Partners*, which address sex differences in intimacy in a fashion similar to Rubin's).

RECOMMENDED

★ ★ ★ ★   *Shyness* (1987) by Philip Zimbardo. Reading, MA: Addison-Wesley.

Shyness gives advice about how to overcome social isolation and become more gregarious. Author Philip Zimbardo, Ph.D., is a highly respected professor of psychology at Stanford University. He has written over a hundred research articles for scientific journals.

According to Zimbardo, shyness is a widespread problem that affects as many as four out of every five people at one time or another in their lives. He explores how and why people become shy and examines the roles that parents, teachers, spouses, and culture play in creating shy people. What does Zimbardo say shy people can do about their situation? First, they have to analyze their shyness and figure out how they got this way. Possible reasons include negative evaluations, fear of being rejected, fear of intimacy, or lack of adequate social skills, among others. Second, they need to build up their self-esteem. To help with this, Zimbardo spells out fifteen steps to becoming more confident. Third, shy people need to improve their social skills. To accomplish this, Zimbardo describes several behavior modification strategies, tells how to set realistic goals, and advocates working hard toward achieving these goals.

Shyness received a 4-star Recommended rating in the national survey, coming very close to making the 5-star Strongly Recommended rating. It is a well-known book and was the most frequently rated book in this category (164 respondents). This is an excellent self-help book for shy people. It gives sound advice, is free of psychobabble, and is easy to read.

★ ★ ★ ★   *Intimate Connections: The New Clinically Tested Program for Overcoming Loneliness* (1985) by David Burns. New York: William Morrow.

Intimate Connections presents a program for overcoming loneliness. Author David Burns, M.D., is a clinical psychiatrist, teacher, and researcher at the Presbyterian Medical Center of Philadelphia. Burns is also the author of *Feeling Good*, which was very positively evaluated in the national survey (Chapter 14, Depression).

Burns believes that loneliness is essentially a state of mind primarily caused by the faulty assumption that a loving partner is needed before one can feel happy and secure. Burns says that the first step in breaking free from the loneliness pattern is learning to like and love oneself. He also makes a distinction between two types of loneliness: situational loneliness, which lasts for only a brief time and can be healthy and motivating, and chronic loneliness, which persists and results from problems that have plagued people for most of their lives.

In *Intimate Connections*, Burns says that to overcome chronic loneliness a person has to change the patterns of perception that created the loneliness and continue to perpetuate it. Among the topics Burns touches upon are how to make social connections, how to get close to others, and how to improve one's sexual life. Checklists, worksheets, daily mood logs, and a number of self-assessments are found throughout the book.

Intimate Connections received a 4-star Recommended rating in the national survey. The book is not nearly as well known as Burns's *Feel-*

ing Good (evaluated by 254 respondents, compared to only 46 evaluations of *Intimate Connections*). Most mental health professionals who know about *Intimate Connections* find it to be a good self-help book for helping people overcome their loneliness. It is easy to read and includes straightforward advice that, if followed, can help people break away from their lonely feelings.

★ ★ ★ ★   *Just Friends: The Role of Friendship in Our Lives* (1985) by Lillian Rubin. New York: Harper & Row.

Just Friends examines the nature of intimacy and friendship. Author Lillian Rubin also wrote *Intimate Strangers*, evaluated earlier in this chapter.

Rubin analyzes the nature of the valued yet fragile bond of friendship between women, between men, between women and men, between best friends, and in couples. She says that unlike many other relationships, friendship is a private affair with no rituals, social contracts, shared tasks, role requirements, or institutional supports of any kind.

When people are asked about their relationship with a friend, they often struggle in trying to explain it, many times simply responding, "Well, we're just friends." Yet Rubin believes friends are central players in our lives, not just in childhood but in adulthood as well. Friends give us a reference outside our families against which we can judge and evaluate ourselves; they help us develop an independent sense of self and support our effort to adapt to new circumstances and stressful situations.

Just Friends received a 4-star Recommended rating in the national survey. Most mental health professionals thought that Rubin's book provides an insightful analysis of the important and often overlooked role that friends play in our lives. However, some critics said that Rubin exaggerates sex differences in the intimacy of friendships and implies that females have exclusive rights to intimacy.

NEUTRAL

★ ★ ★   *Living Alone and Liking It* (1981) by Lynn Shahan. New York: Stratford Press.

Living Alone and Liking It is a guide to living on your own. Author Lynn Shahan is a counselor, educator, and administrator who has herself lived alone for many years.

The purpose of *Living Alone and Liking It* is to help readers develop ways to meet their own needs without depending on someone else, to experience the pleasure of living a productive life on their own, and to make the time of living alone a time of personal fulfillment. The book is divided into three main sections. Section I, The Adjustment to Living Alone, describes what people are likely to feel when they suddenly find themselves alone and how to combat loneliness. Section II, Making Your Own Fun, presents ideas about self-entertainment, hobbies and activities, and going places unaccompanied. Section III, Practical Aspects of Living Alone, describes how to cook for one person, the best places to live, and how to manage money.

Living Alone and Liking It received a 3-star Neutral rating in the national survey. This book is a practical, easy-to-read guide for living alone.

★ ★ ★   *The Art of Living Single* (1988) by Michael Broder. New York: Avon Books.

The Art of Living Single provides advice about living alone. Author Michael Broder, Ph.D., is a clinical psychologist who practices in Philadelphia. He also conducts research on the transitions involved in divorce.

This book presents strategies for coping with life as a single adult: how to appreciate time spent alone and how to make use of time in social situations. The book is divided into six main sections. Section I, Social Strategies, offer advice on making new friends and keeping old ones. Section II, Why No One Has to Be Lonely, offers coping strategies for dealing with feelings of loneliness. Section III, Romantic Strategies, explores barriers to establishing a love relationship and how to overcome them; Section IV, Getting Involved and Nurturing a Relationship, suggests ways to increase the likelihood of finding the right person; Section V, The Perils of Sex, urges evaluation of the risks of a sexual relationship. Section VI, Survival Strategies, focuses on health and security needs, how to balance work and play, and planning for the future.

The Art of Living Single received a 3-star Neutral rating in the national survey. This book provides a great deal of practical advice on living alone happily and effectively. It is similar to Lynn Shahan's book, *Living Alone and Liking It*, but examines single-adult issues in greater depth.

NOT RECOMMENDED

★ ★   *How to Start a Conversation and Make Friends* (1983) by Don Gabor. New York: Simon & Schuster.

How to Start a Conversation and Make Friends dispenses advice on how to meet people and make friends. Author Don Gabor has taught classes under the same title as his book.

Gabor presents strategies that he says will help readers "connect with people." He describes the importance of body language, gives tips for starting conversations naturally and keeping them going, provides recommendations for how to get across ideas, and counsels how to close a conversation naturally. Gabor also offers advice on how to remember names and overcome various conversational hang-ups.

How to Start a Conversation and Make Friends received a 2-star Not Recommended rating in the national survey. Critics said that the book is somewhat superficial and is not well organized. Some of the concrete examples of conversational openers and comebacks, however, are well done.

★   *How to Win Friends and Influence People* (rev. ed., 1981) by Dale Carnegie. New York: Simon & Schuster.

How to Win Friends and Influence People, as its title implies gives advice about, how to develop friendships, meet people, get along with them better, and influence them. Author Dale Carnegie has no professional mental health background or affiliation. He is a famous motivational speaker and, because of this book, one of the most successful self-help authors of all time in terms of book sales. Dale Carnegie courses are taught throughout the world to help people improve their lives and have been taken by more than three million people.

The book itself was derived from a stenographer's notes taken during a Dale Carnegie Course in Effective Speaking offered in the Eastern United States in the 1930s (the first edition of the book was published in 1936). *How to Win Friends and Influence People* is divided into six main parts: Fundamental Techniques in Handling People, Six Ways to Make People Like You, Twelve Ways to Win People to Your Way of Thinking, Nine Ways to Change People Without Giving Offense or Arousing Resentment, Letters of Testimony, and Seven Rules for Making Your Home Life Happier.

Although *How to Win Friends and Influence People* has sold more than 15 million copies in hardback alone and ranks close to the Bible among all-time nonfiction best sellers, the book was not well received in the national survey of mental health professionals. It was given a 1-star Not Recommended rating. As early as 1937, people like famous novelist James Thurber detected problems in Carnegie's approach. Thurber said that the disingenuities in Carnegie's approach "stand out like ghosts at a banquet." Other critics say that Carnegie's book is essentially a sales tool for the Dale Carnegie courses and that it clearly contradicts virtually all the strategies mental health professionals today believe are best for developing sincere friendships. For Carnegie, friendship is merely a practical tool to be used to attain higher status for oneself. Most mental health professionals today prefer to think of friendship as a support system for people living in a stressful world and as an important source of intimacy.

CONCLUSIONS

In summary, we recommend:

- On sex differences in intimacy:
    - ★★★★★ *Intimate Strangers* by Lillian Rubin

- On overcoming shyness and being less lonely:
    - ★★★★ *Shyness* by Philip Zimbardo
    - ★★★★ *Intimate Connections* by David Burns

- On friendship and its important roles in our lives:
    - ★★★★ *Just Friends* by Lillian Rubin

- For a practical guide for adult single life:
    - ★★★ *The Art of Living Single* by Michael Broder

CHAPTER TWENTY-ONE

Infant Development
and Parenting

In this chapter we evaluate self-help books that focus on parenting infants. In other chapters we examine parenting and other periods of development: child development in Chapter 10, pregnancy in Chapter 25, and adolescence in Chapter 32.

Infancy is a special period of growth and development, requiring extensive time and support by caregivers. Unlike the newborn of some species (the newborn wildebeest runs with the herd moments after birth!), the human newborn requires considerable care. Good parenting requires long hours, interpersonal skills, and emotional commitment. Many parents learn parenting practices and baby care from their parents—some they accept, some they discard. Unfortunately, when parenting practices and baby care are passed on from one generation to the next, both desirable and undesirable practices are perpetuated.

Many parents want to know the answer to such questions as How should I respond to the baby's crying? Is there a point at which I can spoil the baby? Which is better, breast feeding or bottle feeding? What are the normal developmental milestones for babies? How should I stimulate my baby intellectually? Many parents turn to self-help books on infancy and parenting for answers to the questions and advice on the best way to handle the new arrival in their family. And those who do find no shortage of books. It is not unusual for expectant parents or the parents of young infants to buy four or five books on infancy and parenting.

Some parents are more confused after reading the sometimes conflicting strategies of infant experts than they were before they bought the books. I (J. S.) was recently in a bookstore purchasing some self-help books to review for *The Authoritative Guide to Self-Help Books*. He had a list of the ratings of the books with him and placed it on the counter while he was purchasing the books. A woman behind him in line asked him what the list and ratings were all about. She was pregnant and had

Infant Development and Parenting
BOOK RATINGS IN THE NATIONAL SURVEY

Strongly Recommended	★★★★★	*Infants and Mothers* by T. Berry Brazelton
	★★★★★	*What Every Baby Knows* by T. Berry Brazelton
	★★★★★	*Dr. Spock's Baby and Child Care* by Benjamin Spock and Michael Rothenberg
	★★★★★	*The First Three Years of Life* by Burton White
Recommended	★★★★	*Babyhood* by Penelope Leach
	★★★★	*The First Twelve Months of Life* by Frank Caplan
	★★★★	*Dr. Spock on Parenting* by Benjamin Spock
Diamonds in the Rough	◆	*What to Expect the First Year* by Arlene Eisenberg, Heidi Murkoff, and Sandee Hathaway

five or six books on infancy and parenting in her arms. The woman said that her parents had done a poor job of rearing her and that she wanted to make sure her infant got a great start in life. When she asked Dr. Santrock what he thought about the books, he told her that some of them would give her conflicting advice and that she really needed only one or two excellent ones. Amazingly, one of the books she was going to buy was an inner child book (for adults whose parents did not adequately rear them as children) — but she thought it was about *her* inner child — the fetus in her womb!

A number of self-help books have been written that give advice about many issues related to parenting infants. In the national survey, four types of books on infancy and parenting were rated: broad-based approaches organized mainly by topics; broad-based approaches organized by age (weeks or months) and developmental milestones; books about the infant's temperament, developmental milestones, and the parents' (especially the mother's) role; and books about child rearing.

Two books that present a broad-based approach to infancy and parenting organized by topic were rated: *What Every Baby Knows* by T. Berry Brazelton and *Dr. Spock's Baby and Child Care* by Benjamin Spock and Michael Rothenberg.

Four books that take a broad-based approach to infancy and parenting organized by age or developmental milestones were rated: *The First Three Years of Life* by Burton White, *Babyhood* by Penelope Leach, *The First Twelve Months of Life* by Frank Caplan, and *What to Expect the First Year* by Arlene Eisenberg, Heide Murkoff, and Sandee Hathaway.

One book that deals exclusively with child rearing and how to improve a child's social and emotional development was rated: *Dr. Spock on Parenting* by Benjamin Spock.

One book on infant temperament, developmental milestones, and the parents' (especially the mother's) role was rated: *Infants and Mothers* by T. Berry Brazelton.

STRONGLY RECOMMENDED

★ ★ ★ ★ ★   *Infants and Mothers* (rev. ed., 1983) by T. Berry Brazelton. New York: Delta/Seymour Lawrence

Infants and Mothers is about the infant's temperament, developmental milestones in the first year of life, and the parents' (especially the mother's) role in the infant's development. Author T. Berry Brazelton, M.D., is a pediatrician, a professor at Harvard University Medical School, and chief of the Child Development Unit of Boston's Children's Hospital Medical Center. He has recently been crowned "America's baby doctor," a title once reserved for Benjamin Spock, as an outgrowth of his widespread television appearances and the numerous popular books on infant and child development he has written in the last several decades.

Infants and Mothers, published initially in 1969, was Brazelton's first self-help book. Brazelton describes three different temperamental or behavioral styles of infants: active baby, average baby, and quiet baby. Brazelton takes readers through the developmental milestones of these three different types of babies as they age from birth to 12 months. Most of the chapters are titled with the month of the babies' ages—The Second Month, The Third Month, and so on. In every chapter, Brazelton tells mothers about the best way to parent the three different types of babies. The author advises mothers to be sensitive observers of their baby's temperament and behavior, believing that this strategy will help them chart the best course for meeting the infant's needs. The 1983 edition includes more attention to the father's role and that of working mothers.

Infants and Mothers received a 5-star Strongly Recommended rating in the national survey. Brazelton's approach is well-informed, warm, and personal. In a foreword to the book, esteemed former Harvard professor of psychology Jerome Bruner said that *Infants and Mothers* does an excellent job of presenting the contrasts between different types of babies. He also commented that Brazelton's book is a gift for parents.

★ ★ ★ ★ ★   *What Every Baby Knows* (1987) by T. Berry Brazelton. Reading, MA: Addison-Wesley.

What Every Baby Knows is a broad approach to parenting infants that is organized according to the experiences of five different families. The book is based on the Lifetime cable television series Brazelton hosts, endorsed by the American Academy of Pediatrics. Brazelton presents in-depth analyses of five families and their child-rearing concerns, such as how to handle crying, how to discipline, how to deal with the infant's fears, sibling rivalry, separation and divorce, hyperactivity, birth order, and the child's developing sense of self.

The descriptions of each family include the circumstances of the family's visits to Dr. Brazelton and lengthy excerpts of pediatrician–parent dialogues, interspersed with brief explanatory notes. Each family also is portrayed two years later to see how they resolved their child-rearing difficulties and where they are at that point. A very brief final chapter pulls together some of the most important points about being a competent family and what the pediatrician's role should be in helping parents.

What Every Baby Knows received a 5-star Strongly Recommended rating in the national survey. As in *Infants and Mothers*, Brazelton dispenses wise advice to parents. He does an excellent job of helping parents become more sensitive to their infants' needs and of providing parents with sage recommendations on how to handle a host of problems that may arise. One criticism of *What Every Baby Knows* is that its question-and-answer format between pediatrician and parents is better suited for television than for a self-help book. That, however, is a minor flaw in an otherwise excellent self-help book on parenting infants.

★ ★ ★ ★ ★   *Dr. Spock's Baby and Child Care* (1985) by Benjamin Spock and Michael Rothenberg. New York: E. P. Dutton.

Dr. Spock's Baby and Child Care, initially published in 1945, is one of the classics in the self-help literature. Author Benjamin Spock, M.D., was considered America's baby doctor for decades, and this book was perceived by many to be the bible of self-help books for parents of infants and young children. Spock practiced pediatrics from 1933 to 1947, then became a teacher and researcher at the famous Mayo Clinic in Rochester, Minnesota. Coauthor of this edition of the book is Michael Rothenberg, M.D., a pediatrician and child psychiatrist on the faculty of the University of Washington School of Medicine and on the staff of the Children's Orthopedic Hospital and Medical Center in Seattle, Washington.

Dr. Spock's Baby and Child Care is a broad approach to infants' and children's development. It has a stronger dose of medical advice than most of the other books in the infant and parenting category, but it also includes a number of chapters on child-rearing advice. Most of the material in earlier editions has been carried forward into the 1985 edition. This material includes advice on feeding, daily care, illnesses, first aid, nutrition, and a myriad of other topics. The 1985 revision gives more attention to divorce, single-parent families, stepparenting, and the role of fathers in the infant's development. An expanded section on breast feeding for mothers who work outside the home appears in the new edition. And there are new chapters on child abuse, neglect, permissiveness, and children's fears of nuclear war. The book has retained its political flavor. The authors fervently state that children should not play with toy guns or watch cowboy movies, advocate a nuclear freeze, and argue for abolishing competitiveness in our society. These themes coincide with Spock's intense objections to the Vietnam War.

Dr. Spock's Baby and Child Care received a 5-star Strongly Recommended rating in the national survey. Across almost five decades, more than thirty million copies of this book have been sold, placing it second on the nation's overall best-seller list (after the Bible). The book's enthusiasts said that it is extremely well-organized and serves as a handy guide for parents to consult when they run into a problem with their infant or child. The common-sense medical advice is outstanding. However, some critics said that Spock's approach to discipline is still too permissive and is not the best strategy for developing young children's self-control. The book's detractors also thought that Spock's inclusion of his stance on nuclear disarmament and other politically sensitive issues is gratuitous in a book on baby and child care. Because of such criticisms, a number of mental health professionals advocate reading *Dr.Spock's Baby and Child Care* for its medical advice but avoiding the discipline advice and the book's political discussions. In Chapter 10, we recommend several books that give a better perspective on discipline than Spock's book. They include *To Listen to a Child* by T. Berry Brazelton, *Between Parent and Child* by Haim Ginott, and *Children: The Challenge* by Rudolph Dreikurs.

★ ★ ★ ★ ★   *The First Three Years of Life* (rev. ed., 1985) by Burton White. New York: Prentice Hall Press.

The First Three Years of Life presents a broad-based, age-related approach to parenting infants and young children. Burton White, Ph.D., is director of the Center for Parent Education in Newton, Massachusetts, and has been senior consultant to the Missouri New Parents as Teachers Project. He was formerly the director of the Harvard Preschool Project, which focused on young children's learning. White also hosted a television show on the first three years of life.

White strongly believes that most parents in America fail to provide an adequate intellectual and social foundation for their children's development, especially between the ages of eight months and three years of age. White provides in-depth discussion of motor, sensory, emotional, sociability, and language milestones at during the first three years of life. He divides the first three years into seven stages:

- Birth to 6 weeks
- 6 weeks to 14 weeks
- 14 to 23 weeks
- 23 weeks to 8 months
- 8 months to 14 months
- 14 months to 24 months
- 24 months to 36 months

For each of the seven stages, White describes the general behavior and educational development of the infant and young child and recommended and unrecommended parental practices. His goal is to provide parents with the tools to help every child reach his or her maximum level of competence by structuring early experiences and opportunities in appropriate ways. White believes that the 8-month to 3-year period is critically important if a child is to reach a maximum level of competence. Prior to 8 months, White believes, biological development dominates children's existence.

White also presents advice about such child-rearing topics as sibling rivalry, spacing children, types of discipline, and detection of disabilities. Appropriate toys and materials for children are listed and how to obtain professional testing of a child is outlined. The author also provides a list of recommended readings for parents.

The First Three Years of Life received a 5-star Strongly Recommended rating in the national survey. While this has been a very popular self-help book, it has received less than glowing reviews in academic circles. Critics, such as Susan Keyes of Harvard University and Sibylle Escalona of Albert Einstein College of Medicine, fault White for his rigid specification of the critical periods and time frames for certain learning to occur, for his failure to understand the importance of at least some variability in child-rearing patterns, for ignoring the importance of fathers, and for recommending that mothers should spend most of their waking hours monitoring the young child's development and learning. White has especially been hard hit with the last criticism; he essentially does not think mothers should work outside the home during the child's early years. Critics say White's view places an unnecessary burden of guilt on the high percentage of working mothers with infants.

White's book obviously has some strong positive points. Some child development experts feel that White's is the best discussion of how to set limits and how to prevent spoiling of any of the self-help books. His recommendations on which toys parents should and should not buy, how to handle sibling rivalry, and how to discipline children are also excellent.

RECOMMENDED

★ ★ ★ ★   *Babyhood* (2nd ed., 1983) by Penelope Leach. New York: Alfred A. Knopf.

Babyhood presents a broad description of infant development from birth to age 2 that is organized mainly according to developmental milestones. Author Penelope Leach, Ph.D., has lectured on psychology and child development at the London School of Economics. She has also written other successful self-help books on babies and currently is host of the Lifetime cable television show, on which she dispenses child-rearing advise about a wide variety of topics.

Babyhood chronicles the physical, emotional, and mental development of babies from birth to age 2. The book is divided into five chronological segments of the child's life. Part I, The First Six Weeks, focuses on settling into a different life with the new infant. Physical characteristics, feeding, sleeping, crying, special difficulties, and the baby's abilities are charted and elaborated on. Part II, From Six Weeks to Three Months, mainly emphasizes the baby's physical development in feeding, sleeping, elimination, and crying. Development of physical abilities, such as posture control, are covered. Part III, From Three Months to Six Months, discusses the baby's emerging sociability and language development. Part IV, From Six Months to Twelve Months, is subtitled Broadening His World and describes the exciting changes involved as the baby becomes a "biped," "talker," and tool user. Part V, The Second Year, chronicles the infant's development from baby to toddler and discusses special concerns of feeding (problem eaters, overweight infants), sleep, toilet training, mobility, language, and fears. The book includes a number of growth charts.

Babyhood received a 4-star Recommended rating in the national survey. Leach has an excellent feel for children and her approach comes across as warm and sensitive. Her advice is generally sound and sometimes excellent (her very detailed advice on how to handle eating problems is outstanding). In this book she says that mothers should breast feed their infants and that parents should rethink whether they want their sons to be circumcised because of the pain involved. She has been criticized for her attack on day care, even though she acknowledges that some mothers have to work. But she accurately assesses most of the day care for children as it now exists as being of low quality. Leach's English background shows occasionally in her style and terms ("nappy" and "push-chair"), she annoyingly refers to most babies as "he," and she is occasionally long-winded and repetitive.

★ ★ ★ ★   *The First Twelve Months of Life* (1973) by Frank Caplan. New York: Bantam.

The First Twelve Months of Life presents a broad-based, developmental milestone approach to the infant's development in the first year of life. Frank Caplan is the director of the Princeton Center for Infancy and Early Childhood, which was organized to educate parents on children's development and stimulation needs. The center was founded and built by Creative Playthings, Inc., a company Caplan once headed.

The First Twelve Months of Life provides a month-by-month assessment of normal infant development in the first year of life. The timetables in the book are presented in a rather rigid way. The author does warn the reader not to use them in that way but rather as indicators of appropriate sequences of growth. Feeding, sleeping, language, physical skills, guidance, parental emotions, and learning stimulation are among the topics covered in depth. Each chapter contains a detailed developmental chart outlining the appropriate sensory, motor, language, mental, and social developmental milestones for that month. The book also includes 150 photographs.

The First Twelve Months of Life received a 4-star Recommended rating in the national survey. The book is well organized, well written, and easy to follow. Although Caplan warns readers not to take the timetables for developmental milestones as gospel, it's almost impossible not to do so because that is the way the book is organized. Most experts on infant development today do not advocate a rigid month-by-month approach because it simply doesn't adequately address the complex variations and wide individual differences that occur within a normal range. Caplan (with Theresa Caplan as a coauthor) wrote a companion book that follows the same format, *The Second Twelve Months of Life.*

★ ★ ★ ★   *Dr. Spock on Parenting* (1988) by Benjamin Spock. New York: Simon & Schuster.

Dr. Spock on Parenting emphasizes how to become a better parent and improve the social and emotional development of the child. This book is primarily a collection of articles that Spock wrote for *Redbook* magazine in the 1970s and 1980s. Topics of the articles are anxieties in our lives, being a father today, divorce and the consequences, the new baby, sleep problems, discipline, stages of childhood, difficult relationships, behavior problems, influencing personality and attitudes, and health and nutrition.

In a chapter on discipline, Spock rebuts the criticism leveled at *Dr. Spock's Baby and Child Care* that he encourages parents to be too permissive with children. Spock says that he never had such a philosophy and believes that parents should deal with their children in firm, clear ways.

Dr. Spock on Parenting received a 4-star Recommended rating in the national survey. This book is easy to read and generally dispenses sound parenting advice. *Dr. Spock on Parenting* actually fits better with the books reviewed in Chapter 10, Child Development and Parenting. A few topics deal specifically with infancy, but most address general concerns of parents throughout the childhood years. The consensus of the experts in the national survey was that Brazelton's *To Listen to a Child*, Ginott's *Between Parent and Child*, and Dreikurs's *Children: The Challenge* are the best choices on general approaches to parenting.

DIAMONDS IN THE ROUGH

◆ *What to Expect the First Year* (1989) by Arlene Eisenberg, Heidi Murkoff, and Sandee Hathaway. New York: Workman.

What to Expect the First Year presents a broad, developmental milestone approach to infant development in the first year of life. For authors Arlene Eisenberg and Heidi Murkoff, no professional background or affiliations are listed. Coauthor Sandee Hathaway has an undergraduate degree in nursing.

What to Expect the First Year is an encyclopedic (almost 700 pages) volume of facts and practical tips on how babies develop, how to become a better parent, and how to deal with problems as they arise. The authors give chatty answers to hypothetical questions arranged in a month-by-month format. As in Caplan's book, developmental milestones are given for each month of the first year, along with potential health and behavioral problems. The book is full of questions commonly asked by parents. What to buy for a newborn, first aid, recipes, adoption, low birth-weight babies, and the father's role also are discussed.

What to Expect the First Year was positively rated but by only 30 respondents, hence its relegation to the Diamonds in the Rough category. Some of the book's enthusiasts called it the best one on the market for the parents of infants in their first year of life. The book covers an enormous array of topics that concern parents and generally provides sound advice. Far more specific medical advice about the first year is given than in any other book in the category, including *Dr. Spock's Baby and Child Care*. As with Caplan's book, the month-by-month organization inevitably leads to difficulties in describing the wide variations in the rate of infants' development. In a foreword to the book, pediatrician Henry Harris of Albert Einstein Medical Center in New York City is laudatory in his praise of the book, and Michael Levi, a professor of pediatrics at New York State School of Medicine, says that the book is filled with wonderfully sensitive advice.

CONCLUSIONS

As in the child development and parenting category (Chapter 10), the infant development and parenting category had a number of very positively rated self-help books. Although in most categories we recommend at the end of the chapter all the books that were given 4-star and 5-stars in the national survey, in this chapter we exclude several of the 4-star and 5-star books because of the considerable overlap from one book to the next. We also place some cautionary notes with several books.

In summary, we recommend:

- On parenting an infant in the first year who is quiet, average, or active:

  ★★★★★ *Infants and Mothers* by T. Berry Brazelton

- A broad-based approach to parenting an infant:

  ★★★★★ *What Every Baby Knows* by T. Berry Brazelton

- A broad-based approach that is especially good on the medical and health aspects of infancy:

  ★★★★★ *Dr. Spock's Baby and Child Care* by Benjamin Spock and Michael Rothenberg

- A broad-based developmental milestone approach with month-to-month descriptions of infant development and care:

  ◆ *What to Expect in the First Year* by Arlene Eisenberg, Heide Murkoff, and Sandee Hathway

Caveat: The month-by-month guidelines should not be interpreted rigidly because there is a considerable variation in normal development. *(Cont.)*

CONCLUSIONS *(Continued)*

- A broad-based developmental milestone approach to parenting an infant in the first two years of life:

  ★★★★ *Babyhood* by Penelope Leach

- A broad-based nonmedical approach to parenting and educating infants and young children:

  ★★★★★ *The First Three Years of Life* by Burton White

  Caveat: The ideas expressed about working mothers are extreme; the idea of developmental milestones as critical to specific periods is questionable; individual variation is not adequately expressed.

CHAPTER TWENTY-TWO

Love, Intimacy,
and Marriage

For centuries, philosophers, songwriters, and poets have been intrigued by what love is. Only recently, though, have psychologists turned their attention to love and made recommendations for how to improve your love life.

Today, love is to a vast and complex territory of human behavior. Some of the complexity of love has come about because of changes in marriage patterns. Not too long ago, people married in their teens and early twenties, had children, and stayed together for the rest of their lives. Men worked outside the home and were the breadwinners; women worked inside the home and cared for the children. In today's world, many people marry later or not all. When they do get married, many couples postpone children until both partners have developed their careers. Or they choose to remain childless. Divorce has become epidemic in our culture. Couples want their relationship to be deep and loving, and if it isn't, they increasingly see a psychotherapist or marriage counselor or buy one or more self-help books that they hope will improve their love relationship. Women, especially women aged 20 to 45, are the consumers of most of the self-help books in this category.

A person who wants to buy a self-help book on love, intimacy, and marriage finds no shortage of choices. In the national survey, more than 75 books in this category were evaluated by one or more respondents. The focuses of the books can be grouped in nine subcategories: the nature of love and forms of love; how longstanding family relationships influence current intimate relationships; women, love, and intimacy; how love develops, the emotional dimensions of love, and how love relationships can be improved; love/hate relationships; how to save a marriage and prevent divorce; spiritual/religious approaches to love; obsessive love; and the cognitive therapy approach to love problems.

Love, Intimacy, and Marriage
BOOK RATINGS IN THE NATIONAL SURVEY

Strongly Recommended	★★★★★	*The Dance of Intimacy* by Harriet Lerner
Recommended	★★★★	*Getting the Love You Want* by Harville Hendrix
	★★★★	*Intimate Partners* by Maggie Scarf
	★★★★	*The Art of Loving* by Erich Fromm
Diamonds in the Rough	◆	*The Intimate Enemy* by George Bach and Peter Wyden
	◆	*The Triangle of Love* by Robert Sternberg
Neutral	★★★	*Obsessive Love* by Susan Forward
	★★★	*Love Is Letting Go of Fear* by Gerald Jampolsky
	★★★	*Divorce Busting* by Michele Weiner-Davis
	★★★	*Do I Have to Give Up Me to Be Loved by You?* by Jordan Paul and Margaret Paul
	★★★	*Women Who Love Too Much* by Robin Norwood
	★★★	*Going the Distance* by Lonnie Barbach and David Geisinger
	★★★	*Husbands and Wives* by Melvyn Kinder and Connell Cowan
Not Recommended	★★	*Loving Each Other* by Leo Buscaglia
	★★	*Men Who Hate Women and the Women Who Love Them* by Susan Forward
	★★	*Men Who Can't Love* by Steven Carter
	★	*When Someone You Love Is Someone You Hate* by Stephen Arterburn and David Stoop
	★	*What Smart Women Know* by Steven Carter and Julia Sokol
Strongly Not Recommended	†	*Women Men Love, Women Men Leave* by Connell Cowan and Melvyn Kinder
	†	*What Every Woman Should Know about Men* by Joyce Brothers

Two books explore the nature of love and different forms of love: *The Art of Loving* by Erich Fromm and *The Triangle of Love* by Robert Sternberg. A third book — *Love the Way You Want It*, also by Sternberg — is profiled in Worth a Further Look.

Two books analyze the influence of longstanding family relationships on current intimate relationships: *Getting the Love You Want* by Harville Hendrix and *Intimate Partners* by Maggie Scarf.

Seven books focus on women and love: *The Dance of Intimacy* by Harriet Lerner (this book also discusses how longstanding family relationships influence current intimate relationships); *Women Who Love Too Much* by Robin Norwood; *Men Who Hate Women and The Women Who Love Them* by Susan Forward; *Men Who Can't Love* by Steven Carter; *What Smart Women Know* by Steven Carter and Julia Sokol; *Women Men Love, Women Men Leave* by Connell Cowan and Melvyn Kinder; *What Every Woman Should Know about Men* by Joyce Brothers.

Three books primarily describe how love develops, the emotional dimensions of love, and how love relationships can be improved they can be improved: *Do I Have to Give Up Me to Be Loved by You?* by Jordan Paul and Margaret Paul, *Going the Distance* by Lonnie Barbach and David Geisinger, and *Loving Each Other* by Leo Buscaglia.

Two books on love/hate relationships were rated: *The Intimate Enemy* by George Bach, and *When Someone You Love Is Someone You Hate* by Stephen Arterburn and David Stoop.

Two books on improving marital relationships and preventing divorce were evaluated: *Divorce Busting* by Michele Weiner-Davis and *Husbands and Wives* by Melvyn Kinder and Connell Cowan.

One book presents a spiritual/religious approach to love: *Love Is Letting Go of Fear* by Gerald Jampolsky.

One book deals with obsessive love: *Obsessive Love* by Susan Forward.

No books in the final ratings describe a cognitive therapy approach to love problems, but one book in this category — *Love Is Never Enough* by Aaron Beck — is profiled in the Worth a Further Look category.

STRONGLY RECOMMENDED

★ ★ ★ ★ ★   *The Dance of Intimacy: A Woman's Guide to Courageous Acts of Change in Key Relationships* (1989) by Harriet Lerner. New York: Harper Perennial.

The Dance of Intimacy is written for women and is about women's intimate relationships. Author Harriet Lerner, Ph.D., is an internationally acclaimed authority on the psychology of women and is a staff psychologist at the famous Menninger Clinic. She also is the author of the highly rated self-help book *The Dance of Anger*, evaluated in Chapter 6, Anger.

Drawing on a combination of psychoanalytic and family systems theories, Lerner weaves together a portrait of our current self and relationships that she believes is derived from longstanding relationships with mothers, fathers, and siblings. Lerner tells women that if they are having problems in intimate relationships with a partner or their family or origin, they need to explore the nature of their family upbringing to produce clues to the current difficulties. Women learn how not to distance themselves from their family of origin and how not to overreact to problems. Lerner gives women insights about how to define themselves, how to understand their needs and limits, and how to positively change. The positive change involves moving out of relationships that are going nowhere or are destructive to intimacy with others and a solid sense of self. Lerner intelligently tells women that they should balance the "I" and the "we" in their lives and be neither too self-absorbed nor too other-oriented. To explore unhealthy patterns of close relationships that have been passed down from one generation to the next in a family, Lerner helps women create what she calls a "genogram," a familly diagram that goes back to the grandparents or earlier.

The Dance of Intimacy received a 5-star Strongly Recommended rating in the national survey and was the highest-rated book in the love, intimacy, and marriage category. This is an outstanding self-help book for understanding why close relationships are problematic and how to change them in positive ways. It does not give simple, quick-fix strategies. Lerner accurately avows that change is difficult, but she shows that it is possible. Her warm, personal tone helps women gain the self-confidence necessary to make the changes she recommends. The extensive number of examples and case studies are well chosen. Although designed primarily for women, many men could also benefit considerably from the Lerner's insights.

Many mental health professionals said that they recommend this book to clients, especially female clients, who are having problems in intimate relationships. Well-known family relationships self-help author Maggie Scarf said that *The Dance of Intimacy* is like a long, revealing conversation with a wise and compassionate friend. Carol Nadelson, past president of the American Psychiatric Association, commented that Lerner has a remarkable ability to evaluate our intimacy problems. And Lillian Rubin, author of *Intimate Strangers,* applauded Lerner for writing a wise and compassionate book that is excellent for teaching people about the complexity of emotions in their family and love relationships.

RECOMMENDED

★ ★ ★ ★   *Getting the Love You Want* (1988) by Harville Hendrix. New York: Henry Holt.

Getting the Love You Want is a guide for couples to help them improve their relationships. Author Harville Hendrix, Ph.D., is a marriage therapist and pastoral counselor with extensive experience in working with couples and families. He is the director of the Institute for Relationship Therapy, based in Dallas and New York City.

Getting the Love You Want is based on Hendrix's workshop techniques that Hendrix has developed and are designed to help couples construct a conscious marriage, a relationship based on awareness of the unresolved childhood needs and conflicts that cause individuals to select particular spouses. The author tells readers how to conduct a ten-week course in marital therapy in the privacy of their home. In a stepwise fashion he helps readers learn how to communicate more clearly and sensitively, how to eliminate self-defeating behaviors, and how to focus attention on meeting their partners' needs. Hendrix's goal is to transform the downward spiral of the struggle for power into a mutually beneficial relationship of emotional growth.

Getting the Love You Want is divided into three main parts. Part I, The Unconcious Marriage, describes our lack of awareness of why we married who we did. Part II, The Conscious Marriage, discusses how to become conscious of the key factors that have influenced our marital or couple relationships. Part III, The Exercises, presents the steps toward a conscious marriage and sixteen different exercises to engage in at home.

Getting the Love You Want received a 4-star Recommended rating in the national survey. Its average rating was high enough for 5-stars, but it was not evaluated by enough respondents (53). This is a good self-help book for marital partners engulfed in conflict. Hendrix does an excellent job of helping the reader become aware of longstanding family influences on current close relationships. The exercises for his ten-week in-home workshop are ingenious. T. George Harris, editor of *American Health* magazine and former editor of *Psychology Today,* said that *Getting the Love You Want* is the best program he has seen to help a couple turn their love–hate relationship into a mutually rewarding relationship.

★ ★ ★ ★   *Intimate Partners: Patterns in Love and Marriage* (1986) by Maggie Scarf. New York: Random House.

Intimate Partners tells readers how to solve their marital problems, especially by understanding the stages of development we go through and how our relationships with our family of origin have influenced our marital relationship. Author Maggie Scarf is a self-help author who has been awarded fellowships at the prestigious Center for Advance Studies at Stanford University and at Harvard University.

In *Intimate Partners*, Scarf charts the lives of five married couples in depth, categorizing them according to their life stage: idealization, disenchantment, child rearing and career building, child launching, and the retirement years. She starts with the Bretts, who are relative newlyweds, and ends with the Sternbergs, who have finished rearing their children and are free to focus on each other once again. Interviews with 32 couples in all are interwoven through the book. Like Harriet Lerner in *The Dance of Intimacy*, Scarf emphasizes the importance of a couple's birth-family configurations. And like Lerner, Scarf also uses genograms—diagrams of lines of attachment between marital partners and their parents, grandparents, and siblings—to illuminate how people often repeat the past. She calls the genograms "emotional family trees." Scarf believes that what we so frequently seek in a mate is satisfaction of some need unfulfilled by a parent.

Intimate Partners informs us that these unfulfilled needs are powerful, unconscious forces that shape our marriage from the beginning and continue to dominate it throughout the marriage stages. How can we get out of this jungle of unconscious forces? Scarf believes that the answer lies in disentangling the past.

Intimate Partners received a 4-star, Recommended rating in the national survey. Mental health professionals who recommend Scarf's book said that Scarf does an excellent job of encouraging marital partners to examine the stages of marriage and how longstanding relationships with parents continue to exert a strong influence. Carol Nadelson, past president of the American Psychiatric Association, who endorsed Harriet Lerner's *The Dance of Intimacy*, also was laudatory in her praise of Scarf's book. Other Scarf enthusiasts in the mental health field said that she had done her homework well and talked to the right mental health professionals.

★ ★ ★ ★   *The Art of Loving* (1956) by Erich Fromm. New York: Harper & Row.

The Art of Loving is a philosophical and psychological treatise on the nature of love. Author Erich Fromm, Ph.D., is a well-known psychoanalyst and social philosopher. He obtained his doctorate in sociology and then underwent extensive psychoanalytic training. He died in 1980.

In *The Art of Loving*, Fromm describes love in general as well as different forms of love. In Fromm's view, love is an attitude that determines the relatedness of the person to the whole world, not just toward one love object. Love is an act of faith, a commitment, a complete giving of oneself, according to Fromm. Fromm doesn't offer quick fixes for developing love. He argues that learning to love is a long and difficult process, requiring discipline, concentration, patience, sensitivity to one's self, and the productive use of one's skills. Fromm stresses that although the principle underlying capitalistic society and the principle of love are incompatible, love is the only sane and satisfactory solution to the human condition.

Fromm's book is very different from most of the books evaluated in the national survey. It doesn't include the usual exercises, case histories, and clinical examples. Rather, *The Art of Loving* tackles the complex question of what love is and how society can benefit if people learn how to love more effecively.

The Art of Loving received a 4-star Recommended rating in the national survey. It barely made the 4-star category in terms of its average score, but it was easily the most frequently rated book on love, intimacy, and marriage: it was evaluated by 257 mental health professionals. Fromm's thesis that love is a cultivable art instead of something people spontaneous fall into is an important one. This is an intellectually challenging piece of work that is not written as clearly as most books in the survey.

DIAMONDS IN THE ROUGH

♦ *The Intimate Enemy: How To Fight Fair in Love and Marriage* (1968) by George Bach and Peter Wyden. New York: Avon Books.

The Intimate Enemy is about fair fighting in love and marriage. Author George Bach, Ph.D., was one of the pioneers in group psychotherapy. He was the founder and director of the Institute of Group Psychotherapy in Beverly Hills, California. Coauthor Peter Wyden is a professional writer; he was executive editor of *Ladies' Home Journal.*

The Intimate Enemy is based on Bach's theory of constructive aggression. That is, he believes that conflict and fighting in close relationships are inevitable. *The Intimate Enemy* tells us that instead of bottling up problems inside ourselves, the healthiest strategy is to express ourselves through fighting. Bach and Wyden advise partners that a fight a day keeps the doctor away. They believe that what ails marriages is couples' inability to fight. When marital partners don't fight, say the authors, they play games, get bored, have extramarital affairs, and misunderstand each other.

The Intimate Enemy is not short on entertainment value. The fight tactics discussed include intimate ambush, hit-and-run attacks, stabbing a partner's Achilles' heel, finding the fair belt line, making a fight appointment, avoiding the kitchen sink, fight trainees who are least likely to succeed, and fighting for good sex fit.

The Intimate Enemy was placed in the Diamonds in the Rough Category because it was rated very postitively but by only 10 respondents (the bare minimum of evaluators needed to make this category). The 10 mental health professionals who evaluated *The Intimate Enemy* said that it is especially good at getting people to reveal their feelings and push conflicts out into the open so that they can be dealt with. They also commented that it is a joy to read. Critics worried that many couples who try Bach and Wyden's strategies on their own won't be able to adequately control their aggression. The book's detractors also felt that it has too much jargon and too many catchy phrases—for example, "Don't drop the bomb on Luxemburg," which translates to "Don't have big confrontations over trivial matters." The very long book is also very repetitious.

♦ *The Triangle of Love* (1987) by Robert Sternberg. New York: Basic Books.

The Triangle of Love presents Sternberg's view of different forms of love. Author Robert Sternberg, Ph.D., is a well-known, highly respected cognitive psychologist and IBM Professor of Psychology at Yale University.

According to Sternberg, the three sides of the triangle of love are the fire of sexual, romantic passion, the close emotional sharing of intimacy, and the enduring bond of commitment. The type and quality of a relationship depend on the strength of each side of the triangle in each partner and how closely the partners' triangles match. Sternberg argues that each side has its own timetable. For example, passion dominates the early part of a love relationship, while intimacy and commitment play more important roles as relationships progress. In the author's view, the ultimate form of love combines the ingredients of passion, intimacy, and commitment. Sternberg gives specific guidelines for improving love relationships and includes a "love scale" for measuring the nature of one's own love.

The Triangle of Love was placed in the Diamonds in the Rough category, its average rating (1.00) just easing it out of the 3-star category. Several mental health professionals said that Sternberg provides an insightful perspective on the nature of love and gives good advice about how to achieve consummate love. But some mental health experts also commented that the book vacillates too much between academic discussions of what love is and self-help recommendations for improving love relationships. Nonetheless, you will find Sternberg's analysis of love's nature much easier reading than Fromm's in *The Art of Loving*.

NEUTRAL

★★★   *Obsessive Love* (1991) by Susan Forward. New York: Bantam.

Obsessive Love examines the type of destructive relationship in which passion holds a person prisoner. Author Susan Forward, Ph.D., is a well-known self-help author who has hosted an ABC Talkradio program for a number of years. She also has worked as a group therapist, and she formed the first private sexual abuse treatment center in California.

Obsessive Love is directed at people who are obsessive lovers or their targets. Obsessive love is not really love at all, according to Forward, but rather a relationship compulsion that is pathological. She believes that obsessive love is caused by rejecting parents or separation problems in childhood. According to Forward, obsessive love occurs about equally in women and men and takes different forms—worshiping someone from afar, savior fantasies directed at an addicted or troubled partner, or refusing to let go of a lover who has broken off a relationship. Obsessive behavior can range from relatively harmless efforts (driving by, compulsive phoning, and stalking) to violent and life-threatening acts (destruction of the target's property or homicide attempts).

Forward intelligently tells obsessive lovers who are violence prone to see a therapist immediately rather than simply relying on her self-help book. For obsessive lovers who are not violence prone, she recommends detailed logging of emotions, a two-week vacation from contact with the target, and then a probing self-evaluation in which obsessors ask themselves tough questions about whether anything in the relationship can be salvaged. If the obsessor still thinks there is, he or she is helped to develop a more healthy plan of contact. If the obsessor realizes that the relationship is over, a process of mourning is outlined that will help the person recover.

Obsessive Love received a 3-star Neutral rating in the national survey. The book came out shortly before the survey was conducted and was rated by only 18 respondents. Some mental health professionals thought that this is Forward's best self-help book and that she sheds light on a growing problem in our society—obsession with love and its pathological ramifications.

★ ★ ★   *Love Is Letting Go of Fear* (1979) by Gerald Jampolsky. Berkeley, CA: Celestial Arts.

Love Is Letting Go of Fear is a spiritually based approach to love. Author Gerald Jampolsky, M.D., is a psychiatrist who formerly was a faculty member at the University of California Medical Center in San Francisco. He also has been a consultant to the Center for Attitudinal Healing in Tiburon, California.

Love Is Letting Go of Fear is based on the spiritual psychotherapy of the Course of Miracles offered by the Foundation for Inner Peace in Tiburon. Jampolsky tells readers that he came across the important ideas in this course at a time when his life was falling apart. The teachings in the course transformed Jampolsky by helping him let go of fear and experience the essence of love.

The book is divided into three main parts: Part I, Preparation for Personal Transformation, Part II, Ingredients of Personal Transformation, and Part III, Lessons for Personal Transformation. Part III, the bulk of the book, contains 12 lessons that range from learning that forgiveness is the key to happiness to changing all the thoughts that hurt. *Love Is Letting Go of Fear* is brief (about 100 pages) and contains a number of large, cartoonlike drawings.

Love Is Letting Go of Fear received a 3-star Neutral rating in the national survey. The book's enthusiasts say that Jampolsky is skilled at communicating about the spiritual and emotional dimensions of love. The book's detractors say that Jampolsky's approach to love is overly simple.

★ ★ ★   *Divorce Busting* (1992) by Michele Weiner-Davis. New York: Summit Books.

Divorce Busting advocates a brief, solution-oriented approach to keeping a marriage together. Author Michele Weiner-Davis has a Master's degree in social work and works as a therapist in private practice.

Weiner-Davis says that divorce is not the answer to an unhappy marriage. She says she came to this conclusion after observing that ex-spouses often continue to be unhappy after the divorce. Much unlike the approaches of Harriet Learner in *The Dance of Intimacy*, Harville Hendrix in *Getting the Love You Want,* and Maggie Scarf in *Intimate Partners,* which advocate solving marital problems by analyzing emotions from the past, Weiner-Davis's approach focuses on the present and the future, on actions rather than feelings, and is accomplished in brief rather than lengthy therapy or problem-solving (in her practice she sees most couples for only four to five sessions).

Divorce Busting offers a step-by-step apprach that couples can follow to make their marriage loving again. Brief case histories show how couples have successfuly used Weiner-Davis's approach in solving their marital difficulties. The steps can be followed alone or with a spouse.

Divorce Busting received a 3-star Neutral rating in the national survey. It was published shortly before the national survey was conducted, so only a few respondents (17) evaluated it. Ray Bardill, president of the American Association for Marriage and Family Therapy, calls *Divorce Busting* a book that meets the needs of people in a fast-paced society who want an efficient, short-term problem-solving solution to their unhappy marriages.

★ ★ ★   *Do I Have to Give Up Me to Be Loved by You?* (1983) by Jordan Paul and Margaret Paul. Minneapolis, MN: Compcare.

Do I Have to Give Up Me to Be Loved by You? provides a plan for improving a love relationship by detecting and overcoming hidden motives. Husband and wife authors Jordan and Margaret Paul, both Ph.D.s and therapists, maintain a private practice in marriage and family therapy in Los Angeles.

The Pauls stress that we have to probe and understand the unspoken motivation behind what we do to solve our relationship problems. Using their intention therapy as a base, the authors tell readers how to become aware of self-created obstacles and develop more intimate relationships. A number of exercises help couples work on their power struggles, sexual expectations, and many other marital problems.

Do I Have to Give Up Me to Be Loved by You? received a 3-star Neutral rating in the national survey. Mental health professionals who endorsed the book felt that the Pauls present a helpful approach to controlling harmful emotions and finding out the reasons for a couple's problems.

★ ★ ★   *Going the Distance: Secrets of Lifelong Love* (1991) by Lonnie Barbach and David Geisinger. New York: Doubleday.

Going the Distance explains why monogamy is best and how to make it work. Lonnie Barbach, Ph.D., is a well-known self-help author in the area of sex and relationships (*For Yourself* and *For Each Other*). David Geisinger, Ph.D., has been director of the Behavior Therapy Institute in Sausalito, California. Both authors, who are married to each other, are on the clinical faculty of the Department of Psychiatry at the University of California Medical School in San Francisco.

The advice in *Going the Distance* is appropriate for a wide range of couples, from people just embarking on a close intimate relationship to people who want to renew their commitment to their marital partners. According to Barbach and Geisinger, we bring the scars of old psychic wounds to any new relationship, a good close relationship is a healing one, and even individuals with a long history of troubled relationships can learn the skills needed to make a marriage work. The authors stress the importance of chemistry, courtship, trust, respect, acceptance, and shared values. They also suggest methods for overcoming commitment phobias, strategies to resolve power conflicts and battles for control, and ways to improve a couple's sex life. A 50-item compatibility questionnaire helps couples evaluate how well suited they are.

Going the Distance received a 3-star Neutral rating in the national survey. The book's supporters said that the authors' advice is solid. They also commented that the material is well written, well organized, and occasionally humorous and that the case histories are well chosen and insightful. Critics pointed out that contrary to the book's subtitle, *Secrets to Lifelong Love*, most of the authors' advice is repackaged standard fare.

★ ★ ★   *Women Who Love Too Much* (1985) by Robin Norwood. New York: Pocket Books.

Women Who Love Too Much addresses the problem of relationship addiction in women who choose the wrong man and stay with him, no matter how bad he is. Author Robin Norwood is a marriage, family, and child therapist in private practice in California.

Women Who Love Too Much is one of a number of best-selling self-help books in recent years that blame most of women's problems on men. Among the characteristics of a woman who loves too much are a childhood in which her emotional needs were not met, willingness to assume the majority of blame for a relationship's problems, low self-esteem, and a belief that she has no right to be happy. Such women choose men who need help, inevitably causing their marriage to become troubled. These women are addicted to pain, says Norwood, just as an alcholic is too liquor.

How does Norwood think a woman can recover from a relationship addiction? The first step is to back off from her partner—quit nagging and stop making demands—and start focusing on her own problems instead of wasting energy on his problems. Norwood advocates finding a support group and leaving the relationship if necessary.

Women Who Love Too Much received a 3-star Neutral rating in the national survey. It headed *The New York Times* best-seller list for thirty-seven weeks. The book's enthusiasts say that Norwood's book can inspire women who are trapped in bad relationships to evaluate their situation and chart a better course for their lives. They also say that reading the book can help women to stop blaming themselves exclusively for their relationship troubles and develop better self-esteem. Critics say that *Women Who Love Too Much* and other self-help books that blame women's problems on men don't adequately deal with what happens to a woman once she "recovers." The book assumes that she will eventually find a man who treats her well, but unless men change drastically, her chances are not good.

★ ★ ★   *Husbands and Wives: Exploring Marital Myths* (1989) by Melvyn Kinder and Connell Cowan. New York: Clarkson N. Potter.

Husbands and Wives provides advice about how to make a marriage work. Author Melvyn Kinder, Ph.D., is a clinical psychologist and codirector of the Westridge Psychiatric Medical Group in Los Angeles. Coauthor Connell Cowan, Ph.D., also a clinical psychologist, has a private practice in Los Angeles. Together they also wrote the popular *Smart Women, Foolish Choices* and *Women Men Love, Women Men Leave.*

According to Kinder and Cowan, the major problem in most marriages is that each partner tries to change the other instead of focusing on improving his or her own behavior. They call their approach self-directed marriage, and it emphasizes the importance of each partner taking responsibility for his or her own happiness and replacing other-directed blame with acceptance. The authors tell marital partners to accept their differences, become friends, and rediscover the enjoyment of marital life.

Husbands and Wives barely received a 3-star Neutral rating in the national survey. Mental health professionals who like the book said that its message can help individuals understand the importance of developing one's self instead of trying to change their partner. Critics said that the book's theme of self-development is too simplistic in today's world of complex marital relationships.

NOT RECOMMENDED

★ ★   *Loving Each Other* (1984) by Leo Buscaglia. Thorofare, NJ: Slack.

Loving Each Other attempts to help people become more loving. Leo Buscaglia, Ph.D. is a well-known self-help author who is a professsor of education at the University of Southern California.

Buscaglia argues that our flippant and uncaring society has produced poeple who do not have enough tenderness and compassion. Dr. Hug, as Buscaglia has become known, says that we are afraid of committing ourselves to loving each other. In today's hip society, says Buscaglia, love and commitment are considered old-fashioned, sentimental, and naive. Buscaglia conducted a survey of relationships and bases many of his chapters on the most frequent responses to the question "What qualities are necessary for a strong relationship? The leading answers were communication, compassion, forgiveness, and joy.

Loving Each Other received a 2-star Not Recommended rating in the national survey. In the 1970s and early 1980s, Buscaglia had a cult-like following of disciples (mainly women). Buscaglia struck a chord in people who were fed up with a society (mainly men) that was egocentric and unloving. Buscaglia's popularity has waned in the last decade. Critics say that *Loving Each Other* and many of Buscaglia's other books are a lot of insubstantial fluff. They also point out that while we all would agree that our society would be better if its members were more loving, Buscaglia's book doesn't provide the answers for how to get there.

★ ★   *Men Who Hate Women and the Women Who Love Them* (1986) by Susan Forward. New York: Bantam.

Men Who Hate Women and the Women Who Love Them is about emotionally abusive men (especially husbands) and victimized women (especially wives). Forward, whose credentials appear in the review of her 3-star book, *Obsessive Love,* in this chapter, says that the men are Jekyll-and-Hyde types—charming, loving helpmates one moment, abusive bullies the next. Forward reveals that she was once married to just this type of male. She calls these men who hate women "mysogynists." They are so insecure that they exploit, humiliate, and overly control women. Why do these men hate women? Forward says it is because they were prevented from identifying with their father as a child. The result is a frightened male, full of rage toward an all-powerful mother, who takes out his frustration and aggression on his wife. Such men seek a wife who is all-sacrificing—someone who is a loving and comforting surrogate, in Forward's analysis. The wives have been reared to be submissive and blame themselves for their husband's destructive behavior.

Forward lays out a plan for these victimized women to help themselves become more assertive and develop a healthier relationship. At the same time, Forward acknowledges that healing these marriages has a better chance of occurring under the guidance of a therapist.

Men Who Hate Women and the Women Who Love Them received a 2-star Not Recommended rating in the national survey. This has been an immensely popular book—a multimillion copy best seller. The mental health professionals who recommend this book said that Forward has a gift for opening the lid of destructive marriages in which husbands exploit wives. They said that this book has helped a number of women make important changes in their lives and in their marriages. Critics of the book said that despite Forward's acknowledgment that not every man is a misogynist, she stereotypes men too negatively. The consensus of the mental health experts was that self-help books such as Harriet Lerner's *The Dance of Intimacy* and Maggie Scarf's *Intimate Partners* present a more reasoned and beneficial approach to healing problematic close relationships.

★ ★ *Men Who Can't Love: When a Man's Fear Makes Him Run from Commitment (And What a Smart Woman Can Do about It)* (1987) by Steven Carter. New York: M. Evans.

Men Who Can't Love is about men who can't make a commitment to love. Author Steven Carter's education and experience are not listed.

Men Who Can't Love is based on Carter's interviews with hundreds of men who are commitment phobic. They want love but they are horrified by commitment and run away from any relationship that makes them feel trapped. Carter provides advice for women about how to identify such a man before getting involved with him, how to determine if the man can ever change and if he is worth the effort, and how to allay his fears before he runs away.

Men Who Can't Love barely received a 2-star Not Recommended rating in the national survey. The book's supporters said that Carter provides some valuable advice for women that will help them understand and evaluate men who are afraid of commitment. Critics faulted the book for stereotyping men, for being sensationalist in places, and for inadequate documentation of the interviews on which the book is based.

★ *When Someone You Love Is Someone You Hate* (1988) by Stephen Arterburn and David Stoop. Dallas: Word.

When Someone You Love Is Someone You Hate is about love–hate relationships and how to improve them. Author Stephan Arterburn, M.Ed., is president of New Life Treatment Centers and resides in Laguna Beach, California. Coauthor David Stoop, Ph.D., is a therapist in private practice in Irvine, California.

Arterburn and Stoop tell victims of love–hate relationships how to move beyond the pain in the relationship, how to accept what cannot be changed, and how to get out of the relationship's traps. They especially advocate forgiveness in resolving the relationship's problems.

When Someone You Love Is Someone You Hate received a 1-star

Not Recommended rating in the national survey. It was not well known; only 10 respondents evaluated it. The consensus of the mental health professionals was that self-help books such as Harville Hendrix's *Getting the Love You Want* and Maggie Scarf's *Intimate Partners*, although not focusing exclusively on love–hate relationships, contain better advice on this topic.

★   *What Smart Women Know* (1990) by Steven Carter and Julia Sokol. New York: M. Evans.

What Smart Women Know is a women's guide to romantic relationships. Neither author's education and affiliation is listed.

Carter and Sokol describe women who are caught in various unrewarding relationships with men. A number of catchy aphorisms about men and rules of behavior for dealing with them are provided. Women are warned to stay clear of "any man who wears his napkin like a bib" as well as one who reads Salman Rushdie's *Satanic Verses* on buses and trains.

What Smart Women Know received a 1-star Not Recommended rating in the national survey. Critics said that the book dispenses nothing more than common-sense advise mixed with jargon. The consensus of the few mental health professionals (10) who evaluated the book was that smart women would be wiser to read such self-help books as Harriet Lerner's *The Dance of Intimacy*.

STRONGLY NOT RECOMMENDED

†   *Women Men Love, Women Men Leave* (1987) by Connell Cowan and Melvyn Kinder. New York: Clarkson N. Potter.

Women Men Love, Women Men Leave attempts to explain what men really want in a relationship, which, according to Cowan and Kinder, is intimacy and commitment. Cowan and Kinder are also the authors of *Husbands and Wives*, a 3-star book reviewed earlier in this chapter, and the best-selling *Smart Women, Foolish Choices*.

Cowan and Kinder argue that men need and want lifetime commitment from the women they choose. But when their masculine pride is threatened, males reject women they otherwise are attracted to, say the authors. In the first section of the book, interviews with women who sought counseling on why they had failed to find a husband are profiled.

The interviews reveal such scenarios as affairs abruptly ending when promising partners thought the women were too eager in initiating sex. The second section of the book stresses the importance of partners overcoming selfishness and devoting themselves to each other. A number of self-tests are used to help women understand how their particular styles of loving affect men.

Women Men Love, Women Men Leave is a commercially successful self-help book, but it received a negative average rating in the national survey, placing it in the Strongly Not Recommended category. Critics of the book said that Cowan and Kinder's thesis that men want intimacy and commitment flies in the face of evidence that it is women who primarily bring intimacy and commitment to a relationship and try, largely unsuccessfully, to train men in these important ingredients of love. The book's detractors also faulted its sensationalist tone.

† *What Every Woman Should Know about Men* (1981) by Joyce Brothers. New York: Simon & Schuster.

What Every Woman Should Know about Men tells women, as the title implies, what they need to know to understand and get along with men. Joyce Brothers, Ph.D., is a well-known media psychologist and self-help book author. She formerly taught at Hunter College and Columbia University in New York City.

Brothers tells women that the more they know about men's mental and emotional makeup, the better equipped they will be to interact successfully with them in business, love, and friendship. Brothers presents the physical, pschyological, and emotional differences between men and women and tells readers about the many gender myths. Stages of male adulthood are outlined with advice about how the stages affect men's behavior. Special attention is given to midlife crises in men. Brothers spends considerable time describing men's insecurities and telling women how to deal with them. She also includes a chapter on how to find a husband.

What Every Woman Should Know about Men is not what the mental health professionals in the national survey think women should know about men. The book received a negative average rating, putting it in the Strongly Not Recommended category. Critics said that Brother's book ought to be titled something like *How to Placate, Coddle, and Reassure Men in Today's Society.* They also criticized the book for its excessive stereotyping of women and men, invariably presenting them in traditional gender roles. One critic said that this book sets women's rights back at least a decade.

WORTH A FURTHER LOOK

◑ ◐   *Love Is Never Enough* (1988) by Aaron Beck. New York: Harper & Row.

Love Is Never Enough is a cognitive therapy approach to love. Author Aaron Beck, M.D., is one of the founders of the cognitive therapy approach to helping people cope with problems. He is a professor of psychiatry at the University of Pennsylvania School of Medicine. He also is the author of positively rated books on anxiety (Chapter 7) and depression (Chapter 14).

Beck tells couples how to overcome misunderstandings, resolve conflicts, and improve their relationship by following cognitive therapy strategies. Beck first helps partners to understand the specific self-defeating attitudes that plague their troubled relationship. Then he applies his cognitive therapy approach to what he labels the most common marital problems:

- How negative perceptions can overwhelm the positive aspects of marriage
- The swing from idealization to disillusionment
- The clash of differing perspectives
- The imposition of rigid expectations and rules
- How partners fail to hear what is said and often hear things that are not said
- How personal bias disrupts a relationship
- How automatic negative thinking leads to conflict
- How partners cognitively distort a relationship
- The hostility that drives couples apart

In the last half of the book, Beck presents a number of different cognitive therapy approaches to fit the specific needs of couples.

Love Is Never Enough was positively rated by only 9 respondents, placing it in the Worth a Further Look category. The book was written primarily as a self-help guide to improving love relationships. The few mental health professionals who rated it applauded Beck's insightful applications of cognitive therapy to close relationships. Critics, however, thought that he places too much attention on the individuals' thoughts and not enough on the relationships.

◑ ◐   *Love the Way You Want It* (1991) by Robert J. Sternberg. New York: Bantam Books.

Love the Way You Want It is author Robert Sternberg's second book on love. It is described as a companion to his earlier book, *The Triangle of*

Love (reviewed in Diamonds in the Rough in this chapter). In *Love the Way You Want It*, Sternberg talks about how to improve relationship intelligence and how to make one's love life more exciting, more flexible, and more enduring. Sternberg believes that the rules we learn in school or business often don't work in the world of love. Sternberg's step-by-step lessons for improving one's love life include the following:

- Gaining insight about the enduring qualities of love through a love equation
- Recognizing the triangle of love—passion, intimacy, and commitment
- Dealing with the villians of love, such as partners who are accusers, controllers, and pretenders
- Improving communication and problem-solving skills in a workshop for couples that can be done at home

Love the Way You Want It was published too late to be included in the national survey. Sternberg provides insightful analyses of love relationships, based on sound research and knowledge about love.

CONCLUSIONS

In summary, we recommend:

- On the nature of love and the forms of love:

    ★★★★ *The Art of Loving* by Erich Fromm

    ◆ *The Triangle of Love* by Robert Sternberg

    ◖◗ *Love the Way You Want It* by Robert Sternberg

- On improving a relationship through comprehension of the influence of long-standing relationships on current intimate relationships:

    ★★★★★ *The Dance of Intimacy* by Harriet Lerner

    ★★★★ *Getting the Love You Want* by Harville Hendrix

    ★★★★ *Intimate Partners* by Maggie Scarf

- On a woman's perspective on love:

    ★★★★★ *The Dance of Intimacy* by Harriet Lerner

- A cognitive therapy approach to love:

    ◖◗ *Love Is Never Enough* by Aaron Beck

CHAPTER TWENTY-THREE

Men's Issues

The male of the species — what is he really like? What does he really want and need? At no other point in the history of *Homo sapiens* have males and females been placed under a psychological microscope as they have been in the last 25 years. It began with the emergence of the women's movement and its attack on society's male bias and discrimination against women. As a result of this movement, women have been encouraged to value their sensitive feelings and connectedness with others, to develop their own identity, and to resist men's attempts to dominate and enslave them.

In response to women's efforts to change what defines themselves, and to change men, men developed their own movement. The men's movement has not been as political or as activist as the women's movement. Rather it has been more of an emotional, spiritual movement that reasserts the importance of masculinity and urges men to resist women's efforts to turn them into "soft" males. Or it has been a psychological movement that recognizes that men need to be less violent and more nurturant but still retain their masculine identity. Many men's movement disciples argue that society's changing gender arena has led men to question what being a man really means.

Self-help books on men's issues can be divided into three main categories: men's movement books from the 1970s and early 1980s that focus on a broad set of issues that men have to face and cope with in a society of fluctuating gender roles, men's movement books from the 1990s that rely on mythological and spiritual accounts of man's nature to recapture his true masculinity, and books that focus on the sexual male. Books on gay men's issues are discussed in Chapter 31, Sexuality.

Two books from the 1970s and early 1980s that explore a broad set of men's issues were rated in the national survey: *The Hazards of Being Male* by Herb Goldberg and *The New Male,* also by Herb Goldberg.

Men's Issues	
BOOK RATINGS IN THE NATIONAL SURVEY	
Neutral	★★★ *The Hazards of Being Male* by Herb Goldberg
	★★★ *The New Male* by Herb Goldberg
	★★★ *Fire in the Belly* by Sam Keen
Not Recommended	★★ *Iron John* by Robert Bly
	★ *Why Men Don't Get Enough Sex and Women Don't Get Enough Love* by Jonathan Kramer and Diane Dunaway
Strongly Not Recommended	† *What Men Really Want* by Susan Bakos

Two books from the 1990s that rely on mythological and spiritual accounts of man's nature to encourage men to recapture their true masculinity were rated: *Fire in the Belly* by Sam Keen and *Iron John* by Robert Bly.

Two books that explore the nature of the sexual male were rated: *Why Men Don't Get Enough Sex and Women Don't Get Enough Love* by Jonathan Kramer and Diane Dunaway and *What Men Really Want* by Susan Bakos.

NEUTRAL

★ ★ ★   *The Hazards of Being Male* (1976) by Herb Goldberg. New York: Signet.

Published in 1976, *The Hazards of Being Male* was the first self-help book for men to come out after the woman's movement began to take hold in the 1970s. Author Herb Goldberg, Ph.D., is a clinical psychologist on the faculty of California State University, Los Angeles. He also maintains a private practice in clinical psychology.

Goldberg became a central figure in the early development of the men's movement in the 1970s and early 1980s, mainly as a result of his writings about men's rights in *The Hazards of Being Male* and *The New Male*. Goldberg argues that a critical difference between men and women creates a precipitous gulf between them: women can sense and articulate their feelings and problems; men—because of their masculine conditioning—can't. The result in men is an armor of masculinity that is defensive and powerful in maintaining self-destructive patterns. Goldberg says that most men have been effective work machines and performers but that most else in their lives suffers. Men live about eight fewer years than women on the average, have higher hospitalization rates, and show more behavioral problems. In a word, Goldberg believes that millions of men are killing themselves by striving to be "true" men, a heavy price to pay for masculine "privilege" and power.

How can men solve their dilemma and live more physically and psychologically healthy lives? Goldberg argues that men need to get in touch with their emotions and their bodies. They can't do this by just piggybacking on the changes that are occurring in women's attitudes, says Goldberg. Rather, men need to develop their own realization of what is critical for their survival and well-being. Goldberg especially encourages men to

- recognize the suicidal "success" syndrome and evade it.
- understand that occasional impotence is nothing serious.
- become aware of their real needs and desires and get in touch with their own body.
- elude the binds of masculine role-playing.
- relate to liberated women as their equals rather than serving as their guilty servant or hostile enemy.
- develop male friendships.

The Hazards of Being Male received a 3-star Neutral rating in the national survey. While some important changes in men's roles have occurred in the almost two decades since Goldberg wrote *The Hazards of Being Male*, the book still delivers some important messages for men, among them: Become more tuned into your inner self and emotional make-up, and work on developing more positive close relationships.

★ ★ ★   *The New Male: From Self-Destruction to Self-Care* (1980) by Herb Goldberg. New York: Signet.

The second book on men's issues by Herb Goldberg that was rated in the national survey is subtitled *From Self-Destruction to Self-Care but Still Male. The New Male's* themes are similar to those of *The Hazards of Being Male.*

Goldberg's purpose in writing *The New Male* was to explore what the world of the traditional male has been like in the past, including his relationship with women; what men's worlds are like in today's era of changing gender roles; and what the future can hold in store for men if they examine, reshape, and expand their gender role behavior and self-awareness. Goldberg argues that the way the traditional male role was defined made it virtually impossible for men to explore their inner self, examine their feelings, and show sensitivity toward others.

The New Male is divided into four parts. Part I, He, evaluates the traditional male role and its entrapments, and Part II, He and She, explores the traditional relationship between men and women. Part III, He and Her Changes, analyzes how the changes in roles of women brought about by the women's movement have affected men. Part IV, He and His Changes, provides hope for men by elaborating on how men can combine some of the strengths of traditional masculinity—such as assertiveness and independence—with increased exploration of the inner self, greater awareness of emotions, and more healthy close relationships with others to become more complete, better adjusted men.

The New Male received a 3-star Neutral rating in the national survey. Goldberg says that he never intended to be a voice for the men's movement, but with *The Hazards of Being Male* and then with *The New Male*, he became one. His books have been referred to as the male counterpart of Betty Frieden's *The Feminist Mystique*. He has been accused by some feminists as being antifemale, but he says that kind of criticism misses his message. Goldberg does tell men not to let the new feminist women walk all over them. But his message of challenging men to explore their inner self, get in touch with their feelings, and pay more attention to developing meaningful relationships is hardly antifeminist. Engaging in these activities, says Goldberg, does not mean being less of a male. Rather, doing so makes men more complete, caring human beings. And that is an important message.

★★★ *Fire in the Belly* (1991) by Sam Keen. New York: Bantam Books.

Herb Goldberg's books—*The Hazards of Being Male* and *The New Male*—were the self-help bibles of the men's movement in the 1970s and 1980s. Two authors have ushered in a renewed interest in the men's movement in the 1990s—Sam Keen and Robert Bly (Bly's book, *Iron John*, is evaluated next). Sam Keen has a background in theology: he holds a Master's degree in theology from Harvard Divinity School and a Ph.D. in philosophy of religion from Princeton University. Keen has been a consulting editor for *Psychology Today* magazine, and over the past twenty years he has conducted seminars on personal mythology and written books—*Fire in the Belly* is his twelfth.

Keen adopts the theme that every man is on a spiritual journey to attain the grail of manhood. He strives to provide a road map for the journey, advising men on ways to avoid the dead ends of combative machismo and the blind alleys of romantic obsession.

Keen says that he wrote *Fire in the Belly* because men have lost their vision of what masculinity is. The 1990s man hears voices that tell him, "Men are too aggressive. Too soft. Too insensitive. Too macho. Too wimpy. Too dead to feel." The result: male identity confusion. Keen's answer to the question of men's true identity: fire in the belly and passion in the heart.

Fire in the Belly is divided into five main parts. Part I, Introduction, stresses that men cannot find themselves without first separating from the world of women. Part II, The Rites of Manhood, argues that modern rites of passage—war, work, and sex—impoverish and alienate men. Part III, Taking the Measure of Man, emphasizes that authentic manhood has always been defined by a vision of how a man fits into the universe and by his willingness to undertake an appropriate task or vocation. Part IV, A Primer for Now and Future Heroes, traces the spiritual journey into the self that Keen believes men must undertake in today's world and sketches a portrait of the potential resulting virtues. Part V, Men and Women Coming Together, which examines the reconciliation and common vocation of men and women. An appendix describes the results of a survey Keen conducted (with Ofer Zuer) for *Psychology Today* with 6,000 men and women about what differentiates ideal, good, average, and inferior men.

Fire in the Belly was a *New York Times* best seller, but it received only a 3-star Neutral rating in the national survey. Virtually all men's issues—and women's issues—books are controversial and stir up inflammatory feelings in the opposite sex. Not surprisingly, the male mental health professionals in the national survey rated *Fire in the Belly* more positively than their female counterparts did. They applauded Keen's efforts to get men to reexamine their male identity and to incorporate more empathy into their relationships. They also supported Keen's notion that males need to reduce their hostility.

Several of Keen's critics, especially female critics, didn't like his trashing of androgyny. They argued that authors like Keen exaggerate differences between women and men and perpetrate masculine bias and discrimination against women. (Keen says that we would probably have a better and clearer world if we stopped using the words "masculine" and "feminine" altogether except to refer to gender stereotypes.) Other critics didn't like the mythology and mysticism that permeate *Fire in the Belly*. Keen adopts a Jungian perspective on man's inner journey to find himself, a perspective that is filled with symbols and metaphors that are not always clearly presented. One of Keen's missions, encouraging men to be aggressive but not hostile, sometimes gets lost in the fuzzy forays into Jungian thought.

NOT RECOMMENDED

★ ★   *Iron John: Straight Talk about Men* (1990) by Robert Bly. New York: Vintage Books.

Iron John ushered in a new wave of male consciousness raising the 1990s. It has been a number one national best seller and already has sold almost half a million copies. Author Robert Bly is a poet, storyteller, and translator. His poetry has won numerous awards, including the National Book Award. He lives in Minneapolis, Minnesota.

Iron John includes many of the same themes as *Fire in the Belly*, not surprisingly since Bly and Keen are both Jungian disciples. Kings, Warriors, Flying Boys, Unicorns, Princesses, and a Hairy Giant populate *Iron John's* poems and stories about man's spiritual and mythical journey. Bly says that we live in a society that hasn't had fathers since the Industrial Revolution. With no viable rituals for introducing young boys into manhood, today's men are confused. In line with Keen's beliefs, Bly argues that too many of today's males are "soft males," having bonded with their mother because their father was not available. These "soft males" know how to follow instead of lead, how to be vulnerable, and how to go with the flow. What they don't know is what it's like to have a deep masculine identity.

Developing a deep masculine identity requires learning how to become the Wildman. Who is the Wildman? Bly says he is not savage man—brutal, war-making, earth-destroying. Rather, the Wildman is like a Zen priest, a shaman, or a woodsman. He is spontaneous and sexual, an action taker, a boundary definer, and an earth preserver.

Iron John is the Wildman. And not just a wildman, but a hairy wildman. He inhabits the forests and helps aimless young princes in their desire to achieve fame and fortune. He has untamed impulses and thoughtful self-discipline.

Bly not only writes poetry and books. He and his associates also conduct five-week-long gatherings and weekend workshops for men. At these gatherings, the participants try to capture what it is like to be a true man by engaging in such rituals as drum beating and naming ceremonies.

Despite *Iron John's* enormous popularity, it received a 2-star Not Recommended rating in the national survey. Some critics of the book didn't like Bly's strong insistence on the separateness of the sexes. Only masculine men and feminine women populate Bly's highly differentiated world. Several mental health experts said that while Bly acknowledges the expanded role of women in the world, his program for men, as defined in *Iron John*, depends strictly on women playing their traditional roles at home. Feminist critics deplore Bly's approach, calling it a regression to the old macho model of masculinity. Like Jung before him, Bly also gets caught up in a world of masculine and feminine archetypes, which describe men and women as unchangeable, fixed opposites. Other critics have poked fun at Bly's outings for men.

★   *Why Men Don't Get Enough Sex and Women Don't Get Enough Love* (1990) by Jonathan Kramer and Diane Dunaway.

This book examines the sexual dimensions of men's and women's lives. Author Jonathan Kramer, Ph.D., is a psychologist and marriage and family therapist in LaJolla, California. Coauther Diane Dunaway, Kramer's wife, is a professional writer.

Kramer and Dunaway explain why men feel good about themselves after they have had sex while women have a need to feel good about themselves before they have sex. The authors also describe how men are trained from childhood not to show love and affection. Kramer and Dunaway developed a ten-step "Great Love, Great Sex" program that is designed to help men and women find out what the other sex truly wants. That is, women want men to be a woman's playmate, hero, lover, and friend. Men are told why helping her with the housework will get them more and better sex. Women learn how to get a more romantic relationship without having to do all of the work. The authors also tell women how to get men to enjoy kissing and cuddling.

Why Men Don't Get Enough Sex and Women Don't Get Enough Love is divided into three main parts. Part I, Too Little Sex, Too Little Love, lays out the problems between men and women and provides a background to help understand the nature of the battle between the sexes. Part II, Great Love, Great Sex, outlines Kramer and Dunaway's 10-step program, which can be done together as a couple or individually. Part III, More Happily Ever After, is a brief section that shows how to continue the changes developed through the ten-step program into the future.

Why Men Don't Get Enough Sex and Women Don't Get Enough Love received a 1-star Not Recommended rating in the national survey. The mental health critics felt that this book grossly stereotypes sex differences and sensationalizes its account of women and men.

STRONGLY NOT RECOMMENDED

†   *What Men Really Want: Straight Talk from Men about Sex* (1990) by Susan Bakos. New York: St. Martin's Press.

What Men Really Want, a paperback book, is about men's sexual lives. Author Susan Crain Bakos is a professional writer who in 1985 began an advice column for *Penthouse* magazine under the psuedonym Carolyn Steele. The column was titled "Dear Superlady of Sex," the title of the hardcover version of *What Men Really Want*. Bakos also developed a questionnaire and distributed it to hundreds of men who were contacted through ads in upscale city magazines and to other males through contacts with friends, business associates, and doctors. More than a thousand men responded, telling Bakos about their sexual thoughts and experiences, fears and fantasies. Bakos writes that one of the most important findings to come out of the survey is that sex depends more on male arousal than female arousal and that men know this better than women do.

What Men Really Want is divided into six parts: Part I, The Languages of Lust; Part II, Seduction: Who Has Sex with Whom and When; Part III, Arousal; Part IV, Performance; Part V, Emotional Involvement; and Part VI, Secret Fears and Hidden Obsessions. Throughout the book, Bakos describes men's sexual expectations, fantasies, fears, and pleasures. She also tells women how to accept the dramatic differences between women and men. Bakos believes that acknowledging men's true feelings about sex can help women enjoy more honest and mutually fulfilling relationships with the opposite sex.

What Men Really Want was not well received by the mental health professionals in the national survey. The book was given a negative average score, placing it in the Strongly Not Recommended category. The mental health professionals said that *What Men Really Want* takes one aspect of a man's existence—his sexuality—and isolates it from the rest of his identity. One critic said that it is all too easy to get the impression from this book that men are just sexual animals. Other critics cited the bias and lack of scientific integrity of Bakos's survey.

CONCLUSIONS

In summary, we recommend:

- On the psychological and social changes men are undergoing in contemporary society:

  ★★★ *The New Male* by Herb Goldberg

CHAPTER TWENTY-FOUR

Positive Thinking
and Self-Talk

"Don't worry, be happy" are the words of a popular tune by Bobby McFerrin, " 'Cause when you worry, your face will frown, and that will bring everybody down . . . " Is McFerrin's cheerful optimism a good coping strategy? Most of the time we do want to avoid negative thinking when dealing with stress. A positive mood improves our ability to processs information more efficiently, makes us more altruistic, and gives us higher self-esteem. An optimistic mood is superior to a pessimistic one in most instances, producing a sense that we are in control of our world. A negative mood increases our chances of getting angry, feeling guilty, making mistakes, and magnifying our mistakes.

Despite the popularity of such self-help books as Norman Vincent Peale's *The Power of Positive Thinking*, for many years most psychologists recommended perceiving reality as accurately as possible as the best route to psychological health. Recently, though, a number of psychologists have begun to recommend that having some positive illusions about one's self is adaptive. Psychological researchers have found that happy people often entertain falsely high opinions of themselves, give self-serving explanations for events, and have exaggerated beliefs about their ability to control the world around them. Indeed, for some people, seeing things too accurately can produce depression. An absence of positive illusions about one's self also may restrict people from undertaking risky, ambitious, and creative projects that could yield great rewards.

Positive self-talk can also build the confidence needed to fully use skills and talents. Because self-talk has a way of becoming a self-fulfilling prophecy, unchallenged, unaltered negative self-talk can spell trouble—it can decrease self-confidence, discourage attempts to change behavior, and block a person's perception of improved circumstances.

Self-help books on positive thinking and self-talk in the national sur-

---

Positive Thinking and Self-Talk
BOOK RATINGS IN THE NATIONAL SURVEY

Strongly Recommended	★★★★★	*Learned Optimism* by Martin Seligman
Diamonds in the Rough	◆	*Positive Illusions* by Shelley Taylor
	◆	*What to Say When You Talk to Yourself* by Shad Helmstetter
Neutral	★★★	*Staying Rational in an Irrational World* by Michael Bernard
	★★★	*Positive Addiction* by William Glasser
	★★★	*Talking to Yourself* by Pamela Butler
	★★★	*Self-Defeating Behaviors* by Milton Cudney and Robert Hardy
Not Recommended	★★	*You Can't Afford the Luxury of a Negative Thought* by John-Roger and Peter McWilliams
	★★	*Tough Times Never Last but Tough People Do!* by Robert Schuller
	★★	*The Power of Optimism* by Alan McGinnis
	★	*The Power of Positive Thinking* by Norman Vincent Peale

---

vey can be divided into four main categories: psychologically based positive thinking books; spiritually based positive thinking books; cognitive and behavioral approaches to coping with stress and eliminating self-defeating behaviors; and self-talk books.

Five books on positive thinking from a psychological perspective were rated: *Learned Optimism* by Martin Seligman; *Positive Illusions* by Shelley Taylor; *Positive Addiction* by William Glasser; *You Can't Afford the Luxury of a Negative Thought* by John-Roger and Peter McWilliams; and *The Power of Optimism* by Alan McGinnis.

Two books on positive thinking from a spiritual perspective were rated: *Tough Times Never Last but Tough People Do!* by Robert Schuller and *The Power of Positive Thinking* by Norman Vincent Peale.

One book that presents a cognitive and behavioral approach to reducing self-defeating behaviors was rated: *Self-Defeating Behaviors* by Milton Cudney and Robert Hardy. A second book in the category—*Thoughts and Feelings* by Matthew McKay, Martha Davis, and Patrick Fanning—is evaluated in Worth a Further Look.

Three books on self-talk were rated: *What to Say When You Talk to Yourself* by Shad Helmstetter, *Staying Rational in an Irrational World* by Michael Bernard, and *Talking to Yourself* by Pamela Butler.

STRONGLY RECOMMENDED

★ ★ ★ ★ ★   *Learned Optimism: The Skill to Conquer Life's Obstacles, Large and Small* (1990) by Martin Seligman. New York: Pocket Books

Learned Optimism is a psychologically based approach to positive thinking. Author Martin Seligman, Ph.D., is a professor of psychology at the University of Pennsylvania. He is widely recognized as a leading authority on psychological dimensions of coping and motivation.

Learned Optimism is one of the new breed of positive thinking books, a breed that first began to appear in the late the 1980s and has steadily increased in number. The new breed is based on psychological research rather than spiritual beliefs.

Seligman argues that optimism and pessimism are not fixed, inborn psychological traits but rather are learned explanatory styles—habitual ways we explain things that happen to us. Pessimists, says Seligman, perceive a defeat as permanent, catastrophic, and evidence of personal inadequacy; optimists, in contrast, perceive the same mishap as a temporary setback, something that can be controlled, and rooted in circumstances or luck. Seligman's positive message is that since pessimism is learned, it can be unlearned. Included are self-tests to determine the reader's levels of optimism, pessimism, and depression.

Seligman reviews a great deal of research on explanatory styles, concluding that optimists do better in school, in athletics, and at work because they persist at attaining success even in the face of setbacks, while equally talented pessimists are more likely not to stay the course. Seligman also reviews research to demonstrate that pessimists have weaker immune systems, have more health problems, and are more likely to be depressed.

Learned Optimism received a 5-star Strongly Recommended rating in the national survey. This is an excellent self-help book on positive thinking. It is well documented but not overly academic and psychobabble-free. Leading cognitive therapist Aaron Beck commented that readers of Seligman's book can learn how to develop a more optimistic style and be happier and healthier for it. Wes Roberts, author of *Leadership Secrets of Attila the Hun*, said that *Learned Optimism* contains a wealth of counsel for people who can't seem to get out of negative thinking habits.

DIAMONDS IN THE ROUGH

◆   *Positive Illusions: Creative Self-Discipline and the Healthy Mind* (1989) by Shelley Taylor. New York: Basic Books.

Positive Illusions, like *Learned Optimism*, is a psychologically based approach to positive thinking. Author Shelley Taylor, Ph.D., is a professor of psychology at UCLA and a highly respected authority in the field of health psychology.

Taylor's main themes are similar to Seligman's: Facing the complete truth about ourselves is often not the best mental health strategy; the healthy human mind has a tendency to block out negative information; positive illusions help us cope. Taylor believes that these creative deceptions are especially beneficial when we are threatened by adversity.

Taylor describes research on cancer patients, disaster victims, and other people facing crises to portray how mental and physical well-being can be improved by having an unrealistically positive view of one's self and abilities. For example, she discusses how an inflated sense of self-worth can help a person be more successful on the job and how an illusory sense of self-confidence can prevent a seriously ill person from giving up.

Positive Illusions was positively rated but by too few respondents (only 13) to make the 4-star or 5-star categories, so it was placed in the Diamonds in the Rough category. This is a good book on positive thinking, but self-help readers will find that Seligman's book reads more smoothly. Taylor's book becomes too formal and academic in places. However, the quality of Taylor's documentation is outstanding and intellectually challenged readers will enjoy the book. Well-known self-help author Carol Tavris called *Positive Illusions* brilliant and provocative. Highly respected health psychologist Roy Baumeister said that Taylor's book is an important one that will force psychologists to revise the way they think about mental health.

◆   *What to Say When You Talk to Yourself* (1986) by Shad Helmstetter. Scottsdale, AZ: Grindle Press.

What to Say When You Talk to Yourself provides advice on how to use self-talk to improve competence. Author Shad Helmstetter, Ph.D., is a behavioral psychologist who has been a consultant on self-management to a number of corporations.

What to Say When You Talk to Yourself examines the success literature and concludes that in all of the many recommendations there are some missing ingredients: permanent solutions, knowledge of mind/brain functions, and a word-for-word set of directions for programming the unconscious mind. Helmstetter concludes that the only solution that includes all of the three missing ingredients is self-talk and goes on to outline five levels of self-talk, the highest being the level of universal affirmation. The author spells out the self-talk strategies of silent self-talk, self-speak, self-conversation, self-write, tape-talk, and creating self-talk tapes. And he covers a number of other ideas about self-talk problem-solving strategies for changing attitudes, changing behaviors, and dealing with different situations.

What to Say When You Talk to Yourself made the Diamonds in the Rough: it was positively rated but by only 21 respondents. A number of mental health professionals said that the book presents some very helpful strategies for coping with stressful circumstances, especially for negative thinkers and people low in motivation. Helmstetter spells out what to say to yourself to improve your life instead of just being a cheerleader like so many of the positive thinking, motivational self-help book authors. Critics said that the material about the nonconscious mind and brain is fuzzy.

NEUTRAL

★ ★ ★   *Staying Rational in an Irrational World* (1991) by Michael Bernard. New York: Carol Publishing.

Staying Rational in an Irrational World applies cognitive therapist Albert Ellis's rational emotive therapy to a number of problems. Author Michael Bernard, Ph.D., is an instructor of psychology in the Department of Education, University of Melbourne, Australia. He trained with Ellis in New York.

Bernard presents a comprehensive application of rational emotive therapy to many different domains of life — love, dating, sex, work, children, parents, women's issues, homosexuality, and death and dying. The basic theme of rational emotive therapy is that to cope effectively we need to replace our irrational thinking with rational thinking. The book includes a large number of examples in which individuals learn to talk to themselves more effectively and think in more rational ways. Two final chapters include an interview with Ellis about rational emotive therapy and a long list of Ellis's books, tapes, and talks.

This book received a 3-star Neutral rating in the national survey. Like Ellis's other books, *Staying Rational in an Irrational World* has a number of supporters and some detractors. The book's enthusiasts say that it does a good job of applying Ellis's ideas to many different aspects of life. Ellis himself, in a foreword to the book, calls it a more serious treatment of rational emotive therapy than his own less academic, more rambunctious presentations.

★ ★ ★   *Positive Addiction* (1976) by William Glasser. New York: Harper Perennial.

Positive Addiction is also a psychologically based approach to positive thinking. Author William Glasser, M.D., became famous in the 1960s and 1970s for founding a school of therapy known as reality therapy—a results-oriented therapy designed to help people cope with their immediate environment.

In *Positive Addiction,* Glasser turns from therapy to the problems virtually all of us have in developing our potential. Glasser argues that every person can overcome self-imposed weaknesses by engaging in positive addictions/activities, such as running and meditation, that help people to lose their consciousness. Glasser says that when people do this they "spin free" and almost mysticallly arrive at new strategies for coping with life. By contrast, negative addictions are escapes from the pain of striving for things people want but doubt they can accomplish, such as career or athletic achievements. Glasser's list of negative addictions includes drinking, gambling, work, overeating, and smoking.

Positive Addiction receieved a 3-star Neutral rating in the national survey. Glasser's ideas were much more popular in the 1960s and 1970s than they are today. *Positive Addiction* itself was written in 1976, and frequent references to well-known people of that time—Jimmy the Greek and Tim Galloway (*Inner Tennis*), for example—seriously date the book. Critics also say that in places the book regresses into mystical explanations.

★ ★ ★   *Talking to Yourself: Learning the Language of Self-Affirmation* (1981) by Pamela Butler. New York: Stein and Day.

Talking to Yourself gives advice on improving life through self-talk. Author Pamela Butler, Ph.D., is a clincial psychologist and director of the Behavior Therapy Institute in Mill Valley, California.

Butler says that each of us experiences an inner self as a distinct person speaking to us. Each of us engages this inner person in a dialogue throughout our lives. Through this inner dialogue with ourselves, we make decisions, set goals, and feel satisfied or dejected. Butler believes that our behavior, thoughts, feelings, and self-esteem are strongly influenced by such inner speech. In this book, Butler gives a number of specific strategies for changing our self-talk and making it work better. Topics covered include anger and self-talk, sex and self-talk, and gender and self-talk.

Talking to Yourself received a 3-star Neutral rating in the national survey. The book's supporters said that it is has good advice about how to improve the way we talk to ourselves and consequently improve our ability to cope with difficult circumstances. They applauded the author's specific recommendations about how to change our self-talk.

★ ★ ★   *Self-Defeating Behaviors* (1991) by Milton Cudney and Robert Hardy. San Francisco: Harper.

Self-Defeating Behaviors presents a cognitive and behavioral approach for eliminating a wide range of self-defeating behaviors. Author Milton Cudney, Ph.D., is a professor of counseling at Western Michigan University. Coauthor Robert Hardy, Ed.D., is a counseling psychologist affiliated with the Golden Valley Health Center in Minneapolis, Minnesota.

The authors believe that we develop self-defeating behavior patterns such as procrastination, defensiveness, alcohol and drug abuse, shyness, and smoking becuse they provide us with comfort and protection. While not the healthiest means of coping, these behaviors function well enough to become entrenched in our behavior patterns. Cudney and Hardy argue that people can free themselves from these self-destructive patterns by

- identifying the problem-causing behavior.
- specifying when, where, and with whom the behavior comes into play.
- intercepting the behavior while it is being practiced.
- developing replacement techniques.
- facing fears.
- overcoming setbacks.
- celebrating breakthroughs.

Self-Defeating Behaviors received a 3-star Neutral rating in the national survey. The book was evaluated by only 10 respondents, no doubt because it was published shortly before the survey was conducted. The book's enthusiasts said that it provides an excellent approach to eliminating self-defeating behaviors. Well-known cognitive therapist Albert Ellis said that the book is the most detailed examination of self-defeating behaviors he has ever read and contains some helpful strategies for getting rid of them. And Harville Hendrix, author of the positively evaluated *Getting the Love You Want* (Chapter 22), commented that Cudney and Hardy map out a clear path for eliminating self-defeating behaviors. Critics said that for a self-help book it is difficult reading.

NOT RECOMMENDED

★ ★   *You Can't Afford the Luxury of a Negative Thought* (1988) by John-Roger and Peter McWilliams. Los Angeles, CA: Prelude Press.

You Can't Afford the Luxury of a Negative Thought is a broad-based approach to positive thinking. No mental health affiliations are listed for author John-Roger. He has written a number of self-help books and tapes. Coauthor Peter McWilliams is a poet and self-help book author. He contributed his poetry to the positively evaluated *How to Survive the Loss of a Love* (Chapter 13).

You Can't Afford the Luxury of a Negaive Thought is one of a number of self-help books John-Roger and Peter McWilliams have written for the series they call "The Life 101 Series." The subtitle of this book is *A Book for People with Any Life-Threatening Illness—Including Life.* They begin by discussing the disease of negative thinking and the cure for the disease (death) and then how to accentuate the positive and eliminate the negative in the way we think. The book is long (more than 600 pages) and covers a wide range of ways to improve positive thinking—from visualization to meditation to developing positive attitudes.

You Can't Afford the Luxury of a Negative Thought received a 2-star Not Recommended rating in the national survey. Critics said that the book is a disorganized, confusing hodgepodge of self-help advice. The consensus of the mental health professionals in the national survey was that books such as Seligman's *Learned Optimism* and Helmstetter's *What to Say When You Talk to Yourself* are much better choices.

★ ★   *Tough Times Never Last, but Tough People Do!* (1983) by Robert Schuller. New York: Bantam.

Tough Times Never Last, but Tough People Do! presents a spiritually based approach to positive thinking. Author Robert Schuller is a founder and senior pastor of the famous Crystal Cathedral in Garden Grove, California. His telecast *The Hour of Power* was highly successful for many years. He has written more than twenty books.

Schuller tells readers that no matter what their problem, they can build a positive self-image. Whether they are unemployed, in poor health, lonely, or depressed, Schuller says his program will transform negative thoughts into positive ones, turning their lives around in the process. Spiritual and psychological strategies are combined in Schuller's approach to positive thinking. He tells readers how to take charge of their lives, how to think positively, how faith can move a mountain of problems, and how to use the power of prayer to put the pieces of their lives together.

Tough Times Never Last, but Tough People Do! received a 2-star Not Recommended rating in the national survey. More than a million copies of this book have been sold, and it was on *The New York Times* best-seller list for more than three months. Well-known self-help author Norman Vincent Peale said that this book is upbeat and and will inspire readers to develop a more creative life style. Critics said that today's new wave of research-based, psychologically oriented positive thinking books—such as Seligman's *Learned Optimism*—provide more substance than the cheerleading type of positive thinking books like Schuller's.

★ ★   *The Power of Optimism* (1990) by Alan McGinnis. San Francisco, CA: Harper & Row.

The Power of Optimism is a psychologically based book on positive thinking. Author Alan McGinnis has written a number of self-help books (for example, *The Romance Factor*) and is director of the Valley Counseling Center in Glendale, California.

McGinnis explores the ways in which an optimistic attitiude improves an individual's life, increases success, and attracts other people. McGinnis described twelve characteristics of optimists and he tells the reader how to achieve them. Optimists

- Are rarely surprised by trouble.
- Search for partial solutions.
- Believe they have control over their future.
- Allow for regular renewal.
- Stop their negative thoughts.
- Improve their powers of appreciation.
- Use their imagination to become successful.
- Are cheerful even when they can't be happy.
- Think they have an almost unlimited capacity.
- Incorporate a great deal of love in their life.
- Like to share good news.
- Accept what they cannot change.

The Power of Optimism received a 2-star Not Recommended rating in the national survey. Critics said that McGinnis's book is not as well grounded in research knowledge as Seligman's *Learned Optimism.* They also said that cognitive therapy books such as David Burns's *Feeling Good: The New Mood Therapy* are a much better choice for learning about how to replace negative thinking with positive thinking.

★   *The Power of Positive Thinking* (1952) by Norman Vincent Peale. New York: Ballantine.

The Power of Positive Thinking is a spiritually based approach to positive thinking. Author Norman Vincent Peale, who has a doctorate in theology, was the minister of New York's Marble Collegiate Church. Through his national radio and television programs, his magazine *Guideposts,* lectures in scores of cities, and this book, Peale became a household name around the world. *The Power of Positive Thinking* has been so successful—selling more than five million copies—that Peale's name has become virtually synonomous with a positive thinking philosophy.

There is no problem, difficulty, or defeat that Peale thinks cannot be solved or overcome by faith, positive thinking, and prayer. The book is liberally sprinkled with exerpts from the Bible. Peale cites many examples of his claims, describing in enthusiastic fashion how people he has known and counseled have turned troubled minds into peaceful ones, improved their health, stopped worrying, and become highly successful.

Although *The Power of Positive Thinking* has been a runaway best seller and one of the most successful self-help books in history, the consensus of the mental health experts in the national survey was that positive thinking is served better by other books, especially Seligman's *Learned Optimism* and David Burns's *Feeling Good,* evaluated in Chapter 14. We certainly owe a big debt to Norman Vincent Peale. It was he who first recognized the power of positive thinking in helping people live happier and more productive lives. However, critics of Peale's book say that although he does not completely ignore or minimize hardships and tragedies, he portrays positive thinking and resulting successes in life as too easily attained, problems as too easily solved, and change as too automatic and immediate.

WORTH A FURTHER LOOK

◖◗   *Thoughts and Feelings* (1981) by Matthew McKay, Martha Davis, and Patrick Fanning. Oakland, CA: New Harbinger.

Thoughts and Feelings presents a cognitive behavior approach to improving positive thinking, self-talk, and general behavior. Author Matthew

McKay, Ph.D., is Director of Psychological Services at the Haight-Ashbury Free Medical Clinic in San Francisco. He is coauthor of a number of self-help books, including *The Relaxation and Stress Reduction Workbook*. Martha Davis, Ph.D., coauthor of both books, is a clinical psychologist in the Department of Psychiatry at the Kaiser Permanente Medical Center in Santa Clara, California. Coauthor Patrick Fanning is a professional writer.

Thoughts and Feelings is subitled *The Art of Cognitive Stress Intervention*. This book could have been placed in Chapter 26, Relaxation, Meditation, and Stress, but the few mental health professionals who rated the book listed it in the self-talk/positive thinking category. The book tells readers how to evaluate their stress level, combat distorted thinking, solve problems, and use visualization, and it gives special attention to roadblocks in coping with stress. *Thoughts and Feelings* includes a number of exercises and examples of how to use the cognitive behavior strategies the authors recommend.

Thoughts and Feelings was positively rated in the national survey but by only 6 respondents. They said that the book provides sound advice about a variety of techniques for coping with stress.

CONCLUSIONS

In summary, we recommend:

- On improving life with optimistic thinking:

  ★★★★★ *Learned Optimism* by Martin Seligman

- On using self-talk to cope with life's difficulties:

  ◆ *What to Say When You Talk to Yourself* by Shad Helmstetter

- On eliminating self-defeating behaviors:

  ★★★ *Self-Defeating Behaviors* by Milton Cudney and Robert Hardy

CHAPTER TWENTY-FIVE

Pregnancy

Although Sara and Jim did not plan to have a baby right away, they did not take any precautions to prevent it, and it was not long before Sara was pregnant. They found a nurse–midwife they liked and invented a pet name—Bibinello—for the fetus. They signed up for birth preparation classes, and each Friday night for eight weeks they faithfully practiced contractions. They drew up a birth plan that included their decisions about such matters as the type of care provider they wanted to use, the birth setting they wanted, and other aspects of labor and birth. They moved into a larger apartment so that the baby could have its own room and spent weekends browsing through garage sales and secondhand stores to find good prices on baby furniture—a crib, a highchair, a stroller, a changing table, a crib mobile, a swing, a car seat.

Jim and Sarah also spent a lot of time talking about Sara's pregnancy, what kind of parents they wanted to be, and what their child might be like. They also discussed what changes in their life the baby would make. One of their concerns was that Sara's maternity leave would last only six weeks. If she wanted to stay home longer she would have to quit her job, something she and Jim were not sure they could afford.

These are among the many scripts and questions expectant couples have about pregnancy. And there have been many books written to help expectant parents like Sara and Jim better understand pregnancy and make more informed decisions about their offspring's health and well-being, as well as their own. Self-help books on pregnancy can be divided into three categories: month-by-month (in some places, week-by-week) guides to pregnancy; general guides to pregnancy issues that emphasize options, planning, and preparation; and books on special pregnancy topics, such as what to eat during pregnancy and becoming pregnant after the age of 35.

One month-by-month guide to pregnancy was rated: *What to Expect*

Pregnancy
BOOK RATINGS IN THE NATIONAL SURVEY

Recommended	★★★★	*The Complete Book of Pregnancy and Childbirth* by Sheila Kitzinger
Diamonds In The Rough	◆	*What to Expect When You're Expecting* by Arlene Eisenberg, Heidi Murkoff, and Sandee Hathaway
	◆	*What to Eat When You're Expecting* by Arlene Eisenberg, Heidi Murkoff, and Sandee Hathaway
Neutral	★★★	*Pregnancy after 35* by Carole McCauley
	★★★	*The Well Pregnancy Book* by Mike Samuels and Nancy Samuels
	★★★	*From Here to Maternity* by Connie Marshall

When You're Expecting by Arlene Eisenberg, Heidi Murkoff, and Sandee Hathaway.

Three general guides to pregnancy were evaluated: *The Complete Book of Pregnancy and Childbirth* by Sheila Kitzinger; *The Well Pregnancy Book* by Mike Samuels and Nancy Samuels; and *From Here to Maternity* by Connie Marshall.

Two books that focus on specific aspects of pregnancy were rated: *What to Eat When You're Expecting* by Arlene Eisenberg, Heidi Murkoff, and Sandee Hathaway and *Pregnancy after 35* by Carole McCauley. Another book — *Will It Hurt the Baby?* by Richard Abrams — is evaluated in the Worth a Further Look section.

RECOMMENDED

★★★★   *The Complete Book of Pregnancy and Childbirth* (1985) by Sheila Kitzinger. New York: Alfred Knopf.

The Complete Book of Pregnancy and Childbirth is a comprehensive guide to pregnancy and childbirth. Author Sheila Kitzinger is a social anthropologist who has studied methods of childbirth education all over the world and has been developing and refining her own approach to childbirth since 1958. She is on the Advisory Board of England's National Childbirth Trust and has been a longstanding champion of women's rights in childbirth.

Kitzinger says that more women are deciding that they want to be active birthgivers rather than passively deliver their newborn. The expectant mother prepares for an active role in childbirth by learning about the changes that are occurring in her body, pregnancy and childbirth options, and who does what to her and why.

In *The Complete Book of Pregnancy and Childbirth,* expectant mothers learn about the early weeks of pregnancy and the emotional and physical changes they are likely to experience at this time. Kitzinger educates expectant mothers about prenatal care and how to understand medical charts. She describes common worries and problems of expectant mothers, lovemaking during pregnancy, and the father's role in the pregnancy. The author recommends relaxation and breathing exercises and provides advice about medical checkups. She covers what happens during stages of labor, support during labor, coping with pain, the option of "gentle birth," and what to expect in the first few hours and days after birth. The book has numerous charts, drawings, and photographs.

The Complete Book of Pregnancy and Childbirth received a 4-star Recommended rating in the national survey. The book's enthusiasts especially liked Kitzinger's holistic approach to pregnancy, her emphasis on women's choices, and her ideas about relaxation and breathing techniques. The book's critics from the medical community said that her portrayal of drug influences are inaccurate in places.

DIAMONDS IN THE ROUGH

♦   *What to Expect When You're Expecting* (2nd ed., 1988) by Arlene Eisenberg, Heidi Murkoff, and Sandee Hathaway. New York: Workman.

What to Expect When You're Expecting is a month-by-month, step-by-step guide to pregnancy and childbirth. For authors Arlene Eisenberg and Heidi Murkoff, no professional background or affiliations are listed. Coauthor Sandee Hathaway has an undergraduate degree in nursing. The authors have written several other self-help books on pregnancy and infant development (*What to Expect the First Year* is profiled in Chapter 21).

The authors are a mother–daughters team. The book was the result of the unnecessarily worry-filled pregnancy of the second author (Heidi Eisenberg Murkoff). The book tries to put expectant parents' normal fears into perspective by giving them comprehensive information and helping them to enjoy this transition in their lives.

What to Expect When You're Expecting is divided into three main parts. Part I, In the Beginning, covers expectant parents' concerns about their medical histories and possible environmental harm to the fetus (cigarette smoking, air pollution, household parents, and the like), how to choose a practitioner, and providing a healthy diet for the expectant mother. Part II, Nine Months and Counting, devotes a chapter to each month of pregnancy from conception to delivery. Each month's chapter informs expectant parents what to expect at a monthly checkup, describes what they are probably feeling, addresses what they may be concerned about, and presents a special topic, such as weight gain (third month), making love (fourth month), and facts about breast feeding (eighth month). Part II also includes a chapter on birth and delivery, which focuses on concerns about stages of labor and childbirth. Part III, Last but Not Least, examines the first week postpartum, the first six weeks postpartum, fathers, and preparing for the next baby.

What to Expect When You're Expecting was placed in the Diamonds in the Rough category—it was very positively rated but by only 30 respondents. The low number of evaluations is surprising given this book's popularity; it is easily the top-selling self-help book on pregnancy and has been a national best seller. But then, none of the pregnancy books were rated by many respondents; even *The Complete Book of Pregnancy and Childbirth* was evaluated by only 39 respondents. The low frequency of ratings of pregnancy books in the national survey undoubtedly occurred because the evaluators were mental health professionals, not obstetricians.

What to Expect When You're Expecting is an excellent self-help book for expectant parents. It is reassuring and thorough. The authors do an outstanding job of walking expectant parents through the nine months of pregnancy and childbirth. One of the book's supporters said that *What to Expect When You're Expecting* is like having an experienced mother nearby whom you can call for answers to questions like "Hey, did you get leg cramps in the fifth month?" The book is filled with charts and lists that make understanding pregnancy easier for expectant parents.

◆   *What to Eat When You're Expecting* (1986) by Arlene Eisenberg, Heidi Murkoff, and Sandee Hathaway. New York: Workman.

What to Eat When You're Expecting focuses on a special aspect of pregnancy: diet and nutrition. The book was written by the authors of *What to Expect When You're Expecting*. It is based on twenty years of practical application in the Eisenberg family. They present the "best odds" diet, which they believe increases the probability of having a healthy baby by controlling the factors that can be influenced and minimizing the risk and worry about factors that cannot be controlled.

The book is divided into four parts. Part I describes nutritional needs during pregnancy and how they affect the baby. Daily recommended portions are given (four servings of protein, two servings of vitamin C, four servings of calcium, three servings of green leafy and yellow vegetables and yellow fruits, one to two servings of other vegetables and fruits, four to five servings of complex carbohydrates, two servings of high-fat foods, eight glasses of fluids, some iron-rich foods, and a daily pregnancy-formulated vitamin supplement. The expectant mother learns how to assess her current eating habits and how to alter them if they are not good.

Part II describes practical solutions for cooking and enlisting the whole family in the eating plan. Safe and unsafe foods are also listed. Part III contains almost 100 pages of recipes, and Part IV is a lengthy appendix of nutritional charts.

What to Eat When You're Expecting made the Diamonds in the Rough category in the national survey. The book is well written and easy to read, and the nutritional plan for expectant mothers is sound.

NEUTRAL

★ ★ ★   *Pregnancy after 35* (1976) by Carole McCauley. New York: Pocket Books.

Pregnancy after 35 is about a special type of pregnancy, that of mothers over the age of 35. Author Carole McCauley is a medical reporter.

The older mother faces certain unique medical and emotional problems during her pregnancy. This book was based on medical journal articles and interviews with physicians, psychologists, midwives, and older couples to address the special concerns of pregnancy in older women. Women over 35 learn about genetic counseling, risk factors, and psychological issues that arise throughout pregnancy.

Pregnancy after 35 received a 3-star Neutral rating in the national survey. The book was written in 1976 and is dated, especially in terms of nutritional advice. And of course it does not cover a number of tests that have been developed in recent years to assess the likelihood of having a healthy baby.

★ ★ ★   *The Well Pregnancy Book* (1986) by Mike Samuels and Nancy Samuels. New York: Summit Books.

The Well Pregnancy Book is a comprehensive guide to pregnancy and childbirth that emphasizes a holistic approach. Author Mike Samuels, M.D., has worked with the U.S. Public Health Service on the Hopi Indian reservation and helped to establish one of the first holistic medicine clinics in northern California. Nancy Samuels, a former nursery school teacher, has cowritten several other self-help books with her husband.

This book focuses on wellness during pregnancy. It provides an overview of childbirth practices in different cultures and serves as an expectant parents' guide to pregnancy, childbirth, and the postpartum period. It covers nutrition and fitness, physical changes in the expectant mother and the offspring, and the medical aspects of hormonal and bodily changes in pregnant women.

The Well Pregnancy Book received a 3-star Neutral rating in the national survey. This book is better for uncomplicated pregnancies rather than high-risk ones. Critics also said that the book is too simplistic and is poorly organized.

★ ★ ★   *From Here to Maternity* (1986) by Connie Marshall. Citrus Heights, CA: Conmar.

From Here to Maternity is a general guide to pregnancy that emphasizes childbirth preparation and selection of a health care team. Author Connie Marshall has a graduate degree in nursing.

This book explores issues and options in prenatal planning. Its purpose is to improve the expectant couple's ability to communicate knowledgeably with their health care team. The book's three parts deal with (1) emotions during pregnancy, the expectant mother's body and prenatal growth, drug use, and choosing breast or bottle feeding, (2) selecting a doctor, and (3) labor and delivery.

From Here to Maternity received a 3-star Neutral rating in the national survey. Critics said that the book is superficial, poorly illustrated, and gives little sound advice.

WORTH A FURTHER LOOK

◑ ◑   *Will It Hurt the Baby?* (1990) by Richard Abrams. Reading, MA: Addison-Wesley.

Will It Hurt the Baby? examines the safe use of medication during pregnancy and breast feeding. Author Richard Abrams, M.D., is the attending physician at Rose Medical Center and a professor of Medicine and Obstetrics at the University of Colorado School of Medicine in Denver.

Abrams describes the trend toward eliminating medication during pregnancy, but he believes that a drug's benefits sometimes outweigh its risks. He discusses 15 common medical problems women may face during pregnancy, their symptoms, and special concerns about them. He also describes nine other possible hazards during pregnancy, such as food additives, pesticides, and physical exertion. In the final section of almost 300 pages, hundreds of drugs from acetaminophen (Tylenol) to zidovudine (AZT) are evaluated. For each drug, Abrams lists common brand names, type of drug (prescription/nonprescription, and use), FDA risk classification, general information, possible maternal side effects, use during pregnancy, use during breast feeding, and alternatives to the medication.

Will It Hurt the Baby? received a positive rating in the national survey but was evaluated by only five respondents. The drug list is extensive and the clinical information easy to understand. The book's enthusiasts said that it is a good reference guide for expectant and breast-feeding mothers. Infancy expert T. Berry Brazelton said that the book is extremely timely and very useful.

CONCLUSIONS

In summary, we recommend:

- A month-by-month, step-by-step guide to pregnancy:
  - ◆ *What to Expect When You're Expecting* by Arlene Eisenberg, Heidi Murkoff, and Sandee Hathaway

- A guide to nutrition during pregnancy:
  - ◆ *What to Eat When You're Expecting* by Arlene Eisenberg, Heidi Murkoff, and Sandee Hathaway

- On the effects of drugs and medications during pregnancy and breast feeding:
  - ◑◑ *Will It Hurt The Baby?* by Richard Abrams

CHAPTER TWENTY-SIX

Relaxation, Meditation, and Stress

We live in a stress-filled world. According to the American Academy of Family Physicians, two-thirds of all office visits to family doctors are for stress-related symptoms. Stress is also thought to be a major contributor to coronary disease, cancer, lung problems, accidental injuries, cirrhosis of the liver, and suicide, six of the leading causes of death in the United States. Two of the five best-selling drugs in the United States are an antianxiety drug (Xanax) and an ulcer medication (Zantac).

There are many ways to cope effectively with stress, just as there are many ways to cope ineffectively with stress. An important point about coping strategies is that we can use more than one to help us deal with stress. For example, heart attack victims are usually advised to change more than one aspect of their lives. The advice might go something like this: Practice relaxation, lose weight, make sure you have one or more friends in whom you can confide, quit smoking, get to the point at which you can exercise vigorously several times a week, develop a more trusting attitude, reduce your anger, and take vacations on a regular basis. One of these alone may not turn the tide against stress, but a combination may be effective.

In this chapter we evaluate books that deal only with relaxation, meditation, and stress. Other books that provide advice on coping with stress are reviewed in the following chapters: Chapter 6, Anger; Chapter 7, Anxiety; Chapter 8, Assertiveness; Chapter 24, Positive Thinking and Self-Talk; Chapter 27, Self-Esteem; Chapter 28, Self-Fulfillment and Happiness; Chapter 29, Self-Improvement and Motivation; and Chapter 30, Sexual Issues and Problems. Also, for stress stemming from a particular source, such as divorce, loneliness, career problems, or the death of a loved one, the recommended books in those chapters may be appropriate.

The books in the national survey on relaxation, meditation, and stress can be divided into the following four categories: broad-based approaches to coping with stress; books on men and stress; spiritually based approaches to coping with stress; and books on relaxation and meditation.

Two books that present a broad-based approach for dealing with stress made the final ratings: *The Relaxation and Stress Reduction Workbook* by Martha Davis, Elizabeth Eshelman, and Matthew McKay and *Thoughts to Live By* by Maxwell Maltz. Three books that merit attention are evaluated in the Worth a Further Look section: *Staying On Top When Your World is Upside Down* by Kathryn Cramer, *Minding the Body, Mending the Mind* by Joan Borysenko, and *The Wellness Book* by Herbert Benson and Eileen Stuart.

One book examines the topic of men and stress: *The Male Stress Syndrome* by Georgia Witkin-Lanoil.

Two books provide a spiritually based approach to coping with stress: *Each Day a New Beginning* and *Touchstones*, both by the Hazelden Foundation.

Three books focus on the roles of relaxation and meditation in combatting stress: *The Relaxation Response* and *Beyond the Relaxation Response*, both by Herbert Benson, and *How to Meditate* by Lawrence LeShan.

Relaxation, Meditation, and Stress
BOOK RATINGS IN THE NATIONAL SURVEY

Strongly Recommended	★★★★★ *The Relaxation Response* by Herbert Benson
	★★★★★ *Beyond the Relaxation Response* by Herbert Benson
Recommended	★★★★ *How to Meditate* by Lawrence LeShan
	★★★★ *Each Day a New Beginning* by the Hazelden Foundation
Diamonds in the Rough	◆ *The Relaxation and Stress Reduction Workbook* by Martha Davis, Elizabeth Eshelman, and Matthew McKay
Neutral	★★★ *Touchstones* by the Hazelden Foundation
	★★★ *The Male Stress Syndrome* by Georgia Witkin-Lanoil
	★★★ *Thoughts to Live By* by Maxwell Maltz

STRONGLY RECOMMENDED

★ ★ ★ ★ ★   *The Relaxation Response* (1975) by Herbert Benson. New York: William Morrow.

The Relaxation Response presents a specific strategy for reducing stress—learning how to relax. Author Herbert Benson, M.D., is a professor of medicine at Boston's Beth Israel Hospital, a teaching hospital of Harvard University, and director of Beth Israel's division of behavioral medicine and hypertension.

Benson believes that the Relaxation Response can significantly improve a person's ability to cope with stressful circumstances and can reduce the likelihood of a number of diseases, especially heart attacks and strokes. Benson says that the Relaxation Response has been used for centuries in the context of religious teachings, usually in Eastern cultures, where it often is practiced on a daily basis. Benson developed a simple method of attaining the Relaxation Response and explains how to incorporate it into daily life. The Relaxation Response consists of four essential elements: (1) locating a quiet context, (2) developing a mental device, such as a word or phrase (such as *om*) that is repeated in a precise way over and over again, (3) adopting a passive attitude, which involves letting go of thoughts and distractions, and (4) assuming a comfortable position. Practicing the Relaxation Response 10 to 20 minutes one or two times a day improves well-being, according to Benson.

The Relaxation Response received a 5-star Strongly Recommended rating in the national survey. Benson's technique may sound too simple to combat stress effectively, but many mental health professionals said that his approach is a very important one. Benson developed the Relaxation Response at a time when Americans were skeptical about spiritual and psychological practices in Eastern cultures. Through his analysis and translation, Benson demystified the strategies that helped people in these cultures cope effectively with stress. Well-known self-help book author Maggie Scarf (her book *Intimate Partners* is reviewed in Chapter 22) says that Benson's strategy is like transcendental meditation without the beads. Benson's research led him to realize that transcendental meditation is but one of a number of techniques that can be used to achieve the Relaxation Response and its deeply relaxed but wakeful bodily state. Many mental health professionals recommend Benson's approach to their clients because they have found that it works. The Relaxation Response is a simple, effective, self-healing technique for reducing the negative effects of stress.

★ ★ ★ ★ ★   *Beyond the Relaxation Response* (1984) by Herbert Benson. New York: Times Books.

Beyond the Relaxation Response is Herbert Benson's sequel to *The Relaxation Response*. A decade after Benson coined the term "Relaxation Response," he concluded that combining the Relaxation Response with another strategy is even more powerful in combatting stress than the Relaxation Response alone. The other strategy is faith in a healing power either inside or outside the self. Benson arrived at this conclusion because of his own clinical observations and studies of Tibetan monks in the Himalayas, which are described in detail in *Beyond the Relaxation Response*. The healing power can be belief in a certain dogma or a traditional religious system, or it can be faith in yourself, in the state attained while exercising, or in the Relaxation Response itself. Benson tells you how to harness the power of faith in a number of different situations — while jogging or walking, swimming, lying in bed, or praying.

Beyond the Relaxation Response received a 5-star Strongly Recommended rating in the national survey. Paul Rosch, M.D., President of The American Institute of Stress, commented that *Beyond the Relaxation Response* is a very practical book that clearly conveys the power of mental strategies, beliefs, and attitudes in influencing our health and the healing process.

RECOMMENDED

★ ★ ★ ★   *Each Day a New Beginning* (1982) by the Hazelden Foundation. New York: HarperCollins.

Each Day a New Beginning is a book of daily meditations for women. The Hazelden Foundation is located northeast of Minneapolis, Minnesota, and it is best known for its approach to treating alcoholism.

The format of *Each Day a New Beginning* is similar to that of *One Day at a Time in Al-Anon* and *A Day at a Time*, the daily meditative books described in Chapter 3, Addiction and Recovery. Each page of the book is devoted to one day — from January 1 through December 31 — and has three elements: a beginning quotation, a paragraph or two about some aspect of daily thought and meditation, and an ending self-affirmation. However, *Each Day a New Beginning* is not designed specifically for alcoholics. Rather, the book is a spiritually oriented approach for women to coping with a wide variety of difficulties in life. Each day is perceived as a new opportunity for growth and successful coping.

Each Day a New Beginning received a 4-star Recommended rating in the national survey. Some of the mental health professionals said that this book is well-conceived and presents thought-provoking ideas in a warm, personal tone. The book is especially appealing to women with a spiritual orientation.

★ ★ ★ ★   *How to Meditate: A Guide to Self-Discovery* (1974) by Lawrence LeShan. Boston: G. K. Hall.

How to Meditate describes a number of different meditative strategies. Author Lawrence LeShan is a practicing psychotherapist and has served as head of the Department of Psychology at the Institute of Applied Biology and as a research psychologist at Union Theological Seminary.

How to Meditate is subtitled *A Guide to Self-Discovery*. LeShan explains what meditation is and what it does. The book traverses the landscape of meditative practices, from Zen, Yoga, and Sufi through Jewish and Christian approaches. The author examines the physiological and psychological effects of meditation and suggests a number of practical ways to use meditation. He warns against instant enlightenment and concludes that every individual must find out which is the best meditative route for him or her. The best strategy never involves consulting charts of the universe or withdrawing from the mainstream of society.

How to Meditate just barely received a 4-star Recommended rating in the national survey. Some mental health professionals found *How to Meditate* a very good overview of different meditative strategies. They also applauded LeShan's presentation of detailed instructions for carrying out a variety of meditative approaches and encouraging readers to select which approach best suits them. Critics said that the book is not as well-documented as Benson's books and that its extremely large type size is annoying.

DIAMONDS IN THE ROUGH

♦   *The Relaxation and Stress Reduction Workbook* (1988) by Martha Davis, Elizabeth Eshelman, and Matthew McKay. Oakland, CA: New Harbinger.

The Relaxation and Stress Reduction Workbook presents a comprehensive set of strategies for coping with stress. Author Martha Davis, Ph.D., is a psychologist in the Department of Psychiatry of Kaiser Permanente Medical Center in Santa Clara, California, where she conducts psychotherapy. Elizabeth Eshelman, who has a Master's degree in social work, teaches stress reduction and relaxation techniques in the Social Work Department of the Kaiser Permanente Center in Redwood City, California. Matthew McKay, Ph.D., is founding director of Haight-Ashbury Psychological Services and codirector of Families in Transition in San Francisco. Both Davis and McKay have written a number of other self-help books.

The Relaxation and Stress Reduction Workbook covers a number of valuable strategies for coping with stress: relaxation, meditation, self-hypnosis, thought stopping, assertiveness training, time management, biofeedback, nutrition, and exercise. This how-to guide has detailed instructions about how to carry out each stress-reduction technique.

The Relaxation and Stress Reduction Workbook received a very high positive rating (almost 2.00) in the national survey but was evaluated by only 12 respondents, so it was placed in the Diamonds in the Rough category. This is an excellent self-help book for people who want to learn about a variety of strategies that will help them cope effectively with stress. It is well written and well organized, it and presents sound advice. Several mental health professionals said that this is the best book in the relaxation, meditation, and stress category, better even than Benson's books, because it presents a variety of coping mechanisms.

NEUTRAL

★ ★ ★   *Touchstones* (1986) by the Hazelden Foundation. New York: Harper Collins.

Touchstones is the male counterpart of *Each Day a New Beginning*. It is a spiritually based approach to coping with stress for men. The organization is the same as that of *Each Day a New Beginning*. Each page is devoted to a day of the year—from January 1 through December 31—and contains a quotation, a meditative commentary, and a self-affirming statement. The breadth of the quotations is extensive, ranging from comments by former New York Yankees baseball manager Billy Martin to passages from D. H. Lawrence to poems by Emily Dickinson. The meditative thoughts also are broad, from awareness of one's problems to letting go to confession.

Touchstones received a 3-star Neutral rating in the national survey. Many of the quotations are well-chosen, the meditative commentary warm, sensitive, and supportive, and the self-affirmations motivating. This book will especially appeal to men with a spiritual orientation who are having difficulty coping with life's stress.

★ ★ ★   *The Male Stress Syndrome* (1986) by Georgia Witkin-Lanoil. New York: Berkley.

The Male Stress Syndrome was written by a woman for men and presents strategies for helping men cope effectively with stress. Author Georgia Wikin-Lanoil, Ph.D., is a professor of psychology at Westchester Community College in New York and a lecturer in the Psychiatry Department at Mt. Sinai Medical College. She also conducts stress reduction workshops, and she wrote an earlier book for women titled *The Female Stress Syndrome.*

Combining the results of a survey administered to more than 500 men and the women closest to them with examples from her own clinical practice, Witkin-Lanoil isolates the key stress factors common to most men. She also gives suggestions for how to recognize these factors and how to manage them. Relaxation exercises are among the stress management strategies for males she recommends. Some stress-reduction strategies are tailored to specific male problems, such as sex therapy for sex-related problems.

The Male Stress Syndrome received a 3-star Neutral rating in the national survey. Several mental health professionals felt that this book provides a good understanding of male-related stress factors and ways to reduce them.

★ ★ ★   *Thoughts to Live By* (1975) by Maxwell Maltz. New York: Pocket Books.

Thoughts to Live By presents coping advice on a wide range of problems. Author Maxwell Maltz is a medical doctor. He also wrote the best-selling book *Psychocybernetics.*

Maltz believes that everyone was born to succeed and that everyone has a great deal of untapped creative potential. The book is divided into two parts. Part I, the bulk of the book, covers an array of topics ranging from courage to relaxation to sincerity to faith, approximately 100 in all. Several pages are devoted to each topic with Matz's advice present throughout. Part II consists of 365 one- or two-line thoughts to live by created by Maltz.

Thoughts to Live By received a 3-star Neutral rating in the national survey; it was evaluated by only 12 respondents. The approach of this book is similar to that of *Each Day a New Beginning* and *Touchstones,* but it does not have the strong spiritual flavor of those books.

WORTH A FURTHER LOOK

❶ ❶ *Staying On Top When Your World Is Upside Down* (1990) by Kathryn Cramer. New York: Viking.

Staying On Top When Your World Is Upside Down provides advice about how to cope with stressful life events and how life's traumas can be turned into growth opportunities. Author Kathryn Cramer, Ph.D., has a health psychology consulting firm and she founded the Stress Center at St. Louis University in Missouri.

Cramer believes that you can increase physical stamina, build self-confidence, and improve personal satisfaction even during times of devastating change. She describes coping strategies that help people make it through such tough times as the loss of a job, divorce, the death of a loved one, and other highly stressful circumstances. The tragic loss of her brother when he was a senior in college inspired her to change directions and make stress management the focus of her life's work.

Staying On Top teaches how to move through shock and confusion to acceptance, mastery, and growth when a traumatic event occurs. The book includes a number of self-tests, charts, and advice on developing a journal for assessing and recording progress in self-evaluation and coping.

Staying On Top was positively rated in the national survey but by only eight respondents. Cramer does a good job of helping readers learn how to turn threats into challenges and how to develop future options.

❶ ❶ *Minding the Body, Mending the Mind* (1987) by Joan Borysenko. New York: Bantam Books.

Minding the Body, Mending the Mind is mainly about the positive effects of meditation and relaxation on the mind and body. Author Joan Borysenko, Ph.D., is a cell biologist and psychotherapist who teaches at Harvard Medical School and directs the Mind/Body Clinic at the New England Deaconess Hospital.

Borysenko discusses how deep relaxation and meditation can shift disease-promoting physiological mechanisms into a healing mode. While the book's main emphasis is on reducing anxiety and stress and developing control over one's life, it also serves as a guide for conditioning the mind to function as a healer and health enhancer.

Minding the Body, Mending the Mind was positively rated but by only six respondents. Some mental health professionals said that this book provides valuable advice about how to use your mind to take control of your own physical and psychological well-being. Highly respected health researcher Herbert Benson, who developed the concept of the Relaxation Response, said that *Minding the Body, Mending the Mind* can help many people cope effectively with stress and disease.

◑ ◑   *The Wellness Book* (1992) by Herbert Benson and Eileen Stuart. New York: Birch Lane Press.

The Wellness Book is a comprehensive guide to maintaining health and treating stress-related diseases. Author Herbert Benson's two very positively rated books on the Relaxation Response were reviewed earlier in this chapter. Coauthor Eileen Stuart is a cardiac nurse specialist and director of cardiovascular programs at the New England Deaconess Hospital. She also lectures at Boston College.

The Wellness Book covers many different aspects of health, psychology, and behavioral medicine, fields that examine the relation between mind and body and explore psychological approaches to preventing illness and improving health. In reality Benson and Stuart are the book's editors, and the chapters are written by experts from Harvard Medical School and the New England Deaconess Hospital. *The Wellness Book* is divided into six main parts: Part I, The Mind/Body Connection; Part II, Exercise; Part III, Nutrition; Part IV, Stress Management (which includes discussion of such topics as how thoughts affect health and problem-solving strategies); Part V, Specialties (such as improving sleep, infertility and women's health, and cardiovascular disease); and Part VI, Relapse Prevention. The book includes participatory exercises, charts, and cartoons.

The Wellness Book was published after the national survey was conducted. It provides sound advice for preventing disease and improving health, presents up-to-date material on the role of stress in disease, and is especially good at describing the powerful role of relaxation and other techniques that help people reduce their chances of incurring life-threatening diseases such as heart disease, cancer, and AIDS. For an edited book with so many different authors, the chapters are surprisingly well-coordinated, and variations in authors' writing styles have been smoothed out.

CONCLUSIONS

In summary, we recommend:

- On using relaxation or meditation to help cope with stress:
    - ★★★★★ *The Relaxation Response* by Herbert Benson
    - ★★★★★ *Beyond the Relaxation Response* by Herbert Benson
    - ★★★★ *How to Meditate* by Lawrence LeShan

- On different strategies for coping with stress:
    - ◆ *The Relaxation and Stress Reduction Workbook* by Martha Davis, Elizabeth Eshelman, and Matthew McKay
    - ◑◑ *The Wellness Book* by Herbert Benson and Eileen Stuart

- For a spiritually based approach to coping with stress:
    - ★★★★ *Each Day a New Beginning* by the Hazelden Foundation (for women)
    - ★★★ *Touchstones* by the Hazelden Foundation (for men)

CHAPTER TWENTY-SEVEN

Self-Esteem

What is self-esteem? Self-esteem, also referred to as self-worth or self-image, is the evaluative and affective dimension of your self-worth. Some psychologists, especially humanists, believe that self-esteem is a critically important dimension of adjustment and well-being. Understanding self-esteem requires acknowledging its complexity; a person has not only a general level of self-esteem but also specific perceptions of self in different domains of life. A person might have, for example, high self-esteem about intellectual and relationship skills but not about physical and athletic skills. Critics of self-help books on self-esteem believe that too often authors address only general self-esteem and fail to adequately evaluate its complex dimensions and varying contexts.

Psychologists disagree about how important self-esteem is to adjustment and well-being and also about how to improve self-esteem, but an increasing number of psychologists believe that the following are important aspects of improving self-esteem:

- Identification of the causes of low self-esteem and which domains of competence are important to the person (i.e., social, intellectual, or physical)
- Emotional support and social approval
- Achievement. Self-esteem can be enhanced by the straightforward learning of skills; people develop higher self-esteem because they know how to do important tasks that will help them accomplish goals.
- Coping. Self-esteem often improves when we face a problem and try to cope with it rather than avoiding it.

In this chapter, we evaluate only books in which the focus is self-esteem. Self-esteem is part of the self-help formula in many of the books

---

Self-Esteem

BOOK RATINGS IN THE NATIONAL SURVEY

Neutral ★★★ *Advice from a Failure* by Jo Coudert

★★★ *Revolution from Within* by Gloria Steinem

★★★ *The Psychology of Self-Esteem* by Nathaniel Brandon

★★★ *How to Raise Your Self-Esteem* by Nathaniel Brandon

---

evaluated in Chapter 28, Self-Fulfillment and Happiness, and Chapter 29 self-improvement, as well.

The self-esteem books in the national survey can be divided into three main categories: general approaches to self-esteem that view low self-esteem as the main cause of many of life's problems; cognitive therapy approaches to self-esteem; and books on women and self-esteem.

Three books that take a general approach to solving self-esteem problems were rated: *Advice from a Failure* by Jo Coudert; *The Psychology of Self-Esteem* by Nathaniel Brandon; and *How to Raise Your Self-Esteem,* also by Nathaniel Brandon.

No books that take a cognitive approach to improving self-esteem made the final ratings. However, one book—*Self-Esteem* by Matthew McKay and Patrick Fanning—is evaluated in the Worth a Further Look section.

One book on women and self-esteem was rated: *Revolution from Within* by Gloria Steinem. A second book—*Women and Self-Esteem* by Linda Sanford and Mary Donovan—is profiled in Worth a Further Look.

NEUTRAL

★ ★ ★ *Advice from a Failure* (1965) by Jo Coudert. New York: Stein and Day.

Advice from a Failure is a general approach to self-understanding. Author Jo Coudert is a mental health professional in the fields of psychiatry and medicine and has been editor of *The International Journal of Group Psychotherapy.* She also has tried her hand as a playwright.

Coudert dispenses advice on the well-lived life. She believes that becoming a competent, comfortable, well-functioning person requires considerable insight about oneself. Not about other people. Just oneself. Coudert urges readers to be friends with themselves, love themselves, and develop a positive view of themselves.

Early in the book, Coudert reveals the failings in her life—divorced parents, an alcoholic mother in a mental hospital, divorced herself, a precariously healed ulcer, and ten years as an unsuccessful playwright. In the book's remaining pages, the author traverses the psychological landscape of many different domains in life—from coping with anger to making friends to dealing with depression to understanding money and sex problems. Throughout the book, Coudert tries to convince you that becoming aware of your self and increasing your self-worth can lead to an improved sense of well-being and happiness in spite of failure.

Advice from a Failure received a 3-star Neutral rating in the national survey. This book was written almost three decades ago, but some mental health professionals thought that it still contains valuable insights about self-understanding and self-worth. Critics said that *Advice from a Failure* tries to cover too much territory and is too general.

★ ★ ★   *Revolution from Within* (1992) by Gloria Steinem. Boston: Little, Brown and Company.

Revolution from Within is about women and self-esteem. Author Gloria Steinem has been a writer and an activist for almost 30 years. She has written several other books and currently is the consulting editor of *Ms.* magazine, which she cofounded in 1972. She also helped to found *New York* magazine. She has been extensively involved in the feminist movement as a lecturer and an organizer. In most quarters, Steinem is recognized as one of the founders of contemporary feminism.

For years Steinem believed that inner change was secondary to societal change. However, she says that she kept encountering women with too little self-esteem to take advantage of hard-won, if still incomplete, opportunities. How did low self-esteem in women come about? Steinem cites totalitarian gender roles, obsession with romantic love, devaluation of feminine qualities, emotional damage caused by IQ testing, stereotypes of sex and race, estrangement from nature, and male-imposed standards of feminine beauty. Steinem declares that there is a sort of national self-esteem crisis in today's female. Personal crises in her own life made Steinem realize that she too was lacking something internally. While crusading for feminism, the author says she created a mythical creature—sophisticated, confident, powerful—while inside, she felt like a plump brunette from Toledo. Her personal recipe for change included yoga, painting, and writing, along with guided meditation and informal support groups (which she calls "psychic families"), among other self-help techniques. Threaded through the recommendations for personal change is the belief that the next key step for women is to nurture their damaged self.

The Revolution from Within received a 3-star Neutral rating. This is a controversial book. The book's enthusiasts said that it highlights an important dimension of today's woman—low self-esteem—that is keeping her from living a satisfied life and from seeking opportunities. They also thought that the message of inner healing—especially coming from someone as famous as Steinem—can benefit many women. Critics faulted the book as having little to set it apart from other self-help books on self-esteem and self-fulfillment. They also blasted the book for its frequent regressions into psychobabble: Steinem promises to take women "in concentric circles," help them hear inner "clicks," and "return [them] to their inner child." One critic called the book "a derivative jumble."

This book could just as readily have been placed in the women's issues section of the national survey. Readers interested in reading further about women and self-esteem should take a look at Chapter 34.

★ ★ ★ *The Psychology of Self-Esteem* (1969) by Nathaniel Brandon. Los Angeles: Nash.

The Psychology of Self-Esteem presents a general approach to the importance of self-esteem in people's lives. Author Nathaniel Brandon is best known as a lecturer on Ayn Rand's views (*Atlas Shrugged*). He also has written many articles on philosophy and psychology for *The Objectivist*. And he is a practicing psychologist at the Biocentric Institute in Los Angeles.

In this book, Brandon explains what he calls "biocentric psychology." He says that neither psychoanalytic theory nor behaviorism concentrate on the most important human qualities: reasoning and the power of volitional consciousness. Mental health, according to Brandon, depends on self-esteem, which is genuine only when people are aware that they are using reason in coping with problems and dealing with people.

The Psychology of Self-Esteem received a 3-star Neutral rating in the national survey. Some mental health professionals said that Brandon's book presents an important theme in mental health, namely, that the route to improved living is through the use of reasoning to raise self-esteem. Critics said that Brandon's approach is overly simplified and that self-esteem per se is not as critical as Brandon thinks in helping people cope with problems. This book is also very difficult to read. It is not only written at a high level, it is also disjointed in many places.

★ ★ ★   *How to Raise Your Self-Esteem* (1987) by Nathaniel Brandon. New York: Bantam.

How to Raise Your Self-Esteem presents a general approach, as the title suggests, to raising self-esteem. Brandon describes the components of healthy self-esteem, uses personal anecdotes and brief observations to illustrate healthy self-esteem in action, and relies on a series of sentence-completion exercises to help readers discover what is blocking their efforts to improve their self-esteem. Brandon also gives examples of everyday situations in which individuals have been able to gain high self-esteem.

How to Raise Your Self-Esteem received a 3-star Neutral rating in the national survey, nearly landing in the 2-star Not Recommended category. A positive virtue of the book is Brandon's energetic optimism. This book is also better written than Brandon's earlier book, *The Psychology of Self-Esteem*, and the influence of contemporary cognitive therapy approaches on his thinking is more apparent. However, the book tends to ramble and the author's self-esteem message is repetitive. Some critics said that once you cut through the optimistic enthusiasm there is not much substance to the book.

WORTH A FURTHER LOOK

◑ ◑   *Self-Esteem* (1987) by Matthew McKay and Patrick Fanning. Oakland, CA: New Harbinger.

Self-Esteem presents a cognitive therapy approach to improving self-esteem. Author Matthew McKay, Ph.D., is a founding director of Haight-Ashbury Psychological Services and codirector of Families in Transition in San Francisco. He also is coauthor of several other books in the national survey, including *The Relaxation and Stress Reduction Workbook* (Chapter 26). Coauthor Patrick Fanning is a professional writer in the mental health field.

The book begins by describing the nature of self-esteem, then introduces the pathological critic, the voice inside that criticizes and keeps self-esteem low. The authors explain to readers how to disarm the critic, accurately assess strengths and weaknesses, think more rationally, handle mistakes, react to criticism, ask for what they want, visualize how to achieve goals, and engage in self-hypnosis. The authors astutely tell readers to be patient in developing higher self-esteem. Each of us has spent our whole life developing the level of self-esteem we have now. It takes time to tear self-esteem down and it takes time to build it up.

Self-Esteem received a high positive rating, but it was evaluated by only seven respondents, hence its relegation to Worth a Further Look. Several mental health professionals commented that this book has more realistic and clearly articulated strategies about improving self-esteem than the other books in this category. It is well-organized and includes a number of helpful exercises.

◑◑ *Women and Self-Esteem* (1984) by Linda Sanford and Mary Donovan. New York: Anchor Doubleday.

Women and Self-Esteem explains why women often have low self-esteem and how they can improve the way they think and feel about themselves. Author Linda Sanford is a psychotherapist and the coordinator of a sex abuse treatment center in Massachusetts. Mary Donovan has had a number of writing jobs, and while working on this book, she and Linda Sanford conducted self-esteem enhancement workshops for women.

Sanford and Donovan draw on research, interviews, and workshop information to address a wide range of issues concerning the development and expression of self-esteem in women. They examine the causes of low self-esteem in women and give suggestions for its prevention and remediation. The authors argue that low self-esteem translates into other problems, such as as depression, negative body image, fear of intimacy, and overinvestment in romantic relationships. They provide readers with exercises that will help them engage in self-evaluation, reduce their negative self-images, and decrease their self-destructive behaviors.

Women and Self-Esteem received a high positive rating in the national survey but was evaluated by only five respondents. This is a good book for women with low self-esteem. It does not regress into psychobabble and does not ramble the way Steinem's recent book, *The Revolution from Within*, does. *Women and Self-Esteem* provides excellent insights into how many women think and feel about themselves and ways they can improve their lives.

CONCLUSIONS

In summary, we recommend:

- For a cognitive therapy approach to improving self-esteem:
  ◑◑ *Self-Esteem* by Matthew McKay and Patrick Fanning

- For women who want to improve their self-esteem:
  ◑◑ *Women and Self-Esteem* by Linda Sanford and Mary Donovan

CHAPTER TWENTY-EIGHT

Self-Fulfillment
and Happiness

Everybody wants to be self-fulfilled and happy, but many people aren't. They feel that life should be better and that something is missing in their life. But, before we reach the positive emotional state of happiness, we have to know what it is we are seeking, and not everyone agrees about what happiness is. For French philosopher Jean-Jacques Rousseau, happiness meant a good bank account, a good cook, and a good digestion.

In recent reviews of research on happiness, psychologists have found reason to disagree with Rousseau. A good cook and a good digestion are not on most people's lists of what makes them happy, and neither is a good bank account. Even winning a large amount in a lottery doesn't usually provide the long-term happiness the winners thought it might. Having enough money to buy life's necessities does seem to be a factor that is related to happiness. Happy people also have high self-esteem, a satisfying marriage or other love relationship, and a meaningful religious faith and they are optimistic and outgoing, sleep well, exercise, and are employed. But self-fulfillment and happiness are not always the same for everyone; what makes you self-fulfilled and happy may not make your parents, siblings, friends, or colleagues feel that way. And that's the main reason that self-fulfillment and happiness have remained so elusive for experts who have sought to pin them down.

Self-help books on self-fulfillment and happiness in the national survey can be classified in the following ways: general approach, spiritually and emotionally based approaches, cognitive approach, existential approach, transactional analysis approach, and scientology approach.

Two books that take a general approach to self-fulfillment and happiness were rated: *Flow* by Mihaly Csikszentmihalyi and *Discovering Happiness* by Dennis Wholey. A third book—*The Pursuit of Happiness* by David Myers—is evaluated in Worth a Further Look.

Self-Fulfillment and Happiness
BOOK RATINGS IN THE NATIONAL SURVEY

Strongly Recommended	★★★★★	*Man's Search for Meaning* by Victor Frankl
Recommended	★★★★	*A New Guide for Rational Living* by Albert Ellis and Robert Harper
	★★★★	*The Road Less Traveled* by M. Scott Peck
	★★★★	*When All You Ever Wanted Isn't Enough* by Harold Kushner
Diamonds in the Rough	◆	*The Search for Significance* by Robert McGee
Neutral	★★★	*How to Be Your Own Best Friend* by Mildred Newman and Bernard Berkowitz
	★★★	*A Guide to Personal Happiness* by Albert Ellis and Irving Becker
	★★★	*I'm OK—You're OK* by Thomas Harris
	★★★	*How to Live 365 Days a Year* by John Schindler
	★★★	*Flow* by Mihaly Csikszentmihalyi
Not Recommended	★	*The Be (Happy) Attitudes* by Robert Schuller
	★	*Discovering Happiness* by Dennis Wholey
Strongly Not Recommended	†	*Clear Body, Clear Mind* by L. Ron Hubbard
	†	*Dianetics* by L. Ron Hubbard
	†	*Scientology* by L. Ron Hubbard

Six books that present a spiritually and emotionally based approach to self-fulfillment and happiness were rated: *The Road Less Traveled* by M. Scott Peck; *When All You Ever Wanted Isn't Enough* by Harold Kushner; *How to Be Your Own Best Friend* by Mildred Newman and Bernard Berkowitz; *The Search for Significance* by Robert McGee; *How to Live 365 Days a Year* by John Schindler; and *The Be (Happy) Attitudes* by Robert Schuller.

Two books that emphasize a cognitive approach to self-fulfillment and happiness were rated: *A New Guide to Rational Living* by Albert Ellis and Robert Harper and *A Guide to Personal Happiness* by Albert Ellis and Irving Becker.

One book that argues for an existential approach to becoming self-fulfilled and happy was rated: *Man's Search for Meaning* by Victor Frankl.

One book that provides a transactional analysis approach to self-fulfillment and happiness was rated: *I'm OK—You're OK* by Thomas Harris.

And three books, all by L. Ron Hubbard, that describe a scientology approach to self-fulfillment and happiness were rated: *Clear Body, Clear Mind; Dianetics;* and *Scientology.*

STRONGLY RECOMMENDED

★ ★ ★ ★ ★   *Man's Search for Meaning* (1984) by Victor Frankl. New York: Pocket Books.

Man's Search for Meaning presents an existentialist approach to the pursuit of self-fulfillment and happiness. Author Victor Frankl, M.D., has been a professor of neurology and psychiatry at the University of Vienna Medical School and distinguished professor of logotherapy at U.S. International University in San Diego. He has published more than twenty books and is a world-renowned psychiatrist.

After Victor Frankl survived the German concentration camp at Auschwitz, he founded a school of psychotherapy he called logotherapy, which maintains that the desire to find a meaning in life is the primary motive in human beings. Frankl's mother, father, brother, and wife died in the concentration camps or gas chambers. Frankl emphasizes each person's uniqueness and the finiteness of life. He thinks that examining the finiteness of existence and the certainty of death adds meaning to life. If life were not finite, says Frankl, we could spend our time doing just about whatever we please because time would continue forever.

Frankl believes that the three most distinct human qualities are spirituality, freedom, and responsibility. Spirituality, in his system, does not have a religious underpinning. Rather, it refers to a human being's uniqueness—to spirit, philosophy, and mind. Freedom refers to the freedom to make decisions. And with the freedom to make decisions comes the responsibility for those decisions. Logotherapists often ask clients such questions as why they exist, what they want from life, and what the meaning of their life is.

Man's Search for Meaning received a 5-star Strongly Recommended rating in the national survey. Published originally in 1946 in Austria,

Man's Search for Meaning still commands a great deal of respect among mental health professionals. Gerald Kreyche of DePaul University commented that this book tells the incredible story of a man who became a number who became a person. Famous psychologist Gordon Allport said that Frankl's book represents one of the most significant psychological movements of the time. This book challenges readers to think about the meaning of their lives. The reading is rough going at times, but for those who persist and probe Frankl's remarkable insights, the rewards are well worth the effort.

RECOMMENDED

★ ★ ★ ★   *A New Guide to Rational Living* (1975) by Albert Ellis and Robert Harper. Englewood Cliffs, NJ: Prentice-Hall.

A New Guide to Rational Living describes a cognitive approach to self-fulfillment and happiness. Author Albert Ellis, Ph.D., is a well-known psychologist and one of the creators of the cognitive therapy approach to problems and disorders. He developed rational emotive therapy and has published more than fifty books on the topic. Robert Harper, Ph.D., is a psychotherapist in Washington, DC, and has served as president of the American Academy of Psychotherapists and of the American Association of Marriage and Family Counselors.

Rational emotive therapy states that people develop psychological problems because they use irrational beliefs to interpret what happens to themselves and their world. In this view, people disturb themselves by thinking in self-defeating, illogical, and unrealistic ways. In rational emotive therapy, the therapist takes an active role in interpreting the client's flawed thinking, explaining how thinking should proceed if the client is to cope with stress successfully and be happy. According to Ellis and Harper, years of long, drawn-out psychotherapy are not needed to attack the root of emotional problems. They believe that rational emotive therapy can quickly help people learn how to detect their irrational thinking, overcome the influence of the past, erase dire fears of failure, conquer anxiety, and acquire self-discipline. The book is filled with conversations between irrational thinkers and therapists and the subsequent interchanges that led to successful living.

A New Guide to Rational Living received a 4-star Recommended rating in the national survey—it is widely known (evaluated by 238 respondents) and came close to making the 5-star rating. The book's enthusiasts say that Ellis's approach is very effective in motivating people to restructure their thinking and rid themselves of harmful irrational beliefs, in the process helping them to cope more effectively with stress and develop a happier life. Some critics say that Ellis's book is prone to overstatement and that some people's problems are not as easily solved as the ones he presents. The approach is also most effective with verbal and well-educated individuals.

★ ★ ★ ★   *The Road Less Traveled* (1978) by M. Scott Peck. New York: Simon & Schuster.

The Road Less Traveled presents a spiritual and psychological approach to self-fulfillment and happiness. Author M. Scott Peck, M.D., is a psychiatrist and has been medical director of New Milford Hospital Mental Health Clinic in New Milford, Connecticut, where he also has a private practice. He also has written *People of the Lie* and *The Different Drum.*

The Road Less Traveled is subtitled *A New Psychology of Love, Traditional Values, and Spiritual Growth.* Peck begins the book by stating that life is difficult and that we all suffer pain and disappointment. He counsels us to face up to life's difficulties and not be lazy. Indeed, Peck equates laziness with original sin, going on to say that people's tendency to avoid problems and emotional suffering is the root of mental disorders. Peck also believes that people are thirsting for integrity in their lives. They are not happy with a country that has "In God We Trust" as a motto and at the same time leads the world in the arms race. They also can't tolerate being just Sunday morning Christians. To achieve integrity, says Peck, people need to move spirituality into all aspects of their daily lives.

Peck speaks of four important tools to use in life's journey: delayed gratification, acceptance of responsibility, dedication to the truth, and balance. After a thorough analysis of each, Peck explores the will to use them, which he calls love. Then, he probes further and analyzes the relation of growth and religion, which leads him to examine the final step of the "road less traveled": grace. By grace, Peck means the whole range of human activities that support the human spirit. Grace operates at the interface between God and man, in Peck's view, at a frontier between our conscious and unconscious selves.

The Road Less Traveled received a 4-star Recommended rating in the national survey. Peck's book has been immensely popular, on *The New York Times* best-seller list for more than ten years. Peck has developed a cultlike following, especially among young people, some of whom follow him around on his lecture tours and ask to touch the hem of his garment. The book's supporters said that Peck recognized important voids in many people's lives, especially the need for an integrated, spiritually oriented existence. Some critics said that many of Peck's ideas are not new, that the writings of some religious authors—such as Ignatius Loyola and Catherine of Siena—also stressed the importance of an inner journey that requires effort, honesty, and fidelity. But what Peck has succeeded in doing is to package those ideas in contemporary American language that has enormous appeal to wide audiences ranging from conservative "Bible belters" in small southern towns to "Yuppies." Some mental health professionals fault Peck for the fuzziness of his ideas, especially when he arrives at the meeting point between God and man and between conscious and unconscious worlds.

★ ★ ★ ★   *When All You Ever Wanted Isn't Enough* (1986) by Harold Kushner. New York: Summit Books.

When All You Ever Wanted Isn't Enough presents a spiritually based approach to self-fulfillment and happiness. Harold Kushner is the rabbi of Temple Israel in Natick, Massachusetts. He also wrote *When Bad Things Happen to Good People,* evaluated in Chapter 13, Death, Dying, and Grief.

When All You Ever Wanted Isn't Enough is subtitled, *The Search for a Life That Matters.* Kushner believes that material rewards create almost as many problems as they solve. He believes that sooner or later we come face to face with a big question, "What am I supposed to do with my life?" We want to be more than just a brief biological flash in the universe and then disappear forever. Kushner argues that there is no one big answer to the meaning of life and self-fulfillment but that there are answers. And the answers are found in filling our day-to-day existence with meaning, with the love of friends and family and with striving for integrity, instead of with reaching for a pot of gold. Kushner spends considerable time analyzing the book of Ecclesiastes in the Bible. He thinks it is an important book because it asks us to think about life. Kushner believes, like Ecclesiastes, that life is its own reward.

When All You Ever Wanted Isn't Enough received a 4-star Recommended rating in the national survey. Mental health professionals who like the book said that in our materialistic world of greed for power and money, this book is a breath of fresh air. They thought that *When All You Ever Wanted Isn't Enough* presents an insightful collection of ideas that can serve as a spiritual survival manual for many individuals.

DIAMONDS IN THE ROUGH

◆   The Search for Significance (1990) by Robert McGee. Houston, TX: Rapha Publishing.

The Search for Significance is a spiritually based approach to self-fulfillment and happiness. Author Robert McGee is a counselor who founded Rapha, a health care organization that provides in-hospital and outpatient care with a Christ-centered perspective.

McGee believes that instead of building our self-worth on our ability to please others, we should build it on the love and forgiveness of Jesus Christ. *The Search for Significance* is divided into two parts. In Part I, McGee discusses our search for significance, good and evil, the process of hope and healing, and how a Christ-based approach is the only answer to self-fulfillment and happiness in life. Part II is an extensive workbook with many religious-based exercises.

The Search for Significance made the Diamonds in the Rough category; it was positively rated but by only 11 respondents. This is a much stronger religious approach to life's meaning than the other spiritually based books in this category—for example, M. Scott Peck's *The Road Less Traveled* and Harold Kushner's *When All You've Ever Wanted Isn't Enough*. The book will appeal mainly to Christians who seek self-fulfillment through religious commitment.

NEUTRAL

★ ★ ★   *How to Be Your Own Best Friend* (1971) by Mildred Newman and Bernard Berkowitz. New York: Random House.

How to Be Your Own Best Friend presents ideas about how to like yourself more and feel more self-fulfilled. Author Mildred Newman, M.A., and Bernard Berkowitz, Ph.D., are married to each other and are both practicing psychoanalysts in New York City.

In less than 100 pages, the authors try to convince us that we need to be more aware of our accomplishments, to have compassion for ourselves, to praise our own achievements, and to be responsible for our choices. The format of the book is one long conversation in which soul-searching questions are followed by uplifting, thoughtful answers.

How to Be Your Own Best Friend received a 3-star Neutral rating in the national survey. Some mental health professionals were effusive in their praise of the book, calling it a modern classic that contains page after page of uplifting messages of self-love and encouragement.

★ ★ ★   *A Guide to Personal Happiness* (1982) by Albert Ellis and Irving Becker. North Hollywood, CA: Wilshire Book Company.

A Guide to Personal Happiness is the second book by Albert Ellis in this category. Coauthor Irving Becker, Ed.D, has worked as a psychologist for the New York City Board of Education and practices psychotherapy in New York City.

Ellis and Becker say that if we don't search for personal happiness, no one else is going to do it for us. They believe that each of us has a right to personal happiness but that we need to go after it, even if it means putting ourselves first. The book includes the usual dose of Ellis's rational emotive therapy and views life in problem-solving terms. People's problems are caused by irrational beliefs that need to be disputed and replaced with rational ones.

A Guide to Personal Happiness received a 3-star Neutral rating in the national survey. This book is very similar to Ellis's other book in this category—*A New Guide to Rational Living*, and the same evaluative comments there apply here as well.

★ ★ ★ *I'm OK—You're OK* (1967) by Thomas Harris. New York: Harper & Row.

I'm OK—You're OK presents a transactional analysis approach to self-fulfillment and happiness. Author Thomas Harris, M.D., has been a practicing psychiatrist in the Sacramento, California, area and was one of the pioneering therapists to apply transactional analysis to the treatment of mentally disordered individuals.

Transactional analysis argues that people are responsible for their behavior in the present and future regardless of what has happened to them in the past. It distinguishes three main components in each person's makeup: the Parent, the Adult, and the Child. The Parent involves the many dont's and a few do's of our early years. The Child represents spontaneous emotion. Both Parent and Child have to be kept in proper relation to the Adult, whose function is that of maintaining reality through decision making. Transactional Analysis's goal is the strengthening and emancipation of the Adult from the Parent and the Child.

Harris identifies four life positions that underlie people's behavior: (1) I'm not OK—You're OK, the anxious dependency of an insecure person; (2) I'm not OK—You're not OK, a position of despair or giving up; (3) I'm OK—You're not OK the "criminal position"; and (4) I'm OK—You're OK, the response of mature adults, at peace with themselves and others. Harris believes that most people unconsciously operate from the I'm not OK—You're OK position.

Harris applies the Parent–Adult–Child system to many areas of life, including marriage and childrearing, violence, prejudice, religion, and international problems. He advises about when psychotherapy might be needed to solve problems.

I'm OK—You're OK received a 3-star Neutral rating in the national survey. This is an extremely well-known book that was immensely successful when it was published. At that time transactional analysis and the I'm OK—You're OK approach were so popular that it was estimated that 3,000 mental health professionals around the world were practicing this type of therapy. Despite its popularity, however, *I'm OK—You're OK* is not without its detractors. A past president of the American Psychiatric Association calls Harris's approach superficial. Other critics say that it trivializes everything it touches. Today, *I'm OK—You're OK* is nowhere near the rage it once was. Its neutral rating in the national survey reflects the mixed posture of mental health professionals about the book. Some experts still praise the book, others are very glad that it has lost much of its luster.

★ ★ ★ *How to Live 365 Days a Year* (1975) by John Schindler. Englewood Cliffs, NJ: Prentice-Hall.

How to Live 365 Days a Year presents an emotionally based approach to self-fulfillment and happiness. Author John Schindler, M.D., is chairman of the Department of Medicine at the Monroe Clinic in Monroe, Wisconsin.

  How to Live 365 Days a Year takes the stance that our illnesses and problems in life arise out of our emotions. The book is divided into two main parts. In Part I, How Your Emotions Make You Ill, readers learn that emotions produce most physical diseases and they also learn about the good emotions and the bad emotions. Part II, How to Cure Your Emotionally Induced Illness, describes how to attain emotional maturity in many different areas of life—with family, sexually, and at work, for example.

  How to Live 365 Days a Year received a 3-star Neutral rating in the national survey. The book's supporters felt that it presents some important ideas about how emotional difficulties cause illness and how to get control of our emotional life. Critics said that the book is somewhat dated and that books such as Martin Seligman's *Learned Optimism* (Chapter 24, Positive Thinking) and Herbert Benson's *The Relaxation Response* (Chapter 26, Relaxation, Meditation, and Stress) are better choices in this area.

★ ★ ★ *Flow: The Psychology of Optimal Experience* (1990) by Mihaly Csikszentmihalyi. New York: Harper & Row.

Flow is about the optimal experiencing of life. Author Mihaly Csikszentmihalyi, Ph.D., is a highly respected professor of psychology at the University of Chicago.

Csikszentmihalyi (pronounced "chik-*sent*-mee-high-yee") has been investigating the concept he calls "flow" for more than two decades. Flow is the state of deep enjoyment and happiness that people feel when they have a sense of mastering something. Flow is a state of concentration in which a person becomes absorbed while engaging in an activity. The author says that flow can be controlled and should not be left to chance. We can develop flow by setting challenges for ourselves, by stretching ourselves to the limit to achieve something worthwhile, by developing competent coping skills, and by combining life's many experiences into a meaningful pattern. Flow is the antidote to the twin evils of boredom and anxiety, says Csikszentmihalyi.

Flow can be found in many different experiences and walks of life. Rock climbers can become so absorbed that they feel at one with the cliff face. Some soldiers say that they are never more alive than on the front line of a battle. Chess masters play in a trancelike state. Artists dab paint on a canvas for hour after hour in a state of immersed concentration. The famous humanistic psychologist Abraham Maslow described a similar sense of euphoria in the early 1960s. What distinguishes Csikszentmihalyi's concept of flow from Maslow's peak experiences is the frequency of flow experiences. Maslow thought people were fortunate if they caught a peak experience several times in their entire lives. Csikszentmihalyi, by contrast, says that if people cultivate flow experiences they can have them several times a day.

Flow received a 3-star Neutral rating in the national survey. Some mental health professionals praised the book. Well-known self-help book author Carol Tavris said that *Flow* is an important book because it documents that the path to happiness does not lie in mindless hedonism but rather in mindful challenge, is not found in unlimited opportunities but in focused possibilities, and is not experienced by having it done for you but by doing it yourself. Roy Baumeister, a professor of psychology at Case Western Reserve University and a widely recognized expert on optimal experience in life, commented that *Flow* is wise, timely, and profound.

This is an excellent book. Why was it not rated higher by the mental health professionals in the national survey? First, it is not well known (it was evaluated by only 43 respondents), and second, people who were not familiar with the book may have lumped it together with shallower New Age books because of its title. Nonetheless, it is a serious, thoroughly documented, and well-researched book that conveys some extremely important messages about how to achieve self-fulfillment and happiness during our stay on this planet.

NOT RECOMMENDED

★ *The Be (Happy) Attitudes* (1985) by Robert Schuller. Waco, TX: Word
Publishers.

The Be (Happy) Attitude is a spiritually oriented approach to self-fulfillment and happiness. Author Robert Schuller is founder and senior minister of the famous Crystal Cathedral in Garden Grove, California (it's an
18-million-dollar church two freeway exits south of Disneyland). His telecast, *The Hour of Prayer,* is one of the most widely viewed programs in
television history. He is the author of more than twenty other books.
   Schuller probes why happiness is so elusive. He believes that few
people find happiness because they look for it in the wrong places—in
wealth, fame, relationships, or recreational drugs. He believes that the
answer to the pursuit of happiness can be found in the most famous section of the Sermon on the Mount, known as the Beatitudes. Schuller takes
the eight Beatitudes and elaborates on them to arrive at eight universal
principles that make real happiness possible—hence his name for the
principles; the "Be (Happy) Attitudes."
   The Be (Happy) Attitudes received a 1-star Not Recommended rating in the national survey. Schuller's religious supporters say that he has
a remarkable talent for translating important religious messages into today's language and experiences. His conservative religious critics complain that his message is too individual-centered and glosses over the
troublesome doctrine of original sin. Some of his critics from the mental health field said that he places too much emphasis on faith and
religion in telling people how to find happiness. They also said that attaining happiness and genuine positive self-worth is a much more complicated and arduous journey than Schuller leads readers to believe.

★ *Discovering Happiness* (1986) by Dennis Wholey. New York: Avon
Books.

Discovering Happiness attempts to discover what happiness is through
conversations with more than 50 prominent men and women. Author
Dennis Wholey also wrote *The Courage to Change.*
   Wholey interviewed a wide range of people to get their thoughts on
the elusive topic of happiness, including Benjamin Spock, Carol Chan-
ning, Jack Anderson, Joyce Brothers, Dick Gregory, Leo Buscaglia, Wil-
lard Scott, Julia Child, and some other people we have not heard of and
you probably haven't either. Their interview responses are arranged in
chapters on happiness, self-worth, love/work/hope, health, spirituality,
humanness, and change, among others.

Discovering Happiness received a 1-star Not Recommended rating in the national survey. Critics said that contrary to what it purports, the book does not have the answer to what happiness is. The answers given by the circus of interviewees are far-flung and never synthesized.

STRONGLY NOT RECOMMENDED

† *Clear Body, Clear Mind* (1990) by L. Ron Hubbard. Los Angeles, CA: Bridge Publications.

Clear Body, Clear Mind is about how the pollution of our bodies blocks clear thinking and happiness. Author L. Ron Hubbard had no professional mental health training. Before turning to self-help book writing and church development, Hubbard was a moderately successful science fiction writer. He started the Church of Scientology to cleanse people of their unhappiness. The Church of Scientology says that it has 700 centers in 65 countries. The group claims to have 8 million active members, although outsiders' estimates are more in the range of 50,000 to 100,000. Hubbard died in 1986.

Clear Body, Clear Mind was published in 1990, four years after Hubbard's death. The book presents a detoxification program of running, saunas, natural oils, and specific vitamins and minerals. Testimonials by people who have successfully used this body detoxification program to become physically and mentally healthy are included. According to the testimony, Hubbard's detoxification program helped them to recover from such afflictions as substance abuse, radiation illness, Agent-Orange-related diseases, and others.

Clear Body, Clear Mind received a low negative rating in the national survey, placing it in the Strongly Not Recommended category. Critics said that the efficacy of megavitamins to cleanse the body is medically unproven. Some critics called Hubbard's approach a ruthless scam and money-making scheme.

† *Dianetics: The Modern Science of Mental Health* (1950) by L. Ron Hubbard. Los Angeles, CA: The Church of Scientology of California.

Dianetics is one of Scientology's sacred texts. It was written in 1950 and is subtitled *The Modern Science of Mental Health*. In this book, Hubbard argues that unhappiness springs from mental aberrations called "engrams" that are produced by early traumas in life. To measure people's electrical changes in the skin while they are discussing intimate details of their past, he created a simplified lie detector, which he called the

"E-meter." Hubbard claims that counseling sessions with the E-meter can destroy the engrams and even improve a person's intelligence and appearance.

Dianetics received a low negative rating in the national survey, placing it in the Strongly Not Recommended category. Most mental health professionals found nothing in Hubbard's *Dianetics* that will help people cope with problems and gain happiness.

† *Scientology: The Fundamentals of Thought* (1988) by L. Ron Hubbard. Los Angeles, CA: Bridge Publications.

Scientology, like the other two Hubbard books, seeks to convince readers that they can achieve happiness by adopting the philosophy of Scientology and abiding by its principles. It is designed to help people better understand themselves, develop self-confidence, and attain a greater sense of personal integrity.

Scientology is subtitled *The Fundamentals of Thought*. It consists of an introduction and eight chapters that discuss the basic principles and goals of scientology. According to Hubbard, scientology is an applied religious philosophy, and any comparison of scientology with psychology is nonsense. Hubbard believes that only through scientology can people find out who they really are.

Like the other Hubbard books, *Scientology* did not fare well in the national survey: It received a very low negative rating, which places it in the Strongly Not Recommended category. Not only did some critics fault Hubbard's antipsychology, cult approach in *Scientology*, they also said that the book is poorly written, meanders, and is unreadable in places. For a more complete list of criticisms, see the review of Hubbard's approach by Richard Behar in *Time* magazine, May 6, 1991.

WORTH A FURTHER LOOK

◑ ◑ *The Pursuit of Happiness* (1992) by David G. Myers. New York: William Morrow.

The Pursuit of Happiness describes who is happy and why. David G. Myers is a highly respected social psychologist who is a professor of psychology at Hope College in Holland, Michigan. He is a leading author of academic textbooks in psychology. His introductory psychology book—*Psychology*—is the most widely used undergraduate text in psychology.

Myers conducted an extensive review of research on happiness. He concluded that happy people have four main characteristics:

- *Self-Esteem.* Happy people like themselves.
- *Optimism.* Happy people are hope-filled.
- *Extroversion.* Happy people are outgoing.
- *Personal control.* Happy people believe that they choose their own destinies.

The author tells readers the best ways to attain these traits and helps readers measure their own levels of satisfaction.

Myers concludes that a number of factors thought to be related to happiness really aren't. Among his findings: Money can't buy happiness; age is not related to happiness, and men aren't happier than women. The book is also full of other valuable information about happiness: what makes a happy marriage, the value of spirituality, the importance of attitude, love, friendships, and meaningful work.

The Pursuit of Happiness was published after the national survey was conducted. This is an excellent book on happiness. It recognizes that happiness is determined by a number of factors, not a single magic bullet; it highlights the important role of beliefs, attitudes, and perceptions in determining whether someone is happy or not; and it is based on extensive research rather than a personal philosophy or a handful of clinical observations. Mihaly Csikszentmihalyi, whose book *Flow* was reviewed earlier in this chapter, commented that Myers has amassed a masterful compendium of what researchers have discovered about happiness. He also said that *The Pursuit of Happiness* is a book that every reader can profit from and enjoy. And highly respected University of Arizona psychologist Robert Cialdini said that *The Pursuit of Happiness* provides engaging and brilliant insights about happiness.

CONCLUSIONS

In summary, we recommend:

- For a general approach to self-fulfillment and happiness:
    - ★★★ *Flow* by Mihaly Csikszentmihalyi
    - ◗◗ *The Pursuit of Happiness* by David Myers

- For a spiritually based approach to self-fulfillment and happiness:
    - ★★★★ *The Road Less Traveled* by M. Scott Peck
    - ★★★★ *When All You Ever Wanted Isn't Enough* by Harold Kushner

- For a cognitive approach to self-fulfillment and happiness:
    - ★★★★ *A New Guide to Rational Living* by Albert Ellis and Robert Harper

- For an existential approach to self- fulfillment and happiness:
    - ★★★★★ *Man's Search for Meaning* by Victor Frankl

CHAPTER TWENTY-NINE

Self-Improvement
and Motivation

In a way, all self-help books are about self-improvement. In some cases, the books describe general ways to attain self-improvement, in others advice is given about specific problems. In this chapter we discuss books that dispense general strategies for self-improvement, along with books devoted to an important aspect of self-improvement— motivation. To change to a new, better, more competent self, we have to become energized and directed, which is what motivation is all about.

Self-help books in the national survey on self-improvement and motivation can be grouped into the following categories: general approaches, books on inner resources and self-healing, behavioral approaches, humanistic approaches, cognitive approaches, books on women and self-improvement, and books on time management and procrastination.

Five books present a general approach to self-improvement: *The 7 Habits of Highly Effective People* by Steven Covey; *Unlimited Power* by Anthony Robbins; *Your Erroneous Zones* by Wayne Dyer; *How to Stop Worrying and Start Living* by Dale Carnegie; and *Steps to the Top* by Zig Zigler.

Two books that take an inner resources, self-healing approach to self-fulfillment were rated: *Peace, Love, and Healing* by Bernie Siegel and *Your Maximum Mind* by Herbert Benson.

One book presents a behavioral approach to self-improvement: *Making Life Right When It Feels All Wrong* by Herbert Fensterheim.

One humanistic book on self-improvement was rated: *Gentle Roads to Survival* by Andre Auw.

One book that takes a cognitive therapy approach to self-improvement was rated: *Feel the Fear and Do It Anyway* by Susan Jeffers.

One book on women and self-improvement was rated: *Don't Blame Mother* by Paula Caplan.

Self-Improvement and Motivation
BOOK RATINGS IN THE NATIONAL SURVEY

Recommended ★★★★ *The 7 Habits of Highly Effective People* by Steven Covey

★★★★ *Peace, Love, and Healing* by Bernie Siegel

★★★★ *How to Get Control of Your Time and Your Life* by Alan Lakein

★★★★ *Overcoming Procrastination* by Albert Ellis and William Knaus

Diamonds in the Rough ◆ *Feel the Fear and Do It Anyway* by Susan Jeffers

◆ *Don't Blame Mother* by Paula Caplan

Neutral ★★★ *Making Life Right When It Feels All Wrong* by Herbert Fensterheim

★★★ *Gentle Roads to Survival* by Andre Auw

★★★ *Unlimited Power* by Anthony Robbins

Not Recommended ★★ *Your Maximum Mind* by Herbert Benson

★★ *Your Erroneous Zones* by Wayne Dyer

★ *How to Stop Worrying and Start Living* by Dale Carnegie

★ *Steps to the Top* by Zig Zigler

And two books on time management and procrastination were rated: *How to Get Control of Your Time and Your Life* by Alan Lakein and *Overcoming Procrastination* by Albert Ellis and William Knaus.

RECOMMENDED

★ ★ ★ ★   *The 7 Habits of Highly Effective People* (1989) by Steven Covey. New York: Simon & Schuster.

The 7 Habits of Highly Effective People tells readers how to harness their potential to achieve their goals. Author Steven Covey is the chairman of Covey Leadership Center and the Institute for Principle-Centered Leadership. His firm advises over a hundred of the Fortune 500 companies on leadership. He is also the author of several other books, including *Principle-Centered Leadership.* Covey's book is different from the many self-help books on self-improvement and motivation that offer quick-fix solutions. It provides an in-depth examination of how people's perspectives and values determine how competently they perform in their business and personal lives.

Covey argues that in order to be quality leaders in an organization, people must first become quality oriented, identifying the underlying principles that are important in their lives and then evaluating whether they are living up to those standards. Covey lists seven basic habits that are fundamental to anyone's efforts to become quality oriented. The first three are dubbed private victories and the next three public victories. The seven habits:

- Be proactive instead of reactive.
- Begin with the end in mind.
- Put first things first.
- Think win/win.
- Seek first to understand, then to be understood.
- Synergize.
- Sharpen the saw (renewal).

The 7 Habits of Highly Effective People received a 4-star Recommended rating in the national survey. Several mental health professionals said that in an area populated by too many slick, quick-fix, get-rich motivation books, *The 7 Habits of Highly Effective People* is a breath of fresh air. They further commented that Covey's choices of personal, family, educational, and professional examples to illustrate the habits of highly effective people are excellent. Critics said that no research has been conducted to document that these are the core seven habits of competent individuals.

★ ★ ★ ★   *Peace, Love, and Healing* (1989) by Bernie Siegel. New York: Harper & Row.

Peace, Love, and Healing presents an inner resource, self-healing approach to self-improvement. Author Bernie Siegel, M.D., is a surgeon who has a strong interest in humanizing medical education and making medical professionals aware of the mind–body connection. He also is the author of *Love, Medicine and Miracles.*

Siegel believes that the medical field has ignored the power of self-healing for too long. He argues that modern medicine and self-healing do not need to be mutually exclusive. Siegel challenges readers to think about how the mind can influence the body and to use this information to their advantage. Among the self-healing techniques he recommends are meditation, visualization, relaxation, and developing peace of mind. Siegel describes a number of exceptional patients who used self-healing to improve their physical and mental well-being.

Peace, Love, and Healing received a 4-star Recommended rating in the national survey. Siegel's book is a controversial one in the medical field. Some physicians felt that Siegel overexaggerates the power of self-healing and that his ideas may in some cases keep people from getting adequate medical treatment for illnesses. They also said that he cites only evidence that supports his view and ignores research that contradicts his beliefs. Siegel's most passionate boosters are his patients with serious illnesses who have been told by their doctors that modern medicine can't do anything for them. His supporters among the mental health professionals said that he has inspired many patients, nurses, medical students, and even some doctors to look at healing in a larger context and to look at illnesses in new ways.

★ ★ ★ ★   *How to Get Control of Your Time and Your Life* (1973) by Alan Lakein. New York: Signet.

How to Get Control of Your Time and Your Life focuses on how to use time management to improve your life. Author Alan Lakein is a professional time management consultant to a number of business executives.

Lakein says that time is life and that to be competent, we have to manage time effectively. He gives advice on scheduling, how to find time we never knew we had, how to make the most out of priorities, how to determine which tasks should be left undone, how to create quiet time for ourselves, when to speed up and when to slow down, the price of delay, and how to do better the next time.

How to Get Control of Your Time and Your Life received a 4-star Recommended rating in the national survey. Written two decades ago, this was one of the early, very successful books on time management. It still contains valuable advice about time management, but its age shows in gender stereotyping: Males invariably are depicted as playing golf, writing reports for the boss, and belonging to the Lions Club. Females drive their children in car pools, sew buttons on shirts, and belong to the League of Women Voters. And one bad piece of Lakein advice: Don't read magazines or newspapers.

★ ★ ★ ★   *Overcoming Procrastination* (1977) by Albert Ellis and William Knaus. New York: Institute for Rational Living.

Overcoming Procrastination applies Ellis's cognitive therapy approach of rational emotive thinking to performing life's tasks in a timely fashion.

Author Albert Ellis, Ph.D., is a well-known cognitive therapist and author of a number of other self-help books on cognitive therapy. Coauthor William Knaus, Ed.D, has worked as a therapist at Ellis's Institute for Rational Living in New York City and has made procrastination his main area of interest.

Overcoming Procrastination is subtitled *How to Think and Act Rationally in Spite of Life's Inevitable Hassles.* Ellis and Knaus begin by explaining what procrastination means and then turn to its main causes—self-downing, low frustration tolerance, and hostility. The authors recommend a cognitive approach to overcoming procrastination and outline the basic ideas of Ellis's rational emotive therapy. The last chapter includes a psychotherapy transcript between therapist and procrastinator and shows how rational emotive therapy helped the client. *Overcoming Procrastination* just barely received a 4-star Recommended rating in the national survey. The book's advocates said that Ellis and Knaus present a creative, practical approach to solving procrastination problems in many areas of life.

DIAMONDS IN THE ROUGH

♦ *Feel the Fear and Do It Anyway* (1987) by Susan Jeffers. San Diego, CA: Harcourt Brace Jovanovich.

Feel the Fear and Do It Anyway presents a cognitive approach, much of it based on Ellis's rational emotive therapy, for coping with fear. Author Susan Jeffers, Ph.D., is a psychologist, and her book is based on a course she taught at the New School for Social Research in New York.

Jeffers believes that most people's inaction, whether it involves changing jobs, breaking off a relationship, starting a relationship, and so on, stems from the fear of not being able to handle whatever comes along. She says that fear never completely goes away. Fear should be a sign to us that we are being challenged, and we should confront the fear by taking reasonable risks.

Feel the Fear made the Diamonds in the Rough category in the national survey. The book's supporters say that Jeffers does a good job of showing how faulty thinking is the source of most people's unreasonable fears and that she gives valuable advice about how to modify such irrational thinking.

♦ *Don't Blame Mother: Mending in the Mother–Daughter Relationship* (1989) by Paula Caplan. New York: Harper & Row.

Don't Blame Mother argues that society and psychology have short-changed mothers, blaming them far too often and too much for their children's problems. Author Paula Caplan, Ph.D., is a clinical and research psychologist. She is a professor of psychology at the Ontario Institute for Studies in Education and a lecturer in women's studies at the University of Toronto.

Caplan argues that daughters are taught to criticize the work of mothering and to make their mothers the scapegoats for any problems the daughters might have as adults. Caplan believes that myths of idealization give rise to impossible expectations and set mothers up for failure. However, Caplan says that mothers and daughters can move beyond these troublesome stereotypes and negative perceptions and gain a new appreciation for each other and their relationship. She gives advice on identifying conflicting messages and myths that weaken the mother–daughter bond. Caplan also underscores the value of women sharing experiences with other women as a means of personal change and self-improvement.

Don't Blame Mother was placed in the Diamonds in the Rough category. A number of respected mental health professionals applauded Caplan's efforts in *Don't Blame Mother*. Leading gender authorities Jeanne Marecek of Swarthmore College and Rachel Hare-Mustin of Villanova University said that at a time when many self-help books, especially those with a codependency perspective, promote mother-blaming as a means of psychological growth, *Don't Blame Mother* is a much-needed antidote. Well-known self-help author and respected mental health professional Harriet Lerner commented that Caplan's sensitive and compassionate book helps us to move away from our deep-rooted tendency to blame our mothers for every problem we have. She goes on to say that the book teaches women how to know and love their mothers better. This is an excellent self-help book on mother–daughter relationships, especially how to improve them in the adult years. *Don't Blame Mother* is also appropriate for consideration under other topics, such as adult development (Chapter 4) and women's issues (Chapter 34).

NEUTRAL

★ ★ ★   *Making Life Right When It Feels All Wrong* (1988) by Herbert Fensterheim. New York: Rawlins Associates.

Making Life Right When It Feels All Wrong presents a modified behavioral approach to self-improvement. Author Herbert Fensterheim, Ph.D., is a clinical professor at Cornell University Medical College. He also wrote *Don't Say Yes When You Want to Say No* (profiled in Chapter 8, Assertiveness).

Fensterheim recommends a cognitive behavioral approach to self-improvement that combines changing actions with conquering long-standing, buried problems. This unusual approach to self-improvement actually combines behavioral and psychoanalytic strategies. Fensterheim tells you that you may not be able to control what happens to you, but you can control your reaction to it. The author applies his ideas to many different domains of life: love, assertiveness, work, friendships, and sports. The book includes many vignettes, anecdotes, and case studies.

Making Life Right When It Feels All Wrong received a 3-star Neutral rating in the national survey. Some mental health professionals praised Fensterheim's unique attempt to integrate behavior therapy principles and psychoanalytic concepts of needs and blocks. However, critics said that behavioral and psychoanalytic approaches make strange bedfellows and that the integration doesn't always work.

★ ★ ★   *Gentle Roads to Survival* (1991) by Andrew Auw. Boulder Creek, CO: Aslan.

Gentle Roads to Survival presents a humanistic approach to self-improvement. Author Andre Auw, Ph.D., is a psychologist and was a close associate of the famous humanistic psychologist Carl Rogers.

In *Gentle Roads to Survival,* Auw presents a guide to making self-healing choices in difficult circumstances. Auw tells you how to become a survivor. He believes that while some people may be born survivors, most of us have to learn survival skills. Auw addresses personal crises in religion, morality, parenting, marriage, cross-cultural adaptation, and many other stressful life circumstances. He especially advocates that each person has to discover his or her own unique path of adaptation and coping.

Gentle Roads to Survival received a 3-star Neutral rating in the national survey. Several mental health professionals, especially those with a humanistic orientation, said that this is a very good self-help book for people facing highly stressful circumstances in their lives. They called Auw's tone warm, sensitive, and compassionate. Before his death, Carl Rogers commented that Andre Auw's ideas contain a great deal of wisdom, wisdom gained from experience. Well-known family therapist Virginia Satir said that Auw's advice captures the humanistic spirit of Carl Rogers, a spirit of respect and caring.

★ ★ ★   *Unlimited Power* (1986) by Anthony Robbins. New York: Fawcett Columbine.

Unlimited Power presents a general approach to self-improvement and motivation. Author Anthony Robbins is a self-made millionaire who conducts motivational and life change seminars. He directs the Robbins Research Institute in La Jolla, California.

Unlimited Power is based on a concept called neurolinguistic programming. According to neuro-linguistic programming enthusiasts like Robbins, people can be programmed in ways that will keep them being highly successful. Robbins advocates a host of mental, emotional, and physiological programming strategies, especially developing confidence in the mind's power. To convince people of their mental powers, Robbins strongly recommends firewalking, a barefoot jaunt over hot coals. A basic step in becoming successful, he says, is selecting a successful person as a model and learning about how the person became successful and how they conduct their lives. Essential to Robbins's "ultimate success formula" are clarity of desired goals, energy, passion, persistence of action, effective communication skills, and altruistic motives.

Unlimited Power barely received a 3-star Neutral rating in the national survey. Mental health professionals said that this book has some good points mixed with some bad points. The good: Robbins's enthusiastic approach can motivate people with talent to develop their talent. And Robbins is better than most authors in this category at pinpointing strategies for self-improvement. Few people could quibble with his recommendations for selecting a competent model to emulate or the desired goals he advocates. The bad: Many critics were less than enthusiastic about the concept of neurolinguistic programming (one mental health professional called it a fancy, catchy term that doesn't mean anything); the mind-over-matter firewalking demonstrations are misleading (scientists have demonstrated that anyone can walk across hot coals without getting burned if they move quickly enough); and Robbins's rash claims that just about anyone can be a rich tycoon or superstar with "unlimited power" made many mental health professionals cringe.

NOT RECOMMENDED

★ ★   *Your Maximum Mind* (1987) by Herbert Benson. New York: Random House.

Your Maximum Mind argues that self-improvement can be attained by tapping our inner resources and understanding the mind–body link. Author Herbert Benson, M.D., is a professor of medicine at Harvard Medical School. He also wrote *The Relaxation Response,* and *Beyond the Relaxation Response,* which were very positively evaluated in the national survey and are profiled in Chapter 26, Relaxation, Meditation, and Stress.

In *Your Maximum Mind,* Benson says that recent studies show that the right and left sides of the brain perform very different types of thinking: The left side does logical thinking, the right side does intuitive thinking. He believes that because the dominant left side of the brain often overrules creative impulses generated by the right side, we tend to repeat old habits and cling to old behaviors, even those we would like to truly change. Benson says that our thought patterns can be changed to achieve more desirable pathways in the brain. The first step in Benson's reprogramming of the brain is to regularly practice the Relaxation Response. A second step is what Benson calls "whole brain" thinking.

Your Maximum Mind received a 2-star Not Recommended rating in the national survey. Why did this book by Benson receive such a low rating and his books that focus exclusively on relaxation such a high rating? Critics said that Benson, like many others, overexaggerates right brain/left brain differences in thinking and that the evidence for many of his assertions in this book is not as well documented as he says. They recommended sticking with either *The Relaxation Response* or *Beyond the Relaxation Response.*

★ ★   *Your Erroneous Zones* (1976) by Wayne Dyer. New York: Funk & Wagnalls.

Your Erroneous Zones presents a general approach to self-improvement. Author Wayne Dyer, Ph.D., is a well-known self-help book author and has been a practicing therapist and professor at St. John's University in New York.

The main message in Dyer's book is that at any given moment you are what you choose to be. He says that most people's thinking takes place in erroneous (that's "erroneous," not "erogenous") zones of self-defeat, which inhibits personal growth. The erroneous zones include guilt, worry, boredom, and procrastination. Dyer tells readers to make choices about their emotions and to take charge of their present life. He then applies these ideas to learning self-love and self-definition, to shifting the emphasis from external approval to self-approval, to avoiding guilt, worry, procrastination, and anger, and to overcoming fear of the unknown and dependence on others.

Your Erroneous Zones was a very popular self-help book in the late 1970s, one of the top ten in self-help book sales, but it did not fare well in the 1990s national survey of mental health professionals. It received a 2-star Not Recommended rating. Critics said that Dyer's book fed the interests of the "me" generation a decade or so ago. Most mental health professionals believe it is important to balance self-direction and self-love with an interest and respect for others rather than being solely self-oriented. Critics, such as respected psychotherapist Silvano Arieti, also thought that Dyer's book tells people that to think or feel deeply is to think tragically, and they do not agree that thinking and feeling superficially will lead to self-improvement.

★ *How to Stop Worrying and Start Living* (1944) by Dale Carnegie. New York: Simon & Schuster.

How to Stop Worrying and Start Living argues that the biggest impediment to self-improvement is worrying. Author Dale Carnegie is the well-known author of *How to Win Friends and Influence People,* and his name is associated with the widely popular Dale Carnegie Course that dispenses a broad array of advice about self-improvement, from becoming a more effective public speaker to winning friends and influencing people to how to quit worrying.

Carnegie says that worry wastes energy, fritters away time, and leads to physical illnesses. He urges people to unwind, relax, take a long-term view of an immediate problem, pray, and learn from others. Carnegie trots out case study after case study of worriers who used his approach and began living more effectively and happily. Quotations from sources ranging from Marcus Aurelius to Babe Ruth dot the pages.

How to Stop Worrying and Start Living received a 1-star Not Recommended rating in the national survey. The book was published almost half a century ago, and its age shows. The many case studies and examples naturally do not reflect the dramatic changes in society that have taken place in the last 50 years—changing gender roles, work and career changes, and so on. Books such as David Burns's *Feeling Good* (see Chapter 14, Depression) and Martin Seligman's *Learned Optimism* (see Chapter 24, Positive Thinking and Self-Talk) are much better choices on the topic.

★ *Steps to the Top* (1985) by Zig Zigler. Gretna, LA: Pelican.

Steps to the Top presents a general approach to self-improvement and motivation. Author Zig Zigler is a well-known self-help author who has conducted nationwide seminars on motivation for many years. He lives in Dallas, Texas.

Steps to the Top is an enthusiastic book in which Zigler assumes a cheerleading role. Zigler lists seven key steps to self-improvement and motivation: attitude, choosing, courage, goals, how to (mainly visualizing success), love, and perseverance.

Steps to the Top received a 1-star Not Recommended rating in the national survey. Critics said that Zigler's book is high on enthusiasm and low on substance.

CONCLUSIONS

In summary, we recommend:

- For a general approach to self-improvement, especially in business:
    - ★ ★ ★ ★ *The 7 Habits of Highly Effective People* by Steven Covey

- For an inner resources, mind–body approach to self-improvement:
    - ★ ★ ★ ★ *Peace, Love, and Healing* by Bernie Siegel

- On managing time and conquering procrastination:
    - ★ ★ ★ ★ *How to Get Control of Your Time and Your Life* by Alan Lakein
    - ★ ★ ★ ★ *Overcoming Procrastination* by Albert Ellis and William Knaus

- On self-improvement for women and why they should not blame their mothers for their problems:
    - ◆ *Don't Blame Mother* by Paula Caplan

CHAPTER THIRTY

Sexuality

Sex has its magnificent moments throughout the animal kingdom. Insects mate in midair, peacocks display their plumage, and male elephant seals have prolific sex lives—all instinctive behaviors. Experience plays an important role in human sexual behavior. We can talk about sex with each other, read about it in books and magazines, and watch it on television and the movie screen.

But although we can talk about sex with each other, we often don't. Sex in America still comes cloaked in mystery and as a nation we are neither very knowledgeable about sex nor very comfortable talking about it. While many people manage to develop a mature sexuality, others don't, and even those who do handle sex maturely and competently have periods of vulnerabilty and confusion. Many people wonder and worry about their sexual attractiveness, their ability to satisfy their sexual partner, and whether they will experience the ultimate sexual fantasy. Our worries are fueled by media stereotypes of sexual potency and superhuman sexual exploits. Sexual concerns also prevail because of our inability to communicate about sex directly with each other.

Sexuality books in the national survey can be divided into the following categories: broad-based approaches to improving sexual enjoyment and skills; books on women and sex; books on men and sex; and books on homosexuality.

Five books that take a broad-based approach to improving sexual enjoyment and skills were rated: *The New Joy of Sex* by Alex Comfort; *More Joy of Sex* by Alex Comfort; *What Really Happens in Bed* by Steven Carter and Julia Sokol Coopersmith; *Dr. Ruth's Guide to Good Sex* by Ruth Westheimer; and *Dr. Ruth's Guide to Erotic and Sensous Pleasures* by Ruth Westheimer and Louis Lieberman.

Three books on women and sex were rated: *For Yourself* by Lonnie Barbach; *For Each Other* by Lonnie Barbach; and *Making Love: A Wom-

---

Sexuality
BOOK RATINGS IN THE NATIONAL SURVEY

Diamonds in the Rough	◆ *Male Sexuality* by Bernie Zilbergeld
	◆ *For Yourself* by Lonnie Barbach
	◆ *For Each Other* by Lonnie Barbach
Neutral	★★★ *The New Joy of Sex* by Alex Comfort
	★★★ *More Joy of Sex* by Alex Comfort
	★★★ *Making Love: A Man's Guide* by Barry White
	★★★ *Making Love: A Woman's Guide* by Judith Davis
	★★★ *What Really Happens in Bed* by Steven Carter and Julia Sokol Coopersmith
Strongly Not Recommended	† *Dr. Ruth's Guide to Good Sex* by Ruth Westheimer
	† *Dr. Ruth's Guide to Erotic and Sensual Pleasures* by Ruth Westheimer and Louis Lieberman

---

an's Guide by Judith Davis. A fourth book—*Becoming Orgasmic* by Julia Heiman and Joesph LoPiccolo—is profiled in Worth a Further Look.

Two books on men and sex were rated: *Male Sexuality* by Bernie Zilbergeld and *Making Love: A Man's Guide* by Barry White. A third book—*The New Male Sexualty* by Bernie Zilbergeld—is profiled in Worth a Further Look.

No books on homosexuality made the final ratings. However, three books on gays and lesbians are evaluated in the Worth a Further Look section: *Permanent Partners* by Betty Berzon; *The New Loving Someone Gay;* and *Lesbian Couples* by D. Merilee Clunis and G. Dorsey Green.

DIAMONDS IN THE ROUGH

◆ *Male Sexuality: A Guide to Sexual Fulfillment* (1978) by Bernie Zilbergeld. Boston, MA: Little, Brown & Co.

Male Sexuality presents a number of ideas about ways to improve male sexuality. Author Bernie Zilbergeld, Ph.D., is a clinical psychologist who formerly headed the Men's Program and was codirector of clinical training in human sexuality at the University of California at San Francisco. He currently is in private practice in Oakland, California.

Male Sexuality presents a number of myths about male sexuality that have victimized men and contributed to unhappy relationships. One common myth that Zilbergeld attacks is that all men really want is sexual intercourse. When men want something else, such as love and sensitivity, they are inhibited by the stereotype. Zilbergeld also feels that men have gotten themselves into a losing situation by adopting superhuman standards by which to measure their genitals, sexual performance, and satisfaction.

Zilbergeld's book is not a sex guide full of gimmicks or gymnastics, it does not try to impose a life style on anyone, and it doesn't accept the premise that all men are the same. Instead, Zilbergeld draws on his extensive background as a sex therapist to portray the real experiences, problems, and needs of men (and women as well). The author describes and explains the most common sex problems, the importance of touching, how to relax in sexual situations, how to be sensitive to your sexual partner, and sex for older adults and medically disabled individuals. A series of exercises—verbal and physical—encourages men to recognize and understand their sexual values, feelings, and preferences.

Male Sexuality made the Diamond in the Rough category in the national survey—it was rated very positively but by only 18 respondents. The book's supporters said that it is far above the crowd of how-to sex books and that it is a literate, thoughtful analysis of male sexuality that can enhance the sexual lives of many men. Sexuality experts Alex Comfort commented that *Male Sexuality* provides enormous reassurance and first aid for victims of cultural stereotypes of male sexuality.

♦   *For Yourself: The Fulfillment of Female Sexuality* (1975) by Lonnie Barbach. New York: Doubleday.

For Yourself is about the fulfillment of female sexuality. Author Lonnie Barbach, Ph.D., is a clinical psychologist who has had extensive experience as a sex therapist specializing in women's sexual problems. Much of her sex therapy has been conducted at the University of California Medical Center in San Francisco.

Barbach addresses the worries that often distress nonorgasmic women and tells them how they can achieve orgasm. Barbach attacks the negative cultural attitudes that women should not enjoy sex. A number of exercises that will enable women to achieve orgasm are presented, and each exercise is accompanied by an explanation of why it can be effective as well as pitfalls to avoid. The book also includes many examples from the sexual lives of women Barbach has counseled in her sex therapy groups. How to achieve an orgasm through masturbation and the eventual transference to orgasms with a partner are covered.

For Yourself was placed in the Diamonds in the Rough category because it was very positively rated but by only 17 respondents. The book's enthusiasts said that Barbach sensitively and clearly explains to women how they can achieve a more satisfactory sex life. Sexuality expert Mary Calderone said that *For Yourself* is an excellent book that should be read not only by the women to whom it is addressed but by their partners as well. She also commented that the book takes a woman step-by-step through the pleasurable sexual sensations that society has unfortunately told her she should not experience.

♦ *For Each Other: Sharing Sexual Intimacy* (1982) by Lonnie Barbach. New York: Doubleday.

For Each Other also addresses women's sexual fulfillment. In *For Yourself,* Barbach focuses most of her attention on women who are preorgasmic — women who have never experienced an orgasm at all. In *For Each Other,* too, she addresses preorgasmic women and how to achieve an orgasm through masturbation, but she devotes more attention to achieving orgasm with a sexual partner. She discusses the communication aspects, women who are orgasmic but not with a partner, women who rarely desire sex, and women who find sex painful. Among the psychological aspects of orgasm that Barbach examines are unresolved anger toward a partner and power struggles with the partner.

For Each Other includes a number of sexual exercises that can be done alone or with a partner that are designed to increase a woman's sexual satisfaction and ability to achieve an orgasm. Barbach recognizes that there are large individual variations in women's sexual desires, all of which are within a normal range.

For Each Other was placed in the Diamonds in the Rough category because it was very postively rated but by only 13 respondents. Most found it to be an excellent book that can help women achieve a more enjoyable sex life. Sexuality expert Bernie Zilbergeld commented that this is the best self-help book on the market on female sexuality.

NEUTRAL

★★★ *The New Joy of Sex* (1991) by Alex Comfort. New York: Crown.

The New Joy of Sex covers a broad range of topics in human sexuality. Author Alex Comfort, M.D., is a physician who has written a number of self-help books on human sexuality. His book *The Joy of Sex* was published two decades ago in 1973 and sold more than eight million copies. Comfort was born in London, spent some time in the United States, and now resides in Kent, England.

The New Joy of Sex is subtitled *A Gourmet Guide to Lovemaking in the Nineties.* Comfort's first book on sexuality—*The Joy of Sex*—was a manual of uninhibited sexual techniques with boldly explicit illustrations. *The New Joy of Sex* includes the uninhibited approach to sexual expression and explicit illustrations that characterized *The Joy of Sex,* along with new material on AIDS and other sexually transmitted diseases (including a stern lecture on the importance of using condoms).

The New Joy of Sex has six main sections, including several with some unlikely titles. The first, Ingredients, covers topics such as love, fidelity, breasts, buttocks, lubrication, and penis. Appetizers examines exercises, kisses, and bites, among other topics. Main Courses includes mouth music, rear entry, standing positions, and the like. Sauces covers such topics as playtime, Chinese style, G-string, leather, vibrators, and bondage. Venues describes locations, such as beds, bathtubs, rocking chairs, railways, and motorcyles. Health and Other Issues explores such topics as AIDS, frigidity, age, bisexuality, fetishes, and transvestitism.

The New Joy of Sex received a 3-star Neutral rating in the national survey, nearly making the 4-star Recommended rating. It is a well-known book—it was evaluated by 173 respondents—even though it was recently published. Some mental health professionals praised Comfort's book, saying that it is educational and can be beneficial in helping people rid themselves of their sexual anxieties and achieve greater sexual satisfaction. However, it's definitely more for liberal thinkers than conservative ones. One conservative critic called the book "educational pornography."

★★★   *More Joy of Sex* (1983) by Alex Comfort. New York: Crown.

More Joy of Sex is described as a lovemaking companion to Comfort's first major book on sex—*The Joy of Sex.* Comfort's goal in *More Joy of Sex* is to go beyond the techniques of lovemaking and provide insight about how to mature sexuality. Like *The Joy of Sex, More Joy* presents an uninhibited view of sexuality with sexually explicit photographs. Comfort continues to try to get people to loosen up sexually and reach a joyful level of sexual satisfaction. He covers positions, threesomes, and group scenes (which, he cautions, are fraught with pitfalls). He explores hot tubs, massages, skin awareness, body image, communication, jealousy, and marriage. He gives special attention to hostility, assertiveness, and dominance, as well as how to read nonverbal behavior in sexual situations. And he examines resources, such as therapy, meditation, and sex surrogates.

More Joy received a 3-star Neutral rating in the national survey. The book's supporters believed that *More Joy,* like Comfort's other books, serves an important function in helping people become more knowledgeable and skillful in achieving sexual satisfaction. This volume includes more information about the psychological and relationship dimensions of sexuality, but it's still "gourmet sex," with frequent discussions and illustrations of a variety of sexual techniques. One reviewer commented that if *The Joy of Sex* was about climbing, then More Joy is about mountaineering, and went on to say that this book is fine for members of the Sexual Himalayan Club, as long as they watch their step, but for others it's a little too liberal.

★ ★ ★   *Making Love: A Man's Guide* (1984) by Barry White. New York: Signet.

Making Love: A Man's Guide is, as its title implies, designed to help men improve their lovemaking and sexual skills. No mental health affiliations are listed for author Barry White.

Making Love advises men about what they can give women, the role of looks in sex, women's sexual hangups, how to make women feel like making love, foreplay, intercourse, women's sexual anatomy, what to do after having sex, how to keep sex exciting, and what to do about sexual problems. This is mainly a how-to book with specific recommendations to men for becoming better lovers.

Making Love received a 3-star Neutral rating in the national survey; it was not well known by the mental health professionals, only 27 of whom responded on it. Critics said that although the book provides some good suggestions in places, too often it regresses to pop-psych descriptions of sexuality. They also criticized the book for its tone of manipulating and at times degrading women (three things every woman craves, for example). The consensus of the mental health professsionals was that Zilbergeld's *Male Sexuality* is a much better choice.

★ ★ ★   *Making Love: A Woman's Guide* (1983) by Judith Davis. New York: Signet.

Making Love: A Woman's Guide gives women advice for becoming more sexually attractive to their male partner. No mental health affiliations are listed for author Judith Davis.

In *Making Love,* Davis says that at one time the woman was supposed to be the passive partner in making love, always waiting for the man to make the move and following his lead after that. She says that the rules have changed in today's world—that women can now take a more active, assertive role and can enjoy sex. This is a how-to sexual guide for women that gives them explicit insructions on how to become a better lover and attract men sexually. The book includes a number of lists of recommendations, such as 20 sure-fire turn-ons, 7 come-love-me hints, and 9 "please-touch" erogenous zone tips.

Making Love received a 3-star Neutral rating in the national survey. Some mental health professionals found it a helpful guide for women who are too inhibited sexually. Critics said that the book contains too many pop-psych sensationalist comments.

★ ★ ★   *What Really Happens in Bed* (1989) by Steven Carter and Julia Sokol Coopersmith. New York: M. Evans.

What Really Happens in Bed presents a broad-based approach to improving sexual competence and relationships for both women and men. Authors Steven Carter and Julia Sokol Coopersmith are writers; no mental health affiliations are listed for them. The also wrote *Men Who Can't Love.*

What Really Happens in Bed is an effort to cut through the sexual expectations of both women and men that too often are based on myths and romantic fantasies. The authors interviewed several hundred women and men to provide a profile of what people are really doing and saying in their sexual lives. The book is divided into two main sections. Section I, Talking About Sex, explodes a number of sexual myths and unrealistic expectations and explores why people are reluctant to talk about what really happens in bed. Section II, Sexual Life Patterns and Stages, examines the single life and temporary sexual solutions, sexual fantasies and experimentation, marriage and sex, extramarital affairs. and what people can learn to improve their sex lives. The book includes a number of excerpts from the interviews the authors conducted.

What Really Happens in Bed received a 3-star Neutral rating in the national survey. Several mental health professionals said that this book does a good job of cutting through many of the sexual myths in our culture. They also applauded the authors for their inclusion of extensive material about communication and relationships instead of focusing only on how-to-do-sex, as so many self-help books on sex do. Critics faulted the authors for the unscientific nature of their interviews; they said that the authors try to explain it away but don't effectively do so.

STRONGLY NOT RECOMMENDED

† *Dr. Ruth's Guide to Good Sex* (1983) by Ruth Westheimer. New York: Warner Books.

Dr. Ruth's Guide to Good Sex presents a broad-based approach to sexual matters. Ruth Westheimer is a sex therapist who has a doctorate in education from Columbia University and has taught in the human sexuality program at the New York Hospital–Cornell Medical Center. She currentlly is an adjunct professor at New York University. Dr. Westheimer is widely known as just "Dr. Ruth" because of her extensive media appearances, first on radio in New York City, then nationally on the Lifetime cable network with *The Dr. Ruth Show.*

Westheimer is convinced that ignorance is at the root of most sexual problems. In *Dr. Ruth's Guide to Good Sex,* Westheimer draws on the questions she fielded on her popular syndicated radio program that deals with sexual issues of all sorts (this book was written before her television show). Like Alex Comfort, Westheimer believes that people are too sexually repressed and that they need to be exposed to frank discussions about sex. Also like Comfort, Westheimer advocates a variety of sexual experiences as long as they are acceptable to both partners. No one, she says, should be pressured into doing any sexual thing they do not want to do. The book tackles a smorgasbord of questions—penis length, sexual positions, orgasm, sex and the disabled, gay sex, and sexually transmitted diseases. Sexual knowledge helps people overcome their shyness, shame, and other negative sexual attitudes, Westheimer says. Her style is explicit, upbeat, and often humorous. She recommends the use of contraception, consultation with a therapist when indicated, and Alex Comfort's *The Joy of Sex* (for people who want to improve and vary their sexual practices).

Dr. Ruth's Guide to Good Sex did not fare well in the national survey, receiving a negative Strongly Not Recommended rating. Critics said that there are more current and more comprehensive sex resources that don't come wrapped in the "Dr. Ruth" hoopla. They criticized the book for being too earthy and too disorganized (the brief question-and-answer format means that she skips from topic to topic often without providing adequate details, descriptions, and explanations of sexual issues) and for the use of transcriptions from the radio program that do not translate well into print. Sandwiched between these problems is practical, if at times too explicit, advice that can benefit some sexually repressed, unknowledgeable people. Although *Dr. Ruth's Guide to Good Sex* received an overall negative evaluation in the national survey, not all mental health professionals criticize the book. Indeed, highly respected sex therapist Helen Kaplan, in a foreword to *Dr. Ruth's Guide to Good Sex,* comments that it contains sound, sensitive, wise advice.

† *Dr. Ruth's Guide to Erotic and Sensuous Pleasures* (1991) by Ruth Westheimer and Louis Lieberman. New York: Warner Books.

Dr. Ruth's Guide to Erotic and Sensuous Pleasures presents a broad-based approach to greater enjoyment of sex. Dr. Westheimer's coauthor on this book, Louis Lieberman, Ph.D., is a professor of sociology at the City University of New York.

   Dr. Ruth's Guide to Erotic and Sensuous Pleasures is a more recent rendition of Westheimer's sexual advice than *Dr. Ruth's Guide to Good Sex.* The newer book does not follow the question-and-answer format that characterized much of the earlier book. The more recent guide also places emphasis on the barriers of everyday stress to sexual fulfillment. The authors prescribe a host of stress-reducing activities to revive and improve people's sexual lives, such as circle dancing, focused nature walks, meditation, poetry, prayer, and skiing. They encourage indulgence in sensuous environments — shower massages, bubble baths, hot tubs, whirlpools, and the like — to improve sexual enjoyment. The book also introduces the art of body mapping for discovering pleasurable body areas. Vibrators, massagers, premature ejaculation, lack of sexual interest, and many other sexual topics are covered.

   Dr. Ruth's Guide to Erotic and Sensual Pleasures, like *Dr. Ruth's Guide to Good Sex,* received a negative Strongly Not Recommended rating in the national survey. While this book is better organized than the first and is not quite as earthy, the mental health professionals still did not feel that it presents human sexuality in a way that will benefit self-help readers.

WORTH A FURTHER LOOK

◖ ◗ *Becoming Orgasmic: A Sexual Growth Program for Women* (rev. ed., 1988) by Julia Heiman and Joseph LoPiccolo. New York: Prentice Hall Press.

Becoming Orgasmic is a guide to sexual and personal growth for women. Auther Julia Heiman, Ph.D., is a professor of psychiatry and behavioral sciences at the University of Washington Medical School in Seattle. She is also director of the Interpersonal Psychotherapy Clinic and the Reproductive and Sexual Medicine Clinic. She is a coauthor of an academic textbook, *Human Sexuality*. Coauthor Joseph LoPiccolo, Ph.D., is a professor and chair of the department of psychology at the University of Missouri. He is a recognized authority on sex therapy. He founded and directed the Sex Therapy Center at the State University of New York at Stony Brook and is a past president of the Society for the Scientific Study of Sex.

Becoming Orgasmic offers women permission, encouragement, and specific behavioral exercises to help them become more sexually fulfilled. The book leads women through a "personal sex history" to understand their own sexual feelings and experiences, includes self-touch exercises for learning how to relax and gain sexual pleasure, and presents advice for sharing pleasures with one's partner. Among the topics that are addressed include looking at oneself, vaginal exercises, erotic literature, fantasizing, using a vibrator, and intercourse.

Becoming Orgasmic received a high positive rating but was evaluated by only nine respondents, barely missing the Diamonds in the Rough category. The mental health professionals who evaluated the book said that it presents extraordinarily good sexual advice for women. Well-known cognitive therapist Albert Ellis found *Becoming Orgasmic* a very good book for women with orgasm problems. Michael Metz, a professor at the University of Minnesota Medical School, said *Becoming Orgasmic* is a very useful and supportive book for women who want to become orgasmic or who seek to improve their sexual responsiveness.

◗ ◗ *The New Male Sexuality* (1992) by Bernie Zilbergeld. New York: Bantam.

The New Male Sexuality is a comprehensive volume on male sexuality. Author Bernie Zilbergeld's background was profiled earlier in this chapter in the review of his book *Male Sexuality*. Why did Zilbergeld write *The New Male Sexuality*? Because, he says, in the last decade we have seen dramatic changes in the sexual landscape from the changing expectations of women to new definitions of masculinity, from the fear of disease to the renewed focus on long-term relationships.

The New Male Sexuality presents encyclopedic coverage of male sexuality. Some of the book is a carryover from the earlier *Male Sexuality*, and some of it is new material. An introductory section tackles male sexual myths and unrealistic expectations, and then the author turns to sexual reality and gives men a brief course in sexual knowledge. The next section explores better sex through topics such as how to be a good lover with your partner, how to be a good listener, touching, arousal, and how to keep the spark alive in long-standing relationships. A final section is devoted to resolving problems and includes discussion of ejaculatory control, erection difficulties, problems of sexual desire, and even advice for fathers on how to communicate more effectively about sex with their sons.

The New Male Sexuality was published after the national survey was conducted. It is an excellent, easy-to-read, well-organized, and authoritative guide to men's sexuality. Sandra Caron, a sexuality professor at the University of Maine, said that *The New Male Sexuality* is the best practical guide she has ever seen for anyone—male or female, young or old, coupled or single—who wants better relationships and better sex. Sexuality self-help author Lonnie Barbach commented that *The New Male Sexuality* presents truly everything there is to know about male sexuality in a clearly written, entertaining format. This book is a giant step above the crass, how-to sex books that have populated the sex self-help shelves in recent years. It is a sensitive and thoughtful map to better and more fulfilling sexual lives for men.

◑ ◑   *Permanent Partners: Building Gay and Lesbian Relationships* (1988) by Betty Berzon. New York: E. P. Dutton.

Permanent Partners is about gay and lesbian relationships. Author Betty Berzon, Ph.D., is a psychotherapist in private practice. A lesbian herself, Berzon lives in Los Angeles with her partner of almost two decades and has counseled same-sex couples for a number of years.

Permanent Partners presents knowledge and understanding that will help gay and lesbian couples make their relationships work, satisfy, and last. Berzon examines the obstacles that same-sex couples face as they try to create a life together. Among the obstacles she explores are lack of visible long-term same-sex couples as role models; absence of support from society—from employers to landlords to insurers—and from the couple's families; a "tradition of failure"; and the guidance gap that has not provided adequate advice for how to effectively build a life with another man or another woman.

Permanent Partners received a high positive rating in the national survey but was evaluated by fewer than 10 respondents, hence its relegation to Worth a Further Look. This is an excellent book on gay and lesbian relationships, both for gays and lesbians who are thinking about becoming coupled or are perplexed about their current relationship, and for others who want to improve their understanding of gay and lesbian couples. Respected sexuality expert John Money, professor of medical psychology at the Johns Hopkins University and Hospital, said that *Permanent Partners* is a timely book that provides good advice about gay and lesbian relationships.

◑ ◑   *The New Loving Someone Gay* (rev. ed., 1987) by Don Clark. Berkeley, CA: Celestial Arts.

The New Loving Someone Gay is a comprehensive guide for gay people and those who care about them. Author Don Clark, Ph.D., is a clinical psychologist and is gay. He has practiced therapy for more than three decades.

In *The New Loving Someone Gay*, Clark cuts through much of the mystery and fear of gay people and gay identity. He shows how gay people can provide support for each other, develop solid relationships, and live in a community of caring individuals who work together. The book also helps families and friends to confront their own prejudices and confusion about gays and to develop more sensitive, supportive relationships with gays. Special attention is given to the AIDS epidemic in this updated version of the book.

This book was not rated in the national survey, but we believe it merits attention by the public and by the mental health profession. *The New Loving Someone Gay* is a sensitive, informed presentation that includes helpful advice for gays and the people who are close to them.

◑ ◑   *Lesbian Couples* (1988) by D. Merilee Clunis and G. Dorsey Green. Seattle: Seal Press.

Lesbian Couples is a guide for lesbian relationships. Authors D. Merilee Clunis and G. Dorsey Green are lesbians who work as therapists and counsel lesbian couples.

The authors chart the stages that most couples go through: romance, conflict, commitment, and collaboration. Some of the topics they cover are common to all couples, such as issues of living arrangements, work, money, and time; others are specific to lesbian couples, such as coming out to family and friends, monogamy and nonmonogamy, separateness and togetherness. Many problem-solving strategies for lesbian issues are interspersed throughout the book.

Lesbian Couples was not rated in the national survey, but we believe it deserves a further look. The authors do an excellent job of analyzing lesbian relationships and providing good problem-solving advice. Laura Brown, an expert on lesbian relationships and a clinical professor of psychology at the University of Washington, said that *Lesbian Couples* is a book that no one who is in, has been in, or might want to be in a lesbian couple relationship will want to be without.

CONCLUSIONS

In summary, we recommend:

- As comprehensive guides to female sexuality and greater sexual fulfillment:
    - ◆ *For Yourself* by Lonnie Barbach
    - ◆ *For Each Other* by Lonnie Barbach
    - ◑◑ *Becoming Orgasmic* by Julia Heiman and Joseph LoPiccolo
- As comprehensive guides to male sexuality and greater sexual fulfillment:
    - ◆ *Male Sexuality* by Bernie Zilbergeld
    - ◑◑ *The New Male Sexuality* by Bernie Zilbergeld
- For gay and lesbians and those close to them:
    - ◑◑ *Permanent Partners* by Betty Berzon
    - ◑◑ *The New Loving Someone Gay* by Don Clark
    - ◑◑ *Lesbian Couples* by D. Merilee Clunis and G. Dorsey Green

CHAPTER THIRTY-ONE

Stepfamilies

The increased variation in American families has included a huge surge in the number of stepfamilies in recent years. Children born today have a 40% chance of living at least part of their lives in a stepfamily before they become 18 years of age. Stepfamilies are a heterogeneous group— about 70% are stepfather families, about 20% are stepmother families, and about 10% are so-called "blended" families to which both partners bring children from a previous marriage. And many stepfamilies produce children of their own.

Remarriage requires a great deal of adjustment, not only for the spouses who remarry but for the children they bring with them to the newly formed stepfamily. Because of their unique makeup, stepfamilies experience certain problems that other families do not. Expectations may be unrealistic, discipline by a nonbiological parent may produce difficulties, stepsibling rivalry may create special problems, family boundaries may produce conflict, and relationships with grandparents may require special attention. Nonetheless, stepfamilies can work well and all members of a stepfamily can live in harmony.

To help stepfamily members make the adjustments needed to be a psychologically healthy stepfamily, a number of self-help books have been written. They fall into four main categories: books about many types of stepfamilies; books about stepfather families; books about stepmother families; and books about blended families to which both adults bring children from previous marriages.

Three books in the national survey are about stepfamilies in general: *Old Loyalties, New Ties* by Emily Visher and John Visher; *The Second Time Around* by Louis Janda and Ellen MacCormack; and *Strengthening Your Stepfamily* by Elizabeth Einstein and Linda Albert.

One book in the national survey focuses on stepfather families: *Step-Fathering* by Mark Rosin.

Stepfamilies

BOOK RATINGS IN THE NATIONAL SURVEY

Recommended   ★★★★ *Old Loyalties, New Ties* by Emily Visher and John Visher

Diamonds in   ◆ *Step-by-Stepparenting* by James Eckler
the Rough   ◆ *Love in the Blended Family* by Angela Clubb
                ◆ *The Second Time Around* by Louis Janda and Ellen MacCormack
                ◆ *Strengthening Your Stepfamily* by Elizabeth Einstein and Linda Albert
                ◆ *Step-Fathering* by Mark Rosin

One book on stepmother families made the final ratings in the national survey: *Love in the Blended Family* by Angela Clubb.

One book on blended families was rated: *Step-by-Stepparenting* by James Eckler.

RECOMMENDED

★ ★ ★ ★   *Old Loyalties, New Ties: Therapeutic Strategies with Stepfamilies* (1988) by Emily Visher and John Visher. New York: Brunner/Mazel.

Old Loyalties, New Ties covers a broad range of topics designed to help stepfamilies cope more effectively. Emily Visher, Ph.D. and John Visher, Ph.D., are widely known for their contributions to psychotherapy with stepfamilies. The Vishers are founders of the Stepfamily Association of America and have conducted an extensive number of workshops for mental health professionals and for stepfamilies. They live in Palo Alto, California.

Old Loyalties, New Ties covers a number of therapy strategies for remarried families and describes how they differ from therapy approaches to so-called nuclear families, those never divorced, never reconstituted. Visher and Visher argue that remarried families are not imperfect copies of nuclear families but rather family systems created from the integration of old loyalties and new ties—hence the title of their book.

The authors first provide an overview of American families in the 1980s and discuss theoretical ideas about stepfamilies. Then they outline special therapeutic strategies they believe are most effective with stepfamilies. Intervention strategies described by Visher and Visher include helping stepfamily members gain or enhance their self-esteem, reducing a sense of helplessness, teaching negotiation, and encouraging mutually rewarding dyadic relationships — all designed to achieve greater integration and stability in the stepfamily.

Old Loyalties, New Ties then presents ways in which therapists can help stepfamilies with specific types of problems, among them how to deal with the many changes and losses in their lives; identify realistic belief systems so that expectations are manageable; resolve loyalty conflicts; develop suitable and adequate boundaries; cope with life cycle discrepancies and complexities in stepfamilies; create a more equal distribution of power; deal with issues of closeness and distance. Many case study examples are interspersed throughout the book to illustrate the authors' therapy strategies.

Old Loyalties, New Ties received a 4-star Recommended rating in the national survey. This is a very good book about remarried families, but it was written primarily for a professional clinical audience rather than a self-help audience. Nonetheless, it is well written, and the self-help reader can gain considerable insight into the dynamics of remarried families and which therapy strategies are most effective. Well-respected family systems therapist Virginia Satir commented that *Old Loyalties, New Ties* is a clear, comprehensive, practical guide to understanding and helping stepparents and stepchildren overcome unique adjustment problems. Clifford Sager, clinical professor of psychiatry at Cornell Medical Center in New York City, said that the Vishers have written a remarkable, readable book on stepfamilies that artfully describes the strengths and weaknesses of stepfamilies and how their members can cope effectively.

DIAMONDS IN THE ROUGH

♦ *Step-by-Stepparenting: A Guide to Successful Living with a Blended Family* (1988) by James Eckler. White Hall, VA: Betterway Publications.

Step-by-Stepparenting is about blended families, to which each adult has brought children from a previous marriage. Author James Eckler has such a family. He is a divorced and remarried Baptist minister who lives in Americus, Georgia, where he is director of music and education for his church.

Step-by-Stepparenting reflects both the adjustments that made author James Eckler's blended family a successful one and his years of experience as a minister and pastoral counselor. A wide array of issues that blended stepfamilies must face are covered, including the games stepchildren play, the rights of the stepparent, name changes, the pros and cons of adoption, discipline, stepsibling rivalries, marital communication, grandparents, and dealing with children at different developmental levels (preschool, elementary school, and adolescence).

Step-by-Stepparenting was placed in the Diamonds in the Rough category in the national survey because it was rated positively but by only 20 respondents. The mental health professionals said that this is a good self-help book for blended families. It presents a balanced approach and includes detailed discussions of blended families' stressful experiences, the variation that exists in blended families, and wise strategies for successful living in a blended family.

♦   *Love in the Blended Family: Stepfamilies* (1991) by Angela Clubb. Deerfield Beach, FL: Health Communications.

Love in the Blended Family is about stepmother families, not blended families in the accepted sense of families to which both adults bring children from a previous marriage. Author Angela Clubb is a professional writer who lives in Muskoka, Canada. She has studied counseling at the Adlerian Institute of Toronto and has conducted counseling workshops in career development and self-motivation.

At the beginning of the book, Clubb tells readers that what they are reading is biased because it is written by a stepmother and second wife. Her husband brought two children to the newly formed stepmother family and the Chubbs subsequently had two children of their own. *Love in the Blended Family* is primarily about relationships and experiences in one stepmother family—Clubb's. Clubb occasionally brings in mental health experts' views on stepfamily issues.

Love in the Blended Family made the Diamonds in the Rough category; it was rated positively but by only 13 respondents. Clubb's background as a professional writer clearly shows in the book, which reads in places like a finely tuned novel Several of the mental health professionals said that this is a very good self-help book for stepmothers. Many of the problems and issues Clubb has experienced in her stepmother family are problems and issues any stepmother has to face.

♦   *The Second Time Around: Why Some Second Marriages Fail* (1991) by Louis Janda and Ellen MacCormack. New York: Carol Pub.

The Second Time Around tackles a wide variety of issues in stepfamilies. Author Louis Janda, Ph.D., is a clinical psychologist on the faculty of Old Dominion University in Norfolk, Virginia, where he also has a private practice specializing in relationship issues. Ellen MacCormack is a doctoral student in clinical psychology at the Virginia Consortium for Professional Psychology.

Janda and MacCormack conducted a study of over a hundred people who were in second marriages, which furnished much of the material for *The Second Time Around.* In this book readers learn that a majority of individuals in stepfamilies find the adjustment to a stepfamily to be more difficult than they anticipated. Janda and MacCormack believe that many people have expectations that are too high when they enter a stepfamily. And they say that stepchildren make any second marriage a challenge. While problems in second marriages can sometimes be overwhelming, the authors argue that a significant number of couples find the love, trust, and security they did not experience in their first marriage.

The Second Time Around was placed in the Diamonds in the Rough category in the national survey because it was positively reviewed but by only 10 respondents. The few mental health professionals who knew about this recently published book felt that it included a number of good examples of stepfamily problems and how to solve them effectively.

♦ *Strengthening Your Stepfamily* (1986) by Elizabeth Einstein and Linda Albert. Circle Pines, MN: American Guidance Service.

Strengthening Your Stepfamily covers many different types of stepfamilies. Author Elizabeth Einstein is a well-known writer and lecturer on stepfamilies. Coauthor Linda Albert, Ph.D., is a family counselor and the author of the *Coping with Kids* series.

Strengthening Your Stepfamily is a 133-page book that contains five comprehensive chapters. Chapter 1 describes stepfamily structure and how it is different from previous family structure. The authors discuss common stepfamily myths and common unrealistic expectations. Chapter 2 focuses on the couple relationship and how to communicate more effectively and share feelings. Chapter 3 examines the basic strategies for creating positive relationships between stepparents and stepchildren. Chapter 4 explores children's feelings and behaviors in stepfamilies along with guidelines for helping children cope more effectively. Chapter 5 discusses the developmental process of making a stepfamily function well along with hints for dealing with issues that range from daily routines to holiday celebrations.

Strengthening Your Stepfamily was placed in the Diamonds in the Rough category because it was positively rated but by only 10 respondents. This is an extremely easy-to-read overview of stepfamily problems and ways to solve them. A number of exercises are included, and readers are asked many questions that will stimulate them to think about applying the knowledge they have learned from *Strengthening Your Stepfamily* to their own stepfamilies. Overall, this book provides easy-to-understand, wise advice for anyone associated with a stepfamily.

♦ *Step-Fathering* (1987) by Mark Rosin. New York: Simon & Schuster.

Step-Fathering gives advice to stepfathers about how to cope with life in a stepfather family. Author Mark Rosin was senior editor of *Parents* magazine for five years and is the stepfather of two sons.

This was the first self-help book to describe the stepfather family experience from the stepfather's perspective. Rosin draws on his own personal experiences as a stepfather and in-depth interviews with more than 50 stepfathers to help men cope effectively in a stepfather family. Chapters take stepfathers through such topics as the adjustment involved in becoming a stepfather, the problems of combining families and some possible solutions, how to handle discipline and authority, communication with the wife/mother, partner, dealing with the other father, money matters, adolescent stepchildren, and the rewards of stepfathering.

Step-Fathering, like most of the other books in the stepfamilies category, was placed in the Diamonds in the Rough category; it was positively reviewed but only by 21 respondents. This is a good self-help book for stepfathers. It is well written and includes insightful examples that most stepfathers will be able to relate to. Paul Bohannon, a nationally recognized expert on stepfamilies, said that Mark Rosin's book provides help and encouragement for stepfathers.

CONCLUSIONS

In summary, we recommend:

- For a wide variety of stepfamily circumstances:
    - ★★★★ *Old Loyalties, New Ties* by Emily and John Visher
    - ♦ *The Second Time Around* by Louis Janda and Ellen Mac-Cormack
    - ♦ *Strengthening Your Stepfamily* by Elizabeth Einstein and Linda Albert
- For stepfathers:
    - ♦ *Step-Fathering* by Mark Rosin
- For stepmothers:
    - ♦ *Love in the Blended Family* by Angela Clubb
- For blended families:
    - ♦ *Step-by-Stepparenting* by James Eckler

CHAPTER THIRTY-TWO

Teenagers and Parenting

Growing up has never been easy. It wasn't for the parents of today's adolescents when they were teenagers. It isn't for today's youth. What will become of today's younger generation? It will grow up and start worrying about the younger generation.

In matters of taste and manners, the youth of every generation have seemed radical, unnerving, and different from adults—different in how they behave, the music they enjoy, their hairstyles, and the clothing they choose. Acting out and boundary testing are time-honored ways in which teenagers move toward accepting, rather than rejecting, parental values. Many parents have a difficult time coping with the acting out and boundary testing of their adolescents. They want to know why their adolescents talk back to them and challenge their rules and values. They want to know if they should be authoritarian or permissive with their young charges. They want to know why adolescents have such mercurial moods—happy one moment, sad the next. They want to know the best way to transmit their values to their teenagers. And they want to keep their adolescents from drinking, taking drugs, delinquency, dropping out of school, becoming depressed, getting involved with the wrong peer group, choosing the wrong career, and being sexually permissive.

As parents worry about all of these temptations and treacherous roads adolescents can follow, adolescents have their own concerns. For them, the transition from childhood to adulthood is a time of evaluation, of decision making, of commitment, and of carving out a place in the world. They try on one face after another, trying to find a face of their own. They want to find out who they are, what they are all about, and where they are going in life. They move through a seemingly endless preparation for life. They play furiously at "adult games" but are confined to a society of their own peers. They want their parents to understand them but often feel they don't. And in the end, there are two

| **Teenagers and Parenting** |
| BOOK RATINGS IN THE NATIONAL SURVEY |

Strongly Recommended	★★★★★	*Between Parent and Teenager* by Haim Ginott
Recommended	★★★★	*All Grown Up and No Place to Go* by David Elkind
Diamonds in the Rough	◆	*You and Your Adolescent* by Laurence Steinberg and Ann Levine
Neutral	★★★	*Surviving Adolescence* by Larry Dumont
	★★★	*Tough Love* by Phyllis York, David York, and Ted Wachtel

paradoxical gifts they hope parents will give them—one is roots, the other is wings.

Self-help books on teenagers and parenting fall into two main categories: books that provide an overview of the nature of adolescence and cover a number of different topics, along with parenting recommendations; and books that focus exclusively on parent–adolescent relationships, with recommendations for how to parent more effectively.

In the national survey of self-help books, three books that present an overview of adolescence, educate parents about a number of aspects of adolescence, and include parenting recommendations made the final list of ratings: *All Grown Up and No Place to Go* by David Elkind; *You and Your Adolescent* by Laurence Steinberg and Ann Levine; and *Surviving Adolescence* by Larry Dumont. A fourth book, *Caring for Your Adolescent* by Donald Greydanus, was published too recently to be included in the survey and is profiled in the Worth a Further Look category.

Two books in the national survey focus exclusively on the nature of parent–adolescent relationships: *Between Parent and Teenager* by Haim Ginott and *Tough Love* by Phyllis York, David York, and Ted Wachtel.

STRONGLY RECOMMENDED

★ ★ ★ ★ ★   *Between Parent and Teenager* (1969) by Haim Ginott. New York: Avon.

Despite the fact that *Between Parent and Teenager* is well past adolescence in its own years (it was published in 1969), it continues to be one of the most widely read and recommended books for parents who want to communicate more effectively with their teenagers. In its 25 years of existence, *Between Parent and Teenager* has sold several million copies. Haim Ginott, also author of the Strongly Recommended *Between Parent and Child* (Chapter 10), was a clinical psychologist at Columbia University and conducted workshops in child psychotherapy and parental guidance. Ginott died in 1973.

Ginott describes a number of common-sense solutions and strategies for parents who are having difficulty understanding and communicating with their teenagers. At the same time parents are trying to intervene and "shape up" their teenagers, the teenagers are fighting to be the masters of their own destiny. For Ginott, parents' greatest challenge in the teenage years is to let go when they want to hold on; only by letting go can a peaceful and meaningful coexistence be reached between parent and teenager.

The first part of *Between Parent and Teenager* helps parents to understand the basic nature of the changes that take place during the adolescent years. Then Ginott quickly moves into parenting recommendations for how to handle parent–adolescent conflict, how to engage in healing dialogue, how to reduce criticism, how to deal with anger without insulting the teenager, and how to praise. In later chapters, Ginott tailors parenting recommendations to the adolescent's social life (peers, dating), sex and values, and driving, drinking, and drugs. A final chapter presents a number of wide-ranging examples of how parents and teenagers can learn, grow, and change.

Between Parent and Teenager is easy and enjoyable reading. Throughout the book, Ginott connects with parents through catchy phrases such as "Don't collect thorns" and "Don't step on corns." "Don't collect thorns" shows parents that in areas where they see imperfections in themselves, they often expect perfection on the part of their teenagers. "Don't step on corns" educates parents to be sensitive to the imperfections in adolescents that the adolescents are sensitive about (ranging from zits to dimples); teenagers don't need parents to remind them of these imperfections. Other "Ginottisms" that make sense include "Don't talk in chapters," that is, don't lecture, but rather be a good listener and discuss with rather than talk down to the adolescent; "Accept teenagers' restlessness and discontent," which reminds parents that normal adolescents experience a great deal of uncertainty and difficulty; "Don't put down their wishes and fantasies," which underscores that normal adolescents are idealists and dreamers; and "Don't futurize," which advises parents not to say things like, "You are so immature; you will never grow up." Such statements only make adolescents more hostile toward their parents and widen the parent–adolescent communication gap.

Between Parent and Teenager was the highest-rated book in the teenagers and parenting category, receiving the 5-star Strongly Recommended accolade. Many of Ginott's suggestions for parents will help them understand and communicate more effectively with their teenagers. His nontechnical, easy-to-read writing style and many examples of interchanges between parents and adolescents give parents a sense of what to say (and how and when to say it) when conflict and tension begin to build up. His strategies can make the life of parents and teenagers a kinder, gentler world. *Between Parent and Teenager*'s one negative is its age. The book's age doesn't harm many of Ginott's general suggestions for improved parent–adolescent communication, but it shows in applications of parenting to specific areas of adolescents' lives. For example, there is of course no discussion of AIDS or cocaine, and Ginnott's discussion of programs to help adolescents is seriously dated.

RECOMMENDED

★ ★ ★ ★   *All Grown Up and No Place to Go: Teenagers in Crisis* (1984) by David Elkind. Reading, MA: Addison-Wesley.

Author David Elkind, Ph.D., who also wrote the Strongly Recommended *The Hurried Child* (Chapter 10), has a background in clinical and child psychology. He currently is a professor of child development at Tufts University in Medford, Massachusetts.

Elkind believes that raising teenagers is more difficult than ever. He argues that today's teens are expected to confront adult challenges too early in their development. By being pressured into adult roles too soon, today's youth are all grown up with no place to go—hence the title of his book. Elkind says that the main reason teenagers are pressed into adult roles too early is that parents are more committed to their own self-fulfillment than to their children's. Today's parents are of the "me generation" and are often too quick to accept their teenagers' outward sophistication as a sign of emotional maturity. Teens' emotional needs are also neglected by a school system that is up to date in computer gadgetry but is bankrupt in the personnel, time, and money it takes to respond to adolescents' emotional needs and individual differences. Elkind also believes the media exploit adolescents by appealing to their vulnerability to peer pressure.

All Grown Up and No Place to Go is divided into three main parts. Part I, Needed: A Time to Grow, describes today's teenagers as in the midst of a crisis, informs parents about how adolescents think, outlines the perils of puberty, and provides details about peer shock. Part II, Given:

A Premature Adulthood, analyzes American society and informs parents that adolescents don't have any rites of passage to guide them, how the hodgepodge of American family structures has made adolescence a difficult transition, and how bad secondary schools really are. Part III, Results: Stress and its Aftermath, examines the effects of these family and societal problems on teenagers' identity and ability to cope with stress and other problems. A very helpful appendix provides a list of services available for troubled teenagers.

All Grown Up and No Place to Go received the 4-star Recommended rating in the national survey. Elkind is a well-respected psychologist and provides important recommendations for how parents, teachers, and other adults could communicate and interact more effectively with teenagers. He does an especially good job of presenting parents with an understanding of how adolescents develop and how our society has neglected their needs. Parenting recommendations are scattered through the book, embedded in discussions of different areas of adolescents' lives. In Ginott's *Between Parent and Child*, parents learn specific things to do and say through extensive interchanges and conversations; in Elkind's *All Grown Up and No Place to Go*, parents learn about what adolescents are like and are given general parenting recommendations.

All Grown Up and No Place to Go provides more up-to-date discussion of adolescent problems than Ginott's *Between Parent and Teenager*. Elkind's book also presents more information about the nature of adolescent development in different areas (such as cognitive development, puberty and physical changes, schools, and so on) than *Between Parent and Teenager*, which focuses on parent–adolescent communication. But Ginott's conversational style and focus on parent–adolescent interchanges make his book easier to read than Elkind's.

DIAMONDS IN THE ROUGH

♦ *You and Your Adolescent: A Parent's Guide for Ages 10–20* (1990) by Laurence Steinberg and Ann Levine. New York: Harper Perennial.

You and Your Adolescent presents an excellent overview of many areas of adolescent development and mixes in wise parenting strategies along the way. Steinberg and Levine's book includes more detailed parenting recommendations than Elkind's *All Grown Up and No Place to Go*. But rather than focus exclusively on parent–adolescent communication as Ginott does in *Between Parent and Teenager*. Steinberg and Levine tackle the dual task of giving parents a solid understanding of adolescent development and prescribing parenting strategies. Author Laurence Steinberg, Ph.D., is a leading authority on adolescent development and is a professor of psychology at Temple University in Philadelphia. Ann Levine is a professional writer.

You and Your Adolescent is divided into four main parts. Part I, The Basics, paints the landscape of what makes a good parent, the nature of family communication, and what today's families are like. Part II, The Preteens: From 10 to 13, discusses the nature of physical health and development (puberty, sexual awakening, and drugs), psychological health and development (how young teenagers think and how they feel), and the social world of the young adolescent (peers, dating, middle schools and junior high, and achievement). Part III, The Teens: From 14 to 17, focuses on sex and the high school student, drug and alcohol use in high school, the search for identity, a number of problem behaviors such as delinquency and running away, friends and social life, school, and work. Part IV, Toward Adulthood: From 18 to 20, explores the transition from adolescence to adulthood and how parents can ease this transition for themselves and their offspring.

Two aspects of Steinberg and Levine's book especially set it apart from other self-help books on teenagers and parenting. First, Steinberg and Levine accurately tell readers that some of the horror stories they have heard about adolescents are false. They believe that boundary testing and acting out are time-honored traditions that if not taken to extremes are a normal part of adolescent development. They argue that knowing what to expect is half the battle in making it through life with teenagers. In Steinberg and Levine's view, knowledge is power. Knowing how adolescents develop keeps parents from making any number of mistakes. Second, Steinberg and Levine's book is organized developmentally. Adolescent experts increasingly recognize that the 12-year-old is different in many ways from the 17-year-old. For example, pubertal changes are a major concern in early adolescence but not in late adolescence; career concerns and identity development are more central issues in late adolescence.

Steinberg and Levine's book is more recent than Ginott's or Elkind's books and is not nearly as well known. *You and Your Adolescent* received positive ratings in the national survey of self-help books, but because it was rated too few times, it did not make the 4-star or 5-star classification and was placed in the Diamonds in the Rough category. The mental health experts in the national survey who did know about the book made glowing comments about it. They felt that *You and Your Adolescent* presents a good balance between educating parents about the nature of adolescence and giving insightful parenting recommendations. Several of the experts said that this is the best book available for the parents of adolescents, citing its currency and completeness as superior to Ginott's. In sum, *You and Your Adolescent* is an excellent self-help book for the parents of teenagers and deserves more recognition than it has received.

NEUTRAL

★ ★ ★   *Surviving Adolescence: Helping Your Child through the Struggle* (1991) by Larry Dumont. New York: Villard Books.

Surviving Adolescence presents a general overview of adolescent problems and disorders, along with parenting recommendations. Larry Dumont, M.D., is a psychiatrist and a member of the American Academy of Child Psychiatry. He specializes in the treatment of adolescent depression and is director of an adolescent treatment unit at a hospital.

Surviving Adolescence is especially geared toward educating parents about the early-warning signs of adolescent problems and disorders ranging from substance abuse and eating disorders to learning disabilities, depression, and suicidal behavior. In addition, Dumont describes a number of treatment strategies for troubled teens, including in- and out-patient hospital sessions, psychiatric counseling, group therapy, dynamic psychotherapy, behavioral therapy, and drug therapy. The author spends considerable time explaining to parents how to make a decision about whether or not to hospitalize their adolescent.

Surviving Adolescence received a 3-star Neutral rating in the national survey. Several of the mental health professionals said that Dumont's book is especially good for helping to make a decision about hospitalizing a teenager with a serious behavioral problem. They also commented that *Surviving Adolescence* provides excellent coverage of a number of adolescent disorders. Critics argued that *Surviving Adolescence* may cause some parents to overreact to adolescent misbehaviors that are not serious but rather part of the normal course of adolescent development.

★ ★ ★   *Tough Love: How Parents Can Deal with Drug Abuse* (1982) by Phyllis York, David York, and Ted Wachtel. New York: Bantam.

Tough Love, like Ginott's *Between Parent and Teenager*, focuses almost exclusively on the nature of parent–adolescent communication. Authors Phyllis York, David York, and Ted Wachtel are the founders of the national Toughlove movement. Toughlove is a self-help movement that now has over a thousand groups in the United States and Canada.

Tough Love squarely places the blame for adolescents' problems on the adolescents, not the parents. The book communicates that many parents are victimized by the guilt caused by their teenagers' behavior. According to the authors, many parents are too hard on themselves instead of on the teenager and the adolescent peer group when their adolescent takes drugs, fails at school, engages in promiscuous sex, commits delinquent acts, and many other negative behaviors. *Tough Love* teaches parents how to face crises, take stands, demand cooperation, and meet challenges by getting tough with teenagers. Although tough love may in the short run cause the gulf between parents and teenagers to widen, in the long run it is the only way the teenager will develop maturity, according to tough love advocates.

Tough Love barely received a 3-star Neutral rating in the national survey of self-help books. Most of the mental health experts in the national survey preferred the gentler, more balanced approach of Ginott, Elkind, and Steinberg and Levine, to the harsh approach of *Tough Love.* The testimony of some parents and their teenagers indicates that the tough love approach has worked for them, but, no research has been conducted to document the success or failure of tough love. According to the mental health critics, one of the problems with approaches such as tough love is that you hear about only its successes, not its failures. Another problem is that many parents exaggerate their teenagers' problems, viewing normal behaviors as abnormal ones. Not understanding the nature of how adolescents develop, parents who adopt a tough love approach when it is not needed may unnecessarily drive teenagers away from them. Most adolescent experts recommend a combination of parental involvement, give-and-take discussion, and warmth rather than the punitive approach of tough love.

WORTH A FURTHER LOOK

◑ ◑   *Caring for Your Adolescent: Ages 12 to 21* (1991) edited by Donald Greydanus. New York: Bantam.

This book was published too recently to have been included in the national survey. *Caring for Your Adolescent* was edited by distinguished pediatrician Donald Greydanus, and it brings together more than 30 experts on adolescent medicine who share their insights about helping adolescents successfully make the long journey from childhood to adulthood. *Caring for Your Adolescent* falls into the same category as Elkind's and Steinberg and Levine's books: It provides an extensive overview of adolescent development for parents along with prescriptions for better parenting.

Greydanus's book is divided into seven main sections: (1) Parenting an Adolescent, (2) Physical Growth, (3) Psychological Development (including communication problems, drugs, suicide, and death), (4) Sexual Growth, (5) Social Growth (peers, friends, and dating), (6) Education, and (7) Care and Feeding of Adolescents (nutrition and eating disorders, exercise, and chronically ill teenagers).

Caring for Your Adolescent is at its best when describing the physical and medical aspects of adolescence. The final section—The Care and Feeding of Adolescents—is especially good, with details about such topics as sports, exercise, gynecological problems, and medical disorders that are not found in any of the other books in this section.

CONCLUSIONS

In summary, we recommend:

- On improving parent–adolescent relationships:

  ★★★★★ *Between Parent and Teenager* by Haim Ginott

- On the nature of adolescence and how adolescents develop, accompanied by recommendations for parenting:

  ★★★★ *All Grown Up and No Place to Go* by David Elkind

  ◆ *You and Your Adolescent* by Laurence Steinberg and Ann Levine

- A broad overview of adolescence from a medical perspective:

  ◗◗ *Caring for Your Adolescent,* edited by Donald Greydanus

CHAPTER THIRTY-THREE

Women's Issues

Many feminists believe that historically, psychology and mental health professionals have portrayed human behavior and well-being with male-dominant themes. They also believe that sexism is still rampant in society and that women continue to be discriminated against in the workplace, in politics, at home, in therapy, and in self-help books.

Critics argue that self-help books in general have perpetuated and continue to perpetuate many stereotypes and myths harmful to women. What are some of these stereotypes and myths? We can journey through the chapters of *The Authoritative Guide to Self-Help Books* and find books that characterize women as having dysfunctional profiles, codependency as a woman's disease, some addictions as women's afflictions (eating disorders, for example) or inflicted by women's problems, mothers as responsible for children's problems and blamed for their adult children's problems. We can find books that overdramatize sex differences, with the differences invariably favoring men (women are described as overly invested in romantic love, dependent on others, less competent than males, and incapable of controlling their emotions).

Few authors bother to write about the positive aspects of being female and fewer still give credence or respectability to many of the daily tasks and responsibilities women have traditionally performed and continue to manage. The best books on women's issues address such concerns and try to help women become aware that what have been labeled as weaknesses or character defects in the past are actually strengths that should be nurtured, rewarded, and cherished, not only by women but by the male-dominated society.

Many books in other categories address women's issues and provide self-help advice for women. We recommend in other chapters a number of excellent self-help books on specific aspects of women's lives, such

Women's Issues	
BOOK RATINGS IN THE NATIONAL SURVEY	

Diamonds in the Rough	◆ *The Second Shift* by Arlie Hochschild
	◆ *Too Good for Her Own Good* by Claudia Bepko and Jo Ann Krestan
Neutral	★★★ *Backlash* by Susan Faludi
	★★★ *My Mother/Myself* by Nancy Friday
	★★★ *Women, Sex, and Addiction* by Charlotte Kasl
Strongly Not Recommended	† *Secrets about Men Every Woman Should Know* by Barbara DeAngelis

as *The Courage to Heal,* on women's recovery from sexual abuse in childhood (Chapter 2); *The Battered Woman,* on men's abuse of women in close relationships (Chapter 2); *The Assertive Woman,* on how women can stand up for their rights (Chapter 7); *You Just Don't Understand,* on how women and men can learn to communicate more effectively with each other (Chapter 11); *The New Aerobics for Women* on the benefits of exercise for women (Chapter 17); *Infants and Mothers,* on effective maternal child rearing (Chapter 20); *The Dance of Intimacy,* on the role of intimacy in women's lives (Chapter 21); *What to Expect When You're Expecting,* on pregnancy (Chapter 24); *Women and Self-Esteem,* on how women can improve their self-esteem (Chapter 26); and *For Yourself* on women's sexuality (Chapter 30).

In this chapter we evaluate self-help books that address the following topics (some of which overlap with other chapters): women's roles, especially work and parental roles; gender stereotypes, myths, and sex differences/similarities; feminist issues; women's bodies and health; self-esteem; and sexuality.

One book on women's roles, especially work and parental roles was rated: *The Second Shift* by Arlie Hochschild.

No books on gender stereotypes, myths, and sex differences/similarities were rated. However, *The Mismeasure of Women* by Carol Tavris is evaluated in the Worth a Further Look section.

One book on feminist issues was rated: *Backlash* by Susan Faludi.

No books that focus on women's bodies and health made the final ratings, but *Body Traps* by Judith Rodin and *The New Our Bodies, Ourselves* by the Boston Women's Health Book Collective are profiled in Worth a Further Look.

One book on women and self-esteem was rated: *Too Good for Her Own Good* by Claudia Bepko and Jo-Ann Krestan.

And three books on women and sexuality were rated: *My Mother/Myself* by Nancy Friday, *Women, Sex, and Addiction* by Charlotte Kasl, and *Secrets About Men Every Woman Should Know* by Barbara DeAngelis.

DIAMONDS IN THE ROUGH

◆ *The Second Shift* (1989) by Arlie Hochschild. New York: Viking.

The Second Shift focuses on the inequality of gender roles in two-career couples with children. Arlie Hochschild, Ph.D., is a professor of sociology at the University of California at Berkeley.

Hochschild conducted extensive interviews and home observations of 50 two-career couples with children under the age of 6 to discover how they allotted their time and responsibility to careers, child rearing, and household chores. Not surprisingly, she found that women did the bulk of the child care and housework in addition to holding down a full-time job outside the home. Indeed, national surveys find that women work 15 hours longer than men do each week. Hochschild labels married couples as traditional (the husband works and the wife stays at home), transitional (both work, and he does less than she thinks he should around the house), or egalitarian (both spend equal time on work and home responsibilities). In her study, all the families were in the last two categories and the majority were transitional.

Hochschild believes that men and women use gender strategies that are based on deep-seated emotional beliefs about manhood and womanhood as they try to define how to juggle jobs, child rearing, and household responsibilities. She believes that their solutions often prevent progress. The married partners may not even be aware that they are using gender strategies. One of Hochschild's main goals in *The Second Shift* is to bring these gender strategies out into the open so that married couples can discuss and benefit from them.

The author outlines several solutions to the gender trap in working women's lives: cultivation of respect for "women's work"; profamily legislation to equalize women's wages and provide family leave for both sexes; tax breaks to companies who allow job sharing and flextime; government encouragement of child care supplied by students or the elderly; support networks formed by neighbors; modification of working hours of parents with small children; tax-subsidized affordable housing; and traveling day-care vans.

The Second Shift was placed in the Diamonds in the Rough Category based on the mental health professionals ratings in the national survey (it received a positive rating but was evaluated by only 28 respondents). What separates *The Second Shift* from the standard feminist fare is the texture of the reporting and the subtlety of the insights. One male critic said that this book is prickly and irritating but distressingly reasonable. Herbert Gans, a distinguished sociologist at Columbia University, said that the book is thought provoking, insightful, and highly readable. Well-known feminist Betty Friedan commented that the book represents a brilliant analysis of the burden on today's working woman and, further, that every woman should give it to every man.

◆ *Too Good for Her Own Good: Breaking Free from the Burden of Female Responsibility* (1990) by Claudia Bepko and Jo-Ann Krestan. New York: Harper & Row.

Too Good for Her Own Good describes the kind of low self-esteem in women that results from feeling that they are "not good enough." Authors Claudia Bepko and Jo-Ann Krestan are family therapists who specialize in working with clients in the area of gender roles and addiction. They also are members of the editorial board of *The Journal of Feminist Family Therapy* and are codirectors of Family Therapy Associates in Maine.

Too Good for Her Own Good discusses the "Goodness Code" that requires women to be attractive, ladylike (low-keyed, controlled), unselfish and of service to others, the moving force in making relationships work, and competent—all without complaining. The authors argue that goodness comes to most women almost instinctively; they feel they must be competent in virtually everything they do while remaining responsible for the happiness of others around them. Yet no matter how hard women work to please others, they often feel inadequate, because part of being good is knowing that they are never good enough. The results: Far too many women have a low self-image, feel insecure, and are overworked.

The authors discuss how to break free from all of this goodness by changing the balance of various factors. They think women should be responsible for their own happiness and learn about the type of goodness that will ultimately prove to be satisfying to them. They also encourage women to leave the self-sacrifice syndrome. And they think female goodness should be redefined as being comfortable (which puts feeling good ahead of looking good), being honest about feelings, being responsive, being nurturant, and being able to set limits on fulfilling obligations to others and meeting others' expectations. A number of case histories are described to buttress the authors' points.

Too Good for Your Own Good was placed in the Diamonds in the

Rough category; it was positively rated but by only 16 respondents. The book's female enthusiasts said that many women with low self-esteem who have lived their lives in the service of others while not paying enough attention to their own needs and balancing different dimensions of their lives will find themselves described on almost every page of this book.

NEUTRAL

★ ★ ★   *Backlash: The Undeclared War against American Women* (1991) by Susan Faludi. New York: Crown.

Backlash concerns the way women and feminism are portrayed by the media. Author Susan Faludi is a Pulitzer Prize-winning reporter for *The Wall Street Journal*. She also has written for the *San Jose Mercury News*, *Ms.*, and *Mother Jones*.

The subtitle of *Backlash* is *The Undeclared War against American Women*. Faludi uncovers a growing backlash against women and feminism in the United States. This backlash has hurt women in two main ways, first, by convincing women that their feelings of dissatisfaction and distress are the result of too much feminism and independence and second, by simultaneously undermining the minimal progress that women have made at work, in politics, and in their own minds.

She cites the (in)famous "Harvard–Yale" study, which in 1988 reported that a single, college-educated woman over the age of 30 has only a 20% chance of ever getting married, and that by time she is 40, she will have only a 1.3% chance. Faludi says that the "man shortage" is just one of the myths propagated by the media (another is the "infertility epidemic") and finds evidence of other "antifeminist" orientations in movies, television, and fashion advertising. The result is that feminism went on a backslide in the 1980s and early 1990s. In her attacks on the reasons for the backslide, she takes on Robert Bly and his male archetype and all-male workshops, as well as feminist thinkers such as Betty Friedan, Germaine Greer, and others.

Backlash received a 3-star Neutral rating in the national survey. It was published shortly before the national survey but was still well enough known to be evaluated by 47 respondents. The book was a best seller when it was published, but it has been given mixed reviews. Some of the book's supporters say that it makes a brilliantly argued case for feminist backlash in the media. They also found the book wholly convincing and alarming. Famous black author Alice Walker (*The Color Purple*) said that the backlash Faludi talks about is very real and that the book can help women continue their unfinished struggle. Deborah Rhode, professor of law at Stanford University, commented that *Backlash* is a crucial book on a crucial subject that contains masterful insights. However, several critics argue that *Backlash* is just another eighties-type bashing book that, while well-written and scholarly, makes stick-figure stereotypes of relationships between women and men. One critic said that what Faludi wanted to say could have been said in a few words in a pamphlet, instead of being repeated over and over again in a lengthy book. Another critic commented that the book is politically correct in the worst sense because it feeds the "woman as victim" theme. Clearly, *Backlash* is a controversial book about which people hardly feel neutral, yet "Neutral" is just the rating it received in the national survey; the evaluators who rated it had strong feelings about it both ways which canceled each other out..

★ ★ ★   *My Mother/Myself* (1977) by Nancy Friday. New York: Delacorte Press.

My Mother/Myself is about women's sexuality. Author Nancy Friday is a writer who also is the author of two other best-selling books—*My Secret Garden* (about women's sexual fantasies) and its sequel, *Forbidden Flowers.*

My Mother/Myself was based on more than 200 interviews with women (most were mothers and of course all were daughters) as well as consultations with a number of mental health experts. Its basic premise is psychoanalytic in nature: daughters identify with their mother while becoming the mother's rival, and the influence of this complex relationship is felt throughout a daughter's life. Friday also describes conflicting messages daughters receive from their mothers about their body and sexuality, as well as unconscious introjection of the mothers' bad qualities.

The author describes the mother–daughter relationship in early childhood, then moves through a number of women's milestones, such as loss of virginity and menopause. One of her basic themes is that society's denial of women's sexuality often conflicts with their role as mothers. Friday explores the cultural signals that stifle young girls' sexual interests and encourage mothers to muffle their own sexuality.

My Mother/Myself received a 3-star Neutral rating in the national survey. It was easily the most widely rated book in the Women's Issues category, evaluated by 187 respondents. The book's supporters said that it broke new ground when it was published in the late 1970s by providing a probing, insightful analysis of mother–daughter relationships and society's negative portrayal of women's sexuality. They also thought that

Friday accurately paints the emotional dynamics that cause problems to develop for girls. However, critics argued that Friday overdramatizes and stereotypes the body inferiority and sexual difficulties of women.

★ ★ ★   *Women, Sex, and Addiction* (1989) by Charlotte Kasl. New York: Ticknor & Fields.

Women, Sex, and Addiction is about women's sexuality, especially sex addiction. Charlotte Kasl, Ph.D., is a psychotherapist who practices in Minneapolis, Minnesota. She specializes in counseling survivors of child abuse and addicted women.

Women, Sex, and Addiction is based on Kasl's work with two organizations: Sex Addicts Anonymous, a support group modeled after Alcoholics Anonymous, and Codependents of Sex Addicts, mainly composed of women who allow themselves to be sexually used to preserve a relationship. Kasl explores the roots of women's sexual addiction and explains the link between sexual addiction/codependency and sexual abuse, all of which she says are related to a misguided search for security and spiritual fulfillment. Case histories are interwoven through the book to buttress the author's points.

Women, Sex, and Addiction received a 3-star Neutral rating in the national survey and was not very far from the lower 2-star Not Recommended rating. Some of the book's critics said that the author stereotypes women, paints them too broadly as incompetent, and does not espouse the strategies for change that many mainstream mental health experts recommend.

STRONGLY NOT RECOMMENDED

†   *Secrets about Men Every Woman Should Know* (1990) by Barbara DeAngelis. New York: Delacorte Press.

Secrets about Men Every Woman Should Know is about women's sexuality. Author Barbara DeAngelis, Ph.D., is the executive director of a counseling firm called the Los Angeles Personal Growth Center. She also wrote *How to Make Love All of the Time* and is a regular contributor to a number of magazines, such as *Cosmopolitan* and *McCall's*. She currently hosts her own talk show in Los Angeles.

This book claims to be an instruction manual about men. It has three main sections—Secrets about How Women Relate to Men; Secrets about Men; and Secrets about Men and Women Together. Each of the sections is divided into chapters with catchy titles and embellished lists, such as "The Six Biggest Mistakes Women Make with Men." In each case DeAngelis gives the lists and then evaluates the items on them—for example, Mistake 1 is that women act like mothers and treat men like children. She provides descriptions of what women do, why women do it, how the behavior can destroy a relationship, how to stop it, and a testimonial on how the author or someone she knows has stopped the behavior.

Secrets about Men Every Woman Should Know received a negative average rating in the national survey, placing it in the Strongly Not Recommended category. Critics didn't like the manipulation orientation of the book, the importance attached to a woman's appearance, and the calculated strategies of how to get and keep a man. Some useful relationship advice unfortunately is overshadowed by the book's flaws.

WORTH A FURTHER LOOK

◑ ◑   *The Mismeasure of Women* (1992) by Carol Tavris. New York: Simon & Schuster.

The Mismeasure of Women explores the stereotyping of women and similarities and differences between women and men. Author Carol Tavris, Ph.D., is a social psychologist, writer, and lecturer; she lives in Los Angeles. Tavris is the coauthor of a widely adopted college textbook on introductory psychology—*Psychology*—and she also wrote *Anger: The Misunderstood Emotion*, which received a 5-star Strongly Recommended rating in the national survey (Chapter 6).

The Mismeasure of Women explores the following eight main issues:

- Why women are not inferior to men
- Why women are not superior to men
- Premenstrual syndrome, postmenstrual syndrome, and other normal "diseases"
- Why women are "sick" but men have problems
- Fables of female sexuality
- How women cornered the love market
- Speaking of gender—the darkened eye restored

These are the subtitles Tavris uses for the chapters in her book.

Tavris believes that no matter how hard women try, they can't measure up. They are criticized for being too female or not female enough, but they are always judged and mismeasured by how well they fit into a male world. *The Mismeasure of Women* contains a thorough review of research that documents how women continue to be ignored, mis-represented, and even harmed by the still male-dominated health professions, which base their standards of normality on male anatomy, physiology, and psychology. Whether in the study of heart disease, where the effect of female hormones on cholesterol is ignored, or in the study of brain structure, where unsubstantiated research is used to explain the supposed inferiority of female spatial and reasoning skills, Tavris argues that women are continually evaluated from a male vantage point.

Tavris believes that more evidence exists for similarities between the sexes than for differences between them. She does not accept male superiority or female superiority. The author refutes feminists who say that women are more empathic than men, and she rejects the notion that women are less sexual. Tavris explores how society "pathologizes" women through psychiatric diagnoses, sexist divorce rulings, and images of women as moody, self-defeating, and unstable. In her view, if women appear to be different, it is because of the roles they have been assigned. By accepting labels such as PMS or self-defeating personality disorder, women can understand and rationalize behavior without threatening a social system that dislikes angry women.

The Mismeasure of Women was published after the national survey was conducted. This is an excellent analysis of gender stereotyping, similarities and differences between the sexes, and how women should be measured by their own standards, not men's. It is well-documented and captivating, presenting a witty feminist portrayal of women's issues and dilemmas and what can be done about them. Bonnie Strickland, former president of the American Psychological Association, said that in this book Tavris cuts through the myths and misunderstandings about women and arrives at some simple but stunning insights about the nature of how women and men relate to each other. Highly respected psychotherapist and self-help book author Harriet Lerner commented that *The Mismeasure of Women* is a splendid, original, provocative book that will change the way we think about the sexes.

◐◐ *Body Traps* (1992) by Judith Rodin. New York: William Morrow.

Body Traps focuses on the destructive standards society has established for women's perceptions of their bodies and how women can free themselves from these "body traps." Judith Rodin, Ph.D., is a professor of psychology and psychiatry at Yale University. She is also the chair of the MacArthur Foundation Research Network for Studies of Health and Behavior. Rodin has published more than 200 research articles and academic books on perceived control of behavior, women's health, eating disorders, and obesity.

Rodin believes that we have become a nation of appearance junkies and fitness zealots. Women spend more on beauty and fitness aids than on social services and education! She argues that good looks, appearance, and fitness have become the measures women use to evaluate their self-worth. This trend has gone so far that one deviation in diet often spells the difference between confidence and despair.

Rodin describes a number of different body traps women can fall into that cause anguish over appearance, anxiety over whether enough is being done about it, and shame over worrying about it:

1. *The Vanity Trap.* Women are accused of and feel themselves to be vain and conceited if they are concerned about how they look.
2. *The Shame Trap.* Women worry about how they look and that makes them feel guilty and ashamed.
3. *The Competition Trap.* Physical attractiveness and weight are still the main arenas in which women are encouraged to compare themselves with each other; the beauty contest is still going strong.
4. *The Food Trap.* What women eat has taken on moral overtones; they feel corresponding virtuous or guilty depending on what the consume.
5. *The Dieting Rituals Trap.* Dieting has become a ritual that entails far more than losing weight; dieting holds the promise of rejuvenation and new beginnings, but it is not equally easy for all individuals.
6. *The Fitness Trap.* The benefits of exercise are real, but, as with most areas of life, too much of a good thing ceases to be good; exercise also has acquired moral overtones.
7. *The Success Trap.* Success at weight control and looking good is the brass ring, the final reward for many people, yet achieving weight control does not always produce joy—sometimes it even brings unhappiness.

Rodin dispenses a number of recommendations for avoiding these body traps and developing more positive ways for women to relate to themselves as they are.

Body Traps was published after the national survey was conducted. The book is a thoughtful, penetrating look at society's preoccupation with women's appearance and the unrealistic expectations and harmful effects the preoccupation has produced. *Body Traps* is informative and well-written, and it is a very helpful guide to what women's bodies mean to them. Well-known self-help author Maggie Scarf commented that *Body Traps* is intelligent, absorbing, and thoroughly liberating for women. Kelly Brownell, codirector of the Yale Center for Eating and Weight Disorders, commented that this book is a treasure chest of information about what women's bodies mean to them.

◖ ◗ *The New Our Bodies, Ourselves* (rev. ed., 1984) by the Boston Women's Health Book Collective. New York: Simon & Schuster.

The New Our Bodies, Ourselves is subtitled *A Book By and For Women;* it is a guide to women's bodies and health issues. The Boston Women's Health Book Collective is a feminist group that had the modest goal of compiling a list of good doctors to whom they could refer women; ultimately their interests led to developing this broader volume on women's bodies and health.

The topics of *The New Our Bodies, Ourselves* include how women can take care of themselves, their relationships and sexuality, how to control their fertility, childbearing, how to cope with growing older and aging, some common and uncommon medical and health problems, and how to deal effectively with the medical system. Exercise, environmental and occupational hazards, and political organizing are also discussed. This edition contains less emphasis on medical issues and more on what women can do for themselves and for each other than previous editions.

The New Our Bodies, Ourselves was very positively rated in the national survey but by only 7 repondents. This book played an important role in revolutionizing the women's health movement. In many places the book dispenses nonjudgmental advice ("You have a right to remain inactive if you choose"), but strong feminist views permeate the book.

CONCLUSIONS

In summary, we recommend:

- On women's work and parenting roles:
    - ◆ *The Second Shift* by Arlie Hochschild

- On gender stereotypes, myths, and sex differences/similarities:
    - ◖◗ *The Mismeasure of Women* by Carol Tavris

- On women's bodies and health and the self-image traps women can fall into:
    - ◖◗ *Body Traps* by Judith Rodin

- On low self-esteem in women and how to improve it:
    - ◆ *Too Good for Her Own Good* by Claudia Bepko and Jo-Ann Krestan

CHAPTER THIRTY-FOUR

The Twenty-Five Best
Self-Help Books

In Chapters 2–33 we presented the self-help books the mental health professionals in the national survey thought were the best in each of 32 different categories—from abuse and recovery to women's issues. Which self-help books did the mental health experts think were the best regardless of category? What were their choices of the best 25 self-help books overall?

To be eligible for the top 25 list, a self-help book had to be rated by a minimum of 75 mental health professionals in the national survey. Following are the 25 books, listed in order of their average ratings. All are 5-star Strongly Recommended books.

1. *The Courage to Heal* by Ellen Bass and Laura Davis (Chapter 2, Abuse and Recovery)

This is an outstanding self-help book on a very specific topic: women's recovery from sexual abuse as children. Any woman who knows she was sexually abused as a child or has an inkling that she might have been should read this book. The 1992 edition lists a number of resources for women survivors of child sexual abuse. While *The Courage to Heal* carefully leads women to become aware of a painful past, it rings with hope and helps them to heal and recover.

2. *Feeling Good* by David Burns (Chapter 14, Depression)

Feeling Good presents a cognitive therapy approach to coping with depression. Burns argues that the key to coping with depression is to identify and restructure faulty negative thinking. The book includes a number of self-assessments, self-help forms, and charts to help people cope with depression. Burns's enthusiasm gives readers the confidence to try out a number of cognitive therapy techniques. This is an excellent self-help book for learning how to cope more effectively with depression.

3. *Infants and Mothers* by T. Berry Brazelton (Chapter 21, Infant Development and Parenting)

Infants and Mothers gives parents, especially mothers, advice on how to respond to three different types of babies—active, average, and quiet—in their first year of life. Brazelton helps parents to become sensitive observers of and responders to their infant.

4. *What Every Baby Knows* by T. Berry Brazelton (Chapter 21, Infant Development and Parenting)

In *What Every Baby Knows*, Brazelton presents in-depth analyses of five families and their child-rearing concerns, such as how to handle crying, how to discipline, how to deal with the infant's fears, sibling rivalry, and the child's developing sense of self. This book covers a broader range of children's ages than *Infants and Mothers*, which focuses exclusively on the first year of life. Brazelton does a superb job of helping parents handle a host of child problems that may arise.

5. *Dr. Spock's Baby and Child Care* by Benjamin Spock and Michael Rothenberg (Chapter 21, Infant Development and Parenting)

Dr. Spock's Baby and Child Care is one of the classics in the self-help literature. It was first published in 1945. The most recent edition (1985) was written by Spock and Michael Rothenberg, a pediatrician and child psychiatrist. This book presents a broad approach to infant and child care, with special attention given to health and potential medical problems. The book is well-organized and serves as a handy guide for parents when they run into a health or medical problem with their infant or child. The child-rearing and discipline advice have received mixed reviews, but as a comprehensive guide to the health care of infants and children, the book is outstanding.

6. *How to Survive the Loss of a Love* by Melba Colgrove, Harold Bloomfield, and Peter McWilliams (Chapter 13, Death, Dying, and Grief)

How to Survive the Loss of a Love provides messages about how to cope with the loss of a loved one, through death or otherwise. Poetry, common sense, and psychological advice are interwoven through more than 100 very brief topics that include understanding loss, surviving, healing, and growing. This is an excellent self-help book for readers to turn to when they experience a loss of a loved one.

7. *To Listen to a Child* by T. Berry Brazelton (Chapter 10, Child Development and Parenting)

To Listen to a Child addresses development throughout the childhood years. The focus is primarily on problematic events that arise in children's lives—fears, sleeping problems (including bedwetting), and stomachaches, for example—and how parents should respond to them. Brazelton assures parents that it is only when they let their own anxieties interfere that these problems become chronic and guilt-laden. This is an excellent guide for parents when children's problems arise.

8. *The Boys and Girls Book about Divorce* by Richard Gardner (Chapter 16, Divorce)

This book is written for children to help them cope with their parents' separation and divorce. It is appropriate for children of average intelligence who are 10 years of age or older. Gardner talks directly to children about their feelings after the divorce, who is to blame, fear of being left alone, and much more. This is a superb resource for helping children cope with the stress of their family's breakup.

9. *The Dance of Anger* by Harriet Lerner (Chapter 6, Anger)

The Dance of Anger is written mainly for women to help them cope more effectively with their anger and the anger of others. Lerner tells women about which styles of coping don't work in the long run and which ones do. This is a careful, compassionate exploration of anger in relationships and can help women turn anger into a constructive force that can reshape their lives in positive ways.

10. *The Feeling Good Handbook* by David Burns (Chapter 14, Depression)

This is Burns's sequel to *Feeling Good*, the second-highest-rated book in the national survey. *The Feeling Good Handbook* covers a wider array of problems (anxiety and relationships as well as depression), includes daily logs to fill out, and describes more recent developments in cognitive therapy. *The Feeling Good Handbook* is an excellent self-help book for coping effectively with depression, anxiety, and relationship problems.

11. *Toddlers and Parents* by T. Berry Brazelton
(Chapter 10, Child Development and Parenting)

This is Brazelton's fourth book on the top 25 list. It advises parents on how to handle typical problems that arise during the toddler years—at 1 year, 15 months, 18 months, 2 years, and 30 months. Brazelton not only provides parents with a helpful guide to coping with toddler problems but also helps them develop a sense of delight in the struggles and triumphs their toddler is experiencing.

12. *Your Perfect Right* by Robert Alberti and Michael Emmons
(Chapter 8, Assertiveness)

Your Perfect Right presents a number of detailed strategies to help people become more assertive. Step-by-step procedures help individuals get started and get enough confidence to stand up for their rights. Not only can this book help nonassertive people become more assertive, it also can help aggressive people realize that they should respect the rights of others and tone down their hostilities.

13. *Between Parent and Teenager* by Haim Ginott
(Chapter 32, Teenagers and Parenting)

Between Parent and Teenager helps parents understand and communicate more effectively with their teenagers. Ginott gives many examples of parent–adolescent interchanges and tells parents specifically what to say to help them get along better with their teenagers. Although more than two decades old, *Between Parent and Teenager* still dispenses sage advice for parents that will help them make their family life kinder and gentler.

14. *The First Three Years of Life* by Burton White
(Chapter 21, Infant Development and Parenting)

White strongly believes that most parents in America have failed to provide an adequate intellectual and social foundation for their children's development, especially between the ages of 8 months and 3 years. White gives in-depth portrayals of infant and toddler development in the first three years of life and provides specific recommendations for how parents should respond to their infants. Along with *Dr. Spock's Baby and Child Care, The First Three Years* is one of the most controversial books on the top 25 list.

15. *What Color Is Your Parachute?* by Richard Bolles
    (Chapter 9, Career Development)

What Color Is Your Parachute? is a comprehensive guide to job-hunting and career-development issues. Bolles is better than any other author at humanizing job hunting. He chatty comments are witty and entertaining and the book is attractively packaged with cartoons, drawings, and many self-administered exercises. An extensive set of appendices provides valuable advice about further readings, workshops, and more.

16. *Between Parent and Child* by Haim Ginott
    (Chapter 10, Child Development and Parenting)

Between Parent and Child provides parents with excellent advice on how to communicate more effectively with their children. Ginott does an especially good job of helping parents become aware of children's feelings that underlie their words and behaviors. Like Ginott's other top 25 book, *Between Parent and Teenager, Between Parent and Child* is extremely easy to read and humorous, and it gives sound advice to parents.

17. *The Relaxation Response* by Herbert Benson
    (Chapter 26, Relaxation, Meditation, and Stress)

The Relaxation Response presents a specific strategy for reducing stress—learning how to relax. Benson dispenses advice on how to attain the Relaxation Response, which he believes helps people to cope effectively with stress and to reduce the probability that they will develop any number of diseases. The Relaxation Response is a simple, effective, self-administered healing technique that many mental health professionals believe works to calm people, reduce stress, and improve health.

18. *The New Aerobics* by Kenneth Cooper
    (Chapter 18, Exercise)

The New Aerobics is the updated version of Kenneth Cooper's *Aerobics,* both of which offer Cooper's age-adjusted recommendations for aerobic exercise. Cooper developed the concept of aerobic exercise, and in *The New Aerobics* he outlines a fitness program that will reap physical and psychological benefits for people who are not in excellent shape. Another Cooper book that presents the same competent message is *The Aerobics Program for Well-Being.* And women can significantly benefit from *The New Aerobics for Women* by Cooper and his wife Mildred. All of Cooper's books are well-written and well-researched and can help most people develop a healthier life style.

19. *Learned Optimism* by Martin Seligman
    (Chapter 24, Positive Thinking and Self-Talk)

Seligman's positive message is that because pessimism is learned it can be unlearned. He shows people how to develop a more optimistic style and be happier and healthier for it. This is a good book for a pessimist who has unsuccessfully tried to become more optimistic. Seligman's book is one of the new breed of positive thinking books that is based on psychological research rather than on spiritual beliefs or cheerleading.

20. *Man's Search for Meaning* by Victor Frankl
    (Chapter 28, Self-Fulfillment and Happiness)

This book provides advice on how to find self-fulfillment in life. Frankl believes that it is important for people to recognize that each individual is unique and that life is finite. He leads the reader on a journey that examines the certainty of death, in the belief that this exploration will add meaning to life. *Man's Search for Meaning* challenges the reader to think about what life is all about.

21. *Children: The Challenge* by Rudolph Dreikurs
    (Chapter 10, Child Development and Parenting)

Dreikurs tells parents how to discipline children more effectively, how to understand their children, and how to meet their emotional and psychological needs. He believes that the main reason children misbehave is that they become discouraged. He teaches parents how to be loving and firm without being hostile and dominating. This book provides very good advice on disciplining children.

22. *You Just Don't Understand* by Deborah Tannen
    (Chapter 12, Communication)

Tannen shows that friction between women and men in conversation often develops because as girls and boys they were brought up in two virtually distinct gender worlds and continue to live in those different worlds. She says that women like to engage in rapport talk, men in report talk. Tannen believes that women and men can communicate more effectively with each other and get along better by understanding differences in women's and men's communication styles. This is an excellent self-help book on relationships and communication between women and men.

23. *The Dance of Intimacy* by Harriet Lerner
(Chapter 22, Love and Intimacy)

This is Harriet Lerner's second book on the top 25 list—*The Dance of Anger* was nineth. *The Dance of Intimacy* is about women's intimate relationships. Lerner believes that a woman's self and relationships with others are derived from longstanding relationships with mothers, fathers, and siblings. She urges women to explore the nature of their family upbringing for clues to current difficulties. This is a wise and compassionate book that can help women understand the complex intertwining of family-of-origin and current close relationships.

24. *Beyond the Relaxation Response* by Herbert Benson
(Chapter 26, Relaxation)

This is Herbert Benson's sequel to *The Relaxation Response,* the seventeenth best self-help book. In *Beyond the Relaxation Response,* Benson says that combining the Relaxation Response with another strategy is more powerful in combatting stress and improving health than the Relaxation Response alone. The other strategy is faith in a healing power either inside or outside yourself.

25. *The Battered Woman* by Lenore Walker
(Chapter 2, Abuse and Recovery)

The Battered Woman is written for women who have been or continue to be abused by their husband or romantic partner. Any woman who has been in an abusive relationship with a man, who continues to be in such a relationship, or who would like to find out if her male partner is a potential abuser, can benefit from this excellent self-help book.

CHAPTER THIRTY-FIVE

Nine Strategies
for Selecting
a Self-Help Book

When you decide to buy a self-help book, you want to get the one that will help you more than any other. You go to a bookstore and begin to look through the books that address your particular problem—maybe addiction and recovery, or communication, or divorce, or dieting and losing weight, or loneliness, or sexuality, or something else. And you wish you had some guidelines to help you pick the best book.

There is no magic key to the self-help book kingdom, but several strategies can help you select the best book for you and avoid the "clunkers" that are not going to benefit you or anyone else who reads them. By analyzing the mental health experts' comments in the national survey, by surveying the increasing number of articles on self-books in mental health journals, and by brainstorming ourselves, we came up with nine strategies for selecting a good self-help book. In the topic chapters, these strategies were often used to rate the books.

1. Don't select a self-help book because of its cover,
   its title, or its glitzy advertising campaign, or
   because it is this year's so-called "breakthrough" book.

The old saying "You can't tell a book by its cover" probably applies to self-help books more than any other type of book. The self-help book business has become big business. Publishers spend huge sums of money to create splashy covers with sensational titles and to put together glitzy, Madison Avenue advertising campaigns. They describe each year's new crop of self-help books as "phenomenal breakthroughs" in understanding life's problems. Some good self-help books do have fancy covers and catchy titles, but so do the bad ones. The same is true with expensive advertisements—the bad books are just as likely to have huge advertising outlays as the good books.

One category with especially flashy titles, huge advertising outlays, good fodder for talk shows, and an abundance of new books virtually every year is love, intimacy, and marriage. In love, intimacy, and marriage, *What Every Woman Should Know about Men, Women Men Love, Women Men Leave, Men Who Hate Women and the Women Who Love Them,* and *Loving Each Other* all were national best sellers, had huge advertising budgets, and have very catchy titles. And all received Not Recommended or Strongly Not Recommended ratings in the national survey. Based on what you hear on talk shows, the books' covers, and their advertising, there isn't any way people can sort through titles in this category and tell that these books aren't good self-help books and that Harriet Lerner's *The Dance of Intimacy,* Harville Hendrix's *Getting the Love You Want,* and Maggie Scarf's *Intimate Partners* are.

Publishers and bookstores influence your self-help book purchasing habits by how many books they display and where the books are located. However, this year's top-selling book that you see stacked from floor to ceiling often finds its way to next year's wastebasket. Or something worse happens: Lavish advertising, expensive promotional campaigns, and support by national book chains enable some bad self-help books to sell extremely well. With no guidelines, consumers don't know these books are bad. It is not unusual for bookstores to have only one or two copies of some of the best self-help books hidden on the bottom shelves or to not carry them at all. As we evaluated the different categories of books, we told you about some of these gems that have withstood the test of time. Of course, they are not among the books in this year's advertising blitz. *The Boys and Girls Book about Divorce* by Richard Gardner, *Between Parent and Teenager* by Haim Ginott, *The New Aerobics* by Kenneth Cooper, *Man's Search for Meaning* by Victor Frankl, and *The Battered Woman* by Lenore Walker all made the top 25 list of self-help books, yet you won't find them advertised or promoted in bookstores; indeed, Frankl's book has virtually disappeared from bookstores. But all of them have been around for decades and are excellent books.

In sum, don't let the publisher or a bookstore chain or a captivating author on a talk show lure you into buying a self-help book. Publishers, bookstore executives, and fast-talking authors on TV and radio talk shows are not the best sources to listen to when making your self-help book choices. Neither are testimonials from talk-show hosts themselves, stars (actresses, actors, sports stars, rock stars, or business executives), or a few individuals who say the book worked for them and that the author is wonderful. What may work for a few people, especially a famous few people, is not necessarily going to work for you.

When one area of self-help books becomes popular, many authors and publishers jump on the bandwagon and quickly pump out books in rapid succession, hoping to cash in on the latest "in" topic or movement. In recent years, codependency, abuse and recovery, addiction and recovery, the inner child, and dieting have been especially "hot" topics, and authors have whipped out books on them at an astonishing pace. Except for abuse and recovery and to some degree addiction and recovery, none of the other "hot" categories yielded any books that were highly rated by the mental health professionals in the national survey. Look back a decade or two and books on spiritually based approaches to positive thinking, cheerleader approaches to improving your self-esteem, and transactional analysis were "hot"; the topics no longer are, and no books in those categories received recommended ratings in the national survey.

Be an intelligent consumer of psychological knowledge and advice by going beyond the cover, the testimonies by celebrities, the fancy ads, the author who's on every talk show, the book store's elaborate display, and believing everything the publicity campaign concocts to lure you into buying the book. Instead, make your choices based on the next eight strategies.

2. Select a book that makes realistic rather than grandiose claims.

If you have a problem, you want to cope with it as effectively and painlessly as possible. The quicker you can fix the problem the better. Unfortunately, the books that make extravagant claims are the most alluring and sell better than books that are more realistic. Most problems do not arise overnight and most can't be solved overnight. Books that promise you magical, wondrous insights that can easily and painlessly solve your problems should be avoided.

If a book promises that you can raise your self-esteem in one day or one week or one month and keep it raised permanently, don't buy the book. If a book states that a new diet has been discovered that will help you lose one pound of weight per day and keep the weight off permanently, don't buy it. The largest number of low-rated books in the national survey were in the dieting category. Books such as *The Beverly Hills Diet, Dr. Abravanel's Anti-Craving Weight-Loss Diet,* and *Dr. Atkins' Diet Revolution* tend to make extravagant claims and take a very narrow approach to weight loss instead of recommending a balanced diet and a change in life style that includes increased exercise. More reasonable books such as *The New Fit or Fat* by Covert Bailey, *Diets Don't Work* by Bob Schwartz, and *The LEARN Program for Weight Control* by Kelly Brownell are not as eye-catching, not as sensational, but they present a much more balanced approach to weight loss—and tend not to sell as well, even though they are far better self-help books.

Try to make a realistic judgment about the book's claims. Be skeptical of anything that sounds easy, magical, and wondrous. Raising self-esteem, losing weight, solving relationship problems, and becoming more self-fulfilled are not easy tasks. They all take a lot of effort. Coping effectively with virtually all of life's tasks and problems—motivation, stress, exercise, parenting, divorce, addiction, or career development—is a lifelong project.

3. Examine the evidence reported in the book.

Unfortunately, many self-help books are not based on reliable scientific or clinical evidence but rather on the author's biased, anecdotal experiences or testimonials of people who say that the author's ideas worked for them. In some instances, evidence is gleaned from interviews with a narrow range of people or a few clients seen in therapy. Too much of what you read in self-help books is based on intuitions that are highly speculative.

In the Teenagers and Parenting category (Chapter 32), the book *Tough Love* is not based on reliable scientific or clinical evidence. As you read through the book, you come across a number of testimonials by parents who say that the book's philosophy worked wonders for them. But where is the information about all of the parents for whom this very authoritarian, distancing strategy backfired? None of those cases are reported. A book based on solid scientific and clinical evidence in the Teenagers and Parenting category that has not received the attention it deserves is Laurence Steinberg and Ann Levine's *You and Your Adolescent.* The authors carefully review what has reliably worked in helping parents communicate more effectively with their teenagers. They don't make any outlandish claims and don't recommend any quick fixes; they give parents excellent advice based on reliable evidence.

Most of the self-help books in the national survey that were highly rated by the mental health professionals were based on reliable research or clinical evidence. The cognitive therapy approach to depression advocated by David Burns in *Feeling Good* (Chapter 14) has undergone careful scrutiny by the clinical and research community and been found to be effective for many people. The same is true for Herbert Benson's *The Relaxation Response* (Chapter 26), *The New Aerobics* by Kenneth Cooper (Chapter 18), and *Learned Optimism* by Martin Seligman (Chapter 24). These books are not based on the biased opinions of the authors or the personal testimonials of others. They are based on sound research and clinical evidence.

Hardly any self-help books have elaborate research citations. This is by design because lengthy citations make the books difficult to read. However, most authors of the best self-help books describe the research evidence, the clinical evidence, or both on which the book is based. And the good books often have a list of sources on which the book's contents are based in an appendix. In the Self-fulfillment and Happiness category (Chapter 28), two authors who did an extraordinarily good job of putting together the scientific evidence for their assertions and recommendations are Mihaly Csikszentmihalyi in *Flow* and David Myers in *The Pursuit of Happiness*. Both books are well written and the authors do not overwhelm you with academic references. However, they do give you a clear picture of the solid base on which their ideas are founded, both in the main chapters and toward the end of the books in references/notes sections. In stark contrast, author Dennis Wholey in *Discovering Happiness* interviewed a mixed bag of celebrities and self-help authors to discover their thoughts about happiness. This book is not based on any reliable scientific or clinical evidence but on the opinions of a few people, most of whom have no mental health training.

4. **Select a self-help book that recognizes that a problem is caused by a number of factors and has alternative solutions.**

It's not just your imagination. You are a complex being living in a complex world. Your problems are not so simple that they have a single cause and a single solution. Yet the human mind is biased toward simple answers to complex problems. After all, solving a problem is easier if there is one simple solution than if you have to modify a number of factors in your life. Consider the problem of coping with stress. Maybe thinking positively will help you cope more effectively with stress, but self-help books that deal only with positive thinking often oversimplify the coping process. Coping can be influenced by optimistic thinking, rearranging the circumstances of your life, understanding your physical strengths and weaknesses, knowing your personality traits, and joining a stress management program.

Too many self-help books give simplistic solutions to complex problems. Diet books are notorious for giving single-factor solutions to the complex problem of losing weight and keeping it off. One of the most recent best-selling diet books—*The T-Factor Diet*—takes the single-solution approach. Some mental health experts criticized the codependency and inner child books on this ground as well.

5. A self-help book that focuses on a particular problem
   is better than one that is a general approach
   to solving all of your problems.

The best self-help books focus on a specific problem rather than promising to cure all of life's ills with a few simple ideas. Books that try to solve all of life's problems are shallow and lack the precise, detailed recommendations that are needed to solve a particular problem. When authors say that their books will solve all of your problems and will help everybody, don't buy the books.

The more authors can convince the public that their books are for everyone, the greater their chances of selling millions of copies of the books. And that is exactly what far too many self-help authors try to do—write books that are so broad in scope that they will appeal to a huge audience. The codependency concept (Chapter 11) was initially developed to apply to the specific problems of people married to alcoholics, especially women married to male alcoholics. But the concept spread rapidly to apply to a host of other circumstances, and it has gotten to the point at which the leading codependency author Melodie Beattie says that codependency is *anything* and that *everything* is codependent. That is far too broad and all-encompassing for most mental health experts. Susan Forward tells readers in *Toxic Parents* (Chapter 2) that if your parents frightened you as a child then you grew up under the regime of toxic parents. Most parents frighten their children at some point or another because they are so much larger and have to mete out discipline as part of socializing their children and helping them develop self-control. Virtually every parent who ever lived fits into Forward's description of toxic parents at least to some degree.

The number one book in the national survey, *The Courage to Heal*, is about a very specific problem: Women's recovery from child sexual abuse. The number two book, David Burns's *Feeling Good*, explores how a specific form of therapy—cognitive—can help you cope with a specific problem—depression. And the number three book—T. Berry Brazelton's *Infants and Mothers*—focuses on a specific age—infants from birth to one year of age—and how parents should respond to particular types of infants—active, average, or quiet. These books don't try to reel in everyone and don't pretend to be all things to all people. They focus on specific types of problems and offer specific solutions to those problems.

6. Don't be conned by psychobabble and slick writing.

In 1977, R. D. Rosen wrote *Psychobabble*, a sizzling attack on the psychological jargon that fills the space between the covers of many self-help books. Unfortunately, almost two decades later psychobabble is still alive and well. Psychobabble is a "hip" and vague language that will not improve your ability to cope with a problem. Too many self-help authors write in psychobabble, saying things like "You've got to get in touch with your feelings"; "Get with the program"; "You've got to get it"; "the real you"; "To solve your problem you need some high-energy experiences"; "You are sending off the wrong vibes," and on and on.

In a number of chapters we specifically criticized some books for having too much psychobabble and praised others for being psychobabble-free. Examples of books with too much psychobabble are Gloria Steinem's *Revolution from Within* (in contrast to Carol Tavris's *The Mismeasure of Woman* and Judith Rodin's *Body Traps*, which are psychobabble-free; Chapter 33), *Looking Out for Number One* by Robert Ringer (in contrast to *Your Perfect Right* by Robert Alberti and Michael Emmons, which is psychobabble-free; Chapter 8), and *What Men Really Want* by Susan Bakos (in contrast to Harriet Lerner's *The Dance of Intimacy*, which is psychobabble-free; Chapter 22).

Psychobabble is not the only semantic problem of bad self-help books. Some disguise their inadequacies with slick writing that is so friendly that it seems as if the author is personally talking to you. After you have read only a few pages of the book, you say to yourself, "Wow! This book can really help me." All too often such slick books offer little more than one or two basic ideas that could be communicated in two or three pages. The rest of the book is filled with polished writing that provides little additional knowledge. Such books lack the extensive, detailed recommendations and sound strategies needed to cope more effectively with life's problems.

The books characterized by psychobabble and slick writing frequently regress into motivational and inspirational sermons or cheerleading. This approach can get you "pumped up" to solve your problem—but then it lets you down by giving you no precise strategies for coping with life's ills. After a few weeks or months, the "buzz" wears off because the author's recommendations lack depth. Examples of books characterized by this approach are Zig Zigler's *Steps to the Top* (in contrast to Steven Covey's *The 7 Habits of Highly Effective People*, which has detailed, effective strategies; Chapter 28) and Leo Buscaglia's *Loving Each Other* (in contrast to *The Triangle of Love* by Robert Sternberg, which examines the complexity of love and its many different avenues; Chapter 22).

We are not against good writing. However, it takes a lot more than an author's slick language to help you cope effectively with a problem. Buy self-help books that are clearly written in language you can understand and that include detailed recommendations for how to cope with a specific problem. Several books that were highly rated in the national survey are not clearly written—Aaron Beck's books on anxiety and depression, for example (Chapters 7 and 14). By contrast, David Burns's *Feeling Good*, on the same topic with a very similar approach to Beck, is very well-written (Chapter 14).

7. Check out the author's educational and professional credentials.

Not all authors of self-help books are mental health professionals who have gone through rigorous educational training at respected universities and who have spent years helping people solve problems. Just about anyone can get their self-help ideas into print if they can convince an agent or publisher that their ideas will make money. But most of the best self-help books are written by *legitimate* mental health professionals, not professional writers or people with no professional training or experience.

In the national survey, the authors of 9 of the top 10 books have Ph.D.s or M.D.s and have done extensive research and/or have had clinical training. David Burns, the author of *Feeling Good* (Chapter 14), is a highly respected psychiatrist who has an M.D. and is on the staff of the University of Pennsylvania Medical School. T. Berry Brazelton, author of three books in the top ten, an esteemed pediatrician who has experience in working with parents and babies; he is affiliated with Harvard Medical School. Harriet Lerner, author of *The Dance of Anger* (Chapter 6), is a superb psychotherapist who has a Ph.D. and is on the staff of the famous Menninger Clinic. But there are exceptions to the rule. Indeed, the number one book in the national survey—*The Courage to Heal* (Chapter 2)—was written by Ellen Bass and Laura Davis, who do not have graduate educational credentials beside their names. Ellen Bass was a professional writer who began offering workshops for the adult female survivors of sexual abuse as a child. Laura Davis was one of the participants in Bass's workshops. The book is sound, sensitive, and very helpful.

Of course, the reverse can also happen. A Ph.D. or an M.D. does not guarantee a wonderful self-help book. The consensus of the mental health experts in the national survey was that Joyce Brothers (she has a Ph.D.), Ruth Westheimer (she has a Ph.D), Wayne Dyer (he has a Ph.D), and a large number of authors with Ph.Ds or M.D.s in the dieting and eating disorders category have written self-help books that should be avoided.

8. Be wary of authors who complain about or reject the conventional knowledge of mental health professionals.

Mental health professionals—such as psychologists and psychiatrists—don't have the answers to all of life's problems, and if they tell you so, they are simply being intellectually honest.

Some self-help authors attack the mental health professions as being too conservative and overly concerned with scientific or clinical evidence to support strategies for coping with a problem. Consider such attacks a red flag and avoid such authors. These antiestablishment, antiscience mavericks avow that their ideas are way ahead of their time, that it will take years for mental health professionals to catch up with their avant garde thinking and insight. Many New Age authors and scientology authors such as L. Ron Hubbard (Chapter 25) fall into this category.

There is nothing wrong with new ideas. Mental health professionals welcome new ideas, but the ideas have to be supported by reliable evidence. For the most part, the books of self-help authors who condemn the mental health establishment will not help you.

9. Use *The Authoritative Guide to Self-Help Books* as a resource for selecting good self-help books.

Even armed with the first eight strategies for selecting a good self-help book, you may still have trouble sorting through the jungle and picking the best one for you. With practice in using the strategies, you will become a more knowledgeable consumer. However, the most important strategy of all for selecting a good self-help book and avoiding the lemons is accessing the knowledge of the most highly trained and experienced mental health professionals in the United States. We have given you their knowledge in this book. The evaluations are not based on just one or two experts' opinions or judgments but on the consensus of hundreds of experts. Use their knowledge to help you select good self-help books.

Rating of All Books
in the National Survey
of Self-Help Books*

Category and Book Title	Author(s)	Survey Rating	Survey Raters	Guide Rating
Abuse and Recovery				
Abused No More	Ackerman & Pickering	0.48	57	★★
Allies in Healing	Davis	2.00	9	◑◑
Battered Wives	Martin	0.85	56	★★★
Battered Woman, The	Walker	1.22	121	★★★★★
Courage to Heal, The	Bass & Davis	1.53	244	★★★★★
Getting Free	NiCarthy	1.00	38	★★★
Healing the Shame That Binds You	Bradshaw	0.56	192	★★★
Reclaiming the Inner Child	Abrams	0.20	97	★
Toxic Parents	Forward	0.47	119	★★
Victims No Longer	Lew	1.43	7	◑◑
Addiction and Recovery				
Addiction and Grace	May	0.67	26	★★★
Adult Children of Alcololilcs	Woititz	0.52	220	★★★
A Day at a Time	Compcare	0.72	52	★★★
Alcoholic Man, The	Carey	0.35	17	★
Alcoholics Anonymous	Alcoholics Anonymous World Services	1.13	179	★★★★
Healing the Addictive Mind	Jampolsky	−1.05	20	†
It Will Never Happen to Me	Black	1.61	14	◆

*Only those books rated five or more times in the national survey are included in this list. Some books that appear in the text in Worth a Further Look do not appear on this list because they were published after the survey was conducted. Some books appear on this list but were not included in the text because they were rated by fewer than 10 mental health expertis and had ratings lower than 1.00. The survey rating is the book's average rating.

Category and Book Title	Author(s)	Survey Rating	Survey Raters	Guide Rating
Addiction and Recovery, *cont'd*				
One Day at a Time in Al-Anon	Al-Anon Family Group Headquarters	0.93	110	★★★
Twelve Steps and Twelve Traditions	Alcoholics Anonymous World Services	1.02	180	★★★★
Adult Development				
How to Deal with Your Parents	Osterkamp	0.50	24	★★★
Lifelines	Merriam & Clark	0.64	22	★★★
Making Peace with Your Parents	Bloomfield	0.99	69	★★★
Necessary Losses	Viorst	1.10	182	★★★★
Passages	Sheehy	0.72	356	★★★
Seasons of a Man's Life	Levinson	1.05	222	★★★★
When You and Your Mother Can't Be Friends	Secunda	0.60	30	★★★
Aging				
Aging Well	Fries	0.84	16	★★★
Complete Guide to Health and Well-Being after 50	Weiss & Subak-Sharpe	0.88	24	★★★
Diminished Mind, The	Tyler & Anifantakis	0.87	23	★★★
Enjoy Old Age	Skinner & Vaughn	−0.60	5	—
50+ Wellness Program	McIlwain, Fulghum, Fulghum, and Bruce	0.24	17	★
How to Live Longer and Feel Better	Pauling	0.53	46	★★★
It's Better to Be Over the Hill Than Under It	LeShan	1.09	22	◆
Old Folks Going Strong	York	0.61	7	—
36-Hour Day, The	Mace & Rabins	1.53	15	◆
Your Renaissance Years	Veninga	1.00	8	◑◑
Anger				
Anger: Deal with It, Heal with It, Stop It from Killing You	Defoore	0.38	24	★★
Anger: How to Live with and without It	Ellis	0.85	24	★★★

Category and Book Title	Author(s)	Survey Rating	Survey Raters	Guide Rating
Anger: The Misunderstood Emotion	Tavris	1.18	83	★★★★★
Angry Book, The	Rubin	0.52	95	★★★
Dance of Anger, The	Lerner	1.39	211	★★★★★
Dr. Weisinger's Anger Work out Book	Weisinger	1.34	5	◑◑
When Anger Hurts	McKay, Rogers, & McKay	0.92	36	★★★
Anxiety				
Anxiety and Panic Attacks	Handly	0.81	27	★★★
Anxiety Disease, The	Sheehan	0.64	59	★★★
Anxiety Disorders and Phobias	Beck & Emery	1.18	172	★★★★★
Don't Panic	Wilson	1.04	82	★★★★
Good News about Panic, Anxiety, and Phobias, The	Gold	0.59	45	★★★
Obsessive-Compulsive Disorders	Levenkron	1.00	31	★★★★
Panic Attack Recovery Book, The	Swede & Jaffe	0.88	27	★★★
Peace from Nervous Suffering	Weekes	0.88	57	★★★
Assertiveness				
Assertive Woman, The	Phleps & Austin	1.82	11	◆
Control Freaks	Piaget	0.00	11	★
Creative Aggression	Bach & Goldberg	0.43	72	★★
Don't Say Yes When You Want to Say No	Fensterheim & Baer	0.91	150	★★★
Gentle Art of Verbal Self-Defense	Elgin	0.66	61	★★★
Good bye to Guilt	Jampolsky	0.77	31	★★★
How to Take Charge of Your Life	Newman & Berkowitz	0.77	39	★★★
Looking Out for Number One	Ringer	−0.73	67	†
Pulling Your Own Strings	Dyer	0.19	148	★
Stand Up, Speak Out, Talk Back	Alberti & Emmons	1.11	75	★★★★
When I Say No, I Feel Guilty	Smith	1.00	223	★★★★
Winning Through Intimidation	Ringer	−1.11	83	†
Your Perfect Right	Alberti & Emmons	1.37	283	★★★★★
Career Development				
Do What You Love, the Money Will Follow	Sinetar	0.57	38	★★★
Knock 'em Dead	Yate	0.74	15	★★★

Category and Book Title	Author(s)	Survey Rating	Survey Raters	Guide Rating
Career Development, *cont'd*				
100 Best Companies to Work for in America, The	Levering, Moskowitz, & Katz	0.27	33	★★
Portable MBA, The	Collins & Devanna	0.40	15	★★
Shifting Gears	Hyatt	0.85	20	★★★
Staying the Course	Weiss	1.06	33	★★★★
Three Boxes of Life and How to Get Out of Them, The	Bolles	1.89	9	◖◖
Upward Nobility	Edwards	0.00	6	—
What Color Is Your Parachute?	Bolles	1.32	324	★★★★★
Win-Win Negotiating	Jandt	1.02	47	★★★★
Child Development and Parenting				
Between Parent and Child	Ginott	1.30	261	★★★★★
Childhood	Konner	0.67	9	—
Children: The Challenge	Dreikurs	1.27	126	★★★★★
Drama of the Gifted Child, The	Miller	1.90	5	◖◖
Father's Almanac, The	Sullivan	0.90	16	★★★
Good Behavior	Garber, Garber, & Spizman	2.00	7	◖◖
How to Talk so Kids Will Listen and How to Listen so Kids Will Talk	Faber & Mazlish	2.00	10	◆
How to Discipline Your Six- to Twelve-Year-Old Without Losing Your Mind	Wyckoff & Unell	0.57	22	★★★
Hurried Child, The	Elkind	1.17	114	★★★★★
Living with Children	Patterson	1.83	11	◆
Parent Effectiveness Training	Gordon	1.15	259	★★★★
Positive Discipline	Nelson	1.32	18	◆
Preschool Years, The	Gallinsky & David	1.00	11	◆
Systematic Training for Effective Parenting	Dinkmeyer & McKay	1.96	8	◖◖
Tips for Toddlers	Beebe	0.71	7	—
Toddlers and Parents	Brazelton	1.37	101	★★★★★
To Listen to a Child	Brazelton	1.41	89	★★★★★
Your Baby and Child	Leach	1.32	32	★★★★
Codependency and Recovery				
Beyond Codependency	Beattie	0.70	49	★★★
Co-Dependence	Whitfield	0.04	52	★
Codependent No More	Beattie	0.84	197	★★★

Category and Book Title	Author(s)	Survey Rating	Survey Raters	Guide Rating
How to Break Your Addiction to a Person	Halpern	0.49	72	★★
Love Is a Choice	Helmfelt, Minirth, & Meier	0.05	41	★
Communication				
Body Language	Fast	0.20	113	★
Coping with Difficult People	Bramson	0.87	62	★★★
Games People Play	Berne	0.62	350	★★★
Getting to Yes	Fisher & Ury	1.03	69	★★★★
Messages	McKay, Davis, & Fanning	1.42	5	◑◑
Opening Up	Pennebaker	0.91	18	★★★
People Skills	Bolton	1.03	32	★★★★
Peoplemaking	Satir	1.47	7	◑◑
Stop! You're Driving Me Crazy	Bach & Deutsch	0.50	46	★★★
Talk Book, The	Goodman & Esterly	1.03	18	◆
That's Not What I Meant!	Tannen	0.99	61	★★★
You Just Don't Understand	Tannen	1.24	148	★★★★★
Death, Dying, and Grief				
Bereaved Parent, The	Schiff	2.00	5	◑◑
Coming Back	Stern	0.78	9	—
Enigma of Suicide, The	Colt	0.69	13	★★★
Final Exit	Humphrey	−0.33	61	†
Grief Observed, A	Lewis	1.50	8	◑◑
Grief Recovery Handbook, The	James & Cherry	1.73	6	◑◑
Helping Children Grieve	Huntley	1.08	25	◆
How to Go on Living When Someone You Love Dies	Rando	1.25	31	★★★★
How to Survive the Loss of a Love	Colgrove, Bloomfied, & McWilliams	1.41	100	★★★★★
Learning to Say Good-Bye	LeShan	1.22	52	★★★★
Living through Personal Crisis	Stearns	1.06	18	◆
On Death and Dying	Kübler-Ross	0.99	355	★★★
Recovering from the Loss of a Child	Donnelly	1.15	27	◆
Sudden Infant Death	DeFrain, Ernst, Jakub & Taylor	1.00	16	◆
Talking about Death	Grollman	1.23	40	★★★★
Up from Grief	Kreis & Pattie	1.00	14	◆
When Bad Things Happen to Good People	Kushner	1.88	24	◆

Category and Book Title	Author(s)	Survey Rating	Survey Raters	Guide Rating
Death, Dying, and Grief, *cont'd*				
Widowed	Brothers	−0.02	34	†
Widow's Handbook, The	Foehner & Cozart	0.54	13	★★★
Depression				
Cognitive Therapy and the Emotional Disorders	Beck	1.16	198	★★★★★
Feeling Good	Burns	1.51	254	★★★★★
Feeling Good Handbook, The	Burns	1.38	116	★★★★★
From Sad to Glad	Kline	0.58	50	★★★
Getting Un-Depressed	Emery	0.93	42	★★★
Good News about Depression, The	Gold	0.01	50	★
Happiness Is a Choice	Minerth & Meier	0.42	30	★★
How to Cope with Depression	DePaulo & Ablow	0.65	20	★★★
How to Stubbornly Refuse to Make Yourself Miserable about Anything, Yes, Anything	Ellis	1.82	5	◑◑
When the Blues Won't Go Away	Hirschfield	0.62	13	★★★
You Mean I Don't Have to Feel This Way?	Dowling	0.44	16	★★
Dieting and Weight Loss				
Beverly Hills Diet, The	Mazel & Schultz	−1.35	61	†
Carbohydrate Addict's Diet, The	Heller & Heller	−1.09	34	†
Diet Center Program, The	Ferguson	−0.83	35	†
Diet for a Small Planet	Lappe	0.44	78	★★
Diets Still Don't Work	Schwartz	2.00	5	◑◑
Dr. Abravanel's Anti-Craving Weight-Loss Diet	Abravanel & King	−1.05	22	†
Dr. Atkins' Diet Revolution	Atkins	−0.97	58	†
Fat Is a Feminist Issuee	Orbach	1.44	16	◆
LEARN Program for Weight Control	Brownell	2.00	5	◑◑
New Fit of Fat, The	Bailey	0.69	65	★★★
One Meal at a Time	Katahn	0.00	21	★
Pritikin Program for Diet and Exercise, The	Pritikin	0.02	80	★
Rotation Diet, The	Katahn	−0.62	47	†

Category and Book Title	Author(s)	Survey Rating	Survey Raters	Guide Rating
T-Factor Diet, The	Katahn	−0.22	41	†
35 Plus Diet for Women, The	Spodnik & Gibbons	−0.90	19	†

Divorce

Boys and Girls Book about Divorce, The	Gardner	1.39	212	★★★★★
Creative Divorce	Krantzler	0.66	88	★★★
Dinosaurs Divorce	Brown & Brown	1.42	44	★★★★
Going It Alone	Weiss	0.80	27	★★★
Growing Up with Divorce	Kalter	1.00	33	★★★★
How It Feels When Parents Divorce	Krementz	1.09	70	★★★★
Parents Book about Divorce, The	Gardner	1.88	8	◑◑
Rebuilding When Your Relationship Ends	Fisher	1.76	8	◑◑
Second Chances	Wallerstein & Blakeslee	0.99	102	★★★

Eating Disorders

Fat Is a Family Affair	Hollis	0.88	41	★★★
Feeding the Hungry Heart	Roth	1.83	6	◑◑
Food for Thought	The Hazelden Foundation	0.66	32	★★★
Inner Eating	Billigmeier	0.22	9	—
Love Hunger	Minirth, Meier, Helmfelt, Sneed, & Hawkins	0.13	31	★
Love-Powered Diet, The	Moran	−0.91	11	†
Obsession	Chernin	1.40	5	◑◑
When Food Is Love	Roth	0.66	32	★★★
Why Weight?	Roth	0.68	22	★★★
You Can't Quit Eating until You Know What's Eating You	LeBlanc	0.47	17	★★

Exercise

Complete Book of Running, The	Fixx	0.77	98	★★★
Fat-Burning Workout, The	Vedral	−0.09	11	†
Kid Fitness	Cooper	0.80	15	★★★
New Aerobics, The	Cooper	1.28	92	★★★★★
New Aerobics for Women, The	Cooper & Cooper	1.19	28	◆

Category and Book Title	Author(s)	Survey Rating	Survey Raters	Guide Rating
The Family				
Adult Children	Friel & Friel	0.52	49	★★★
Back to the Family	Guarendi	0.91	11	★★★
Bradshaw on the Family	Bradshaw	0.34	129	★★
Families	Patterson	1.78	12	♦
Family Crucible, The	Napier & Whitaker	1.04	108	★★★★
Friendship, Loneliness, and Single Adult Life				
Art of Living Single, The	Broder	0.72	18	★★★
How to Start a Conversation and Make Friends	Gabor	0.42	12	★★
How to Win Friends and Influence People	Carnegie	0.24	161	★
Intimate Connections	Burns	1.08	46	★★★★
Intimate Strangers	Rubin	1.18	82	★★★★★
Just Friends	Rubin	1.07	31	★★★★
Living Alone and Liking It	Shahan	0.82	28	★★★
Making Friends	Matthews	0.67	6	—
Positive Solitude	Andre	0.89	9	—
Shyness	Zimbardo	1.14	164	★★★★
Single File	Dietz	0.50	6	—
Infant Development and Parenting				
Babyhood	Leach	1.37	42	★★★★
Dr. Spock's Baby and Child Care	Spock & Rothenberg	1.43	187	★★★★★
Dr. Spock on Parenting	Spock	1.05	114	★★★★
First Three Years of Life, The	White	1.34	102	★★★★★
First Twelve Months of Life, The	Caplan	1.33	60	★★★★
Infants and Mothers	Brazelton	1.47	114	★★★★★
What Every Baby Knows	Brazelton	1.44	105	★★★★★
What to Expect the First Year	Eisenberg, Murkoff, & Hathaway	1.44	37	★★★★
Love, Intimacy, and Marriage				
Art of Loving, The	Fromm	1.05	257	★★★★
Dance of Intimacy, The	Lerner	1.23	145	★★★★★
Divorce Busting	Weiner-Davis	0.85	17	★★★
Do I Have to Give Up Me to Be Loved by You?	Paul & Paul	0.83	56	★★★
Getting the Love You Want	Hendrix	1.32	53	★★★★
Going the Distance	Barbach & Geisinger	0.67	33	★★★
Husbands and Wives	Kinder & Cowan	0.55	10	★★★

Category and Book Title	Author(s)	Survey Rating	Survey Raters	Guide Rating
Intimate Enemy, The	Bach & Wyden	1.94	10	♦
Intimate Partners	Scarf	1.06	87	★★★★
Love Cycle	Cutler	0.60	5	—
Love Is Letting Go of Fear	Jampolsky	0.88	48	★★★
Love Is Never Enough	Beck	1.69	9	◑◑
Loving Each Other	Buscaglia	0.31	94	★★
Men Who Can't Love	Carter	0.27	141	★★
Men Who Hate Women and the Women Who Love Them	Forward	0.29	141	★★
Obsessive Love	Forward	0.94	18	★★★
Triangle of Love, The	Sternberg	1.00	23	♦
What Every Woman Should Know about Men	Brothers	−0.94	48	†
What Smart Women Know	Carter & Sokol	0.09	11	★
When Someone You Love Is Someone You Hate	Arterburn & Stoop	0.10	10	★
Women Men Love, Women Men Leave	Cowan & Kinder	−0.17	29	†
Women Who Love Too Much	Norwood	0.64	194	★★★

Men's Issues

Fire in the Belly	Keen	0.61	86	★★★
Hazards of Being Male, The	Goldberg	0.81	63	★★★
Iron John	Bly	0.30	158	★★
New Male, The	Goldberg	0.67	39	★★★
Seasonss of a Man's Life	Levinson	1.05	222	★★★★
What Men Really Want	Bakos	−0.12	25	†
Why Men Don't Get Enough Sex and Women Don't Get Enough Love	Kramer & Dunaway	0.10	20	★

Positive Thinking and Self-Talk

Learned Optimism	Seligman	1.27	89	★★★★★
Positive Addiction	Glasser	0.82	89	★★★
Positive Illusions	Taylor	1.23	13	♦
Power of Optimism, The	McGinnis	0.27	11	★★
Power of Positive Thinking, The	Peale	0.22	153	★
Self-Defeating Behaviors	Cudney & Hardy	0.80	10	★★★
Staying Rational in an Irrational World	Bernard	0.91	71	★★★
Talking to Yourself	Butler	0.80	18	★★★
Thoughts and Feelings	McKay, Davis, & Fanning	1.60	6	◑◑
Tough Times Never Last but Tough People Do	Schuller	0.41	42	★★

Category and Book Title	Author(s)	Survey Rating	Survey Raters	Guide Rating
Positive Thinking and Self-Talk, *cont'd*				
What to Say When You Talk to Yourself	Helmstetter	1.10	21	◆
You Can't Afford the Luxury of a Negative Thought	John-Rogers & McWilliams	0.44	6	—
Pregnancy				
Complete Book of Pregnancy and Childbirth, The	Kitzinger	1.41	39	★★★★
From Here to Maternity	Marshall	0.80	10	★★★
Pregnancy after 35	McCauley	0.90	20	★★★
Pregnancy, Childbirth, and the Newborn	Simkin	0.83	6	—
Well Pregnancy Book, The	Samuels & Samuels	0.87	15	★★★
What to Eat When You're Expecting	Eisenberg, Murkoff, & Hathaway	1.00	16	◆
What to Expect When You're Expecting	Eisenberg, Murkoff, & Hathaway	1.54	30	◆
Will It Hurt the Baby?	Abrams	1.00	5	◑◑
Relaxation, Meditation, and Stress				
Beyond Chaos	West	0.83	6	—
Beyond the Relaxation Response	Benson	1.22	135	★★★★★
Each Day a New Beginning	The Hazelden Foundation	1.05	34	★★★★
14-Day Stress Cure	Reuter	−0.44	16	†
How to Meditate	LeShan	1.00	52	★★★★
Male Stress Syndrome, The	Witkin-Lanoil	0.68	22	★★★
Minding the Body, Mending the Mind	Borysenko	1.37	6	◑◑
No Gimmick Guide to Managing Stress	Neidhart	0.88	8	—
Relaxation Response, The	Benson	1.28	212	★★★★★
Relaxation and Stress Reduction Workbook, The	Davis, Eshelman, & McKay	1.97	12	◆
Staying on Top When Your World Is Upside Down	Cramer	1.50	8	◑◑
Stresses	Curran	0.89	9	—
Thoughts to Live By	Maltz	0.67	12	★★★
Touchstones	The Hazelden Foundation	0.90	30	★★★

Category and Book Title	Author(s)	Survey Rating	Survey Raters	Guide Rating
Self-Esteem				
Advice from a Failure	Coudert	0.83	11	★★★
Developing Self-Esteem	Palladino & Crisp	0.75	8	—
How to Raise Your Self-Esteem	Brandon	0.57	57	★★★
Revolution from Within	Steinem	0.79	41	★★★
Psychology of Self-Esteem, The	Brandon	0.72	67	★★★
Self-Esteem	McKay & Fanning	1.89	7	◑◑
Women and Self-Esteem	Sanford & Donovan	1.68	5	◑◑
Self-Fulfillment and Happiness				
Be (Happy) Attitudes, The	Schuller	0.23	21	★
Being Happy	Matthews	0.63	8	—
Choosing Happiness	Ray	0.44	9	—
Clear Body, Clear Mind	Hubbard	−1.62	62	†
Dianetics	Hubbard	−1.77	187	†
Discovering Happiness	Wholey	0.09	11	★
Flow	Csikszentmihalyi	0.57	43	★★★
Guide to Personal Happiness, A	Ellis & Becker	0.82	68	★★★
How to Be Your Own Best Friend	Newman & Berkowitz	0.83	85	★★★
How to Live 365 Days a Year	Schindler	0.58	12	★★★
I'm O.K.—You're O.K.	Harris	0.60	318	★★★
Living Happily Ever After	Sinetar	0.75	8	—
Man's Search for Meaning	Frankl	1.27	260	★★★★★
New Guide to Rational Living, A	Ellis & Harper	1.12	238	★★★★
Road Less Traveled, The	Peck	1.03	285	★★★★
Scientology	Hubbard	−1.88	173	†
Search for Significance, The	McGee	1.15	11	♦
When All You Ever Wanted Isn't Enough	Kushner	1.20	72	★★★★
Self-Improvement and Motivation				
Do It! Let's Get Off Our Butts	McWilliams	−0.06	9	—
Don't Blame Mother	Caplan	1.00	20	♦
Feel the Fear and Do It Anyway	Jeffers	1.24	25	♦
Gentle Roads to Survival	Auw	0.70	10	★★★
How to Get Control of Your Time and Your Life	Lakein	1.14	63	★★★★
How to Stop Worrying and Start Living	Carnegie	0.15	65	★
Making Life Right When It Feels All Wrong	Fensterheim	0.78	18	★★★

Category and Book Title	Author(s)	Survey Rating	Survey Raters	Guide Rating
Self-Improvment and Motivation, *cont'd*				
Overcoming Procrastination	Ellis & Knaus	1.00	69	★★★★
Peace, Love, and Healing	Siegel	1.13	66	★★★★
7 Habits of Highly Effective People, The	Covey	1.28	67	★★★★
Steps to the Top	Zigler	0.13	23	★
Unlimited Power	Robbins	0.54	14	★★★
Your Erroneous Zones	Dyer	0.37	169	★★
Your Maximum Mind	Benson	0.47	25	★★
Sexuality				
Becoming Orgasmic	Heiman & LoPiccolo	1.79	9	◑◑
Dr. Ruth's Guide to Erotic and Sensuous Pleasures	Westheimer & Lieberman	−0.42	47	†
Dr. Ruth's Guide to Good Sex	Westheimer	−0.66	65	†
For Each Other	Barbach	1.59	13	◆
For Yourself	Barbach	1.87	17	◆
Making Love: A Man's Guide	Barry	0.81	27	★★★
Making Love: A Woman's Guide	Davis	0.77	26	★★★
Male Sexuality	Zilbergeld	1.89	18	◆
More Joy of Sex	Comfort	0.94	175	★★★
New Joy of Sex, The	Comfort	0.99	173	★★★
Our Bodies, Ourselves	Boston Women's Health	1.97	7	◑◑
Permanent Partners	Berzon	1.64	5	◑◑
What Every Woman Should Know About Sex	Brothers	−0.51	49	†
What Really Happens in Bed	Carter & Coopersmith	0.80	15	★★★
Stepfamilies				
Love in the Blended Family	Clubb	1.23	13	◆
Old Loyalties, New Ties	Visher & Visher	1.28	42	★★★★
Second Time Around, The	Janda & MacCormack	1.20	10	◆
Step-by-Stepparenting	Eckler	1.30	20	◆
Step-Fathering	Rosin	1.10	21	◆
Strengthening Your Stepfamily	Einstein & Albert	1.10	10	◆
Teenagers and Parenting				
All Grown Up and No Place to Go	Elkind	1.20	49	★★★★
Between Parent and Teenager	Ginott	1.34	181	★★★★★

Category and Book Title	Author(s)	Survey Rating	Survey Raters	Guide Rating
Surviving Adolescence	Dumont	0.95	21	★★★
Tough Love	York, York, Wachtel	0.54	124	★★★
You and Your Adolescent	Steinberg & Levine	1.10	23	◆
Women's Issues				
Backlash	Faludi	0.87	47	★★★
Juggling	Crosby	0.75	8	—
Making It Work	Houston	1.00	6	◑◑
My Mother/Myself	Friday	0.59	187	★★★
Second Shift, The	Hochschild	1.39	28	◆
Secrets about Men Every Woman Should Know	DeAngelis	−0.42	19	†
Too Good for Her Own Good	Bepko & Krestan	1.26	16	◆
Why Women Worry and How to Stop	Handly, Handly & Ness	0.50	6	—

Notes and References

CHAPTER 1: INTRODUCTION TO SELF-HELP BOOKS AND THE NATIONAL SURVEY

We, the authors of this book, strove to avoid a theoretical bias. Each of us is best described as having an eclectic orientation, believing that a number of viable approaches can be used to help people cope effectively with the problems in their lives. The first author, John Santrock, is also the author of a number of leading psychology textbooks, books in which the strengths and weaknesses of a wide variety of theoretical approaches are presented.

One bias of the book is that the survey participants were primarily clinical and counseling psychologists rather than psychiatrists. More psychiatrists adopt a psychoanalytic approach to life's problems than do clinical and counseling psychologists. In the psychoanalytic approach to solving problems, emphasis is often placed on the roles of early experience especially with parents, the unconscious mind, and biology. Some books by psychiatrists, as well as some pediatricians (who also were not included in the survey), appeared on the list of the best 25 self- help books. Nonetheless, had more psychiatrists been included in the survey, it is likely that more books that emphasize psychoanalytically based approaches would have received higher ratings. To our knowledge, no survey of psychiatrists' self-help book ratings has been conducted, so we can only speculate about how their ratings might turn out.

In the actual national survey, 36 categories rather than 32 were used. Because there were so few books rated in several categories, they were combined with other logical categories in the analysis and in the book. Marriage was combined with love and intimacy, motivation with self-improvement, self-talk with positive thinking, and happiness with self-fulfillment.

Overall, the mental health experts were more likely to rate books positively than negatively. The stars (1 to 5) and the dagger given to books were our judgments based on the average rating of the book and how often the book was rated. After extensive discussions and inspections of the ratings, we chose the cutoff points for 1 to 5 stars described in Chapter 1. While the average ratings for the

1- and 2- star books were in the positive range, they were low positive. Most of the 1- and 2-star books received large numbers of zero and negative as well as positive ratings. Because of their low positive average rating and the rather large number of zero and negative ratings they received, we decided to list them as unrecommended. In every category, the consensus of the mental health experts was that other books are much better than the 1- and 2-star books. And, as described in Chapter 1, the worst rating—the dagger— was reserved for the books with a negative rating.

We mailed the survey to 4000 members of the clinical and counseling divisions of the American Psychological Association, almost one- half of all members in those divisions. Almost 800 members returned the surveys, but full ratings of the books were completed by just under 600 of the respondents. Some of the members had died and their spouses returned the unanswered surveys with a note; more than 100 respondents filled out the first part of the survey (demographic information and some general items about self-help books) but did not rate individual books; and some respondents returned the forms unanswered. In many surveys, a follow-up mailing is conducted to increase the sample size. We considered this alternative but did not exercise it for a simple reason: inadequate funds.

Surveys get extremely varied responses depending on the targeted audience, the length of the survey, the motivation of the respondents to answer the survey, and so on. Our survey was very long (indeed, about 20 mental health experts returned the survey with the comment that it was too long and took too much time to fill out). We considered the length factor initially but opted for the longer survey because we felt it necessary to get the detailed ratings needed in many different categories of self-help books. Also, we deliberately sent the survey to academics as well as therapists working outside academia in order to ensure a wide range of respondents. We realized that this strategy would mean a somewhat lower response rate because many academic psychologists, although trained in counseling or clinical psychology, do not see clients at their colleges and universities. On the other hand, many do, and we felt that their evaluations were especially important.

The mental health professionals who did respond with usable ratings all hold doctorates. They live in every state and represent a broad cross-section of clinical and counseling psychologists in the United States. While the respondents are members of the clinical and counseling divisions of the American Psychological Association, the ratings and evaluations of self-help books in the survey and this book are not in any way endorsed by the American Psychological Association itself.

Miscellaneous

Marx, J. A., Gyorky, Z. K., Royalty, G. M., & Stern, T. E. (1992). Use of self-help books in psychotherapy. *Professional Psychology, 23,* 300–305.

    This survey of mental health professionals was published after we conducted our survey. The survey was conducted in the spring of 1987 and obtained the ratings of 209 counseling psychologists of best-selling self-help books. Books that received the highest number of positive evaluations were *What Color Is Your Parachute?* (Bolles), On Death and Dying (Kübler-Ross), *Adult Children of Alcoholics* (Woititz), *The Relaxation Response* (Benson), *When I Say No, I Feel Guilty* (Smith), *Women Who Love Too Much* (Norwood), and *The Road Less Traveled* (Peck). Books that received the highest number of negative ratings were *Smart Women, Foolish Choices* (Buscaglia), *Living, Loving, and Learning* (Buscaglia), *The Cinderella Complex* (Dowling), and *Women Who Love Too Much* (Norwood).

Rosen, G. R. (1987). Self-help treatment and the commercialization of of psychotherapy. *American Psychologist, 42,* 46–51.

Stark, E. (1989, July). Off-the-shelf salvation. *Health,* pp. 28–30.

Starker, S. (1988). Do-it-yourself therapy: The prescription of self-help books by psychologists. *Psychotherapy, 25,* 142–146.

    Steven Starker of the VA Medical Center in Portland, Oregon, conducted a small survey of 121 psychologists in Seattle, Washington, and Cambridge, Massachusetts. Books were ranked according to how frequently a book was prescribed by therapists. The books recommended most (by seven therapists) were *The Relaxation Response* (Benson), *Your Perfect Right* (Alberti and Emmons), and *What Color Is Your Parachute?* (Bolles). *Feeling Good* (Burns) was prescribed by six therapists.

Starker, S. (1988). Psychologists and self-help books: Attitudes and prescriptive practices of clinicians. *American Journal of Psychotherapy, 42,* 448–454.

    In a second study, Starker obtained the self-help book ratings of 123 psychologists in 36 states. In this study, the 10 most widely prescribed self-help books by clinicians were *The Relaxation Response* (Benson), *On Death and Dying* (Kübler-Ross), *Parent Effectiveness Training* (Gordon), *Between Parent and Child* (Ginott), *Your Perfect Right (Alberti and Emmons), What Color Is Your Parachute?* (Bolles), *When I Say No, I Feel Guilty* (Smith), *The Boys and Girls Book About Divorce* (Gardner), *Feeling Good* (Burns), and *How to Survive the Loss of a Love* (Bloomfield and others). Many of these books also showed up when the clinicians rated self-help books for their quality and their helpfulness. Books were not rated in different categories (such as addiction and recovery, divorce, and communication).

CHAPTER 2: ABUSE AND RECOVERY

The Courage to Heal

Bass, E., & Davis, L. (1990, October). The courage to heal. *Cosmopolitan,* 252–255.

James, J. (1988, May 15). Review of *The Courage to Heal. Library Journal,* p. 86.

Koss, M. P. (1990, March). The women's mental health research agenda: Violence against women. *American Psychologist, 45,* 374–380.

The Battered Woman

Ferraro, K. J. (1986). Opening closed doors. *Contemporary Sociology, 15,* 50–52.

Hertzberger, S. (1984, December). Review of *The Battered Woman. Choice,* p. 623.

Steinmetz, S. K. (1986). Battered women: A study of violent histories. *Contemporary Psychology, 31,* 51–52.

Battered Wives

Bernard, J. (1977). Battered wives: Coming out of the closet. *Contemporary Psychology, 22,* 398–399.
Gelman, D. (1990, November 26). Making it all feel better. *Newsweek,* pp. 66–68.
Nichols, B.B. (1977). Review of *Battered Wives. Social Casework,* 182–183.

I Never Called It Rape

Koss, M. P. (1988). Afterword: The methods used in the *Ms.* project on campus sexual assault. In R. Warshaw, *I Never Called It Rape.* New York: Harper & Row.

CHAPTER 3: ADDICTION AND RECOVERY

Alcoholics Anonymous

Gelman, D., Leonard, E. A., & Fisher, B. (1991, July 8). Clean and sober—and agnostic. *Newsweek,* pp. 62–63.
McCarthy L. F. (1991, July/August). Beyond AA. *Health,* pp. 40–44.

Twelve Steps and Twelve Traditions

Hamma, R. M. (1989, July/August). Review of *The Twelve Steps. The Catholic World,* pp. 179–182.
Orrock, B. G. (1989, June 9). Alcoholics Anonymous. *Journal of the American Medical Association, 261,* 3315–3316.
Skinner, B. F. (1987, July/August). A humanist's alternative to A.A.'s Twelve Steps: A human-centered approach to conquering alcoholism. *The Humanist, 47,* p. 5.

The Truth about Addiction and Recovery

Ellis, A. (1991). Cover notes.
Tavris, C. (1991). Cover notes.

CHAPTER 4: ADULT DEVELOPMENT

Necessary Losses

Spock, B. (1986). Cover notes.

Seasons of a Man's Life

Newton, P. (1978). Cover notes.

Sears, R. R. (1979). Midlife development. Review of Seasons of a Man's Life. Contemporary Psychology, 234, 97–98.

Passages

Neugarten, B. L. (1980). Must everything be a midlife crisis? Annual editions, *Human Development, 80/81.* Guilford, CT: Dushkin.

The Silent Passage

Ehrenreich, B. (1992, October 20). Chronicling the change. *Time,* pp. 80–82.

McKinlay, S. M., & McKinley, J. B. (1984). *Health Status and Health Care Utilization by Menopausal Women.* Unpublished manuscript, Cambridge Research Center, American Institutes for Research, Cambridge, MA.

Miscellaneous

Santrock, J. W. (1992). *Life-Span Development* (4th ed.). Dubuque, IA: Wm. C. Brown.

CHAPTER 5: AGING

Miscellaneous

Cavanaugh, J. C. (1990). *Adult Development and Aging.* Belmont, CA: Wadsworth.

Rybash, J. W., Roodin, P. A., & Santrock, J. W. (1991). *Adult Development and Aging* (2nd ed.). Dubuque, IA: Wm. C. Brown.

Santrock, J. W. (1992). *Life-Span Development* (4th ed.). Dubuque, IA: Wm. C. Brown.

CHAPTER 6: ANGER

The Dance of Anger

Gordon, T. (1985). Cover notes.

Tavris, C. (1985). Cover notes.

Anger: The Misunderstood Emotion

Montagu, A. (1989). Cover notes.

Tavris, C. (1989). Cover notes.

When Anger Hurts

Ellis, A. (1989). Cover notes.

Patterson, G. (1989). Cover notes.

Dr. Weisinger's Anger Work Out Book

Gordon, T. (1985). Cover notes.
Podell, R. (1985). Cover notes.

Miscellaneous

Butcher, J. N., & Spielberger, C. D. (1983). *Advances in Personality Assessment* (Vol. 2). Hillsdale, NJ: Erlbaum.

CHAPTER 7: ANXIETY

Anxiety Disorders and Phobias

Klerman, G. (1985). Cover notes.
Strupp, H. (1985). Cover notes.

Don't Panic: Taking Control of Anxiety Attacks

Beck, A. (1986). Foreword.

Obsessive-Compulsive Disorders

Kenin, M. (1991). Cover notes.
Vaith, R. (1991). Cover notes.

Miscellaneous

Santrock, J. W. (1991). *Psychology* (3rd ed.). Dubuque, IA: Wm. C. Brown.

CHAPTER 8: ASSERTIVENESS

Miscellaneous

Simons, J., Kalichman, S., & Santrock, J. W. (1993). *The Psychology of Adjustment.* Dubuque, IA: Wm. C. Brown.

CHAPTER 9: CAREER DEVELOPMENT

Win–Win Negotiations

Phillips, J. J. (1986, Winter). Review of *Win-Win Negotiations.Personnel Psychology, 39,* 917–919.

Staying the Course

Kimmel, M. S. (1990, September 9). Guys you can count on: A review of *Staying the Course. The New York Times Book Review,* p. 28.

The Three Boxes of Life

Aston, S. (1980, May/June). Review of *The Three Boxes of Life. The Humanist*, p. 40.

Miscellaneous

Simons, J., Kalichman, S., & Santrock, J. W. (1993). *The Psychology of Adjustment*. Dubuque, IA: Wm. C. Brown.

CHAPTER 10: CHILD DEVELOPMENT AND PARENTING

Toddlers and Parents

Donavin, D. P. (1989, September 15). Review of *Toddlers and Parents. Booklist*, p. 127.

To Listen to a Child

The New York Times. Cover notes.

Between Parent and Child

Booklist. (1989, January 15). Review of *Between Parent and Child*, p. 823.
Choice. (1982, September). Review of *Between Parent and Child*, p. 184.
Lincoln, R. D. (1982, December). Review of *Between Parent and Child. Phi Delta Kappan*, p. 291.

Children: The Challenge

Shulman, B. H., & Dreikurs, S. G. (1978, November). Contributions of Rudolf Dreikurs. *Journal of Individual Psychology, 34*(2), 153–169.

The Hurried Child

Cole, J. (1982, September). Review of *The Hurried Child. Parent's Magazine*, p. 46.
Kirkus Review. (1978, August 1). Review of *The Hurried Child*, p. 859.
Wilder, R. (1978, August). Review of *The Hurried Child. Parent's Magazine*, p. 43.

Your Baby and Child

Ames, L. B. (1982, December). Review of *Your Baby and Child*. In Books in Brief, *Journal of Learning Disabilities*, p. 630.
Booklist. (1982, February 15). Review of *Your Baby and Child*, p. 727.
Brazelton, T. B. (1991). Cover notes.
May, C. L. (1982, March). Review of *Your Baby and Child. The New York Times Book Review*, p. 22.

How to Talk So Kids Will Listen and Listen So Kids Will Talk

Christian Science Monitor. (1980). Cover notes.
Heavenrich, R. M. (1980). Cover notes.

The Preschool Years

Brazelton, T. B. (1988). Cover notes.

Solve Your Child's Sleep Problems

Brazelton, T. B. (1985). Cover notes.
Publisher's Weekly, (1985). Cover notes.

CHAPTER 11: CODEPENDENCY

Miscellaneous

Chion-Kenney, L. (1992, April 2). Putting the past in its place. *The Washington Post,* p. D5.
Goodchilds, J. (1989). Commentary in Tavris article in *Vogue.*
Haaken, J. (1990, November). A critical analysis of the codependency construct. *Psychiatry, 53,* 396–406.
Lawler, A. C. (1992, August). A Feminist Perspective on Codependency. Paper presented at the meeting of the American Psychological Association, Washington, DC.
Lerner, H. (1989). Commentary in Tavris article in *Vogue.*
Rapping, E. (1990, March 5). Hooked on a feeling. *Nation,* pp. 316–319.
Tavris, C. (1989, December). Do codependency theories explain women's unhappiness—or exploit their own insecurities? *Vogue,* pp. 220–226.
Taylor, E. (1990, December 10). Taking care of herself. *Time,* pp. 106–107.
Tiefer, L. (1989). Commentary in Tavris article in *Vogue.*

CHAPTER 12: COMMUNICATION

You Just Don't Understand

Scarf, M. (1990). Cover notes.

The Talk Book

Smith, M. B. (1986). Cover notes.

That's Not What I Meant

Campbell, J. (1986). Cover notes.

Opening Up

Leary, M. R. (1992). Confession is good for the soul and a lot of other things. *Contemporary Psychology, 37,* 290–291.
Ornstein, R. (1990). Cover notes.
Wegner, D. M. (1990). Cover notes.
Weiten, W., Lloyd, M. A., & Lashley, R. L. (1990). *Psychology Applied to Modern Life* (3rd ed.). Pacific Grove, CA: Brooks/Cole.

Messages

Satir, V. (1983). Cover notes.

CHAPTER 13: DEATH AND DYING

How to Survive the Loss of a Love

The New York Times. (1991). Cover notes.
The Pittsburgh Press. (1991). Cover notes.

Learning to Say Good-Bye

Ames, L. B. (1976). Cover notes.

Talking about Death

Kirkus Review. (1982, September 15). Review of *Recovering from the Loss of a Child,* p. 1082.
The New York Times. (1976). Cover notes.

When Bad Things Happen to Good People

The New York Times Book Review. (1982, January). Review of *When Bad Things Happen to Good People,* p. 10.
Publisher's Weekly. (1981, August). Review of *When Bad Things Happen to Good People,* p. 74.
Schwartzer, A. (1981, September 1). Review of *When Bad Things Happen to Good People. Library Journal,* p. 1639.

On Death and Dying

Garvey, J. (1977, July 22). Review of *On Death and Dying. Commonweal,* pp. 471–473.
John, H. J. (1979, April). Review of *On Death and Dying. Choice,* pp. 179–181.
Publisher's Weekly. (1969, March 31). Review of *On Death and Dying,* p. 51.

Rosis, L. D. (1969, July). Review of *On Death and Dying*. *Kirkus Review*, pp. 2622–2623.

Times Literary Supplement. (1971, February 5). Review of *On Death and Dying*, p. 162.

Up from Grief

Publisher's Weekly. (1969, March 3). Review of *Up from Grief*, p. 54.

The Enigma of Suicide

The New York Times Book Review. (1991, April 7). Review of *The Enigma of Suicide*, p. 9.

Widowed

Glatt, C. R. (1990, November 1). Review of *Widowed*. *Library Journal*, p. 115.

Final Exit

Angelo, B. (1991, November 18). Review of *Final Exit*, *Time*, pp. 14–16.

Campbell, P. (1991, November). Review of *Final Exit*. *Wilson Library Bulletin*, pp. 104–105.

Donavin, D. P. (1990, October 1). Review of *Final Exit*. *Booklist*, p. 201.

Henry, W. A., III. (1991, August 19). Review of *Final Exit*. *Time*, p. 55.

Kass, L. R. (1991, December). Review of *Final Exit*. *Commentary*, pp. 19–24.

A Grief Observed

Loades, A. (1988). Review of *A Grief Observed*. *Theology Today*, 269–276.

Wilson, L. (1984, November). Review of *A Grief Observed*. *English Journal*, pp. 78–82.

CHAPTER 14: DEPRESSION

Cognitive Therapy and Emotional Disorders

Mahoney, M. J. (1977). Cognitive therapy—A revolutionary contender? *Contemporary Psychology, 22*, 104–105.

Happiness Is a Choice

Marsh, D. S. (1979, January 1). Review of *Happiness Is a Choice*. *Library Journal*, pp. 115–116.

Miscellaneous

Rosenhan, D. L., & Seligman, M. E. P. (1989). *Abnormal Psychology* (2nd ed.). New York: Norton.

Russo, N. F. (1985). *A Women's Mental Health Agenda.* Washington, DC: American Psychological Association.

Santrock, J. W. (1991). *Psychology* (3rd ed.). Dubuque, IA: Wm. C. Brown.

Showalter, E. (1992, March 9). Ladies sing the blues. *The New Republic,* pp, 44–45.

Simons, J., Kalichman, S., & Santrock, J. W. (1993). *Human Adjustment.* Dubuque, IA: Wm. C. Brown.

CHAPTER 15: DIETING AND WEIGHT LOSS

Fat Is a Feminist Issue

Dixler, E. (1980, May). Fat liberation. *Psychology Today,* pp. 110–115.

Howard, J. (1980, March 16). Fat women. *The New York Times Book Review,* p. 12.

Polivy, J., & Herman, C. P. (1979). Functions of fat. *Contemporary Psychology,* 24(4), 321–322.

Resources. (1985, May). Review of *Fat Is a Feminist Issue. Ms.,* p. 144.

Vandershaf, S. (1989, Fall). Antidotes to dieting. *The Whole Earth Review,* pp. 100–101.

Fit or Fat

Publisher's Weekly. (1978, June 26). Review of *Fit or Fat,* p. 114.

Wilder, R. (1978, October). Review of *Fit or Fat. Parent's Magazine,* p. 43.

Diet for a Small Planet

Blanchard, B., & Watrous, S. (1990, February). Frances Moore Lappe: Something new is possible under the sun. *The Progressive,* pp. 34–37.

Mueller, R. (1982, June 1). Review of *Diet for a Small Planet. Library Journal,* p. 1097.

Publisher's Weekly. (1982, May 21). Review of *Diet for a Small Planet,* p. 74.

The Pritiken Program for Diet and Exercise

Epstein, J. (1980, February 21). Help. Review of *The Pritiken Program for Diet and Exercise. The New York Review of Books,* pp. 7–9.

Kirkus Review. (1986, May 15). Review of *The Pritiken Program for Diet and Exercise,* p. 783.

Monaghan, C. (1985, September 1). Classics in the Kitchen. *Washington Post,* Book World section, pp. 1, 11.

Publisher's Weekly. (1986, April 18). Forecasts: Review of *The Pritiken Program for Diet and Exercise,* p. 58.

Publisher's Weekly. (1989, December 15). Review of *The Pritiken Program for Diet and Exercise,* p. 64.

One Meal at a Time

Kirkus Review. (1991, February, 1). Review of *One Meal at a Time*, p. 169.
Publisher's Weekly. (1991, February 22). Review of *One Meal at a Time*, p. 224.

The Beverly Hills Diet

Hegsted, D. M. (1983, January). Rating the diets. *Health*, pp. 21–23.

Dr. Abravanel's Anti-Craving Weightloss Diet

Kirkus Review. (1989, December 1). Review of *Dr. Abravanel's Anti-Craving Weightloss Diet*, pp. 1739–1740.
Publisher's Weekly. (1989, December 15). Review of *Dr. Abravanel's Anti-Craving Weightloss Diet*, pp. 64–65.

Dr. Atkins' New Diet Revolution

Publisher's Weekly. (1992, June 22). Review of *Dr. Atkins' New Diet Revolution*, p. 59.

The 35-Plus Diet for Women

Publisher's Weekly. (1987, March 20). Review of *The 35-Plus Diet for Women*, p. 62.

The Diet Center Program

Lezak, C. S. (1990, May 1). Review of *The Diet Center Program. Library Journal*, p. 104.

The Rotation Diet

Unger, S. M. (1986, May 1). Review of *The Rotation Diet. Library Journal*, p. 126.

The T-Factor Diet

Publisher's Weekly. (1989, April 21). Review of *The T-Factor Diet*, p. 89.

CHAPTER 16: DIVORCE

Dinosaurs Divorce

Abeel, E. (1986, November 9). After brontosaurus moves out. Review of *Dinosaurs Divorce. The New York Times Book Review*, p. 41.

How It Feels When Parents Divorce

Brazelton, T. B. (1984). Cover notes.
Crow, E. (1984, November 11). Caught in the crossfire. Review of *How It Feels When Parents Divorce, Washington Post,* Book World section, p. 17.
Nelms, B. & Horton, L. (1985, September). Broken circles: Adolescents on their own. *British Journal,* pp. 84–85.

Growing Up with Divorce

Brazelton, T. B. (1990). Cover notes.
Enzer, N. B. (1990). Review of *Growing Up with Divorce. Journal of the American Academy of Child and Adolescent Psychiatry, 29,* 842.
Spock, B. (1990). Cover notes.
Wallerstein, J. (1990). Cover notes.

Second Chances

Arendell, T. (1991). Review of *Second Chances. Contemporary Sociology, 20,* 308–310.
Chodorow, N. (1989). Cover notes.
Erikson, E. H. (1989). Cover notes.
Markham, H. (1990). Review of *Second Chances. Contemporary Psychology, 35,* 846–847.
Viorst, J. (1989). Cover notes.

Going It Alone

Rubin, L. (1979). Cover notes.

Creative Divorce

LeShan, E. (1973). Cover notes.
Ziegler, M. P. (1973). Review of *Creative Divorce. Library Journal,* p. 3620.

Rebuilding When Your Relationship Ends

Satir, V. (1981). Foreword.

Miscellaneous

Santrock, J. W. (1992) *Life-Span Development* (3rd ed.). Dubuque, IA: Wm. C. Brown.

CHAPTER 17: EATING DISORDERS

Fat Is a Family Affair

Journal of Clinical Child Psychology. (1990). Review of *Fat Is a Family Affair, 19,* 186.

When Food Is Love

Kirkus Review. (1991, January 15). Review of *When Food Is Love*, p. 96.
Publisher's Weekly. (1991, January 25). Review of *When Food Is Love*, p. 44.

Obsession

Atlantic Monthly. (1981, November). Review of *Obsession*, p. 89.
McFall, G. (1982, January). Review of *Obsession*. *Ms.*, pp. 42–43.
Publisher's Weekly. (1981, August 28). Review of *Obsession*, p. 384.
Witzel, C. N. (1982, May). Review of *Obsession*. *Contemporary Sociology, 11*(3), 342.

CHAPTER 18: EXERCISE

The New Aerobics

Segal, E. (1977, December). The Pheidippides Complex. *The New York Times Book Review*, p. 22.
Swardson, A. (1978, January 16). Health and happiness in the long run. *Business Week*, p. 13.

Kid Fitness

Snider, B. (1991, August 7). Ken Cooper targets kids, older adults. *USA Today*, p. 1D.

Miscellaneous

Allen, L., & Santrock, J. W. (1993). *Psychology: The Contexts of Behavior.* Dubuque, IA: Wm. C. Brown.
Simons, J. A., Kalichman, S., & Santrock, J. W. (1993). *The Psychology of Adjustment.* Dubuque, IA: Wm. C. Brown.

CHAPTER 19: THE FAMILY

The Family Crucible

Library Journal. (1978, February 15). Review of *The Family Crucible*, pp. 467–468.

Families

Coe, T. D., & Wahler, R. G. (1976). Something old, something new. *Contemporary Psychology, 21*(8), 537–538.
Havens, R. I. (1976, October). Review of *Families. Personnel and Guidance Journal, 55*, 68.

Back to the Family

Kirkus Review. (1990, August 1). Review of *Back to the Family*, p. 1080.
Stabiner, K. (1990, October 7). Review of *Back to the Family. Los Angeles Times Book Review*, p. 6.

Miscellaneous

Mitchell, E. (1991, November 25). Father of the child within. *Time*, pp. 82–82.

CHAPTER 20: FRIENDSHIP, LONELINESS, AND SINGLE ADULT LIFE

Intimate Strangers

Allen, M. B. (1983, April 1). Review of *Intimate Strangers. Library Journal*, p. 750.
Brown, E. M. (1983, March/April). Books and Films: Review of *Intimate Strangers. Science*, p. 191.
Scarf, M. (1983, August 15). The gender gulf. *The New Republic*, pp. 34–35.

Shyness

Stern, B. L. (1988, February). Your well-being. *Vogue*, p. 432.

Intimate Connections

Aronofsky, J. (1984, November 1). Review of *Intimate Connections. Library Journal*, p. 2070.
Seyfert, W. (1985, January 2). Review of *Intimate Connections. The Christian Century*, p. 24.

Just Friends

Arensberg, A. (1985, September). Talking about books. *Vogue*, p. 504.
Jones, W. H. (1987). A friend in need is more than likely a woman. *Contemporary Psychology, 32*(3), 226–227.
Kennedy, M. (1985, September 15). Intimacy men can never know. *The New York Times Book Review*, p. 35.
Miller, H. (1987, Fall). Review of *Just Friends. Journal of Marriage and the Family*, pp. 217–218.
Scholar, N. (1985, November). Review of *Just Friends. Wilson Library Bulletin*, p. 67.

How to Win Friends and Influence People

Baida, P. (1985, February/March). If you want to gather honey. *American Heritage*, pp. 18–19.

Coniff, R. (1987, October). The so-so salesman who told millions how to make it big. *Smithsonian*, pp. 82–93.

Hilbert, A. (1982, April). Friends for now. *Harper's*, pp. 101–103.

Nelton, S. (1986, December). How to win friends—for half a century. *Nation's Business*, pp. 40–41.

CHAPTER 21: INFANT DEVELOPMENT AND PARENTING

Infants and Mothers

Fasick, A. (1969, November 1). Review of *Infants and Mothers. Library Journal*, p. 50.

Finlayson, A. (1985, May 20). Successor to Dr. Spock. *MacLean's*, p. 54.

Kantrowitz, B., with Wingart, P. (1989, February 13). Somersaults and sympathy. *Newsweek*, p. 72.

What Every Baby Knows

Kirkus Review. (1987, October 1). Review of *What Every Baby Knows*, p. 1452.

Library Journal. (1987, November 1). Review of *What Every Baby Knows*, p. 118.

Weber, K. (1987, November 13). T. Berry Brazelton. *Publisher's Weekly*, pp. 57–58.

Dr. Spock's Baby and Child Care

Changing Times. (1985, July). Review of *Dr. Spock's Baby and Child Care*, p. 48.

Leo, J. (1985, April 8). Bring Dr. Spock up-to-date. *Time*, pp. 76–78.

Seligman, D. (1992, April 6). Keeping up: Baby talk. *Fortune*, p. 119.

The First Three Years of Life

Choice. (1976, March). Review of *The First Three Years of Life*, p. 141.

Church, J. (1975, December 28). Review of *The First Three Years of Life. The New York Times Book Review*, pp. 4–5.

Eliot, J. (1977, October). Review of *The First Three Years of Life. Childhood Education*, p. 36.

Escalona, S. K. (1976). Do-it yourself books on early childhood. *Contemporary Psychology*, 21(12), 886–888.

Keyes, S. (1976, May). Review of *The First Three Years of Life. Harvard Educational Review*, pp. 272–275.

Library Journal. (1975, November 1). Review of *The First Three Years of Life*, p. 2058.

Babyhood

Choice. (1977, June). Review of *Babyhood*, p. 565.

Kirkus Review. (1976, August 1). Review of *Babyhood*, pp. 883–884.

Publisher's Weekly. (1976, September 20). Review of *Babyhood*, p. 68.

Schuman, W. (1985, May). The best child-care books for new parents. *Parent's Magazine*, pp. 46–52.

USA Today. (1991, November 27). Your baby sits tight, pp. D1–D2.

The First Twelve Months of Life

Changing Times. (1978, March). Books to make you a better parent, pp.19–20.

Charnley, L. (1975, February). Review of *The First Twelve Months of Life. Childhood Education*, pp. 224–225.

Kalisch, B. (1973, June 1). Review of *The First Twelve Months of Life. Library Journal*, pp. 1829–1830.

Kirkus Review. (1973, April 15). Review of *The First Twelve Months of Life*, p. 485.

Dr. Spock on Parenting

Booklist. (1988, July). Review of *Dr. Spock on Parenting*, p. 1757.

Kirkus Review. (1988, June 15). Review of *Dr. Spock on Parenting*, p. 894.

Publisher's Weekly. (1988, June 24). Review of *Dr. Spock on Parenting*, p. 100.

What to Expect the First Year

Green, M. (1989). Cover notes.

Publisher's Weekly. (1989, April 28). Review of *What to Expect the First Year*, p. 71.

Rosenberg, L. (1992, May). Best books for new parents. *Parent's Magazine*, pp. 87–89.

Sullivan-Fowler, M. (1989, May 15). Review of *What to Expect the First Year. Booklist*, p. 1590.

CHAPTER 22: LOVE, INTIMACY, AND MARRIAGE

Dance of Intimacy

Nadelson, C. (1989). Cover notes.

Rubin, L. (1989). Cover notes.

Scarf, M. (1989). Cover notes.

Getting the Love You Want

Booklist. (1988, June 15). Review of *Getting the Love You Want*, p. 1694.

Harris, T. G. (1988). Cover notes.

Levinger, G. (1990). How shall we communicate about love? *Contemporary Psychology, 35*, 347–348.

Trotter, R. J. (1986, September). The three faces of love. *Psychology Today*, pp. 46–54.

The Art of Loving

Davidson, H. A. (1956, October 29). A cultivable art: Review of *The Art of Loving. The New Republic*, pp. 21–22.

Intimate Partners

Hersch, P. (1987, March). The pathology of marriage. *Psychology Today*, pp. 68–70.
Nadleson, C. (1986). Foreword.
Tavris, C. (1987, March 1). Scenes from a genogram. *The New York Times Book Review*, pp. 15–16.

The Intimate Enemy

Kitman, M. (1969, April 6). What marriages need is more or less a number of things. *The New York Times Book Review*, pp. 8–9.
Shaffer, J. B. P. (1970, February). Review of *The Intimate Enemy. Harvard Educational Review*, pp. 165–174.

Obsessive Love

Glatt, C. R. (1991, April 15). Review of *Obsessive Love. Library Journal*, p. 112.
Kirkus Review. (1991, March 1). Review of *Obsessive Love*, p. 298.

Divorce Busting

Bardill, R. (1992). Cover notes.
Publisher's Weekly. (1991, November 22). Review of *Divorce Busting*, p. 43.

Going the Distance

Kirkus Review. (1991, August 15). Review of *Going the Distance*, p. 1080.

Women Who Love Too Much

Kapp, I. (1986, April 6). Where the boys are. *The New Republic*, pp. 38–41.
Leerhesen, C. (1987, March 9). Loving too much. *Newsweek*, pp. 52–53.

Husbands and Wives

Kirkus Review. (1989, April 1). Review of *Husbands and Wives*, p. 525.

Loving Each Other

Booklist. (1984, September 15). Review of *Loving Each Other*, p. 91.

Men Who Hate Women and the Women Who Love Them

Kirkus Review. (1986, July 1). Review of *Men Who Hate Women and the Women Who Love Them*, p. 992.

Roberts, Y. (1988, June 22). Hungry people make poor shoppers. *The New Statesman*, p. 22.

Shapiro, L. (1987, June 1). Advice givers strike gold: New experts tell women what's wrong with men. *Newsweek*, pp. 64–65.

Women Men Love, Women Men Leave

Publisher's Weekly. (1987, May 22). Review of *Women Men Love, Women Men Leave*, p. 63.

What Every Woman Should Know About Men

Spence, J. (1982, October). Review of *What Every Woman Should Know About Men. Contemporary Psychology*, 27, 823–824.

Miscellaneous

Santrock, J. W. (1991). *Psychology* (3rd ed.). Dubuque, IA: Wm. C. Brown.

CHAPTER 23: MEN'S ISSUES

Iron John

Csikszentmihalyi, M. (1990, December 9). Bring on the hairy mentor. *The New York Times Book Review*, pp. 15–16.

Gaines, C. (1991, October). Robert Bly, wild thing. *Esquire*, pp. 125–128.

Johnston, J. (1992, February 23). Why *Iron John* is no gift to women. *The New York Times Book Review*, pp. 3–4.

Miscellaneous

Doyle, J. A., & Paludi, M. A. (1991). *Sex and Gender* (2nd ed.). Dubuque, IA: Wm. C. Brown.

Gelman, D. (1990, November 26). Making it all feel better. *Newsweek*, pp. 66–68.

Levine, A. (1991, April 8). Masculinity's champion. *U.S. News & World Report*, pp. 61–62.

Morrow, L. (1991, August 19). The child is father to the man. *Time*, pp. 52–54.

Stengel, R. (1991, July 8). Bang the drum quickly. *Time*, p. 58.

CHAPTER 24: POSITIVE THINKING AND SELF-ESTEEM

Learned Optimism

Beck, A. (1990). Cover notes.

Roberts, W. (1990). Cover notes.

Sandmaier, M. (1991, January 20). Don't worry, be happy. *The New York Times Book Review*, p. 9.

Positive Illusions

Baumeister, R. (1989). Cover notes.
McAuliffe, K. (1991, September). Think positive. *Self*, pp. 170, 179.
Ray, T. (1989, December 24). Permission to lie to yourself. *The New York Times Book Review*, p. 8.
Tavris, C. (1989). Cover notes.

Positive Addiction

Peele, S. (1976, April). Review of *Positive Addiction. Psychology Today*, p. 36.
Rowe, W. (1978, January). Review of *Positive Addiction. Personnel and Guidance Journal*, pp. 299–300.

Tough Times Never Last but Tough People Do

Peale, N. V. (1983). Cover notes.

Self-Defeating Behaviors

Ellis, A. (1991). Cover notes.
Hendrix, H. (1991). Cover notes.
Weinstein, F. (1991, September 15). Review of *Self-Defeating Behaviors. Library Journal*, p. 133.

The Power of Positive Thinking

Stephenson, G. R. (1952, October 26). A pastor's prescription. *The New York Times Book Review*, p. 36.

Miscellaneous

Santrock, J. W. (1991). *Psychology* (3rd ed.). Dubuque, IA: Wm. C. Brown.

CHAPTER 25: PREGNANCY

The Complete Book of Pregnancy and Childbirth

Block, B. S. (1990). Book Reviews. *New England Journal of Medicine, 322*(18), 1324–1325.
Booklist. (1981, February 15). Review of *The Complete Book of Pregnancy and Childbirth*, p. 785.

What to Expect When You're Expecting

Brinley, M. (1988). Cover notes.

Fugett, C. (1988, Spring). Review of *What to Expect When You're Expecting*. *Whole Earth Review*, p. 91.

Kelly, K. (1986, June). Nine months' reading. *Parent's Magazine*, pp. 48–55.

Kirkus Review. (1984, October 15). Review of *What to Expect When You're Expecting*, p. 988.

What to Eat When You're Expecting

Miller, P. (1986, November 15). Review of *What to Eat When You're Expecting*. *Library Journal*, pp. 106–107.

Pregnancy After 35

David, H. P. (1977, June). Review of *Pregnancy After 35*. *Contemporary Psychology, 22*(6), 474.

Kirkus Review. (1976, July 1). Review of *Pregnancy After 35*, p. 774.

The Well Pregnancy Book

Crampon, J. E. (1986, February 15). Review of *The Well Pregnancy Book*. *Library Journal*, p. 189.

From Here to Maternity

Carpenter, K. H. (1991, May 1). Review of *From Here to Maternity*. *Library Journal*, p. 94.

Will It Hurt the Baby?

Brazelton, T. B. (1990). Cover notes.

Sullivan-Fowler, M. (1990, July). Review of *Will It Hurt the Baby?*. *Booklist*, p. 2056.

CHAPTER 26: RELAXATION, MEDITATION, AND STRESS

The Relaxation Response

Scarf, M. (1975, December 6). Maggie Scarf on the behavioral sciences. *The New Republic*, pp. 19–22.

The Male Stress Syndrome

Jacquay, R. L. (1986, June 1). Review of *The Male Stress Syndrome*. *Library Journal*, p. 128.

Minding the Body, Minding the Mind

The New York Times Book Review. (1988, March 27). Review of *Minding the Body, Minding the Mind*, p. 43.

CHAPTER 27: SELF-ESTEEM

The Psychology of Self-Esteem

Wadsworth, C. E. (1970, February 1). Review of *The Psychology of Self-Esteem*. *Library Journal*, p. 503.

The Revolution from Within

Carlson, M. (1992, January 20). Even feminists get the blues. *Time*, p. 57.
English, D. (1992, February 2). She's her weakness now. *The New York Times Book Review*, p. 13.
King, F. (1992, March 2). Gloria in excelcis. *The National Review*, pp. 47–58.
Ross, C. (1992, February 17). The neglected self. *MacLean's*, p. 69.
Shapiro, L. (1992, January 13). Little Gloria, happy at last. *Newsweek*, pp. 64–65.

Miscellaneous

Abbott, L. M. C. (1987, October). Women, work, and self-esteem. *Choice*, pp. 265–268.
Bednar, R. L., Wells, M. G., & Peterson, S. R. (1989). *Self-Esteem*. Washington, DC: American Psychological Association.
Simon, J., Kalichman, S., & Santrock, J. W. (1993). *The Psychology of Adjustment*. Dubuque, IA: Wm. C. Brown.

CHAPTER 28: SELF-FULFILLMENT AND HAPPINESS

Man's Search for Meaning

Allport, G. W. (1984). Cover notes.
Bolotin, S. (1985, December). What makes a bestseller? *Vogue*, p. 317.
Kreyche, G. F. (1984). Cover notes.
Leerhsen, C. (1985, November 18). Peck's path to inner peace. *Newsweek*, p. 79.

The Road Less Traveled

Peck, M. S. (1988, October). Interview. *Omni*, pp. 125–133.

When All You Ever Wanted Isn't Enough

Boyer, A. (1986, June 22). Review of *When All You Ever Wanted Isn't Enough*. *The New York Times Book Review*, p. 27.
Sussman, V. (1986, May 11). Answers to life's big questions. *Washington Post*, p. 10.

I'm OK—You're OK

Time. (1973, August 20). T.A.: Doing OK, pp. 44–46.
Todd, R. (1973, November). I'm nobody—who are you? *Atlantic Monthly*, pp. 108–114.

Flow

Baumeister, R. (1992). Thoughtful reflections on optimal experience. *Contemporary Psychology, 37*, 291–292.

The Be (Happy) Attitudes

The Christian Century. (1987, September 30). Problems for Schuller, p. 818.
DeDubovay, D. (1987, April). Dr. Robert Schuller: TV's minister of hope. *McCalls*, pp. 33–51, 111.
Stengel, R. (1985, March 18). Apostle of sunny thoughts. *Time*, p. 70.
Tavris, C. (1990, March 18). Contentment is hard work. *The New York Times Book Review*, p. 7.

Scientology

Behar, R. (1991, May 6). The thriving cult of greed and power. *Time*, pp. 50–57.

The Pursuit of Happiness

Cialdini, R. (1992). Cover notes.
Csikszentmihalyi, M. (1992). Cover notes.

Miscellaneous

Begley, S. & McCormick, J. (1986, June 2). Going with the flow. *Newsweek*, pp. 68–69.
Myers, D. G. (1992). *Psychology* (3rd ed.). New York: Worth.
Santrock, J. W. (1991). *Psychology* (3rd ed.). Dubuque, IA: Wm. C. Brown.
Simons, J. A., Irwin, D. B., & Drinnin, B. A. (1987). *Psychology*. St. Paul, MN: West.

CHAPTER 29: SELF-IMPROVEMENT AND MOTIVATION

The 7 Habits of Highly Successful People

Rottenberger, K. (1991, December). The marketer's essential library. *Sales & Marketing Management*, p. 38.

Peace, Love, and Healing

Schwartz, T. (1989, June 12). Doctor love. *New York*, pp. 41–49.

Overcoming Procrastination

Weinrach, S. G. (1978, June). Review of *Overcoming Procrastination. Personnel and Guidance Journal*, pp. 647–648.

Don't Blame Mother

Lerner, H. (1989). Cover notes.
Maracek, J., & Hare-Mustin, R. (1991, Spring). Review of *Don't Blame Mother. Signs*, pp. 625–630.
Tavris, C. (1989, September). How psychology shortchanges mothers. *Psychology Today*, pp. 74–75.

Making Life Right When It Feels All Wrong

Abrams, W. (1988, September 15). Review of *Making Life Right When It Feels All Wrong. Library Journal*, p. 87.

Gentle Roads to Survival

Rogers, C. Cover notes.

Unlimited Power

Kirkus Review. (1986, July 1). Review of *Unlimited Power*, p. 1007.

Your Maximum Mind

Booklist. (1987, October 15). Review of *Your Maximum Mind*, pp. 352–353.

Your Erroneous Zones

Arieti, S. (1977, October). How to read how-to books. *Psychology Today*, pp. 142, 148.
Myers, L. J. (1979). Three prescriptions for overcoming social ills. *Contemporary Psychology, 24,* 386–387.

How to Stop Worrying and Start Living

Time. (1948, June 14). A kick in the shins, pp. 101–102.

CHAPTER 30: SEXUALITY

Male Sexuality

Comfort, A. (1978, March 12). The male animal. *The New York Times Book Review*, pp. 12–13.

For Each Other

Publisher's Weekly. (1982, July 30). Review of *For Each Other*, p. 65.

Zilbergeld, B. (1982, October). Pursuit of the Grafenberg Spot. *Psychology Today*, pp. 82–84.

The New Joy of Sex

Birnbaum, J. (1991, October 7). Tiding of comfort and joy. *Time*, p. 65.

Gelman, D. (1991, October 21). There's still sex to be found in "Joy." *Newsweek*, p. 69.

More Joy

DeMott, B. (1977, April). Sex in the seventies: Notes on two cultures. *Atlantic Monthly*, pp. 88–91.

Kirkus Review. (1974, July 15). Review of *More Joy*, p. 774.

Becoming Orgasmic

Ellis, A. (1977, October). Becoming more becoming by coming. *Contemporary Psychology*, pp. 763–764.

Metz, M. (1990). A quality sexual growth program. *Contemporary Psychology*, 35, 790–791.

Wade, C. O. (1976, November). Women's orgasm: Getting there alone. *Psychology Today*, 94–97.

Dr. Ruth's Guide to Good Sex

Kirkus Review. (1983, February 1). Review of *Dr. Ruth's Guide to Good Sex*, p. 194.

CHAPTER 31: STEPFAMILIES

Old Loyalties, New Ties

Sager, C. (1988). Cover notes.

Satir, V. (1988). Cover notes.

Miscellaneous

Santrock, J. W., & Sitterle, K. A. (1987). Parent–child interaction in stepfamilies. In K. Pasley & M. Ingheimer-Tallman (eds.), *Remarriage and Stepfamilies: Current Theory and Practice.* New York: Guilford Press.

CHAPTER 32: TEENAGERS AND PARENTING

Miscellaneous

Santrock, J. W. (1993). *Adolescence* (3rd ed.). Dubuque, IA: Wm. C. Brown.

CHAPTER 33: WOMEN'S ISSUES

The Second Shift

Allen, C. L. (1989, November). Who scrubs the tub? *Commentary*, pp. 60–62.

Brines, J. (1990, February). Book reviews. *Journal of Marriage and the Family*, pp. 278–279.

Hertz, R. (1990, November). Review of *The Second Shift. American Journal of Sociology*, 776–778.

Library Journal. (1989, April 15). Review of *The Second Shift*, p. 90.

Miller, J. (1989, July 31). Women's work is never done. *Newsweek*, p. 65.

Publisher's Weekly. (1989, May). Review of *The Second Shift*, p. 62.

Skow, J. (1989, August 7). The myth of male housework. *Time*, p. 62.

Stone, N. (1989, October). Mother's work. *Harvard Business Review*, pp. 50–56.

Too Good for Her Own Good

Jurgens, J. (1990, May 15). Review of *Too Good for Her Own Good. Booklist*, p. 1758.

Kirkus Review. (1990, April 1). Review of *Too Good for Her Own Good*, p. 472.

Backlash

Allen, C. (1992, February). New wave feminism. *Commentary*, pp. 62–63.

Gallagher, M. (1992, March 30). Exit, stage back. *The National Review*, pp. 141–142.

Goodman, E. (1991, October 27). The "man shortage" and other big lies. *The New York Times Book Review*, pp. 35–36.

Morgenson, G. (1992, March 16). Careers. *Forbes*, pp. 152–153.

New Yorker. (1991, December 23). Review of *Backlash*, p. 108.

Pogash, C. (1992, April). The brains behind *Backlash. Working Woman*, pp. 64–67.

Publisher's Weekly. (1991, October 4). Review of *Backlash*, p. 76.

Wheelwright, J. (1992, April 3). The new avengers. *New Statesman & Society*, pp. 44–45.

My Mother/Myself

Booklist. (1977, October 15). Review of *My Mother/Myself*, p. 341.

Gardiner, J. K. (1978, Fall). The new motherhood. *The North American Review*, pp. 72–76.

Kirkus Review. (1977, July 1). Review of *My Mother/Myself*, p. 703.

Library Journal. (1977, September 15). Review of *My Mother/Myself*, p. 1857.

The Progressive. (1978, May). Review of *My Mother/Myself*, p. 45.

Publisher's Weekly. (1977, July 18). Review of *My Mother/Myself*, p. 134.

Spurling, H. (1979, March). Bloody Mama. *New Statesman*, pp. 453–454.

Women, Sex and Addiction

Banas, M. (1989, April 1). Review of *Women, Sex, and Addiction. Booklist*, p. 1330.

Kirkus Review. (1989, April 15). Review of *Women, Sex, and Addiction*, p. 617.

Publisher's Weekly. (1989, April 21). Review of *Women, Sex, and Addiction*, p. 78.
Vincent, S. (1990, May 25). Nymphos or doormats? *New Statesman and Society*, pp. 36–37.

Secrets about Men Every Woman Should Know

Kirkus Review. (1989, December 15). Review of *Secrets About Men Every Woman Should Know*, p. 1797.
Publisher's Weekly. (1989, December 22). Review of *Secrets About Men Every Woman Should Know*, p. 51.

The New Our Bodies, Ourselves

Booklist. (1984, November 15). Review of *The New Our Bodies, Ourselves*, p. 405.
Ehrenreich, B. (1985, January). Body language. *Vogue*, pp. 239–282.
Henig, R. M. (1985, January 20). The body politic. *Washington Post*, Book World section, p. 4.
Kirkus Review. (1984, November 15). Review of *The New Our Bodies, Ourselves*, p. 1077.
Napoli, M. (1985, May). Women's health. *Ms.*, p. 96.
Randall, F. (1985, January 13). Feeling both well and good. *The New York Times Book Review*, p. 16.
Seligman, J. (1985, February 4). A book of body politics. *Newsweek*, p. 9.
Tavris, C. (1985, April 20). Healthy permissiveness. *The Nation*, pp. 437–438.

The Mismeasure of Woman

Banas, M. (1992, March 15). Review of *The Mismeasure of Woman*. *Booklist*, p. 1322.
Burton, M. (1992, April 15). Review of *The Mismeasure of Woman*. *Library Journal*, pp. 113–114.
Jacoby, S. (1992, March 29). Calipers of the patriarchs. *The New York Times Book Review*, pp. 9–10.
Morgan, D. (1992, April 5). Caught in a double bind. *Bookworld*, p. 6.
Publisher's Weekly. (1992, January 27). Review of *The Mismeasure of Woman*, p. 80.

CHAPTER 35: THE NINE KEYS TO SELECTING A SELF-HELP BOOK

Miscellaneous

Halliday, G. (1991). Psychological self-help books—how dangerous are they? *Psychotherapy*, *28*, 678–680.
Quackenbush, R. L. (1991). The prescription of self-help books by psychologists: A bibliography of selected bibliotherapy resources. *Psychotherapy*, *28*, 671–677.

Rathus, S. A. & Nevid, J. S. (1991). *Psychology and the Challenges of Life* (4th ed.). Fort Worth, TX: Holt, Rinehart and Winston.

Rosen, R. D. (1977). *Psychobabble.* New York: Atheneum.

Scogin, F., Jamison, C., & Gochnearu, K. (1989). Comparative efficacy of cognitive behavioral bibliotherapy for mildly and moderately depressed older adults. *Journal of Consulting and Clinical Psychology, 57,* 403–407.

Weiten, W., Lloyd, M. A., & Lashley, R. L. (1991). *Adjustment in the 90s* (3rd ed.). Pacific Grove, CA: Brooks/Cole.

Author Index

Subject Index